Renovating Politics in Contemporary
VIETNAM

Renovating Politics in Contemporary
VIETNAM

Zachary Abuza

LYNNE
RIENNER
PUBLISHERS

BOULDER
LONDON

JQ
898
.D293
A25
2001

Published in the United States of America in 2001 by
Lynne Rienner Publishers, Inc.
1800 30th Street, Boulder, Colorado 80301
www.rienner.com

and in the United Kingdom by
Lynne Rienner Publishers, Inc.
3 Henrietta Street, Covent Garden, London WC2E 8LU

© 2001 by Lynne Rienner Publishers, Inc. All rights reserved

Library of Congress Cataloging-in-Publication Data
Abuza, Zachary.
    Renovating politics in contemporary Vietnam / Zachary Abuza.
    Includes bibliographical references and index.
    ISBN 1-55587-961-6 (alk. paper)
    1. £Đng còng sàn Viòt Nam. 2. Vietnam—Politics and government—
1945–1975. 3. Vietnam—Politics and government—1975– 4. Vietnam—
Economic policy—1975– 5. Dissenters—Vietnam. 6. Government, Resistance
to—Vietnam. 7. Civil rights—Vietnam. 8. Democratization—Vietnam.
9. Political culture—Vietnam. I. Title.
JQ898.D293 A25   2001
320.9597—dc21   00-066502

British Cataloguing in Publication Data
A Cataloguing in Publication record for this book
is available from the British Library.

Printed and bound in the United States of America

⊗   The paper used in this publication meets the requirements
     of the American National Standard for Permanence of
     Paper for Printed Library Materials Z39.48-1984.

    5 4 3 2 1

CONTENTS

Introduction: Dissidents and Democratization in Vietnam   1

1   Politics in Vietnam   9

2   The *Nhan Van–Giai Pham* Affair, the 1967 Purge,
and the Legacy of Dissent   41

3   The Debates over Democratization and Legalization   75

4   The Battle over Intellectual Freedom and Freedom
of the Press   131

5   The Club of Former Resistance Fighters:
Dissension from Within   161

6   Religious Freedom and Civil Society   183

7   The VCP: Coping with Internal Dissent and
External Pressure   211

8   Conclusion   235

Bibliography   245
Index   259
About the Book   273

INTRODUCTION:
DISSIDENTS AND
DEMOCRATIZATION IN VIETNAM

The Vietnamese Communist Party (VCP) has ruled continuously in the northern half of the country since 1954 and throughout Vietnam since May 1975. In that time, it has tolerated no dissent, monopolizing all political power and decisionmaking. In the twenty-five years since the end of the war, the standard of living for the vast majority of the population has improved negligibly, though Vietnam is situated in the heart of the most economically dynamic region in the world. The VCP has survived the collapse of communism in Eastern Europe and its former patron the Soviet Union. It has embarked on a program of limited economic reform in an attempt to raise the standard of living to regain its tarnished legitimacy, but it has countenanced no political liberalization or reform.

Since the onset in 1986 of the economic reform program known as *doi moi* (renovation), there has been a growing chorus of dissent directed toward the party and its policies. That any dissent has emerged in the authoritarian, one-party state of Vietnam is surprising, but there is something even more extraordinary. Most of the dissent comes from an unlikely source: within the party's own ranks. Although opposition has been voiced by former members of the Republic of Vietnam regime and by the historically political clergymen of the many religions and sects in the country, the most vociferous criticism has come from senior members of the party who are upset at the country's development or lack thereof. Despite twenty-five years since achieving national unification, Vietnam at the turn of the century remains one of the poorest and least developed countries in the world.

Vietnam is a paradox in many ways. It is a richly endowed country, but average per capita GDP has remained at $300 per year for nearly a decade. Vietnam has one of the highest literacy rates in the world, yet draconian press and culture laws limit all freedom of expression and intellectual freedom. Vietnam's most important authors remain banned, read only abroad, while the film industry has all but collapsed. The visual arts, especially modern art, have blossomed, but they have only a small domestic audience and are appreciated primarily abroad.

The collapse of communism in Eastern Europe and in Vietnam's principal patron, the Soviet Union, shocked Hanoi, but Vietnam has remained doggedly committed to socialism. Unwilling to embark on any degree of political reform, Hanoi asserts that it simply will not make the same mistakes that its comrades in Eastern Europe made. Yet the inherent corruption of the Eastern European regimes is even more prevalent in resource-scarce Vietnam. Although the country has been in relative peace since 1989, its leadership still maintains its clandestine decisionmaking style. The Communist Party—whose members comprise only 3 percent of the population—continues to monopolize political power, asserting that it alone represents the interests of all Vietnamese people. The military, too, commands a disproportionate share of government resources and has a powerful voice in policymaking. The National Assembly remains for the most part a rubber stamp for party decisions. Despite assertions of collective decisionmaking and political consensus, policymaking is riddled by factionalism. Since the Communist Party's Eighth National Congress in 1996, the country has experienced the worst infighting and political deadlock in its history. Vietnam's hallmark collective leadership has all but broken down, leaving the country unable to adequately respond to the economic crisis that rocked Southeast Asia from 1997 to 2000.

The Communist Party, which led popular anticolonial wars against France and the United States, also led the country into quagmires with the Chinese and Cambodians that left the country bankrupt and diplomatically isolated. The party that had so much legitimacy that it could call on the Vietnamese people to make continued and repeated sacrifices has squandered much of its popular support. The aging leadership remains profoundly influenced by the war and continues to believe that the population will support it because of its leadership role in anti-colonial struggles. But Vietnam has a very young population; over half of its citizens were born after the war ended in 1976. Thus the majority knows only of the war through propaganda and has been confronted with a lifetime of economic mismanagement. Widespread food shortages and economic mismanagement forced the regime to embark on an economic reform program in 1986 that did much to revitalize the economy. But as even those reforms have waned since the mid-1990s, the party has not been able to capitalize on performance-based legitimacy.

Hanoi launched a Chinese-style economic reform program in 1986. In the first ten years of the reform program, the economy grew 7 to 8 percent annually. GDP grew from $2.2 billion in 1989 to $20.3 billion in 1997, and averaged 8.2 percent annually from 1991 to 1996. Agricultural reforms that dismantled socialist communes and allowed individuals to lease land and negotiate production contracts with the state turned the country from a net importer into a net exporter of rice. Price and currency reform helped to bring inflation under control, from 400 percent in 1988 to 5 percent in 1996. More importantly, Vietnam shifted its growth strategy from a Stalinist-grounded economy based on central planning, price controls, and heavy industrialization to an outwardly oriented economy based on foreign trade, foreign investment, bi- and multilateral borrowing, and economic interdependence. Vietnam received over $16 billion in foreign investment and $8.5 billion in development assistance, while foreign trade increased from $3.3 billion in 1989 to $17.8 billion in 1996, an average annual growth rate of 16.9 percent in the 1990–1995 period. The World Bank summed up Vietnam's transition this way: "Under *doi moi,* Vietnam began its transition from a centrally planned system towards a market economy by implementing a wide range of macro-economic and structural reforms to create a vibrant economy with several features of a free market system." There was real zeitgeist surrounding Vietnam, which was hailed as the next "tiger" economy. Yet even before the Asian economic crisis hit Vietnam, the economy was in serious trouble. Even though legally a multisector economy was established, the government has hampered the growth of the private sector and continues to pour public funds into the inefficient state-owned sector. Over 50 percent of the 5,200 state-owned enterprises lose money, yet the government refuses to shut them down or allow for wide-scale privatization for fears of exacerbating the country's serious, but underreported, unemployment crisis. The government failed to create a viable private sector that could absorb the surplus labor and the annual million new entrants to the workforce; as a result, foreign investors began to cut their losses, and by 2000 investment rates were below 1992 levels.

Popular unrest has increased, yet the VCP has not come up with any innovative solutions to the country's myriad of woes and increasingly divergent social forces. Fearing that radical economic reform or any political reform will diminish its political monopoly, the party has stubbornly clung to power and punished all dissenters.

Why has Vietnam failed to realized its promise as a nation? There are three main reasons. First and foremost, the leadership's worldview was shaped by thirty years of anticolonial struggle and ten more years of conflict with China and its surrogate, the Cambodian Khmer Rouge. The regime is xenophobic and truly believes that the international system is hostile and threatens its monopoly of power. Put simply, the VCP equates its own survival with national survival. Although the government asserts that the country is so poor because of thirty years of war and a hostile international environment, bad economic policies are much to blame. The party did take some concrete steps in the late 1980s to reform the economy, but it is fearful of any policy that could cause unrest and destabilize the regime. This is a regime that does not rush into anything. Although so much is said of how radical *doi moi* was, Vietnam moved in reality very carefully. The regime intentionally did not use such words as "reconstruction" or "rebuilding" that would imply a fundamental overhaul, because the VCP believes that it only needs to make cosmetic changes. Its style of policymaking is reactive, responding to crises rather than governing with foresight. Finally, despite fundamental structural reforms in the economy, there have been no corresponding political reforms.

Second, the leadership is stagnant. Not only do regular transitions of power not occur frequently enough, but the political "gene pool" is very small: less than 3 percent of the population are members of the VCP. The major decisionmaking body, the VCP Central Committee, has 170 members, while the Politburo currently only has 18 members. Membership in both bodies is overwhelmingly male and ranges in age from fifty to seventy years. Within the party, promotion and advancement are based on the Soviet-style *nomenklatura* selectorate process. Loyalty and slavish subservience to the party and its edicts are the requisites for career advancement; leaders with new ideas do not readily rise to the top of the political system. Even though the party talks about the need to "renovate" its personnel, the structure of the political system makes this nearly impossible.

Third, there is something about Vietnamese political culture: regardless of regime type, communist or noncommunist, Vietnamese political leaders are very uncompromising. Throughout Vietnam's modern history, these leaders have perceived politics as a zero-sum game in which compromise is equated with weakness, a view that has reinforced authoritarian political cultures and made democracy harder to implement. This was true in the south, under Ngo Dinh Diem and his successors, as well as in the north, under the VCP—which to this day countenances no dissent, no opposition, and no criticism. Those who transgress party policies are dealt with harshly. The uncompromising nature of the party (and of the émigré community and dissident opposition) does not bode well for democratic transition.

The Vietnamese Communist Party believes that if it liberalizes the political system, it will lose its monopoly, causing grave instability throughout the country and jeopardizing national sovereignty. Yet, the party's intransigence and refusal to sufficiently liberalize the political and economic systems has led to corruption, abuse of power, authoritarianism, and economic mismanagement by a stagnant, self-sustaining political system. Only by broadening national decisionmaking, using the National Assembly, a free press, and the knowledge of experts, and placing itself on an equal level under the law can the VCP begin to reform itself and regain popular support.

This book concludes that the party is incapable of doing so and that it has become the prerogative of a handful of senior party members to advocate such reforms. These members are not counterrevolutionaries; indeed most are loyal, lifelong party members who have dedicated themselves to the revolution and only wish for the party to renovate its governing style and win back the overwhelming support of the people. They want to reform the existing political system, not replace it. They see themselves as patriots who can put national interests above their class interests. They are members of the ruling elite and beneficiaries of the current political system, but they are dissatisfied with the entrenched, corrupt, authoritarian nature of the party, which they feel is responsible for the country's economic mismanagement and poverty. To this end, they are willing to speak out.

Organization of this Book

Chapter 1 begins by analyzing the political and economic context that saw the rise of dissent. It provides a brief overview of the VCP's rise to power and contemporary political institutions in Vietnam. It then examines who the dissidents are and their concerns and demands, and examine why they are so important. The chapter concludes that unlike Eastern Europe or in the Asia-Pacific region, where there were such independent agents of change as unions, independent churches, opposition political parties, large student groupings, and a middle class, Vietnam has none. Dissidents and some members of the clergy are the only individuals willing to confront the state. Even though the dissidents are without an alliance to one or more autonomous groups and their power to alter the political process is limited, they nonetheless provide an important first step. As lifelong revolutionaries, they are seen as voices of conscience.

The book will primarily focus on dissent since *doi moi* was launched in December 1986, but it will begin by revisiting the *Nhan Van–Giai Pham* affair of the 1950s and the intraparty purges of 1967. Although this period has been covered in other works, notably those by Georges Boudarel, Neil Jamieson, Hirohide Kurihara,[1] because so many of today's dissidents were victims of the 1950s affair and so many of their demands have remained unchanged, they warrant discussion. The 1967 purge, though written about by historians such as William Duiker,[2] has not been analyzed outside the context of the War of National Liberation. Here it will be analyzed as an event with a fundamentally transformative effect on the Vietnamese political system. The two events continue to be a major source of friction between dissidents and the party, and many of the issues that sparked the incidents back in the 1950s to 1960s continue to ring true today, notably demands for intellectual freedom, reimplementation of intraparty democracy, and democratic centralism. Chapter 2 also analyzes the crackdown on intellectuals and the intraparty purge in the context of today's dissidents who demand redress and rehabilitation.

Chapter 3 begins with an analysis of the purge of Politburo member Tran Xuan Bach, the Politburo's debates over democratization, and the party's conservative retrenchment in reaction to the collapse of socialism in Eastern Europe. The chapter then analyzes the party's reaction and piecemeal responses to the 1998 Thai Binh peasant protests. The chapter looks at the contending visions of political reform among the dissidents: regardless of their support for a Western-style multiparty democracy, all demand a strengthened and more independent role for the National Assembly. The intellectuals' campaign for the legalization of society and, significantly, the abolition of article 4 of the constitution that places the party above the law and, in effect, creates a "new class" of party members who are alienated from society is also examined here.[3] In short, this is a look at the attempt to rid the country of all its Stalinist influences and to broaden democracy.

Chapter 4 revisits many of the themes found in the earlier discussion of the *Nhan Van–Giai Pham* affair, notably intellectual freedom and freedom of the press. It begins by analyzing how the party controls the press and intellectuals, and how those constraints—or freedoms—have been used by the various VCP general secretaries since *doi moi* was implemented to further their political and economic reform agendas. The chapter also examines the dissidents' rationale for free speech and analyzes their specific demands and suggestions for reform.

Although the underlying theme of Chapter 5 is the continued rift between the north and south and the lingering issue of national reconciliation, the chapter focuses on the role of the Club of Former Resistance Fighters, the country's first and only independent political grouping. Made up of former members of the National Liberation Front, Provisional Revolutionary Government, and Communist Party apparatus in the south, club members were vocal in their anger at the party's mismanagement of the economy, the reconciliation process, and corruption, among other things. The club became the first independent pressure group and sought to serve as a loyal opposition to the party, before the regime cracked down, forcing the club's closure after only four years of existence.

Chapter 6 looks at dissidence, but from a different sector: religion. Religion, especially the main faiths of Buddhism and Catholicism, has always been highly politicized in Vietnam. Although this deviates from the thesis that much contemporary dissent to the party in Vietnam comes from within the intellectual and party elite, the power of the churches to confront the authority of the state is immense and, therefore, must be analyzed. Moreover, the demands of the clergy are, in many cases, the same as those of the secular dissident movement. And the role of the various churches is important for another reason: they help to create civil society, with groupings autonomous from state control. The chapter concludes that the party spends an inordinate amount of energy trying to control religious organizations. The small dissident movement, without links to broader socially based autonomous organizations, is a minimal threat to the regime.

The government's and party's various responses to the critics are the subject of Chapter 7. Responses include attack and persecution, but also openly campaigning on the same concerns as raised by the dissidents. In many cases, what concerns the dissidents often concerns the party—but the latter is angered that the dissidents do not operate through proper party channels. The VCP can be critical of itself and lead rectification campaigns, but it countenances no independent criticism or dissent. All the same, the party's response to external pressures for political reform and improving its human rights conditions is far different: Vietnam is vulnerable to exogenous forces.

Notes

1. Georges Boudarel, *Cent Fleurs aecloses dans la Nuit du Vietnam: Communisme et Dissidence 1954–1956* (Paris: Jacques Bertoin); Boudarel, "Intellectual Dissidence in the 1950s: The Nhan-Van Giai-Pham Affair," *Vietnam Forum* 13 (1994): 154–164; Hirohide Kurihara, "Changes in the Literary Policy of the Vietnamese Workers' Party, 1956–1958," in *Indochina in the 1940s and 1950s* (Ithaca, N.Y.: Southeast Asia Program, Cornell University, 1992), 165–196; Neil Jamieson, *Understanding Vietnam* (Berkeley: University of California Press, 1993), 257–284.

2. William Duiker, *The Communist Road to Power* (Boulder, Colo.: Westview Press, 1981).

3. Milovan Djilas, *The New Class* (New York: Praeger, 1974).

I

POLITICS IN VIETNAM

In inner-party politics, these methods lead, as we shall see, to this: the party organization substitutes itself for the party, the central committee substitutes itself for the organization, and, finally a dictator substitutes himself for the central committee.

—Leon Trotsky

Even a purely moral act that has no hope of any immediate and visible political effect can gradually and indirectly over time, gain in political significance.

—Vaclav Havel in a letter to President Alexander Dubcek, 1968

Agents of Change: Why Dissidents Matter

The mere rise of dissidence in Vietnam is not a harbinger of the collapse of communist rule. The Communist Party in Vietnam is not large but it is entrenched and it has a near monopoly of coercive powers. The party has deep roots in society, having won its authority on both the international and domestic battlefields and not being installed by the Soviet Red Army. There are some dissidents who are outspoken and articulate a vision of political reform, but they do not yet form a critical mass with links to the broader population. Many in society may sympathize with them, but few are willing to challenge the authoritarian regime. In short, Vietnam lacks agents of change: organized and autonomous groups with their own authority system and ability to organize, articulate views, and represent the interests of their constituency. For political change to occur, there needs to be a broad alliance between different classes and sectors, such as the intellectual-peasant alliance

9

that defeated the French in the mid-1940s to 1950s that brought the VCP to power.[1] This is evident not just in Vietnam but across the region and in Eastern Europe, which saw a profound political transformation as liberal democracies emerged from authoritarian regimes.

The Economic Crisis, the Middle Class, and Agents of Change in Asia

The Asian economic crisis, which began in the summer of 1997 following the Thai government's failed defense of the baht, caused a reevaluation of the region's political systems, but political change was only possible because of the development of society and the rise in the number of agents of change. Although much of the crisis can be explained by easy access to short-term foreign capital used for long-term projects or speculative investments, in many ways the crisis can be explained also by the existing and opaque political systems in the region. It was not that capitalism was excessive, but that there were no checks on the economic players who had close ties with their governments. To this end, although 1997–1999 was overshadowed by the economic collapse of the Asian economies, there were very important political reforms throughout the region. For the first time an opposition figure, Kim Dae Jung, was elected president in Korea. Popular pressure in Thailand resulted in the resignation of the government of Premier Chaovalit and the passage of sweeping constitutional changes following the election of Chuan Lekpai's Democratic Party. Most striking were the student-led protests in Indonesia that ended President Suharto's 32-year authoritarian reign and the continued protests that dogged his successor, B. J. Habibie right through the June 1999 election, Indonesia's first free and fair election since 1955. In Malaysia, following the sacking and arrest of reformist Deputy Prime Minister Anwar Ibrahim, students and protestors took to the street daily to protest the capricious and authoritarian rule of Prime Minister Mahathir Mohammed. Anwar Ibrahim's wife, Wan Azizah Wan Ismail, and other associates founded a popular opposition party. In Taiwan, opposition parties surged ahead in local elections and, for the first time, led the country at the national level. In the Philippines, Joseph Estrada was elected president on a populist platform, reinforcing the concept of a peaceful, regularized transition of power.

Three points should be noted. First, throughout the region democracy is taking hold. This flies in the face of the "Asian values" argument, propounded constantly throughout the 1990s, which argued that

Asians give preference to "order-supporting values" and needed a strong government that could ensure societal harmony.[2] There is little validity to the notion that democracy is anathema to Asia and at odds with "Asian values."

Second, in all these cases the force for political change came from outside the ruling circles; there were strong independent agents of political change, whether unions, religious entities, students, political parties, or societal groupings. In the Philippines, the Catholic Church was a key political actor, but Corazon Aquino's People Power revolution could never have occurred without the support of the armed forces, especially General Fidel Ramos, her successor in Malacañang Palace. Students forced Suharto from power in Indonesia, but with the help of an independent party led by Sukarno's daughter Megawati and Abdurrahman Wahid's Nahdlatul Ulama. In Burma, the students and an independent, though harassed, political party, the National League for Democracy, led by Nobel Prize winner Aung San Suu Ky, continue to be a thorn in the side of the military junta that runs the country. In Taiwan, political change was driven by the legalization of the outlawed Democratic People's Party. In Malaysia, protests are being conducted by the student and religious wings of the ruling political party UMNO, as well as the Islamic party PAS and several smaller opposition parties such as the Democratic Action Party and the National Awakening Party. In China, students and the potential of independent labor unions threatened the regime during the Tiananmen Square massacre in June 1989. In South Korea, students were also active, but independent and very militant labor unions were the key actors in forcing political change.

Third, the growth of an urbanized middle class facilitated political reform.[3] A key requisite for democracy is a large urbanized middle class, for it is the middle class, with greater mobility (physical and social), better communication, and higher education and literacy that push for the establishment of the rule of law, property rights, and political rights to protect individual freedoms. Eventually members of the middle class enter politics to implement policies that benefit their class interests. Moreover, with economic development, society shifts from being one "class" of people involved in agriculture to a complex society with many different and competing groups and interests. With the development of the economy, "a centrally-dominated social order is increasingly difficult to maintain" as new groups compete to articulate their interests.[4] The opening of an economy serves as a catalyst to this process because the bourgeoisie will demand greater liberalization and transparency in decisionmaking.[5] Regimes that maintain authoritarian political systems, impede transparent decisionmaking, restrict a free press, and are in general paternalistic may be able to offer rapid economic development for a time, but not over the long run. This was brought to the fore across East and Southeast Asia during the economic crisis of 1997–1999.

The Development of Civil Society in Eastern Europe

Likewise, in the former socialist bloc, there were strong institutions that served as agents of political change. In Poland there was a solid alliance between the Catholic Church, which was strong and autonomous enough to resist the Communist Party dictates, the Solidarity labor movement, and intellectuals. Professional associations, such as networks of physicians, also provided a forum for the middle class and intellectuals to organize. In East Germany, in addition to the example of a more successful and less repressive model of governance in West Germany, the Catholic Church was also strong. In Hungary, a fairly successful economic reform program begun in 1962 had created new sectors of society, and indeed factions in the ruling Communist Party, that had a vested interest in continued reform. Across much of Eastern Europe there was a large, disgruntled urban middle class that was fed up with the "overwhelming bureaucratization of every aspect of daily life," constant shortages, and the barrage of lies and ideological exhortations that came from a corrupt, despotic, and sometimes nepotistic communist oligarchy.[6] Daniel Chirot argues that although the poor economic conditions were a factor, "What happened was that the moral base of communism had vanished" as "educated urbanites living in a highly politicized atmosphere where there are constant pronouncements about the guiding ideological vision of fairness, equality, and progress could not help but react with growing disgust" at the corruption and nepotism that plagued society.[7]

Moreover, throughout Eastern Europe there slowly emerged civic organizations that acted independently of the respective communist parties. For Robert Putnam, this is a far greater indicator of democratization than mere economic development,[8] though clearly there is a correlation between development and the number of civic organizations because economic development creates new sectors and groups.

This is not to say that there were no exogenous forces at work in Eastern Europe. There was constant pressure from the West and the successful socioeconomic models they offered. One of the most important "outside" forces was Soviet President Mikhail Gorbachev's October 1989 Berlin speech in which he not only announced his support for reform in Eastern Europe, but avowed that the Soviet Union would never again intervene to alter the course of such reforms as it had done in Hungary in 1956 and Czechoslovakia in 1968. Nonetheless, the real cause of the collapse, according to Chirot, was the urban middle class that could no longer tolerate the "utter moral rot."

But much of the impetus for reform came from within the parties themselves. Adam Przeworski argues that socialist regimes liberalize for two reasons: first, because of factionalism and divergent interests among institutions and, second, from social pressure.[9] But it is factionalism that is the key, because social pressure alone rarely causes change. What is to stop the unified state from cracking down as happened in June 1989 in Beijing? In the competitive political arena, factions need supporters, members of the elite, interest groups, institutions, and even classes. To this end, according to Przeworski, each faction tries to reduce state pressure on these groups or institutions and, in return for loyalty, they are given more autonomy. As the societal forces and groups organize and expand, the regime is ultimately faced with a choice between a brutal crackdown or a transition to democracy.[10] In Eastern Europe, the costs of repression became too high as civil society sprang from the competition among social forces, new and old political and economic actors, and autonomous groupings. As Samuel Huntington argues, democratic transitions are only possible when the leaders of these new social forces form key alliances with moderates in the government. Both groups negotiate the transition and shun the more radical positions of their colleagues, whether radicals in society who want to overthrow the existing system or government hardliners who want to crack down to maintain absolute power.[11]

Agents of Change in Vietnam

Unlike Eastern Europe where the forces of change were autonomous groups in society, Vietnam has no such groups. There is no independent labor movement, for instance, even an underground one (moreover, the size of the urban proletariat is quite small). The VCP-controlled Vietnam General Confederation of Labor has over 3.3 million members in some 35,184 separate unions, comprising half of the industrial and manufacturing workforce. A radical and politicized student movement as in South Korea, Indonesia, or Malaysia does not exist in Vietnam. As one graduate student told an American journalist:

> Foreigners ask me why students don't go to the street as they did in China or Indonesia. It's simple. If you're in college, you're either the child of a cadre and you think that the system is O.K. Or your family is wealthy and is benefiting from the system. Or you're the first kid from a poor farmer's family ever to go to college. You're not going to ruin your family's chance for a better life by demonstrating for democracy.[12]

Even if Vietnam had a radical student movement, its effects would likely be small because their numbers would impose limitations: only 2 percent of the population graduates from institutions of higher education.[13] The church is divided between the state-controlled religious establishment and the underground and besieged Buddhist and Catholic churches (the subject of Chapter 6). This is of concern to the regime, which has gone to great lengths to maintain firm control of all religious activity. The urbanized middle class is still small, though it is growing, and its economic position has not been threatened in any way that would galvanize it into challenging the state. There is an active intellectual community, but perhaps most significant has been the growth of civil society in Vietnam. Carlyle Thayer argues that the marketization of the Vietnamese economy has led to the rapid establishment of a civil society: all of a sudden, there is a need for new organizations to represent new sectors of society. Although these professional organizations and associations, according to Thayer, are first authorized by the government, their importance to the government gives them significant autonomy, and increasingly the professional organizations are not responsible to the Vietnam Fatherland Front, the party's umbrella organization.[14]

The VCP has the capacity and the will to maintain its monopoly of power through coercive force and has little reason to back down. Under the 1992 constitution, the military is obligated to defend not just the Vietnamese nation but the socialist regime as well. It is a regime that continues to imprison thousands of political and religious prisoners and deny its population press freedom and the right to organize. The Ministry of the Interior, under the directive 31/CP is authorized to detain people without trial for up to two years, while directive 89/CP authorizes military and security forces to set up temporary detainment camps to fight popular unrest. Vietnam claims to not have any political or religious prisoners, but simply common criminals; but as Amnesty International notes, in violation of its own constitution "Vietnamese law criminalizes the right to freedom of expression."[15] Although the Vietnamese government annually commemorates its signing of the Universal Declaration of Human Rights, the leadership has warned not only that "we need to selectively absorb human values in accordance with Vietnam's political, economic, cultural and social conditions," but that "we also have to take measures to prevent those who take advantage of 'human rights and democracy' to interfere in Vietnam's internal affairs and sovereignty."[16] Vietnam has repeatedly asserted that "each country has its own way to deal with its own problems in order to maintain stability."[17] To that end it has refused to allow foreign monitoring of its human rights conditions.[18] Nonetheless, there has not been enough coercion on a wide enough scale to push the people into challenging the state. There are committed and articulate critics of the regime in Vietnam, but they have no alliances with any other segments of society. Autonomous actors, what I term *agents of change,* just do not exist in critical numbers at this point in Vietnam, so the dissidents remain isolated and unable to broaden their base of support. As Brantly Womack noted, "Vietnam's social forces are less autonomous and aggressive than in Europe."[19]

The Vietnamese Political System

The VCP's Consolidation of Power

The origins of the Vietnam Communist Party date back to 1925, when Comintern official and Vietnamese nationalist leader Ho Chi Minh founded the Revolutionary Youth League in southern China. Hobbled by factionalism, the group was defunct by May 1929.[20] After uniting feuding communist groups operating in southern China, Ho founded the Indochina Communist Party (ICP) in 1930. The group operated clandestinely because French colonial authorities imprisoned many of its leaders. The ICP grew, however, into the preeminent anticolonial force in French Indochina.

To widen the ICP's appeal, Ho created a broad nationalist united front, known as the Viet Minh, under this party's leadership in 1941. Viet Minh troops waged a guerrilla war against Japanese and Vichy French troops and cooperated with U.S. forces. Following Japan's surrender, Ho's Viet Minh marched into Hanoi and declared the founding of the Democratic Republic of Vietnam (DRV) on 2 September 1945. Ho then dissolved the ICP in order to assuage fears that communist forces would dominate the new coalition government. With the return of French colonial forces and the breakdown of a series of negotiations in 1946, the Viet Minh began a guerrilla war, culminating in the historic 1954 defeat of French forces at Dien Bien Phu. Materially aided by the People's Republic of China after April 1950, the Viet Minh leadership was strongly encouraged to restore the Communist Party to power. In February 1951, the Lao Dong [Workers] Party (LDP) was founded.

Under intense Chinese, Soviet, and French pressure, the DRV was forced to accept the temporary division of Vietnam at the 17th parallel as part of the Geneva Accords, although it anticipated winning nationwide elections scheduled for 1956–1957. The LDP was the sole political force in the north and began to implement an authoritarian political system and Stalinist economic program. The LDP implemented a two-stage land reform program from 1954 to 1960 that was particularly brutal and had an adverse effect on production. At the advice of Chinese advisors, "people's courts" were established and "class labels" were applied to all members of society to identify and liquidate the landlord class.[21] Widespread violence and peasant unrest led the LDP to sack its general secretary, Truong Chinh, and revise its policies. The LDP also imposed a strict system of control over its writers and artists, beginning in 1954.

Dismayed at the continued division of the country, in May 1959, the LDP Politburo authorized support for southern revolutionaries to defeat the regime of Ngo Dinh Diem. In 1963, the LDP ordered the infiltration of North Vietnamese troops into the south of the country. The LDP continued its policy of liberating the south following Ho's death in 1969, and eventually negotiated peace with the Americans in 1973. In 1974, the Politburo again ordered the use of force to liberate the south, which fell on 30 April 1975. Formal reunification occurred at the VCP's Fourth National Congress in October 1976, at which point the LDP changed its name to the Vietnam Communist Party. From 1976 to 1986, the VCP consolidated its rule but led the country into an economic malaise and diplomatic isolation following the December 1978 invasion of Cambodia and the March 1979 war with China.

The rapid push to collectivize the southern economy after 1976, including the disastrous currency reform and flight of ethnic Chinese, caused severe economic imbalances in a system that for thirty years had been geared solely to the war effort. Thirty years of war against the French, Japanese, and Americans, as well as ten years of war in

Cambodia and a brief war against China in 1979, had nearly bank-rupted the economy. Over one-third of the national budget went to the military, on top of an average of $1 billion in annual Soviet military aid. War communism had crippled Vietnamese industry that was further reeling from the cessation of Chinese aid after 1978. Membership in the Soviet trade bloc, the Council on Mutual Economic Assistance, and Soviet aid simply created greater distortions in the national economy, and things were just as bad in the countryside. The collectivization of agriculture in the south—the country's ricebasket—led to a net de-crease in per capita output, and by 1982 much of collective farming had to be scrapped. Inflation, by 1986, was in the triple digits.[22] This was the context in which Vietnam embarked on a course of economic and limited political reform at the VCP's Sixth National Congress in December 1986.

Nguyen Van Linh, the Ho Chi Minh City (Saigon) party chief, who had been dropped from the Politburo at the Fifth Congress in 1982, was quietly brought back onto the Secretariat and the Politburo in 1985 in acknowledgment of his reform program in the south that had already seen tangible results. At the Sixth Party Congress, he was appointed general secretary and his reforms were implemented at the national level. Most important, Chinese-style family-level agriculture contracts replaced collective farming, turning Vietnam in one year from a net im-porter of foodstuffs to one of the world's leading exporters of rice. For-eign investment was courted and exports encouraged; policymaking was decentralized; private enterprises were legalized, creating an entire class of small-scale traders; and centrally planned pricing was scrapped as market reforms took hold. These reforms had real results: inflation was brought down from triple digits, budget deficits fell, the currency was stabilized, and the country's balance of payments improved.

Nonetheless, Linh had a lot of trouble getting the entrenched com-munist bureaucracy, which gained its power and privileged position in society by controlling the distribution of money and resources, to im-plement his reforms. To counter this formidable and recalcitrant bu-reaucracy, Linh tried to decentralize decisionmaking, giving the provinces more autonomy. Second, Linh used *coi moi* ("openness") to liberalize the press and empower intellectuals whom he hoped would rally to his side, expose corruption and graft, and cajole the bureau-cracy into implementing the necessary reforms.[23]

For the most part, journalists, writers, artists, and other intellectu-als did just that. Investigative reporting was permitted, though there were still sacred cows. An incredible degree of artistic freedom was tolerated and encouraged; during the late 1980s, Vietnamese literature and art hit the world stage to near universal acclaim. Socialist realism was dropped and intellectual boundaries expanded, empowering many in becoming even bolder in their criticism of Vietnamese society, culture, and politics. This caused alarm among party conservatives who remembered the intellectually liberal period in the mid-1950s that had nearly caused a split in the party and resulted in a brutal crackdown on writers, artists, and intellectuals (the subject of Chapter 2).

With the collapse of communism in Eastern Europe in 1989, Linh and the party conservatives rejected all movement toward intellectual and political liberalization. Writers who had flourished in the mid- to late 1980s could no longer publish their works. Journalists were constrained by fears of being prosecuted for "revealing state secrets" and publishing "antisocialist material." Advocates of political reform, including senior party members, were fired, imprisoned, or put under house arrest.

At the VCP's Seventh National Congress in 1991, the party further cemented its ties with China and the remaining socialist community by adopting the Chinese model of continued economic reform with no concurrent political reform. In other words, the party would continue *doi moi*, but reject *coi moi* and anything that could possibly lead to the dissipation of the party's monopoly of power and the collapse of socialism in Vietnam. This resulted in another wave of dissidence, this time broader than the first. Encompassing more than disgruntled writers and artists who wanted greater intellectual freedom and freedom of speech, dissidence in the 1990s centered around disaffected high-ranking party members angered by the slow pace and narrow scope of the reform program and the lack of any meaningful reform of Vietnam's political institutions.

Vietnamese Political Institutions

Vietnam is a one-party state in which the VCP monopolizes all economic and political decisionmaking. The party's penetration of society is deep and "there can be no doubt that officials still intend the state to play an interventionist role in society, on all fronts at every level."[24] Like most other socialist states, Vietnam is characterized by interlocking directorates by which every government unit has a party component (*ban can su dang*) down to the village level. Although there is a state bureaucratic apparatus, it is controlled by the party through membership, appointments, and policy directives. Overall membership in the party is small, approximately 2.5 million members, or 3 percent of the population. Although 1999 saw a massive recruitment drive, the party was concerned that it was unable to attract youth into its ranks, and most who joined did so for reasons of career advancement and not ideology or a commitment to public service. Power is concentrated in the VCP's elite Central Committee, which has grown from the 101 members of the Fourth Congress Central Committee that saw the reunification of the country in 1976, to 170 members of the Eighth Congress in 1996. The Central Committee is a uniform organization dominated by middle-aged men. The committee meets at least twice a year, while the VCP's national congress is held approximately every five years. Within the Central Committee power is concentrated in the hands of the Politburo, which itself has expanded from thirteen to nineteen members, having dropped alternate members in 1990. The VCP's Secretariat was abolished in 1996 due to too much overlap in the concurrent membership of the Politburo, and replaced by a five-member Standing Committee of the Politburo. Since the death of Ho Chi Minh in 1969, there has been no paramount leader and the standard operating code of the Politburo has been collective leadership. Decisions are now based less on consensus than on factionalism and ideological differences over the pace and scope of reform, but the decisionmaking process in the Politburo retains its wartime clandestine nature.[25] As David Marr sums up, "Although the 1992 Constitution enjoins the party to fulfill its leading role within the law, old habits persist; a great deal of state affairs are still conducted secretly by a party hierarchy which is internally self-justifying and self regulating."[26]

The Vietnam People's Army (VPA) is one of the country's key political institutions.[27] Though nominally under the command of the state, since 1992 it is constitutionally responsible, in addition to national defense, to the maintenance of the party's monopoly of power. The VPA has been cut in size from over a wartime high of 1.5 million men, to around 500,000–600,000 men. The VPA is guaranteed a block of seats in the Central Committee (10–13 percent) and currently has four of eighteen members on the Politburo, and usually more. The senior party organization that controls the VPA is the Party Military Affairs Commission, chaired by the VCP's general secretary.

The National Assembly has traditionally been nothing more than a rubber stamp for party decisions, though it has fought to expand its role and autonomy since *doi moi* was implemented in 1986. By the late 1990s, it had become far more powerful and assertive, often challenging the party and government line, although it still does not have true autonomy. The party has traditionally controlled membership in the National Assembly. Although "independent" candidates are technically eligible, the party must first vet them. The National Assembly has become more assertive and has rejected party policies and candidates, but its power is still limited.

The government would like to assert strong central control over all parts of the country, but this is countered by a strong tradition of regionalism compounded by poor communications and infrastructure and the war that saw the country divided into military zones, and regions maintain considerable autonomy. The traditional maxim that "the emperor's rule stops at the village gate" continues to ring true in part. After reunification, some provinces were consolidated to facilitate the center's management over them, but the provincial leaders became too powerful and, in the 1990s, they were broken up again. Prime Minister Vo Van Kiet tried to limit provincial authority by maintaining the central government's right to appoint and fire provincial leaders, but failed to wrest total control from them.[28] To date, the center seems willing to tolerate regional autonomy as long as it retains the power to overrule any single provincial decision.

The party maintains its links with the people through a number of mass organizations, which are controlled by the VCP's Fatherland Front. By 1990, there were some 124 center-level mass organizations, and over 300 provincial- and municipal-level organizations.[29] The four largest are the Vietnam General Confederation of Labor, with 3.3 million members in 1989, or half the industrial workforce; the Vietnam Peasants Association, with 7 million members and 10,000 chapters; the Ho Chi Minh Communist Youth Union, with chapters in every school; and the Vietnam Women's Union. Greg Lockhart contends that "the national network of mass organizations faded after the war, in the late 1970s and early 1980s, partly, it is sometimes said, because the Communist Party of Vietnam feared the growing influence of some of them."[30] Yet once *doi moi* was under way and there were calls for increased democratization and political reform, the party "began to revive mass organizations and reestablish mass mobilization as a central element in the Vietnamese political process."[31] As any democratization had to be contained, the existing communist-controlled associations and unions were the appropriate bodies and forums. This, according to

Yeonsik Jeong, has given Vietnam the characteristic of a corporatist society.[32]

In Vietnam, democracy is viewed through a Marxist-Leninist lens: Western democracy is not really democracy because it only represents the interests of a single class, the bourgeoisie, and not the working class. The VCP asserts that it is democratic because it represents the interests of the majority of the population, the peasants and the proletariat. This justifies the state monopoly of the press: independent news organs would not represent the interests of the majority of the population but only the narrow interests of the owners' class. Democracy in Vietnam, though, runs from the top down and not from the bottom up, just as it is in the VCP and its mass organizations that represent the people's interests. The standard operating procedure is based on the concept of democratic centralism (*tap trung dan chu*). In short, democratic centralism allows for limited debate within party ranks until a decision has been made, at which point no member is allowed to stray from or criticize the party line. There have been gradual reforms, and particularly in the Communist Party's own ranks greater levels of democratic participation have emerged. Even the National Assembly has become slightly more democratic, though the party still controls membership and many of the outcomes.

The concept of political legitimacy in Vietnam was traditionally based on the imperial Chinese concept of the "mandate of heaven" as well as two Vietnamese concepts: *duc* and *the*. *Duc* refers to personal morality, or rectitude, as well as charisma. Stephen Young contends that it was to acquire legitimacy that the VCP appealed to Ho Chi Minh's *duc* and propagated an entire hagiography and "cult" of Ho.[33] *The* refers to the ability to master circumstances and control the external environment, that is, win wars against superior enemies, develop the economy, and become a powerful state in the region. The regime continues to base its mandate to rule on its leadership in the wars of national liberation and the reunification of the country, as well as "performance legitimacy" in improving the lives of the people. In terms of the former it has had tremendous success, never failing to remind its people that it was the party that led the people to victory over the foreign imperialists. However, because over 60 percent of the population was born after the reunification of the country in 1976, the party has increasingly had to switch to performance legitimacy. In this regard the regime is losing popular support, and will continue to do so until meaningful and sustainable economic reforms are implemented and corruption is effectively dealt with. Despite calls by the party for thrift and the implementation of upright socialist values, corruption in the party is really causing the leadership to lose its *duc*-based legitimacy.

Vietnamese leaders have also framed their concept of democracy in the rhetoric of the "Asian values" debate.[34] While there is no clear definition of Asian values, most advocates speak of four themes: (1) the need for an orderly society and societal harmony, in which individual rights never take precedence over the rights of the group; (2) social duties rather than rights; (3) group membership and community rather than the individual; and (4) unquestioned and unchallenged respect for authority. In short, proponents of Asian values see democracy as a Western import that is anathema to Asian values and culture.

The Vietnamese political system, in sum, is primarily geared to the maintenance of the VCP's political monopoly. In terms of policymaking it tends to be very reactive to problems. The system is geared toward maintaining the status quo, rather than leading the country forward.

The Vietnamese Perception of Threat

The Vietnamese leadership has identified two distinct threats and tailored its political institutions to addressing them. The first is a menace from China to Vietnam's territorial integrity along their 400-mile land border, in the Gulf of Tonkin, and around Spratly and Paracel Islands in the South China Sea. The second threat is less easily identifiable, often labeled "peaceful evolution."[35] This is the threat from the growth of democratization, human rights, and other Western values that will cause the dissipation of Marxist-Leninist-Ho Chi Minh ideology and the monopoly of power held by the VCP. "After socialism collapsed in the former Soviet Union and other Eastern European countries," warned one commentator, "Vietnam has become a vital place for carrying out peaceful evolution by imperialism."[36] Therefore, "today, defending the fatherland is not only defending the land, airspace and territorial waters; it is also the defense of Marxism-Leninism and Ho Chi Minh Thought, the party leadership, and the socialist revolutionary path chosen by our party and people."[37]

In the short run, the Vietnamese believe the Chinese are too focused on building up their domestic economy to pose a major threat to Vietnam even though tensions over the Spratly Islands remain high. That leaves the Vietnamese to concentrate on the threat of subversion to VCP rule. The party has identified "four dangers" to the regime's existence:

economic underdevelopment, deviation from the socialist path, corruption, and spiritual pollution. This concern was made explicit in the VPA white paper issued in September 1998. In this document, the VPA revealed that its utmost national security concern is not on its northern border. "The plots to interfere in Vietnam's internal affairs in the disguise of 'human rights' and 'democracy,' the intrusion into this country by means of culture and ideology, activation of subversion and destabilization for the purpose of replacing the current political and social system are all great menaces to Vietnam's security and national defense."[38]

The VCP is determined not to surrender any political power: after watching with horror in 1989 to what happened to its Eastern European counterparts, the VCP has spent much of its energy since then consolidating its power. Even political moderates such as President Tran Duc Luong have put the reform process in the context of unchallenged party rule: "Renovation and stability are two unified faces of development, compounding each other and the effect of each other. In other words, there can not be one without the other."[39] Former Politburo member Tran Xuan Bach argued that there could not be stability without some political reform. For Bach, economic liberalization could only be successful when coupled with political liberalization: "You can't walk with one long leg and one short one, and you can't walk with only one leg," he said in a January 1990 interview.[40] This is the central concern confronting the Vietnamese leadership: Does economic liberalization necessarily lead to political pluralism, and, if so, can the VCP maintain its dominance over the political process?

It is an insecure regime, one that realizes it has rested on its laurels for too long, thought itself to be infallible, and not delivered economic development to its people. It is this single point that has led many senior party members, many with impeccable revolutionary credentials, to join the ranks of dissent.

Who Are the Dissidents?

Calls for political reform within Vietnam are interesting for a number of reasons. First, demands for political reform come not from outside but from within the polity, and often from the highest echelons. The leading dissidents are not electricians, the disenfranchised, or those who have been alienated for years. In general they are lifelong party members with irreproachable revolutionary records. And unlike outsiders who have nothing to lose by challenging the state, Vietnamese dissidents could be stripped of everything: their positions and status, which includes those of their children. The major exceptions to the makeup of the dissidents are those in the Unified Buddhist Church and a few in the south, many of whom gained their political consciousness by protesting against the Ngo Dinh Diem regime and others in the former Republic of Vietnam. These dissidents without long-standing ties to the VCP have been persecuted harshly.

For the purpose of this study, I primarily analyze the writings and views of well-known political dissidents and several senior members of the Buddhist and Catholic clergies. There are approximately thirty well-known dissidents with followings both inside and outside the country who have caught the attention of the human rights and international community for their continued articulation of political reform. No doubt, there are far more. Amnesty International reports that as of the beginning of 1998 "at least 54 prisoners of conscience and possible prisoners of conscience arrested in previous years were known to be detained throughout the year, although the figure may have been higher."[41] Countless others are under surveillance, harassed or detained by the police. The U.S. Department of State's annual human rights report for Vietnam estimated that there were at least 200 political prisoners in Vietnam,[42] while some overseas Vietnamese exile groups claim the number to be over 1,000. With the September 1998 presidential amnesty that saw Thich Quan Do, Doan Viet Hoat, and Nguyen Dan Que's release, there are only a few prominent dissidents still imprisoned.

Of the 25 most prominent secular dissidents, 16 are or were party members. Of those 16, five joined during the Indochina Communist Party era, that is, before 1950. Of the 16 members, 9 were expelled from the party, while 2 resigned. Several others were censured. Only 7 of the dissidents have served lengthy prison sentences.

The average age is in the mid- to late 60s, and all but two are men. Geographically they are predominantly southerners: 9 live in Ho Chi Minh City (Saigon) while 4 more live in Dalat. Eight live in Hanoi, while 1, Bui Tin, lives in exile in France, and several others now reside in the United States. The five leading religious dissidents are all based in the south.

They represent a wide range of occupations, but seven of them are writers, journalists, editors, or former propaganda officials. Other intellectuals include two doctors, a geologist, historian, mathematician, and economist. There are also several former security officials and military officers, including the chief of cabinet in the Ministry of the Interior and a high-level official in the Central Committee's Internal Security Bureau. Three were members of the VCP's Central Committee, while two others were high-level officials in the Central Committee's various departments.

Over half of the dissidents served in the military during the War of National Liberation, either as cadres, soldiers, or propaganda officials; one was second in command of Hanoi's forces in the south. Four participated in the anti-French war. Several were members of the National Liberation Front (NLF), including one of its original founders, Dr. Duong Quynh Hoa. She, and one other dissident, Lu Phuong, were Provisional Revolutionary Government ministers and deputy minister, respectively.

Among the most notable are Bui Tin, a colonel in the VPA who served in the south and then in Cambodia, who later became an editor at the party daily, *Nhan Dan*. Lt. Gen. Tran Do was a top ideologue in the party, a long-time head of the Central Committee's Culture Committee, and second in command of Hanoi's forces in the south during the war. For his letter-writing campaign in 1998, the Central Committee censured him and then expelled him from the party in January 1999. Duong Quynh Hoa, who served as the minister of health in the Provisional National Government, resigned from the party in 1995. Duong Thu Huong is an internationally acclaimed novelist, who was labeled by General Secretary Nguyen Van Linh the "dissident whore" after the publication of her second novel, *Paradise of the Blind,* for which she was expelled from the party and later arrested.

Other leading dissidents include Do Trung Hieu, a party member for thirty-six years before being expelled in 1992. He was the former head of the party's Mass Mobilization Department in Saigon and thus responsible for organizing students and intellectuals. Nguyen Thanh Giang, a prominent intellectual and geologist, gained notoriety for his attempts to run for a seat in the National Assembly as an independent candidate. He was arrested in March 1999. Two younger academics, both nonparty members, Ha Si Phu, a biologist, and Phan Dinh Dieu, a mathematician, have written some of the sharpest intellectual attacks on ideology.

One of the most important dissidents is a veteran revolutionary from the south, Nguyen Ho, who founded the Club of Former Resistance Fighters (CFRF) in 1986. The club, which was comprised of hundreds of war heroes and members of the "Viet Cong," was critical of Hanoi's treatment of the south after the war, Hanoi's downplaying of the role of the Viet Cong, and Hanoi's handling of the economy since reunification in 1976. Other CFRF officials include Nguyen Phong Ho Hieu, Nguyen Van Tran, and La Van Lam.

With the exception of the religious leaders and a few southern-based dissidents, the above were all members of the ruling elite. These are people with a deep commitment to the revolution and the Vietnamese nation. They had nothing to gain and everything to lose by embarking on their various courses of action. Almost all gave most of their lives to working for Vietnam's independence and sovereignty, and are patriots above all else. As Hue-Tam Ho Tai so elegantly wrote about Duong Thu Huong, "She continues to believe that the ten years she spent dodging bombs and bullets in the central highlands were the best years of her life. They are the inspiration of her many themes and one source of the moral authority she brings to her new role as a political dissident."[43]

Most acknowledge the important role the VCP played in liberating the country, but are unhappy with its policies implemented since reunification. This attitude is summed up succinctly by Do Trung Hieu who complained that "for 40 years I had fought under the flag of the VCP out of love for this country and people and out of hope that the party would build a powerful country with social justice. Reality has proved otherwise. The party leads the country closer to a dead end. The VCP must seriously review its methods."[44]

Ha Si Phu used the analogy of a boat (the party) to cross the river (independence). But on the far shore it is simply encumbering the country, and not allowing it to catch up to its fellows who are further down the road of development. He does not denigrate the importance of "crossing the river," for without independence the Vietnamese nation would not be able to develop itself. "The boat has helped us cross the river, but continuing our journey on foot with it is only cumbersome and cannot avoid criticism. That 'abnormal equipment' in our journey is truly useless to our people. If it could be dropped, we will be lightened and able to catch up with our friends on the long road."

Many are at odds with the notion that what is in the party's interest is in the nation's interest. Because they are (or were) members of the ruling elite and do have such strong revolutionary credentials, they are safer than the average dissident, members of the former South Vietnamese regime, or religious leaders. Although many, including their family members, have been detained or harassed, only seven served lengthy prison terms. This puts them with odds with other dissidents such as the southerners Nguyen Dan Que and Doan Viet Hoat who, though critical of the governments of South Vietnam, had no links to the Communist Party, and both served long prison terms.

For all these reasons, the regime considers the prominent individuals to be very dangerous. They are respected enormously and are seen as the voice of moral authority in the country: they have been in positions of leadership; they have protégés, supporters, and loyalists, many of whom are still within the regime, and as writers and leaders they are charismatic. However, they are mostly an aging group; it is to be seen whether another generation will emerge. But a group of older people, even a small one that is no longer in power, can be a catalyst. The Vietnamese leadership only has to look at the outpouring of popular feelings for Imre Nagy in Hungary or Alexander Dubcek in Czechoslovakia in the late 1980s that helped fuel the political reform process and the end of the communist monopoly of power.

The second and related point is that because most of these dissidents are (or until recently were) party members, in many ways they appear to be a nascent loyal opposition rather than a subversive counterrevolutionary grouping. These dissidents do not want to be dissidents. Having dedicated most of their lives to the revolution, wars of liberation, and the party, they are enormously patriotic, and many remain loyal to the party. And even if they are more critical of the party, few deny the important role the party played in the nation's independence. For the most part, these dissidents want to be a loyal opposition within the party, wanting to raise issues and policies that will strengthen Vietnam and, in some cases, rejuvenate the party. In the Sinic-Confucian-Marxist tradition, the intellectuals are bound to the state; traditionally through the imperial examination system, and in the Marxist-Leninist era through factionalism. Career advancement is linked to loyalty to the regime. Therefore, their demands are generally reasonable and fairly moderate.

For them, serving as a loyal opposition and making demands on the party and government is not only a right but a duty. As Merle Goldman writes about the obligations of intellectuals in Confucian societies: "Confucianism did not legally guarantee a loyal opposition, but it justified one ideologically. To criticize government misdeeds was not the literati's right, as in the West, but their responsibility."[45] Writing about the intellectual elite in Vietnam, the historian Alexander Woodside suggests similarities between the literati's role in pre- and postrevolutionary public life. Reform-minded intellectuals believed they were serving the people by serving the state. "Under both Confucian dynasties and communist dictatorships, policy-makers were not necessarily intellectuals, would encourage such state service by intellectuals through their patronage, the better to promote their own programs within an almost eternally factionalized political world."[46]

But this type of system has drawbacks for the process of democratization. In the context of Confucianism and communism, few intellectuals will stick their necks out to challenge the state, because it is the state that controls their careers and livelihood. Those few intellectuals who have defied the state are not mere intellectuals, but lifelong party members and veterans of the revolution. And this is a potential problem for gaining a broader base of elite support to compel the state to alter its current policies. As one dissident, Tieu Dao Bao Cu, complained:

> Up to now, intellectuals have been individuals, without organized forces, followers, and support. In today's struggle for democracy, intellectuals are supposed to be the leading flag. But is that really so, or the opposite true? Could it be, that deep down, intellectuals themselves are afraid of democracy; that with democracy they might lose certain privileges, immunity and interests considered exclusively theirs through the ages?[47]

In this observation is an important point. But perhaps the explanation for this phenomenon has more to do with the dissidents' inability to gain a wider following and to convince others, who are not in the elite, to sacrifice themselves. Perhaps a larger number would be willing to give up the trappings of being in the elite if there were greater popular support for the cause or links with independent agents of change.

Until that happens, dissent will continue to be in the purview of intellectuals and members of the political elite. For example, one who joined the chorus of dissidents was Mai Chi Tho, a former Politburo member, minister of the interior, and brother of Le Duc Tho, who wrote to the Politburo in October 1998 complaining of corruption and the deterioration of society and the party. Likewise, the loudest protest about the party's decision to oust Tran Do came from a fellow military intellectual, Col. Pham Que Duong, a former official in the military's History Department and editor in chief of the journal *Tap Chi Lich Su Quan Su (Military History Journal)*. The most recent critic has been Gen. Vo Nguyen Giap, the country's greatest living hero, who orchestrated Vietnam's military defeat of the French and Americans. The ninety-year-old general lashed out at the party for not reforming: "To be successful in these endeavors," he thundered, "the party must be truly democratic and learn from its mistakes, listen to the opinion of the people, reform its leadership methods and build a state based on the rule of law."[48] That this chastisement appeared in the official press is telling: there are many in the top echelons of the party who share his views, but few have his stature and are willing to openly challenge the state.

There is one additional shortcoming to the dissident movement in Vietnam: its members have real trouble in working together. This is not hard to fathom when one understands all the quarters that dissent comes from. Dissidents include lifelong Communists frustrated by current government policies; supporters of the old Saigon regimes; Buddhist monks and Catholic clergy; and artists, writers, and poets simply wanting freedom of expression. There is considerable mistrust among these groups, and they have no history of working together. Because they are divided, it is easier for the regime to isolate and dominate them and dissipate pressure for political reform. But as dissent now emerges from so many sources, it invites the question of why a critical mass of dissidents is emerging today.

Why Have They Emerged Now?

What has emboldened a critical mass of dissidents? As this book will show, there has always been some intellectual dissent confronting the VCP, beginning in the 1950s when intellectuals began to chafe under the rigid socialist system of arts and letters. But the party's crackdown was brutal, and with the exception of the brief period following the fall of Saigon, there was almost no dissent until *doi moi* was implemented in late 1986. *Doi moi* and the short-lived *coi moi* did lead to greater freedoms, and today dissent appears to be louder and to come from more sectors of society. There are four reasons for this. First, exogenous forces play an important role: the collapse of socialism in Eastern Europe and the former Soviet Union profoundly influenced both the VCP and the dissident community. While the VCP contends that its fraternal parties failed because they did not understand "reform" or they misapplied Marxist-Leninist doctrine, liberals believe that Vietnam is holding on to an outdated and failed ideology, placing it in the ranks of economic basket cases like North Korea. The demonstrated effects of the economic success, until late, of its ASEAN and "Asian tiger" neighbors is also important. Vietnam emerged from years of struggle as one of the poorest states not only in the region but in the world, yet it is in an area experiencing some of the most rapid economic growth the world has ever seen. With its opening up to the West, Vietnam has also become more vulnerable to foreign pressure. With the hosting of the November 1997 Francophone Summit, for example, Hanoi found itself under intense French pressure to release forty dissidents, whose names the French foreign minister presented to his Vietnamese counterpart. To present a better face to the international community foreign journalists were less restricted, which allowed one French TV crew to film the remote prison camp where a prominent dissident was being held. Likewise, human rights dominate every meeting between Vietnam and the United States. As Secretary of State Madeleine Albright told her Vietnamese hosts, "Human rights is a permanent issue for us. It is not going to go away."[49] And, of course, the Internet is changing the way that Vietnamese are able to communicate both among themselves and with exile and dissident groups abroad. This has caused great consternation in the Interior Ministry, which sees the Internet as a subversive force that must be thoroughly controlled.[50] Outside forces are not going to change the nature of the Vietnamese political system, but they do embolden critics.

Second, there is a malaise that has taken hold of Vietnam that contains a few elements. First is the economic reform program, which started in 1986 and had such wonderful initial results, that has died. The Vietnamese economy, by all measures, has been in dismal shape since 1997. Even though the first ten years of the reform program saw tangible improvements as the economy grew at an average annual rate of 7 to 8 percent, today the country is struggling to achieve 4 percent growth; barely enough to keep pace with the country's rapid population growth and a paltry figure for such an underdeveloped country.[51] Foreign investment has fallen by 85 percent since 1996, and between 1998 and 1999 investment fell from $4.06 to $1.48 billion.[52] The Asian economic crisis hit Vietnam hard: the region was the source of 70 percent of foreign investment and the recipient of 60 percent of Vietnam's exports. The Vietnamese leadership, fearful of the Asian contagion, tried to mobilize $7 billion in domestic capital, but this failed to stimulate the economy. Exports fell because the currency remained overvalued, and the government announced a $1 billion trade deficit, 150 percent higher than predicted in 1999. The financial sector is embroiled in a triangular debt crisis involving the 5,200 debt-ridden state-owned enterprises (SOEs). Estimates of indebtedness range from 46 to 66 percent, a figure that Hanoi conservatively puts at $14.2 billion.[53] Hoping to revive the moribund SOE sector, the government has channeled the bulk of foreign investment to it, yet foreign investors are fleeing and cite corruption, red tape, and mounting losses. The government fears that any attempt to reform the SOE sector will lead to massive unemployment, and so it continues to subsidize the SOEs at enormous public expense. Ironically the private sector, which could go a long way in hiring the estimated 1 million new entrants to the workforce each year, has been hindered in its development. There has been minimal equitization (the official term for privatization)—only 400 firms of the 1,600 planned.[54] The private sector accounts for only 7.1 percent of GDP, and its share of the national total is falling. The World Bank and the International Monetary Fund (IMF) withheld $500 million and $700 million in lending in 1999 and 2000, respectively, until Hanoi adopted "a more comprehensive approach to reform."[55] But the leadership has resisted any attempt to reform the economy, preferring to ride out the storm and not jeopardize political stability.

Vietnam's future economic growth is dependent on continued and deepened reform, such as privatization of state-owned assets that will challenge the authority of the state as well as its ideological underpinnings. There is tremendous resistance to implementing these necessary reforms from within the party; thus dissidents are becoming bolder in supporting the advocates of economic liberalization. Not reforming presents a great risk: as the respected economist Ari Kokko recently warned, "Without growth, but with increasing unemployment and poverty, political stability may be at risk."[56] Herein lies the problem: reform has never gone far enough for fear of creating social instability, but not reforming could cause the same effect.

Another cause of malaise has been the peasant protests throughout the countryside, centered primarily in Thai Binh, since the end of 1997 (and discussed in detail in Chapter 3). That peasants, the traditional base of the VCP's support, are up in arms, quite literally, has caused consternation among the political elite. Many realize that the party must reform its methods of governance or it will continue to lose popular support and legitimacy.

The economic downturn, including foreign investor flight and the peasant protests, are centered on one issue: corruption. Because Vietnam has a weak legal infrastructure and few of the necessary tools to regulate the marketplace, the incentive for corruption is enormous. Vietnam is one of the most corrupt societies in Asia, according to international watchdog groups, and commentators estimate that corruption adds 5 to 15 percent to project costs for foreign investors. As the former prime minister, Vo Van Kiet, complained: "The state of corruption plus incapabilities, red tape and domineering behavior, and the lack of a sense of discipline among numerous officials in various state machines at all levels and branches . . . have . . . jeopardized the renovation process and brought discredit to the party's leadership."[57] As stated above, political scientists such as Daniel Chirot contend that the single greatest factor in understanding the collapse of communism in Eastern Europe was corruption, what he called the "utter moral rot" that communist societies bred.[58] The current VCP general secretary, Le Kha Phieu, seems genuinely concerned at the pervasiveness of corruption and in May 1999 launched a two-year anticorruption campaign. But because the party itself is the source of the corruption, few believe that the party can effectively reform itself, especially above the lower echelons.

Many dissidents are simply frustrated that the country has developed at such an abysmally slow rate. Saigon fell twenty-five years ago, and the government cannot continue to blame war and foreign aggressors for the country's poverty. For that and all the other reasons listed above, high-level dissenters have emerged and begun to boldly attack the regime, demanding political reform—though few have called for the complete dismantling of the existing system. Most dissidents are angered by the lack of political reform and the party's stubborn clinging to power. And most feel that the communist regimes of Eastern Europe collapsed because they monopolized decisionmaking and did not consult with other groups or classes, or practice democratic centralism, thus stifling all open debate. The heart of this problem lies in the Vietnamese political system.

What Are the Issues at Stake?

Despite the vast differences within the political opposition, the dissidents have tried to focus their demands on seven major issues. First, they demand redress of both the *Nhan Van–Giai Pham* affair of the 1950s and the intraparty purge of 1967, as well as the complete rehabilitation of the victims of these campaigns. In this, what they are really trying to do is to get the party to live by its own laws and the constitution it promulgated and to observe the tenets of democratic centralism, which allow for greater debate and consensual style decisionmaking within the party. This is all to improve transparency and eliminate the secretive nature of governance.

Second, they call for greater democratization. But we must be precise. Few actually call for a Western-style multiparty democracy in Vietnam, and even fewer call for the disbanding or the overthrow of the VCP. Their demands focus on establishing a greater role for the National Assembly in national decisionmaking and, more important, the complete independence of the National Assembly from VCP control. The dissidents want independent candidates, but few advocate a strong multiparty system of governance.

Democracy is a broad political term, encompassing many different types of political systems, but there are many shared components and institutions in all democratic regimes. At the top of the list, there needs to be an authority structure based on the rule of law, not of individuals. Adherence to a constitution allows a legal continuity between different governments. Next, individuals and groups must have the ability to formulate preferences, which takes place at several levels. Any number of parties must be allowed to organize, run candidates for office, and promote their views; in all cases, individuals must be allowed equally to organize and run for office.

Free and fair elections must be held at regular intervals; there must be clear conditions for eligibility for office; and there must be universal suffrage, with all adults having the right to vote and individuals not having their political rights denied. Of course, there must be a regularized transition of power between governments: an exit pattern must be defined, whereby outgoing rulers must know that they will not be prosecuted by the next government for what they did in office. And, as Robert Dahl argues, there need to be "institutions for making government policies depend on votes and other expressions of preference."[59] Governments must have the capacity to formulate policies based on popular aspirations and then the power to implement them.

Concomitantly, there must be a free press and freedom of expression so that different groups in society are allowed to promote their beliefs and counter the arguments put forth by their adversaries. More important, a free press serves as a watchdog for the society to ensure that a government does not abuse its power and undermine the constitution and democratic institutions. A free press is the only safeguard against the government's monopoly on the flow of information.

Along with all this, there must be a strong and meaningful civil society.

> The realm of organized social life that is voluntary, self-generating, (largely) self-supporting, autonomous from the state, and bound by a legal order or set of shared rules. It is distinct from society in general in that it involves citizens acting collectively in a public sphere to express their interests, passions, and ideas, exchange information, achieve material goals, make demands on the state, and hold state officials accountable.[60]

The dissidents are divided over their conception of what Vietnamese democracy should look like. This is not surprising considering the vast range of interests they represent. Some would want to adopt a Western-style multiparty system, in which the Communist Party would simply be one of many competing parties. Most, however, do not believe the Western model is appropriate at this time: they have, instead, an elitist concept of democracy. They see a preeminent role for the National Assembly, independent and freed from party dictates and interference, but they feel that the parliamentarians should be members of the intellectual, social, and political elite. Whereas they want an independent National Assembly, they see it as a forum for individuals and not institutionalized parties, at least for the short term.

Third, the key to the implementation of democracy, unanimously according to the dissidents, is the abolition of article 4 of the 1992 constitution, which enshrines a "leading role" for the party and places it above the law. Hence, their third demand is for the legalization of political, economic, social, and intellectual life. Putting it simply, they are calling for the establishment of the rule of law, the abolition of governing by party decree, and the cessation of the party's ability to stand above the law. The 1992 constitution guarantees freedom of religion, speech, organization, and assembly, but there are numerous loopholes that allow the party to curtail these rights and freedoms. Article 4 is the most egregious of them.

Fourth, there are the longstanding demands for greater intellectual freedom and artistic expression and license, especially the independence of the press. The demand for an independent press, which could serve as a watchdog to prevent government corruption and abuse of power, is unanimous among the intellectuals. All see the exchange of ideas to be essential for both the formulation of sound public policy and economic development.

Fifth, they are highly critical of corruption. Although some critics would like to see the VCP completely surrender economic decision-making to market forces, many others are very critical of unbridled capitalism. As corruption-inspired peasant protests throughout the country have been at the top of the party's agenda, the critics' attacks on corruption have not fallen on deaf ears. Many, especially at the highest echelons of the party, are gravely concerned about corruption and there have been countless campaigns since the late 1980s to root it out. But the party and government want to lead the attack, and not let the agenda fall into the hands of outsiders who could use it to further their own political agenda. For example, dissidents have used the issue of corruption to attack the party for having become a "new class," a corrupt elite alienated from the masses.

The sixth issue centers around the CFRF in Ho Chi Minh City. Among their many concerns is the resentment by southerners of northern dominance in politics and economics as well as the lingering sense of victor versus vanquished; despite twenty-five years of unification, there is still a chasm between the two halves of the country. These are important issues, but they are simply symptoms. The issue of the CFRF is more important for another reason: the development of civil society. Until individuals have the legal right to organize, publicize their views, lobby, hold officials accountable, and challenge the state, political reform is a moot point. The CFRF was the first and only independent organization to openly debate and question party and state policies. Without independent civic organization, there cannot be substantial political reform: this is at the heart of religious freedom issues. There has been an unprecedented degree of religious freedoms for individuals since *doi moi* was launched, but the state goes to great lengths to prevent the autonomy of religious organizations. The organizations are treated as arms of the state because as independent organizations, with an internal authority structure and nationwide grass-roots network, they have the potential to challenge the party's authority and monopoly of power.

A common thread that runs throughout has to do with the party's linkage of its own interests and survival with those of the state. In other words, can one be a patriot without being a supporter of the VCP? These critics are aghast at the arrogance of the party, whose membership constitutes less than 3 percent of the population, which believes that it represents the interests of all the people of Vietnam.

Yet, these critics are not out to undermine the system or to overthrow the communist party, quite the opposite. They seek to broaden the political spectrum, scope of political debate, and political participation—all in order to strengthen the party and restore its legitimacy.

Despite their calls for "democracy," in general they are not advocating a Western-style multiparty bourgeois democratic system. They have a very elitist concept of democracy, whereby the party more actively consults with intellectuals, experts, and members of the National Assembly. They are against Stalinism, not necessarily ideals of communism for which so many fought.

Notes

1. Christine Pelzer White, "The Vietnamese Revolutionary Alliance: Intellectuals, Workers, and Peasants," in John Wilson Lewis, ed., *Peasant Rebellion and Communist Revolution in Asia* (Palo Alto, Calif.: Stanford University Press, 1974), 77–98.

2. The Malaysian prime minister, Mahathir Mohammed, elucidated six key "Asian values": an orderly society, societal harmony, accountability of public officials, openness to new ideas, freedom of expression, respect for authority. See Mahathir Mohammed, "Let's Have Mutual Cultural Enrichment," *New Straights Times,* 16 March 1995: 10-11.

3. Seymour Lipset, "Some Social Requisites of Democracy: Economic Development and Political Legitimacy," *American Political Science Review* 53 (1959); Robert Dahl, *Polyarchy* (New Haven, Conn.: Yale University Press, 1971), 62-80. See, for example, the sections by Lo Shiu Hing, "Liberalization and Democratization in Taiwan: A Class and Functional Perspective"; Chung-Si Ahn, "Economic Dimensions of Democratization in South Korea"; and Surin Masirikrod, "The Making of Thai Democracy: A Study of Political Alliances Among the State, the Capitalists, and the Middle Class," in Anek Laothamatas, ed., *Democratization in Southeast Asia* (Singapore: Institute of Southeast Asian Studies, 1997), 141–166, 215–236, 237–258.

4. Dahl, *Polyarchy,* 78.

5. Nigel Harris, "New Bourgeoisie?" *Journal of Development Studies* 24 (January 1988): 237–249.

6. "Economic modernization did, indeed, produce a larger middle class (not in the sense of bourgeois ownership, of course, but in the cultural and educational sense, as well as in its style of life)." Daniel Chirot, "What Happened in Eastern Europe in 1989?" in Daniel Chirot, ed., *The Crisis of Leninism and the Decline of the Left: The Revolution of 1989* (Seattle: University of Washington Press, 1991), 11, 20.

7. Ibid., 11.

8. Robert D. Putnam, *Making Democracy Work: Civic Traditions in Modern Italy* (Princeton, N.J.: Princeton University Press, 1992), 152-154.

9. Adam Przeworski, *Democracy and the Market* (New York: Cambridge University Press, 1991).

10. Ibid., esp. 66–88.

11. Samuel P. Huntington, *The Third Wave* (Norman: University of Oklahoma Press, 1991), 109–163.

12. Cited in Tim Larimer, "Disquiet Among the Quiet," *Time*, Asia Edition, 18 January 1999.

13. David Marr and Stanley Rosen, "Vietnamese and Chinese Youth in the 1990s," *China Journal* 40 (July 1998): 154.

14. Carlyle Thayer, "Mono-Organizational Socialism," in Benedict J. Tria Kerkvleit and Doug J. Porter, eds., *Vietnam's Rural Transformation* (Boulder, Colo.: Westview Press, 1995): 52–53.

15. "Vietnam Must Return to Secure Human Rights-Amnesty," Reuters, 6 January 1999.

16. "Vietnam Says Must Be Selective Over Rights," Reuters, 10 December 1998.

17. "Vietnam Justifies Clampdown on Dissidents," Reuters, 18 March 1999.

18. According to Foreign Ministry spokesman, Le Sy Vuong Ha, "We will not accept any foreign individual or organizations that wish to travel in Vietnam to carry out rights investigations into religious or human rights issues." The statement came after the UN Special Rapporteur on Religious Intolerence Abdelfattah Amor released his report on Vietnam, which accused the regime of restricting religious freedom. Amor accused Hanoi of hindering his investigation in October 1998. Reuters, "Hanoi Says Human Rights Investigators Unwelcome," *South China Morning Post*, 18 March 1999.

19. Brantly Womack, "Political Reform and Political Change in Communist Countries: Implications for Vietnam," in William S. Turley and Mark Selden, eds., *Reinventing Vietnamese Socialism* (Boulder, Colo.: Westview Press, 1993), 277-308, esp 290–298.

20. The definitive history of the VCP in this period is Huynh Kim Khanh, *Vietnamese Communism, 1925–1945* (Ithaca, N.Y.: Cornell University Press, 1982); also see William Duiker, *The Communist Road to Power* (Boulder, Colo.: Westview Press, 1981).

21. Andrew Vickerman, *The Fate of the Peasantry: The Premature "Transition to Socialism" in the Democratic Republic of Vietnam* (New Haven, Conn.: Yale Center for International and Area Studies, Monograph No. 28, 1986).

22. Adam Fforde and Stefan de Vylder, *From Plan To Market: The Economic Transition in Vietnam* (Boulder, Colo.: Westview Press, 1996), 125–160.

23. Gareth Porter, "The Politics of 'Renovation' in Vietnam," *Problems of Communism* 39 (May–June 1990): 72–88.

24. David G. Marr, "The Vietnamese Communist Party and Civil Society," Vietnam Update Conference, "Doi Moi, the State and Civil Society," 10–11 November 1994, Australian National University, Canberra: 9.

25. Douglas Pike, "Political Institutionalization in Vietnam," in Robert Scalapino, Seizaburo Sato, and Jusuf Wanandi, eds., *Asian Political Institutionalization* (Berkeley, Calif.: Institute of East Asian Studies, 1986), 42–58. For more on factionalism during the war-time era, see P. J. Honey, ed., *Communism in North Vietnam: Its Role in the Sino-Soviet Dispute* (Cambridge, Mass.: MIT Press, 1963); *North Vietnam Today: Profile of a Communist Satellite* (New York: Praeger, 1962); Hoang Van Hoan, *A Drop in the Ocean: Hoang Van Hoan's Revolutionary Reminiscences* (Peking: People's Liberation Army Press, 1987).

26. Marr, "The Vietnamese Communist Party and Civil Society," 8.

27. Carlyle A. Thayer, *The Vietnam People's Army Under Doi Moi* (Singapore: Institute of Southeast Asian Studies, 1995); Douglas Pike, *PAVN: People's Army of Vietnam* (New York: Da Capo Press, 1984).

28. Kiet failed to get this legislation through the provincially dominated National Assembly. In the end, the center was given the right to fire provincial leaders, but could only appoint them at the recommendation of the provincial people's committee.

29. Thayer, "Mono-Organizationalism Socialism and the State," 45.

30. Greg Lockart, "Mass Mobilization in Contemporary Vietnam," *Asian Studies Review* 21 (November 1997): 176.

31. Lockart, "Mass Mobilization in Contemporary Vietnam," 176.

32. Yeonsik Jeong, "The Rise of State Corporatism in Vietnam," *Contemporary Southeast Asia* 19 (September 1997): 152–171.

33. Stephen B. Young, "Vietnamese Communism in the 1990s: The End is in Sight," *Vietnam Commentary* (November–December 1989): 5–6.

34. Proponents of "Asian values" include Bilahari Kausikan, "Asia's Different Standard," *Foreign Policy* 92 (Fall 1993): 24–41; Fareed Zakaria, "Culture Is Destiny: A Conversation with Lee Kwan Yew," *Foreign Affairs* 73 (March/April 1994): 109–126; Mahathir Mohammed, "Let's Have Multicultural Enrichment," *New Straights Times*, 16 March 1995, 10–11. Critics include Charles Freeman, "Human Rights, Asian Values and the Clash of Civilizations," *Issues and Studies* 34 (October 1998): 48–78; Aryeh Neier, "Asia's Unacceptable Standard," *Foreign Policy* 92 (Fall 1993): 42–51; Zachary Abuza, "Human Rights and Culture in Southeast Asia," paper presented to the International Studies Association, 30–31 August 2000.

35. According to the military daily, *Quan Doi Nhan Dan,* peaceful evolution is an attempt to replace Vietnam's "communist economic structure, legal system, and political regime with a multi-party and pluralist regime, thus gradually changing from socialism to capitalism." *Quan Doi Nhan Dan,* 30 July 1994.

36. Le Xuan Luu, "Relations Between Building and Defending the Fatherland in the New Revolutionary Stage," Voice of Vietnam, 11 June 1996, in Foreign Broadcast Information Service, *Daily Reports-East Asia* (hereafter *FBIS-EAS*), 13 June 1996, 85.

37. Luu, "Relations Between Building and Defending the Fatherland," 85.

38. Ministry of Defense, *Vietnam: Consolidating National Defense Safeguarding the Homeland* (Hanoi: Ministry of Defense, 1998), 13-14.

39. Adrian Edwards, "Vietnam's President Says Unrest Prompting Rethink," Reuters, 23 February 1998.

40. Murray Hiebert, "Survival Tactics," *Far Eastern Economic Review* (*FEER*), 1 February 1990, 24-25.

41. Amnesty International, *Annual Report, 1997,* http://www.amnesty.org//ailib/

42. The State Department report can be found online at *http://www.state.gov/www/global/humanrights/1999*

43. Hue-Tam Ho Tai, "Duong Thu Huong and the Literature of Disenchantment," *Vietnam Forum* 14 (1994): 84.

44. "Interview with Do Trung Hieu," *Vietnam Democracy* (October 1996).

45. Merle Goldman, *China's Intellectuals: Advice and Dissent* (Cambridge, Mass.: Harvard University Press, 1981), 3.

46. Alexander Woodside, "Exalting the Latecomer State: Intellectuals and the State During the Chinese and Vietnamese Reforms," *China Journal* 40 (July 1998): 13.

47. Tieu Dao Bao Cu, "Open Letter to Phan Dinh Dieu," *Vietnam Insight* (April 1995).

48. Huw Watkin, "Hero Takes Leadership to Task," *South China Morning Post,* 20 June 2000.

49. Cited in Thomas W. Lippman, "Vietnam Rejects U.S. Reproach on Human Rights," *International Herald Tribune,* 28-29 June 1997, 1.

50. AP, "Internet Must Be Controlled, Advise Police," *South China Morning Post,* 8 April 1999.

51. AFP, "World Bank President to Push Vietnam on Economic Reform," 20 February 2000. Also see World Bank, "Vietnam: Ready for Takeoff?" (Washington, D.C.: December 1999).

52. Reuters, "Foreign Investors Shun Vietnam in Early 2000," 1 March 2000.

53. AFP, "Vietnam Finally Set to Move on Billion-Dollar Reform of State Banks," 4 July 2000.

54. Ibid.

55. AFP, "Vietnamese PM Paints Grim Picture of Economic Prospects," 18 November 1999.

56. For more on the economic situation, see Ari Kokko, "Vietnam: Ready for Doi Moi II," *ASEAN Economic Bulletin* 15 (1998): 319-327.

57. Cited in Benedict J. Tria Kerkvleit, "Rural Society and State Relations," in Kerkvleit and Porter, eds., *Vietnam's Rural Transformation* (Boulder, Colo.: Westview Press, 1995): 80.

58. Daniel Chirot, "What Happened in Eastern Europe in 1989?" in Chirot, ed., *The Crisis of Leninism and the Decline of the Left,* 11, 20.

59. Dahl, *Polyarchy,* 3.

60. Larry Drummond, "Rethinking Civil Society: Toward Democratic Consolidation," *Journal of Democracy* 2 (July 1994): 6.

2

The Nhan Van–Giai Pham Affair, the 1967 Purge, and the Legacy of Dissent

Culture and art, like all other activities cannot stand aloof from economics and politics, but must be included in them.

—*Ho Chi Minh*

The Soviet composer must seek after the heroic, the great and the beautiful, fight against subversive modernism, typical of the decadence of modern bourgeois art. [Music must be] nationalist in form and socialist in content.

—*Maxim Gorky, "On Socialist Realism," 1934*

Some men manage to live a hundred years
just as lime pots do,
The longer they live, the more useless they become.
The longer they live, the more they shrink.

—*Phan Hoi*

From the reunification of the country in 1975 to the Sixth Party Congress in December 1986 when the economic reform program was launched, there was for all intents and purposes no nationwide dissent aside from that of former members of the anticommunist Republic of Vietnam regime. Even that dissent was limited because of the government's heavy-handedness and the extent of its crackdown on former enemies. Those who were not "reeducated" and sent off to the "new economic zones" (over 300,000) were intimidated into submission. The origins of the dissent that emerged during the renovation period predate reunification, and there is a historical context, particularly in regard to two events, that must be examined to understand dissent in the contemporary era. The first event has to do with the treatment of intellectuals, writers, poets, artists, and composers who had joined the Viet Minh in

41

the 1940s and 1950s but were purged and reeducated after demanding greater intellectual freedoms, including the right to publish independent works. Indeed, many of these intellectuals are still leading opposition figures today while the same issues and demands continue to resonate. The second was the intraparty purge of the mid- to late 1960s in which opponents of escalating the war against the Americans were purged in violation of the tenets of democratic centralism. Party members who offered a different approach to the war in the south from the hard-line leadership of the party were ruthlessly persecuted, thereby ending all open and meaningful debate within the party. From 1967 until *doi moi* was implemented, all decisionmaking was monopolized by a handful of unchallenged and unquestioned leaders, thus producing stagnation in public and foreign policy. Although the *Nhan Van–Giai Pham* affair and the 1967 intraparty purge have been covered in other works more thoroughly, I am revisiting the incidents. They were the first and most formative events in political dissidence under the VCP's rule, and the issues raised by dissidents in the 1950s and 1960s remain unchanged. The legacy of these events is attractive, and they have become rallying points for today's dissidents: the *Nhan Van–Giai Pham* affair as a symbol of the party's failed promises of intellectual freedom and the intraparty purge as the demise of intraparty democracy and the deadening of thought in policymaking. Finally, how the regime responds to these events, even today, tells much about the state of political reform in Vietnam.

The *Nhan Van–Giai Pham* Affair

Background of the Affair

In 1950, in the middle of the Viet Minh's war against the French, Ho Chi Minh traveled to China to sign a military aid agreement with the new communist leadership in Beijing. With the introduction of Chinese military aid came the massive influx of Chinese-styled institutions, reforms, and advisors. A crash campaign was launched to study the Chinese revolutionary experience, and 200,000 copies of some forty-three Chinese Communist Party books and articles were translated and printed. Chinese political and economic institutions became increasingly prevalent. By 1952, there were about 7,000 Chinese troops and advisors in the Bac Ho (the northern war zone). In the 1949–1954 period,

China trained and equipped about 50,000 Vietnamese soldiers in camps in Yunnan and Guangxi established in the spring of 1950. At China's insistence, the avowedly socialist Lao Dong Party was founded in February 1951, thereby ending any pretense that the Viet Minh was a broad-based anticolonial organization with no ideological leanings.[1] Truong Chinh's *The Resistance Will Win,* which set forth a three-stage evolution of the war was, according to one historian, Maoist "to the point of being plagiarized."[2] William Duiker succinctly noted that the Viet Minh leadership was simply "stroking the egos of Chinese leaders" because their support was absolutely necessary.[3]

A massive partywide rectification campaign (*chinh huan,* or *cheng feng* in Chinese), modeled on the 1942 Yenan campaign in China, was launched and thousands of cadres were purged; party membership fell from 50,000 in 1950 to 40,000 in 1954. A two-phase land reform campaign modeled on China's was also put into action. A moderate phase from 1953 to 1954 emphasized rent reductions, followed by a more radical phase from 1954 to 1956 that redistributed much of the property in the north.[4] This alarmed many intellectuals because most had some ties to the "feudal" and "reactionary" landowning classes.[5] In March 1953 the list of social classes determined by the government was issued, with the government trying to assuage fears by stating that "intellectuals do not form a distinct class of their own" but that their status would be based on their family's "label." Since many intellectuals were labeled "class enemies," a new label of "progressive personalities" was created for them if they voluntarily surrendered all their property to the state, in addition to serving the revolution.

While Chinese logistical support was necessary, equally important for the Viet Minh's anticolonial struggle was to win the sympathy of the intellectuals. Many intellectuals felt that they had no choice but to go to the Viet Bac and join the resistance; not doing so would be perceived as collaborating with the French. Many intellectuals joined the Viet Minh out of patriotism, not a love of communism. Indeed, as the Viet Minh leadership tried to hide its communist ties, nominally by disbanding the Indochina Communist Party in 1946, it is possible many intellectuals believed the Viet Minh was what Ho Chi Minh avowed it to be, a nationalist and not a communist organization. Indeed, a South Vietnamese scholar argued that the intellectuals were "encouraged by the hope that they might use the resistance organization to assemble nationalist elements and to create a force which would actually tip the scales against the communists within the ranks of the resistance."[6]

Whatever their reasons for joining, the intellectuals applied themselves to the anticolonial struggle with zeal.

> From the very beginning, [the writers] applied themselves with enthusiasm and energy to whatever activity their country demanded of them in time of war. They fought alongside ordinary coolies, resisted their country's enemies side by side with the peasants. They shared with these men the terrible privations of life in the jungle and, like them, they lived and worked in an atmosphere of the most fervent patriotism.[7]

But from the outset, the party was determined to control the intellectuals and prevent them from being too independent. Based on the works of Mao, Lenin, and Maxim Gorky,[8] Vietnamese artists and writers were forced into accepting the tenets of socialist realism and to reexamining their ideological stand. In a 1948 speech, VCP General Secretary Truong Chinh demanded that literature and culture "remain absolutely loyal to the fatherland and the resistance war."[9]

The year 1951 saw two further constraints on the intellectuals: First was the introduction of "democratic centralism" as the party's central operating procedure. This principle became the link between the elite and the masses: once the party had reached a decision it would not tolerate any dissent. Then, in a 1951 letter to artists and intellectuals, Ho adopted the language of Mao's Yenan talk to intellectuals, in which the Chinese leader made clear that "there is in fact no such thing as art for art's sake, art that stands above classes, art that is detached from or independent of politics. Proletarian literature and art are part of the whole proletarian revolutionary cause."[10] Ho elucidated to the intellectuals the concept of socialist realism. "To fulfill his tasks," he said, "the cultural fighter needs a firm political stand and sound ideology: In short you must place the interests of the resistance, the country and the people above all else."[11] To that end, Ho argued that "culture and art, like all other activities cannot stand aloof from economics and politics, but must be included in them."[12] As a result, all artistic license was curbed and, according to the French scholar Georges Boudarel, "their works were expected to revolve around stock characters or 'types' (*dien hinh*) and to serve the political requirements of the movement in a 'timely' fashion (*phuc vu kip thoi*). The catchword was 'hate' (*cam thu*): hate for the foreign imperialists (*de quoc*) and for the native 'feudalists' (*phong kien*) or land owners."[13]

These artistic constraints, along with the implementation of other aspects of communist doctrine, "set in motion a great wave of intellectuals to the French-controlled zone."[14] P. J. Honey asserted that "the more the principles learned from the Chinese communists were applied, the longer became the lines of disillusioned intellectuals, abandoning the ranks of the resistance movement."[15] Those who remained created little more than the texts for the Viet Minh's literacy campaign and were subjected to the rigorous tenets of socialist realism.

In a further attempt to subject the intellectuals to party control, they were pressured to join the party. "They were threatened that if they refused membership, they would be denounced as reactionaries, and, at the same time, were tempted to join by promises of special privileges."[16] Nonetheless, even those intellectuals who stayed in the bush and joined the party had to endure a reeducation campaign led by "special communist cultural cadres" who had been "instructed by their 'elder brothers on the other side of the frontier' [Chinese cadres] in the 'Chinese system of arts and letters.'"[17]

All in all, most intellectuals remained in the bush for patriotic reasons. The anti-French struggle was truly a motivating force. For the sake of independence, writers and artists were willing to accept socialist realism and the dictates of the party that their work had to be part of the overall resistance movement led by the Lao Dong Party. They accepted party control, censorship, and a loss of intellectual freedom for the sake of national independence. As a leading dissident wrote:

> When the [Literary] Association [for National Salvation] was in Viet Bac its lines of conduct seemed very simple. In order to serve the country, the people, and above all the pressing war of resistance, one had to follow Marxism. It cannot be presumed that writers and artists in those days correctly and properly fulfilled their duties, but it was certain that they did their best to follow the above lines of conduct. Did they have any dissatisfaction with their leaders? Scarcely any. Or if there was any, they did not pay much attention to it since their souls were immersed in the greatness and the glorious misery of the Resistance War. They had no leisure to think of other matters.[18]

They were filled with pride and enthusiasm in hoping to build a new and independent Vietnam, and they believed that they had earned their intellectual freedom for their service to the revolution. Their expectation was that, after the struggle, they would enjoy even greater freedoms than under the French and an end to party interference in the arts and letters.

At first it seemed as if they would have their way. The LDP sent cultural cadres into Hanoi in September 1954 to convince those who had left the Viet Bac not to move to the south in the 300-day period as permitted under the Geneva Accords. To regain the support of the intellectuals, in 1954–1955 the LDP took a very liberal attitude toward intellectuals and specialists who had served the French; those who stayed in the north were treated well, often earning more than those who entered Hanoi with the LDP in 1954.[19] To Huu, a leading party intellectual, announced a conciliatory policy in 1955: "The party can supply expert leadership in fighting the enemy, but now is the period for constructive work. The party can no longer lead, but should give way to the intellectuals."[20] But at the same time, the LDP forced all writers and artists to join the official Association of Arts and Letters. The crackdown had begun.

The Opening Salvo

Open dissent began when Tran Dan, a military writer and party member, wrote a book of reportage on the Battle of Dien Bien Phu in February 1955. Foreshadowing later works by Bao Ninh and Duong Thu Huong in the 1990s, his characters were hardly the heroic socialist models that the party had dictated. The book was a grim portrayal of life in the trenches where there was little evidence of the glory of war and the righteousness of the socialist cause. Nonetheless he was sent to China to write the screenplay; there he had a terrible fight with the political commissar who was sent to work with him. Tran Dan returned disillusioned and gathered a group of like-minded intellectuals within the army whose goal was to convince the VCP leadership of the need for intellectual freedom. They wanted freedom from not just the military's censors but from the party's political commissars. According to the platform drawn up and submitted to the Central Committee in 1955 by Tran Dan and almost thirty other intellectuals,

> the highest expression of a writer's responsibility is his respect for and his faithfulness to truth. . . . Truth, with its breadth and scope, transcends all directives, all theories. . . . If it goes against a program or an order, writers should conform to it and not distort it and not force it in the framework of politics. . . . Revolution needs no apostle to burn incense and praise programs and has even less use for shamans who celebrate its cult as they clap cymbals and intone litanies. . . . Today, one finds in our literature much artifice (and even hypocrisy).[21]

He argued that "a writer must be allowed quasi-absolute freedoms in the choice of his subject, of his characters, of his style to express attitudes and feelings. All hindrances and restraints must be proscribed as enemies of realism." While in China, Dan became very influenced by the Chinese literary figure Hu Feng, who wanted to broaden the acceptable bounds of literature. On his return, Dan wrote, "Why does no one write about government officers, for instance? Or about love? Why restrict characters . . . to individuals from a worker or peasant background? Realism encourages a hundred schools to thrive."[22] Such blunt attacks on party controls struck a nerve among intellectuals, who rallied to his defense. Phan Khoi, the father of modern Vietnamese poetry,[23] then 70 years old, wrote that "each of us possesses his own art and reflects his own personality in it. Only this kind of art and personality can create the spectacle of a hundred flowers rivaling each other in charm. On the contrary, if one compels all writers to write in the same style, there may come a day when all the flowers will be changed into chrysanthemums."[24]

Another intellectual, Le Dat, complained that socialist realism was like

> Placing police stations and machinery in the center of the human
> heart
> Forcing feelings to be expressed according to a set of rules promul-
> gated by the government.

The party's initial response to Tran Dan and the other dissidents was to place them under house arrest and then to reeducate them.[25] To Huu, the official poet, then launched a campaign to reinvigorate intellectual life with the tenets of socialist realism. Huu demanded a strict adherence by intellectuals to the parameters defined in Mao's Yenan speeches: "positive characters," "revolutionary heroes," and "peasants and workers as the vanguard." In short, Huu called for the uncompromising synthesis of politics and art because "content determines form."

While many intellectuals read the writing on the wall and toed the party line, others laid low until early 1956 when a collection of writings entitled *Giai Pham Mua Xuan (Works of Beauty for the Springtime)* was published. The boldness of the journal, which included a poem by Tran Dan that described an intolerable malaise in the north, was a catalyst for others.[26] When the party awarded its top literary prize in 1954–1955 to a mediocre piece of socialist realism by party loyalist Xuan Dieu, the intellectuals revolted.[27]

At the August 1956 Conference of the Vietnamese Literary Association, intellectuals openly demanded greater freedom, just as their counterparts in China and the Soviet Union were doing at the time. In

China, for example, Lu Dingyi called for "breaking the stagnation of intellectual activities in China" in his "100 Flowers" speech. Specifically he demanded that the Chinese Communist Party authorize "freedom of independent thought in ideology, artistic and scientific research activities; freedom of expression; freedom to engage in creative work and to criticize the work of others; freedom to express opinions; and freedom to withhold opinions." The scholars were also discussing the changes in Soviet policies toward intellectuals since the Twentieth Congress of the Communist Party of the Soviet Union when Khrushchev gave his de-Stalinization speech.

In an attempt to stop the wave of criticism a senior party official, Hoai Thanh, published a "self-criticism" in the official weekly newspaper for literature and the arts, *Van Nghe*. But it was too late: the intellectuals began publishing their own journals based on the philosophy of the Chinese dissident intellectual Hu Feng, who argued that "socialist realism should turn to a man and assert itself as a kind of humanism (*nhan van*)." On 15 September 1956, the independent journal *Nhan Van* (*Humanism*) received permission to publish. Edited by Phan Khoi, *Nhan Van* was published five times between 20 September and 20 November 1956. In that period, the VCP briefly tolerated the directness of the authors and editors.

The More Things Change . . .

In addition to demands for intellectual freedom and the right to establish independent publications free from party censorship and controls, the dissidents had numerous other complaints. Like many of their counterparts in the 1990s, the intellectuals in the 1950s were very careful to not challenge either socialism or the party's monopoly of power. "But they refused to equate socialism with monolithism and patriotism with totalitarianism," according to the leading scholar of the movement, Georges Boudarel.[28]

Much of their demands focused on the issue of "truth" and the legality of alternative and independent sources of information. The dissidents understood the need for propaganda, but they were alarmed at how the party misinterpreted or lied about events to further its goals. Phung Quan explicitly demanded transparency in a famed poem:

> A man, sincere and true,
>   will laugh when, happy, he wants to laugh,

will cry, when, sad, he wants to cry.
If you love someone, say you love.
If you hate someone, say you hate.
Someone may not talk sweet and flatter you—
    still, don't say hate when you feel love.
Someone may grab a knife and threaten you—
    still, don't say love when you feel hate.[29]

Likewise, Tran Ve Lan accounted the lack of alternative sources of information to disastrous unaccountability and abuse of power by the party. "Had open criticism been applied earlier among the public and in the press, with everyone frankly saying what he thought so that our leaders might gradually tell truth from falsehood in the implementation of policies, many catastrophes would have been avoided."[30]

The paramount mistake was the land reform program that was characterized by the "rise of a ruffianized peasant movement." Dissidents were concerned about the fact that there was less legality in the countryside than in French-controlled Hanoi: Nguyen Huu Dang's editorial in the fourth issue of *Nhan Van,* on 5 November 1956, recalled Khrushchev's denunciation of the violence and terror of Stalin and Beria, but stated that "in our country, this is not a readily accepted fact. It is so because our contempt for bourgeois legality has reached such proportions that, for many of us, it has turned into contempt for legality in general. . . . *It is the absence of legislation that favors abuse of power and authoritarianism.*[31]

To promote a more lawful society, the intellectuals called for a revised constitution, the freedom of the National Assembly from party control, and an independent judiciary. A prominent lawyer, Nguyen Manh Tuong, outlined four basic legal reforms in October 1956 that were needed to prevent such extralegal abuses as those that had occurred during the agrarian reform campaign: establishing statutes of limitations; ending the practice of guilt by association to families and across generational lines; creating a higher standard for evidence; and providing the accused with rights during an investigation. Additional roadblocks, according to Tuong, were "contempt for legality which is subordinated to politics, and contempt for specialists."[32]

The critics were also very vocal about the lack of democracy, the monopolization of power in the hands of a few, and the stagnation of politics in general. Most daring were two works by Phan Hoi and Le Dat, who wrote about the "lime pot," a spittoon used by betel nut chewers, that is filled with lime to stop the smell; in time the lime builds up, rendering the lime pot useless. The implicit allusion to Ho Chi Minh and the top party leadership infuriated the party:

> Some men manage to live a hundred years,
> Just as lime pots do,
> The longer they live, the more useless they become.
> The longer they live, the more they shrink.

Phan Khoi wrote an essay based on this quatrain, entitled "Mr. Lime Pot," to further flesh out Le Dat's allegory. In the essay, he says that as a young man of eighteen he "took down every one of those 'Mr. Lime Pots' from their place of veneration and tossed them on the ground? Why did we do that? We just did it and didn't need any reason." He attacked the aged and useless party leadership: "In summation, people show their reverence and respect to a lime pot by calling it 'Mister' because it has lived a long time, filled up hard and dry inside, its mouth covered over, sitting in melancholy on an altar or up on a wall, like an earthen or wooden statue, speechless and motionless."[33]

The object of the attack was clear. Ho and the top party leadership had become too rigid and too closed and, like old lime pots, had lost their usefulness. It was simply time to put them on a shelf. There they would be respected, but they would be replaced by new and effectual "lime pots." For this, Phan Khoi was attacked as a reactionary and revisionist, a senile old man who was unable to overcome his "bourgeois mentality," but despite the attacks, he continued to edit *Nhan Van* and *Giai Pham* and to assist and support young writers and intellectuals. To the charges by many in the party, he was simply a counterrevolutionary, he responded in the third issue (October 1956) of *Giai Pham* with this poem:

> What sort of rose is without thorns?
> Just let it not be a rose without blossoms.
> If it is to be a rose, it must have blossoms.
> Who would tend a rose with only thorns and no blossoms?
> O rose, I love you very much.
> You have thorns, but a fragrant scent as well.

Nonetheless, Le Dat and Phan Khoi were in a distinct minority, and few were willing to confront communist ideology head on. One exception, however, was Dao Duy Anh, a professor of history, who asserted that the party's rigid adherence to ideology would limit the scope of research and knowledge in the country and thus retard its growth and development. In a passage that would foreshadow the works nearly four decades later of Phan Dinh Dieu and Ha Si Phu, Dao Duy Anh wrote:

> In our country, dogmatism and the personality cult which are even more prevalent have driven people, no matter what subject they treat, to begin by presenting theories of Marx, Engels and Lenin, or the views of Stalin or some other leader in order to develop them at length or to distort the material to make it fit the formal framework built out of those basic ideas. Let me give a recent example. In the debate about the periodization of Vietnamese history and the formation of our country, many researchers did not dare to put forward new ideas that failed to conform to the theses of classical Marxists or of our leaders on these questions. Whoever stepped outside established frameworks found himself accused of some dire deviation and thus effectively shut up. . . . In fact, the debate was undermined in its very foundation. In many fields of research or in discussion about any problem, many people have only one fear, that of inadvertently straying from the beaten paths of orthodox, official thinking. To them, research is just a sport of tightrope walking at the circus. Research must be an immensely broad avenue through which everybody freely comes and goes, not a stretched wire on which ventures a circus artist. One must root out dogmatism and the personality cult to liberate research. One must apply the policy implemented by the Chinese Communist Party in this area, "Let a hundred schools contend."[34]

Orthodoxy was not just leading to intellectual stagnation and dogmatism, but creating an entirely new elite society, a "brahmin" class of party members who had begun to alienate themselves from the masses. Foreshadowing the 1990s, Huu Loan attacked this new class in the poem "The Same Sycophants," in which he accused the new ruling class, which acted much the same as the feudal and colonial ones they replaced, of becoming something that was not supposed to exist in a classless society.[35]

The Party's Response

The party leadership was divided over how to deal with *Nhan Van, Giai Pham,* and the other dissident journals. Many wanted to exonerate the intellectuals. The military, in particular, was fairly sympathetic to their demands perhaps because the VPA, too, felt that the party interfered too much in its own affairs. Many in the VPA, like the intellectuals, were also alarmed at the slavish subservience to Chinese models and doctrines.[36] Indeed, a top ideological commissar in the VPA, Tran Do, who would become a leading dissident in the 1990s, tried to moderate a compromise with party hardliners led by To Huu and his assistant Hoai Thanh.

Others simply did not believe that the intellectuals posed a threat to the regime: the scathing attacks from within intellectual circles infuriated many in the party, but these intellectuals and their criticisms were for the most part unknown to the general public. Bui Tin argues that the movement was tolerated because of its isolation. Socialist realism, usually in the form of Chinese and Soviet books and movies, was far more available to the average Vietnamese than the works of Le Dat or Phan Khoi. As Tin notes, "In those days nobody could get hold of copies of *Nhan Van* or *Giai Pham* to see for themselves what the fuss was about."[37] The appeal of these dissidents was somewhat lost on the broader public because nearly 90 percent of the population was illiterate or semiliterate peasants.

However, party hardliners carried the day, and in February 1956 the crackdown began with the arrest of Tran Dan and several of his colleagues. Although it launched a series of public campaigns against his works the party, in keeping with trends in the communist world such as Khruschev's de-Stalinization speech and Lu Ding Yi's "100 Flowers" speech, allowed *Nhan Van, Giai Pham,* and other journals to come out that summer and fall (*Nhan Van* being published five times between September 20 and November 20). And the Japanese scholar Hirohide Kurihara argues that during this period the party actually admitted mistakes in its literary policies.[38] For example, the party's theoretical journal, *Hoc Tap,* acknowledged that issues raised in *Nhan Van* and *Giai Pham* were "partly in accord with reality," and an article in the party daily, *Nhan Dan,* said that the "100 Flowers" policy was "correct in principle."[39]

Simply raising literary issues did not threaten the party. What did scare the VCP was that the movement sought to turn itself into an independent, permanent, and organized loyal opposition to the party. As summed up by one editor, Chu Ngoc, in the third issue of *Nhan Van*: "We are trying to fight within the framework of the organization [party], but our efforts are always thwarted, and the requests we send to the Central Committee always come back to us treated like those of a coterie."[40] When the attacks in the journals became increasingly more political and less literary oriented, many in the party wanted to crack down.

Exogenous forces changed the tone of intraparty discourse when the Soviets crushed the Hungarian uprising in November 1956 while China was in the midst of the "antirightist" campaign. In the 16 September 1956 issue of the party's daily *Nhan Dan* (*The People*), Le Duan published an article entitled "Smashing the Right," which held up as a shining example the struggle being waged in China against Ding Ling and other intellectuals who voiced criticism during the 100 Flowers movement. In the article, Le Duan wrote that "the [political] right is a poisonous weed and [we should] turn it into a fertilizer to improve the soil of our rice fields."[41] In November, *Nhan Dan* labeled the Hungarian uprising a counterrevolution,[42] and a December conference of communist parties in Moscow led to an overall hardening of ideological views and justified suppressing all enemies of the proletarian dictatorship.

There were also endogenous forces at work, namely the radicalization of society during the brutal 1954–1956 land reform campaign. The LDP "unleashed the might of the masses to destroy the landlord class," a campaign that was enormously unpopular and traumatized much of the countryside. Agricultural collectivization was undertaken in 1956 under Chinese leadership, and Chinese tactics such as people's courts, antilandlord campaigns, mass mobilization, class labeling, and mass executions were zealously applied.[43]

And, of course, there was the concern about the reunification of the country, which had divided since mid-1954. There was fear that if the intellectuals became too outspoken and acquired a public forum they could use to promote their views, then they would be used by the Ngo Dinh Diem regime in the south for propaganda and to discredit the North Vietnamese government.[44] Under the Geneva Accords in 1954, elections were to be held within two years—a compromise decision, because Hanoi had wanted to hold elections immediately to capitalize on the Viet Minh's overwhelming popularity. Although elections were increasingly unlikely, all hope had not yet been abandoned, and the party still wanted to maintain high levels of popular support—especially in the north—since the Viet Minh network and base of support was being quickly wiped out by Diem and his brother, Ngo Dinh Nhu, in the south.

The net effect of international pressure and domestic political needs was a two-pronged response. First was a crackdown on the dissidents, including the suppression of their publications and the arrest and reeducation of their leaders. Second was a vigorous literary campaign led by intellectuals who remained loyal to the party and the dictates of socialist realism.

The campaign began when *Nhan Van* was shut down in November 1956 after a staged strike of printing plant workers, before the sixth issue was published. *Giai Pham* was also closed after only four issues (March, August, October, December 1956). The publishers of both were arrested, and Phan Khoi died in Hanoi in early 1960, just days before he was supposed to go on trial for "deviationism." Other leaders were accused of "plotting to incite the masses to carry out counterrevolutionary demonstrations in order to overthrow the popular democratic regime and the leadership of the party."

In a July 1956 talk to intellectuals, Ho laid down the line that "the Party and Government should help the intellectuals by educating them so as to give them a firm class stand, a correct viewpoint, sound thinking, and democratic manners."[45] Following his lead, in December 1956, a meeting of senior party officials responsible for education and the arts convened to "unify party views and thoughts on the subject of arts and letters, to reach a decision about the journal *Nhan Van,* and to point out the direction of future progress."[46] At this meeting, the decision was made to translate into Vietnamese all the important Chinese and Soviet documents on managing intellectuals.

This meeting was followed up on 20 February 1957, when the LDP held the Congress on Arts and Literature that adopted an "uncompromising stand when it [comes] to the party line, but relaxed somewhat in terms of human relationships."[47] The party invited intellectuals, editors, and writers from *Nhan Van* and *Giai Pham* and was willing to address some practical (that is, nonpolitical) issues with them. Despite the study of Chinese documents that called for reeducation and ideological vigilance, the conference was surprisingly un-ideological. To Huu, the recipient of most of the intellectuals' scorn, was equally conciliatory: "In cultural and artistic activities, we can and should have different tendencies in our common standpoint, for this is of benefit to our country and people. All ideas and artistic tendencies can and must result from discussion."[48]

The conference led to the establishment of a new umbrella organization for intellectuals, the Union of Arts and Letters (UAL), in which leading dissidents, such as Van Cao,[49] were elected to the leadership. The UAL was authorized to publish its own journal *Van* (*Literature*), the first issue of which appeared on 10 May 1957. But only 37 issues were published because of the sentiments of its editorial staff against the party. The 36th issue (10 January 1958) included an allegorical story by the intellectuals' mentor and elder statesmen, Phan Khoi, about a jeweler who chastises an author: "When you know little about a question, you must listen and not break in. I'm not about to hold forth on literary theories with you, so you're not about to come here and teach me my craft." That was apparently the last straw: *Van* was accused of continuing anti-party agitation and a week later, the weekly stopped publication.

At a 6 January 1958 meeting of the Central Committee, To Huu launched a campaign against "saboteurs on the ideological and cultural front."[50] A Politburo resolution of the same date decreed:

> By exploiting the weaknesses of the arts and letters front and in particular the confused nature of thinking of the majority of artists and writers, the saboteurs have contrived to continue their activities and to cause very serious damage. It is clear that the anti-Socialist and anti-Party elements have profited from our laxness to continue their attacks on us in the sphere of ideas under the guise of arts and letters. The activities of these saboteurs among the artists and writers constitute a most dangerous threat and must be dealt with urgently.[51]

The Politburo resolution led to a series of study sessions and rectification courses beginning in January. A reeducation course was organized for nearly 500 writers and artists in January 1958, and from March to April 1958 the LDP Central Committee's Subcommittee for Arts and Letters organized a "study session" for some 304 writers, poets, and other cultural cadres, each of whom was forced to make a "self-criticism." According to the official *Van Nghe,* "All 304 artists, writers, and literary cadres" signed a letter dated 14 April 1958 to the LDP in which they "voluntarily accepted the four principles for reform of intellectuals laid down by the party." The campaign was in full swing by April 13 when a *Nhan Dan* editorial called for a "struggle to eradicate erroneous thoughts." There was no doubt now what was acceptable and what was not. Leading dissidents, especially Dao Duy Anh, Tran Dan, Nguyen Manh Tuong, Le Dat, and Tran Duc Thao were forced to write self-criticisms. All other dissidents were subjected to a barrage of public attacks. According to the party, these intellectuals were

> confronted with the brilliance of proletarian thought, with the clear truth, and by the determined struggle and patient assistance of their fellow literary artists, elements participating in the *Nhan Van–Giai Pham* affair took a first step toward recognizing the errors and crimes of their clique toward each and every one of their brothers and sisters who are literary artists.[52]

The entire April edition of *Van Nghe* was devoted to criticizing the *Nhan Van–Giai Pham* authors. The May edition contained self-confessions, self-criticisms, and retractions.

In June 1958, Ho himself appeared in person to open a 10-month reeducation course for senior intellectuals. And on 13 July, there was a "festival" held to celebrate the departure of 58 of the 92 members of the Union of Arts and Letters "into reality." The first course—"study through manual labor"—saw the intellectuals sent to labor in mines, factories, communes, and new economic zones. The fifteenth issue of *Van Nghe* tried to assuage their unhappiness at their treatment:

> It may be said that you are going into the most strategic places, into the first ranks on the frontiers of production, into the centers of contemporary life. The primary purpose of this phase of travel is not really to create. The primary purpose remains the reform of thought. But through this phase of thought reform, we believe that the enthusiastic spirit of revolution . . . will spread into our literature and our art, will give rise to creations that will make an appropriate contribution to the common task, for this has become a matter of regulation.[53]

Likewise, at the "farewell" reception for the second group sent to reform through labor, Bui Cong Trung, a Central Committee member, said that "this is a reforming of the spirit which will create completely new men, this disciplining of the spirit will, not unnaturally, be hard and painful, and it will extirpate everything from the past."[54]

In the end, four dissenters were expelled from the Union of Arts and Literature and others, such as poets Tran Dan and Le Dat, were suspended. There were thirty-seven dissidents considered by the authorities to be leaders and active, regular contributors of the condemned publications, and in the end 300 of the 476 people reeducated were writers and artists.

Lessons Learned

A harbinger of the government's heavy-handed tactics, used again in the 1990s to arrest such dissidents as Ha Si Phu and Le Hong Ha, was the arrest of journalist Nguyen Huu Dang, the poetess Luu Thi Yen (Thuy An), and the publisher Tran Thieu Bao on the charge that "during the year 1956 this group had disguised itself in the trappings of literature and art in order to carry out anti-government and anti-regime activities, and that since that time they had continued their sabotage activities."[55] One year later, a trial was held in secret at which they were accused of "acting as spies for the U.S.-Diem clique" and were sentenced to fifteen years in prison. In just one trial, an ideological difference was made into a counterrevolutionary criminal offense—a tactic used to control intellectuals and journalists to this day. Vaguely written and broadly interpreted national security laws remain the primary weapon against dissident writers and party critics.

The second instrument to control the intellectuals was a vigorous campaign to promote socialist realism. Despite the widespread desire for greater intellectual freedom, there was a number of intellectuals who embraced the party and its calls for a strict adherence by all intellectuals to the tenets of socialist realism. Ho Chi Minh himself led a real backlash against the champions of individual freedoms and selfish individualism. In a 1958 article, "On Revolutionary Morality," Ho warned that "the worst and most dangerous vestige of the old society is individualism," one of the "three enemies" of the revolution, every bit as dangerous as "capitalism and imperialism" and "backward habits and traditions."[56] Because Ho warned that "the success of socialism cannot be separated from that of the struggle for the elimination of individualism," many establishment intellectuals began to attack the literary dissidents for being egotistical and putting their own freedom ahead of the freedom of society, thus foreshadowing the debate over "Asian values" in the 1990s. In the March issue of *Van Nghe,* leading party critic Xuan Dieu declared that he too disliked dogmatism, and that "we too are awaiting, are encouraging, and are striving for a hundred types of *socialist* poems to blossom like flowers, to show off their freshness." But the emphasis was on the need for strict adherence by authors and artists to socialist realism:

> Yes, we have no need to imitate America, or England, or France, where conflicting literary tendencies are inevitably molded. Here in our Democratic Republic of Vietnam, although conflicting classes still exist, under the leadership of the party, we are advancing toward socialism. We want to have hundreds, thousands of approaches to writing, tens and tens of thousands of creations, but our literature has only one tendency and this is progress toward socialism.[57]

Furthermore, socialist realism was really the "humane" literature because it represented the interests of the proletarian class: "We understand that in previous regimes, basically, the masses had no writers or poets who were of their own class, serving their class directly." Xuan

Dieu gave the intellectuals one last shot at salvation: "Socialism needs technicians who are red, completely red, and not just ones with a pink-ish tinge. We also need writers and poets who are red, completely red, and not just ones with a pinkish tinge" or those who just "carry a card indicating membership in the party." In the same issue, Che Lan Vien published a poem entitled "When You Have Purpose."

> When you have purpose, a common stick can slay the enemy.
> Our brothers of old used their teeth to rend the flesh of opposing
>   troops.
> One leaflet can activate an entire district.
> Dirty hands and muddy feet can overturn even the throne of a king.
> When you have purpose, on those mornings and afternoons without
>   savor,
> Which are molded by fortifications meant to protect the "self."
> In the vale of agony weapons can be found
> To shatter the loneliness and mix it with "people."
> Nothing at all is lost
> When life has clear purpose.
> The tiniest moss-covered crevice will glisten with light,
> When the sunshine of thoughts plumbs the deep caves.[58]

A sense of purpose, a sense of belonging, the psychological reward of being part of a team or group really inspired a lot of poets and writers, for as Neil Jamieson notes, these poets, Huy Can, Xuan Dieu, To Huu, Luu Trong Lu, and Che Lan Vien

> were among the most alienated and disturbed young poets of the 1930s. Their poetry revealed extreme individualism and preoccupa-tion with their own inner feelings. What they seem to have felt, how-ever, was mainly loneliness and despair. They had not celebrated the joys of individualism; they had expressed its anguish. . . . They had been rejuvenated by their participation in the Resistance War and their conversion to communism in the mid-1940s. Party discipline, combined with membership in a tightly knit, highly organized social group had enabled them to slough off the oppressive weight of indi-vidualism and provided them with new and satisfying identities.[59]

Because of collectivism, "they had become integral parts of an effica-cious collectivity that transcended their own lives both sociologically and temporally." They were converts who defended the party with zeal: because of this, for twenty-five years starting in 1960 North Vietnam was all but a cultural wasteland. Not until *coi moi* was initiated in 1986 were the ideological constraints of socialist realism loosened and intellectual freedoms encouraged, with Vietnamese literature and arts earning critical acclaim at home and abroad.

The 1963–1967 Purge

Like the *Nhan Van–Giai Pham* affair, the 1963–1967 purge of high-level party officials continues to resonate and be a source of friction between the party and the dissident community. But unlike the literary events of the late 1950s, the verdict on this purge is unlikely ever to be reversed or its participants ever to be rehabilitated. To do so would attack the party's policies for the reunification of the country, a policy deemed totally correct and vindicated by history. Rather than recounting the history of the liberation of the south, we will simply analyze the purge as an egregious violation of one of the central tenets of communist systems: democratic centralism. Democratic centralism holds that within the party, there can be open debate of any issue until the decision is made. Thereafter, however, no debate or dissension is tolerated. Still, the treatment of those who were against the hardline approach to the liberation of the south was so harsh that it effectively ended all intraparty debate for the next two decades, with all decisions monopolized by a handful of leaders with absolute and unchallenged authority. Today's dissidents see this violation of democratic centralism as a mistake that the party must resolve in order to relegitimize itself.

Roots of the Purge

The cause of the 1963–1967 purge lay in perhaps the party's longest standing ideological and tactical policy considerations: how to reunify the south and whether to "lean" toward the Soviet Union or the People's Republic of China, with both choices made even more difficult in the context of the zero-sum Sino-Soviet rift that began in 1959. Although many scholars have argued that Vietnam's leadership has always been divided along pro-Chinese or pro-Soviet lines, the need for bloc unity for Hanoi's war effort was absolutely necessary regardless of an individual leader's proclivity.[60] Vacillations in Hanoi's relations with its two socialist patrons may have been driven by factional politics and ideology, but from the 1950s to the 1970s, the most important determinant was which country was more willing to support Hanoi's policies and tactics in the reunification of the country.

In the case of the 1963–1967 purge the hawks on the Central Committee, led by Le Duan and Le Duc Tho, were able to implement new policies to increase the military struggle in the south, beginning at the Central Committee's Fifteenth Plenum in May 1959. Such advocates of increased involvement by northern regulars as Le Duan and Gen. Nguyen Chi Thanh were able to impress their views upon their colleagues, while supporters of protracted guerrilla warfare, such as Gen. Vo Nguyen Giap, were either purged or demoted. In November 1960 the international communist movement openly split into two competing camps, one headed by the more militant People's Republic of China, the other led by the more moderate Soviet Union. In 1961, Hanoi openly rejected Khrushchev's policy of "peaceful coexistence" with the United States and began to receive increased amounts of Chinese military aid. When the Soviet Union failed to condemn a report from the International Control Commission that accused Hanoi of aggression in the south, Le Duan declared at the Central Committee's Ninth Plenum, in December 1963, that Soviet objectives with regard to the United States were inconsistent with DRV objectives in the south. "Some people," he said, proposed détente with the West, and "whether you like it or not, the outcome will be only to hamper the development of the revolution." The Central Committee's "resolution 9" authorized a full-fledged commitment to armed struggle in the south. As a result, Khrushchev decided to "disengage" the Soviet Union from Indochina and cut back most aid to Hanoi.

Hanoi was undaunted. Following the Ninth Plenum there was a flood of articles in the press stating that no revisionism would be tolerated, that is, there would be no retreat from the plenum decision to escalate the war in the south. For example, the 21 January 1969 editorial of *Nhan Dan* stated that "the error of the revisionist line is to . . . fear that revolutionary struggle might render the world situation tense and that revolutionary wars might flare up into a world nuclear war." Soon after, Le Duc Tho announced the start of a rectification campaign and in the 3–4 February edition of *Nhan Dan,* the editorial warned that it was "absolutely necessary to compel each and every comrade to submit himself to party discipline." Tho was very concerned about intra-party dissent, an "extreme minority," who disagreed with the Ninth Plenum goals and strategies, and he was not alone. On 27 March 1964, President Ho evoked for the first time article 67 of the constitution, which gave the president the authority to call a "special political conference to examine major political problems." Ho wanted to make sure that all party members were toeing the party line established at the Ninth Plenum; or, as Thomas Latimer put it, "North Vietnam firsters" were forced to publicly support the war.[61]

When the August 1964 Gulf of Tonkin incident led to a massive increase in U.S. troops in South Vietnam and the beginning of the bombing campaign against the north, China again increased its aid and commitments to Hanoi. The purge of Khrushchev in October 1964 led to renewed ties between Moscow and Hanoi, as Premier Pham Van Dong immediately flew to Moscow to confer with Kosygin and Brezhnev, but Hanoi remained bitter toward the Soviets. A March 1965 party document, for example, called Khrushchev a "traitor who distorted revolutionary ideals," and soon afterward, the VCP passed up an opportunity to negotiate with the United States, opting instead to escalate the war in the south. But Soviet weaponry was essential as the United States increased its involvement in the south and intensified its bombing campaign in the north. The decision to match the U.S. escalation in the south was, to a degree, successful. With over a half-million troops on the ground in 1968, the United States was coming no closer to winning the war.

But the party was not unified. Unnamed cadres, notably Gen. Vo Nguyen Giap, were criticized for believing that "the revolution in the south should be allowed to develop itself," which was China's current position.[62] Giap was investigated by the Bao Ve, a division of the army's General Political Department responsible for investigating the loyalty of all soldiers.[63] This department had very close ties to the Central Committee's Organization Commission, headed by Le Duc Tho, which was responsible for all personnel decisions. As a harbinger of things to come, three of Giap's top aides were arrested in 1964 for being "revisionists."[64] With Giap and opponents of direct military intervention in the south weakened, purged, or arrested, the Central Committee's Twelfth Plenum in December 1965 opted for a strategy that entailed small-scale offensives, heavier casualties, a greater risk of escalation, set piece battles requiring Soviet equipment, and larger amounts of aid that could not be provided by China alone.[65]

Once the debate over whether to fight was resolved, the debate shifted to how to fight. Was it to be a protracted guerrilla war that would sap U.S. power or a Dien Bien Phu-style general uprising to shock the U.S. military and people and convince them that the war was unwinnable? At the Central Committee's Thirteenth Plenum in April 1967, advocates of protracted war, led by Gen. Giap, were again defeated by hardliners led by Le Duan, Gen. Nguyen Chi Thanh, and Truong Chinh, who called for a "spontaneous uprising [in the south] in order to win a decisive victory in the shortest possible time." Resolution 13 was made manifest nine months later as the Tet Offensive.

The Purge

The 1963–1967 purge was not an issue of being pro-Soviet or pro-Chinese. It revolved around the conduct of the war in the south. The top party leadership purged all those who questioned its policy, regardless of whether they supported Khrushchev's peaceful coexistence, an attempt to revive the Geneva Accords and negotiate a Laos-like settlement, or whether they supported a Maoist-style protracted people's war. The top party leadership was committed to the military conquest of the south and reunification on Hanoi's terms.

The purge was headed by Le Duc Tho. Nguyen Trung Thanh, the head of the Central Committee's Internal Security Bureau, along with Minister of Public Security Tran Quoc Hoan and Maj. Gen. Song Hao, head of the VPA's Political Affairs Department, was authorized by Le Duc Tho to investigate "antiparty revisionists," or all those who opposed resolution 9, which authorized the use of force in the south, and the subsequent resolution 13, which rejected protracted guerrilla warfare. (Later, the scope of the purge was broadened to include advocates of the more cautious and less costly strategy of protracted warfare.) These men had full investigative powers and were authorized by Tho to go after any "revisionists," no matter how high in rank or party stature. No one was safe: Prime Minister Pham Van Dong got an implicit warning when his private secretary was accused in 1967 of being a "pro-Soviet revisionist."

One of the leading proponents of "peaceful coexistence" in the LDP was Hoang Minh Chinh. Despite being a member of the Hanoi elite, the French-educated Chinh had become an Indochina Communist Party activist at age nineteen and led a youth brigade in the war against the French. After recovering from a war injury, he was sent to Moscow to study Marxist theory for three years. He returned and rose quickly through the party apparatus, culminating with his appointment in 1960 as director of the Marxism-Leninism Institute in Hanoi.[66] His brother, Hoang Minh Giam, served as both the minister of culture and head of the Nguyen Ai Quoc National Academy of Politics for middle- and high-level cadres. Chinh was purged at the Ninth Plenum in 1963 for expressing criticism of "Maoist tendencies" in the party that advocated a greater commitment by Hanoi to armed struggle in the south. Believing that armed struggle in the south would lead to a greater confrontation with the United States, which Hanoi could ill afford, he supported Khrushchev's policy of peaceful coexistence and perhaps a negotiated settlement, along the lines of that in Laos in 1962. Chinh rejected Mao's "antagonistic contradictions" theory of class struggle, as well as the inevitability of conflict with the West, which the party leadership believed was unavoidable and necessary. For Chinh antagonistic class struggle would only slow the revolution. The path to socialism was best achieved not by a costly conflict with the United States, but through cooperation and peaceful coexistence with the West. Between 1967 and 1990, Chinh spent eleven years in prison and nine under house arrest, including a six-year jail sentence, from 1975 to 1981, for his advocacy of democratic reforms.

Nguyen Kien Giang is another contemporary dissident and victim of the 1963–1967 purge. Upon returning from studying at the Higher Political School in Moscow in 1964, this deputy director of the VCP's publishing house, *Su That,* and a member of the State Science Commission was immediately arrested for being a "revisionist." Kien was just one of thousands of party officials and intellectuals who were arrested, purged, or forced into reeducation camps because of an elite debate over the conduct of the war. Other senior officials arrested in September 1967 included Minh Can, the Soviet-trained deputy secretary of the Hanoi Party Committee; Gen. Dang Kim Giang, the deputy minister of state firms; Vu Dinh Huynh, chief of the Ministry of Foreign Affairs Protocol Department; and three senior journalists: Lt. Col. Quoc Doan of *Quan Doi Nhan Dan;* Tran Chau, a correspondent of *Nhan Dan;* and Pham Viet, a correspondent of *Thoi Moi,* as well as more than a dozen others. In January 1968, over 300 more were arrested, including two senior intelligence and security officials, Le Trong Nghia, the head of the Central Research Department, and Senior Col. Tran Hieu, deputy head of both the Supreme People's Control Organ and the Central Research Department.[67]

Revisiting the Purge

The purge reemerged as a divisive issue in the mid-1990s, beginning with an open letter by Hoang Minh Chinh that called for the reexamination of verdicts and labels and for the rehabilitation of victims. Despite eleven years of prison and house arrest he dared to write this letter because "none of the accused in the Revisionist Trial is left in prison today. They are not on this earth either. Dozens of them, including deputy ministers, members of the Party Central Committee, army generals, writers, editors-in-chief, poets, have carried unjust condemnation to their graves. It is my duty to speak out on their behalf so people will know the truth."[68] This letter struck a chord and emboldened several senior party officials to also call for a reexamination of the incident. Nguyen Van Tran, a former Central Committee member and head of the Central Committee's Culture and Education Committee, went so far as to label the "trial of the anti-party revisionists" as one of the many "crimes this regime has committed" in his controversial and banned book, *Writing to Mother and the National Assembly* (1995).

The sharpest criticism of the "antirevisionist" purge came from not the victims, but two former prosecutors, Le Hong Ha and Nguyen Trung Thanh. Le Hong Ha was a high-ranking official in the Ministry of Interior, at one point in his twenty-one-year career, serving as the chief of cabinet.[69] Le Duc Tho appointed Thanh head of the Central Committee's Internal Security Bureau to investigate antiparty revisionists beginning in 1963, which led to the purges of 1967. Upon his retirement in the early 1990s Thanh, with the help of Le Hong Ha, began to research and go through party archives relating to the antirevisionist trial.

This research culminated in December 1993 with an unsolicited report to the Politburo and Secretariat informing them that the evidence used in the prosecution of the dissidents was incorrect. Thanh received no response from the party and wrote another letter fourteen months later, on 3 February 1995, this time distributing copies to the media. When he was summoned to meet with General Secretary Do Muoi on 22 March 1995, he attacked the politicized nature of the indictments and the blatant overreaching of the party: "No one but the Inspectorate [the Central Committee's Central Inspection Commission] and the court can condemn people. Even the Politburo does not have the power to condemn a citizen. The Politburo has no right to strip people of their citizen's rights. . . . Under the State's laws, opposing the Party is not a crime; and supporting revisionism is not a crime."[70]

While Thanh attacked the legality of the purges, Le Hong Ha began to actively campaign for the rehabilitation of the victims the party had mistakenly prosecuted, notably Hoang Minh Chinh.[71] Ha then called for a recounting of those killed during the land reform campaign and demanded that the party accept responsibility for its mistakes during the *Nhan Van–Giai Pham* affair as well.

For their efforts to redress events that the party deemed correct and vindicated by history, Thanh and Ha were expelled from the VCP in July 1995. That December, Ha was arrested and in the following August was given a two-year sentence for "having revealed state secrets."[72] Thanh was only placed under surveillance, even though he had gone further in his attack than Ha. Thanh challenged the legality of article 4 of the constitution that gives the party a monopoly of power and which places it above the law. This will be discussed in detail in the following chapter.

The Legacy of Dissent

Because many of the issues remain the same, the *Nhan Van–Giai Pham* affair and the 1967 intraparty purge are the logical starting points for understanding contemporary dissent in Vietnam. Although a dwindling number of today's dissidents lived through the crackdown on intellectuals and party purge, these two events have been a reference point for those who want political reform, the restoration of intraparty democratization, and greater intellectual freedom. Despite attempts by the party to put these issues behind, they will not go away—indeed, they serve as a rallying point. The *Nhan Van–Giai Pham* affair remains very sensitive in Hanoi to this day because so many of the current dissidents were victims of the purge.

The affair, is course, is not recounted in the current press or in histories. For example, the long-time party historian, Nguyen Khac Vien, clearly toed the party line by not even mentioning the affair or any signs of intellectual dissent in his books. Instead, he only wrote of the "establishment" intellectuals;[73] To Huu was the "leading figure," although Vien also singles out Xuan Dieu, Che Van Lien, Te Hanh, and Huy Can, who "depicted with warmth and skill the heroes and achievements of the advancing revolution."[74] Although "these masters" were in the forefront of revolutionary arts, Vien noted that they "were joined by a host of young poets, often still entangled in clumsy expression," forgivable because many "were born into worker or peasant families." For him, "the literary movements closely followed the revolutionary movement, setting itself revolutionary tasks; during the war the motto was to 'cover the sound of bombs by singing,' so helping to encourage revolutionary heroism among the broad masses. Literature and arts in Vietnam proudly fulfilled this mission."[75] Indeed, the mission of the arts to serve the party and revolution would remain state and party policy until the late 1980s. General Secretary Le Duan made it quite clear, as late as the Fourth Party Congress in 1982, that because of the *Nhan Van–Giai Pham* affair, literature and the arts were "developed on the basis of the perspective of Marxism-Leninism," and the responsibility of all writers and cultural officials was to combat "all bourgeois and opportunistic tendencies in literature and the arts."

Almost all the issues raised by the intellectuals in the 1950s remain the same for the dissidents in the 1990s and at the turn of the century: intellectual freedom, freedom of the press, democratization, greater transparency in the party's and government's decisionmaking, a greater role for the National Assembly, and the implementation of the rule of law for everyone, including the party.

The *Nhan Van–Giai Pham* affair remains important because it continues as a rallying point for those who demand that the party reopen the matter and rehabilitate the victims. It was not a coincidence that when Nguyen Dan Que founded the Vietnamese chapter of Amnesty International that he termed it the "High Tide of Humanism Movement." Several of today's leading dissidents demand redress in the affair, among other things. La Van Lam, for example, demanded in a 2 January 1996 letter to General Secretary Do Muoi that the party reverse the "fabricated charges [against the writers and intellectuals] during the *Nhan Van–Giai Pham* trial." Aside from literary reforms, the affair remains a symbol for the advocates of economic liberalization. For example, both intellectuals and economic reformers were delighted by To Huu's firing before the Sixth Party Congress in July 1986. As a result of his party work in the 1950s and 1960s, Huu had been steadily promoted, eventually becoming first vice premier, and was a candidate to succeed Premier Pham Van Dong who stepped down in December 1986. But Huu was also the leading advocate of the ill-conceived and poorly executed September 1985 currency reform that targeted the black market but instead caused massive inflation, shortages, and a severe economic slowdown.[76]

More important, it is an issue that young artists, writers, and intellectuals can relate to. Although they may not share the personal experience of the older victims of the movement, the rebellion against the tenets of socialist realism transcends generations. The *Nhan Van–Giai Pham* affair, therefore, becomes a bridge that links a new generation of writers, musicians, artists, and intellectuals who have no revolutionary or wartime experience to their predecessors. It allows them all to speak the same language. In a frank October 1987 exchange between General

Secretary Nguyen Van Linh and writers and intellectuals (discussed in detail in Chapter 4), Nguyen Khac Vien, who had become very critical of the party by the mid-1980s, called for an exoneration of those purged during the *Nhan Van–Giai Pham* affair. He warned the general secretary that "for a long time, artists, writers, journalists, and film-makers have been told 'do this,' 'don't do that.' Sometimes works of art have been put on trial, accused of being anti-party or revisionist or provocative. Sometimes artists have gone to prison. But the scars of artists going to prison for cultural crimes carry from one generation to the next."[77]

One does not have to delve deeply into Duong Thu Huong's newest novel, *Memories of a Pure Spring,* also banned by Hanoi, to understand the pent-up anger of artists and intellectuals. This is the story of an artist caught up in a political conflict and his spiritual decay after being labeled a "class enemy."[78] The artists who suffered during this period are lionized: as one Vietnamese journalist wrote, "The luminaries of Aesthetic Humanism are now lionized as 'true intellectuals,' men willing to stand up for what they believed."[79]

Likewise, the antirevisionist purge of 1963–1967 continues to be a sensitive subject for the party. The dissidents' demand that the party acknowledge its mistake cuts to the heart of the regime's legitimacy. It is not simply an issue of the party's infallibility. First, by rehabilitating victims of this purge, by admitting its policy was wrong, the party opens the door to the charge that the entire policy of armed struggle in the south, and thus hundreds of thousands of lives and years of suffering, was incorrect. The War of National Liberation and the reunification of the country are the regime's greatest source of popular legitimacy and the regime will not do anything to jeopardize that. By promoting the war as a "just cause" the regime is able to justify the enormous hardships, in both human and material costs, suffered by the population during the long period of war. Thus the war must still be portrayed as a heroic struggle and a just cause, two of the themes of the twenty-fifth anniversary celebrations in April 2000. Not only was the party's policy correct, but it was glorious. It is for this reason that writers such as Bao Ninh and Duong Thu Huong are reviled for their less-than-heroic characters and depictions of war.[80] And the party is willing to sacrifice anyone who tries to call into question the source of what is left of its legitimacy.

Second, because only a distinct minority of the dissidents want to implement a Western-style system of bourgeois democracy, most of the party-based dissidents, indeed party members, want to improve intra-party democratization. The key to this is to move from a dictatorial system, in which decisionmaking is monopolized by a handful of un-challenged leaders, to an avowed system of consensual decisionmaking based on open dialogue and debate. Yet the legacy of the 1967 purge was the demise of democratic centralism: free debate in the policy for-mulation stage was no longer tolerated if it went against the interests of the top leaders. The harsh crackdown in 1967 forced most into utter si-lence and slavish subservience to the leaders' wishes, effectively end-ing policy debates. Afterward, all decisionmaking and power were con-solidated into the hands of a few. But since 1986, dissidents within the party have fought to restore intraparty democracy and open debates over public policy.

Third, and perhaps more threatening to the regime, the dissidents are challenging article 4 of the constitution. What the dissidents are concerned with is the question of whether opposition to the VCP, or one of its policies, is a crime against the state. As Bui Minh Quoc com-plained, "I could never believe that while my family, like thousands of others, were willing to give up their lives for the independence of our country and freedom for everyone, those who urged our sacrifices took away our freedom and persecuted their comrades because of their opin-ion."[81] Article 4 is the subject of much controversy, and in the redraft-ing of the constitution in 1991–1992, the wording was changed to state that the party was no longer "the leading force," but simply "a leading force." But to most the change is cosmetic, not substantive. A related concern of theirs is the legality of the Politburo's power to condemn in-dividuals. As in the *Nhan Van–Giai Pham* affair, the party was able to circumvent the state by using its own disciplinary tools, not the govern-ment's legal apparatus, which for the most part was inactive. Indeed, the entire Ministry of Justice was disbanded in 1961 and lay dormant until the early 1980s, while the other lawmaking organ, the National Assembly, was nothing but a rubber stamp for the party's decisions. The extralegal powers of the party, which continue to be one of the most controversial aspects of its control, will be discussed in the fol-lowing chapter.

Notes

1. Ho had disbanded the ICP in 1946 when talks with the French over self-rule broke down and Ho was preparing to fight the French. To get other

nationalist groups, especially the staunchly anticommunist VNQDD (Viet Nam Quoc Dan Dang), to join the umbrella organization, the Viet Minh, Ho dissolved the ICP. Ho sought to alleviate any concerns that the Viet Minh was a communist-led or dominated organization. ICP cadres, however, dominated the Vietminh's leadership.

2. Melvin Gurtov, *The First Indochina War: Chinese Communist Strategy and the United States* (New York: Columbia University Press, 1967), 16.

3. William Duiker, *The Communist Road to Power in Vietnam* (Boulder, Colo.: Westview Press, 1981), 141.

4. Andrew Vickerman, *The Fate of the Peasantry: The Premature "Transition to Socialism" in the Democratic Republic of Vietnam* (New Haven, Conn.: Yale Center for International and Area Studies, Monograph No. 28, 1986). Also see Neil Jamieson, *Understanding Vietnam* (Berkeley: University of California Press, 1993), 224.

5. Nhu Phong, "Intellectuals, Writers and Artists," in P. J. Honey, ed., *North Vietnam Today: Profile of a Communist Satellite* (New York: Praeger, 1962), 77.

6. Nhu Phong, "Intellectuals, Writers and Artists," 73.

7. Dang Thai Mao, "Vietnamese Literature," *Europe,* 387–388 (July–August 1961), 91.

8. Mao Zedong, "Talks at the Yenan Forum on Literature and Art," May 1942, in Mao Zedong, *Selected Works,* vol. 3 (Peking: Hanoi Foreign Language Publishing House, 1965), 69–98; Vladimir Lenin, "Party Organization and Party Literature," 1905, in Robert C. Tucker, ed. and trans., *The Lenin Anthology* (New York: Norton, 1975), 148–153; Maxim Gorky, "Soviet Literature," Address delivered to the First All-Union Congress of Soviet Writers, 17 August 1934, in Maxim Gorky, *On Literature: Selected Articles* (Moscow: Foreign Language Publishing House, n.d.), 228–268.

9. Truong Chinh, "Marxism and Vietnamese Culture" (Report delivered at the 2nd National Culture Conference, July 1948) in Truong Chinh, *Selected Writings* (Hanoi: Foreign Languages Publishing House, 1977), 286.

10. Mao Zedong, "Talks at the Yenan Forum on Literature and Art," 86.

11. Ho Chi Minh, "To the Artists on the Occasion of the 1951 Painting Exhibition," in Ho Chi Minh, *Selected Writings (1920–1949)* (Hanoi: Foreign Language Publishing House, 1973), 133.

12. Ibid., 134.

13. Georges Boudarel, "Intellectual Dissidence in the 1950s: The Nhan-Van Giai-Pham Affair," *Vietnam Forum* 13, 155.

14. Nhu Phong, "Intellectuals, Writers and Artists," 74.

15. P. J. Honey, "Introduction," in Honey, ed., *North Vietnam Today: Profile of a Communist Satellite* (New York: Praeger, 1962), 6.

16. Nhu Phong, "Intellectuals, Writers and Artists," 75.

17. Ibid., 76.

18. Phan Khoi, "Criticism of the Leadership in Arts and Letters," *Giai Pham Mua Thu* (September 1956) in Hoang Van Chi, ed., *The New Class in North Vietnam* (Saigon: Cong Dan Publishing Co., 1958), 75.

19. Nhu Phong, "Intellectuals, Writers and Artists," 80.

20. Cited in Nhu Phong, "Intellectuals, Writers and Artists," 80.

21. Cited in Boudarel, "Intellectual Dissidence in the 1950s," 157.

22. Cited in C. K. Nguyen, "Prophets without Honour," *Far Eastern Economic Review* (hereafter *FEER*), 4 April 1991, 31.

23. Khoi was the grandson of the legendary Hong Dieu (who hanged himself when the French overran the citadel in Hanoi) and the father of modern poetry, a veteran revolutionary who spent nine years imprisoned in Paulo Condore and another eight years in the Viet Bac jungles with the resistance forces. He died in disgrace, labeled an enemy of the state.

24. *Giai Pham,* September 1956, cited in Jamieson, *Understanding Vietnam,* 258.

25. Hoang Van Chi asserts that Tran Dan was eventually put on trial, but that "no word for his defense was pronounced," thereby proving that "all their mouths have been filled up." See Hoang Van Chi, *The New Class in North Vietnam* (Saigon, Cong Dan Publishing Co., 1958), 81–83.

26. See Nguyen Ngoc Bich, ed., *One Thousand Years of Vietnamese Poetry* (New York: Columbia University Press, 1975), 187–189.

27. The winning work was Xuan Dieu's "The Star." Dieu became a leading party intellectual closely aligned with To Huu, the revolutionary poet and, later, Politburo member.

28. Boudarel, "Intellectual Dissidence in the 1950s," 164.

29. Cited in Boudarel, "Intellectual Dissidence in the 1950s," 164. When the party warned him about such writings, Phung Quan defiantly responded:

> The honey-strewn road of riches and honors cannot sweeten my
>   tongue,
> A thunderbolt striking my head cannot knock me down. Who then
>   can snatch away my pen and paper?

30. Tran Le Van, "Fear Not that the Enemy Shall Benefit," *Nhan Van* 2 (30 September 1956): 164; cited in Boudarel, "Intellectual Dissidence in the 1950s."

31. Cited in Boudarel, "Intellectual Dissidence in the 1950s," 166.

32. Ibid.

33. Cited in Jamieson, *Understanding Vietnam,* 261.

34. Cited in Boudarel, "Intellectual Dissidence in the 1950s," 167.

35. The poem appeared in the October 1956 edition of *Giai Pham Mua Thu* and can be found in Hoang Van Chi, *The New Class in North Vietnam,* 34–36.

36. Bui Tin, *Following Ho Chi Minh: Memoirs of a North Vietnamese Colonel* (Honolulu: University of Hawaii Press, 1995), 14-16. This was highlighted in the dispute between Vo Nguyen Giap and Truong Chinh. Giap, who won the Battle of Dien Bien Phu, did so by ignoring the advice from his Chinese advisors. It is interesting to note that in his memoir regarding the battle, he barely mentions Chinese support or the help he received from PLA advisors. Also see Cecil Currey, *Victory at Any Cost* (Washington, D.C.: Brassey's, 1997), esp. 145–212.

37. Tin, *Following Ho Chi Minh,* 35.

38. Hirohide Kurihara, "Changes in the Literary Policy of the Vietnamese Workers' Party, 1956-1958," in *Indochina in the 1940s and 1950s* (Ithaca, N.Y.: Cornell University, Southeast Asia Program, 1992), 165–196.

39. See, for example, Nguyen Chuong, "Co Can Cu Hay Khong Co Can Cu," *Nhan Dan,* 15 October 1956. And Nguyen Chuong, "May diem Sai Lam Chu Yen Trong bao Nhan Van va tap Giai Pham Mua Thu," *Nhan Dan,* 25 September 1956.

40. Chu Ngoc, *Nhan Van,* No. 3. Cited in Boudarel, "Intellectual Dissidence in the 1950s," 164.

41. Cited in Boudarel, "Intellectual Dissidence in the 1950s," 171.

42. "Phat Cao Ngon co yeu nuoc va xa hoi chu nghia, nha dan Hung-ga-ri da de bep bon phan cach mang, tay sai cua de Quoc," *Nhan Dan,* 5 November 1956.

43. The land reform campaign was brutal and caused open rebellion in Nghe An, which threatened the survival of the party—as even the loyalty of the VPA was in doubt. Ho was forced to sack Troung Chinh (who underwent public self-criticism) and took over the reins of the party himself. Excesses were acknowledged by Ho himself, and a rectification campaign was launched. The Central Committee admitted that "a number of grave errors had been committed during the execution of the land reforms," and thousands of political prisoners were released as a gesture of good will. But the party's purges had sowed deep mistrust. At the Central Committee's Tenth Plenum, the LDP announced that it would "extend democracy, safeguard democratic liberties and enlarge the system of democratic legality." Lincoln Kaye, "A Bowl of Rice Divided: The Economy of North Vietnam," in P. J. Honey, ed., *North Vietnam Today,* 107–108. A full history of the land reform campaign can be found in Vickerman, *The Fate of the Peasantry.*

44. See, for example, Hoang Van Chi, *The New Class in North Vietnam.*

45. Ho Chi Minh, "A Talk with Intellectuals," in Ho Chi Minh, *Selected Articles and Speeches, 1920–1967,* Jack Woddis, ed. (New York: International Publishers, 1969), 109.

46. *Van Nghe,* 13 (June 1957).

47. Boudarel, "Intellectual Dissidence in the 1950s," 168.

48. *Van Nghe,* 162 (1–7 March 1957), cited in Nhu Phong, "Intellectuals, Writers and Artists," 84–85. The recently deposed Truong Chinh gave the keynote address, "Striving for a Popular Arts and Letters Movement Under the Flag of Patriotism and Socialism."

49. Van Cao, the author of the National Anthem, "March to the Front," was purged and eventually rehabilitated in the mid-1980s.

50. *Van Nghe,* 10.

51. Cited in Nhu Phong, "Intellectuals, Writers and Artists," 85.

52. *Van Nghe,* 12, 59.

53. *Van Nghe,* 15, 7–8, cited in Jamieson, *Understanding Vietnam,* 271.

54. Cited in Nhu Phong, "Intellectuals, Writers and Artists," 88.

55. *Van Nghe* (19 April 1958), cited in Nhu Phong, "Intellectuals, Writers and Artists," 87.

56. Ho Chi Minh, "On Revolutionary Morality," in *Selected Writings,* 197, 201.

57. *Van Nghe* (March 1958), cited in Jamieson, *Understanding Vietnam,* 264.

58. Cited in Jamieson, *Understanding Vietnam,* 266–267.

59. Jamieson, *Understanding Vietnam*, 268–269.

60. Major works on this subject include John Donnell and Melvin Gurtov, *North Vietnam: Left of Moscow, Right of Peking*, Rand Report P-3794 (Santa Monica: The Rand Corporation, 1968); William J. Duiker, *The Communist Road to Power;* Herbert J. Elison, ed., *The Sino-Soviet Conflict: A Global Perspective* (Seattle: University of Washington Press, 1982); P. J. Honey, *Communism in North Vietnam;* Douglas Pike, *Vietnam and the Soviet Union: Anatomy of an Alliance* (Boulder, Colo.: Westview Press, 1987).

61. Some continued to speak out against the north's involvement in the war in the south, most notably Vo Nguyen Giap. In a July 1964 article, he stated that "the liberation war of our people in the south is a protracted and hard war in which they rely mainly on themselves." Thomas Latimer, *Hanoi's Leaders and their South Vietnam Policies, 1954–68*, Ph.D. diss., Georgetown University, 1972.

62. China, which was beginning its Maoist swan song, the Cultural Revolution, argued that the liberation of the south should be undertaken through guerrilla warfare. Lin Biao's "Long Live the Victory of the People's War" was an implicit criticism of the Vietnamese leadership and its failure to understand the nature of a protracted people's war.

63. Bui Tin, *Following Ho Chi Minh*, 55.

64. Do Duc Kien was the head of military operations, Le Minh Nghia was Giap's personal secretary, and Nguyen Minh Nghia was the director of military intelligence.

65. In his "Letter to Southern Comrades," Le Duan blamed the party for not taking advantage of the south's political instability in 1963–1964. He was really blaming Giap and his followers who resisted sending troops to the south. "It was obvious that the situation of the war developed more rapidly than we had anticipated. At that time, we had not yet acquired adequate conditions to cope with the rapid development of the situation."

66. Bui Tin says that Chinh became the director of the Institute of Philosophy in 1962.

67. Nguyen Ngoc Bich, *Six Studies on Vietnam* (Washington, D.C., 1971 n.p.), 64–65.

68. "Interview with Hoang Minh Chinh," in *Vietnam Democracy* (July 1996).

69. Ha also served on the Scientific and Social Commission for three years and was the chairman for ten years of the committee that drafted Vietnam's labor codes.

70. "Still Going," *Vietnam Democracy* (April 1998).

71. Amnesty International, *Country Report—Socialist Republic of Vietnam: The Case of Le Hong Ha and Ha Si Phu* (1996).

72. Ha, like Ha Si Phu and Nguyen Kien Giang, was in possession of a widely circulated letter to the Politburo written by Premier Vo Van Kiet. He later commented, "About my crime of 'revealing state secrets,' I wonder. What is the purpose of 'protecting those secrets' if not the coverup of party members' wrong doings?" He was released on 6 August 1997, four months early.

73. Maurice Durand, a French intellectual with ties to the Democratic Republic of Vietnam and who lived in Hanoi during the 1950s, subscribed to the party line. In his book, *An Introduction to Vietnamese Literature*, he also cites

the leading party writers, such as Xuan Dieu, Luu Trong-Leuu, To Huu, and Che Lan Vien, but gives only cursory treatment of the *Nhan Van–Giai Pham* affair, which he simply described as "a revolt of writers and poets opposed to the regime," and does not include the works of its leading writers. After labeling the affair "reactionary," Durand notes that the "Lao Dong took a firm hold on the situation, and called on writers to make a greater effort to raise their cultural level of their works and learn from the masses." Under the leadership of To Huu, the Second Congress of the National Assembly of Artists and Men of Letters stated that "the people call on all artists to adopt the role of 'spiritual engineer.'" Literature then focused on resistance and agrarian reform, but Durand agrees with Vien that even though the new authors were steeped in socialist realism, "they were lacking in political and cultural maturity, depth of thinking, and skill in presenting." Maurice M. Durand and Nguyen Tran Huan, *An Introduction to Vietnamese Literature* (New York: Columbia University Press, 1985), 134–135.

74. Nguyen Khac Vien, *Vietnam: A Long History* (Hanoi: The Gioi Publishers, 1993), 342.

75. Ibid., 343.

76. The vice premier for currency reform, Tran Phuong, was sacked, but that did not satisfy the critics who wanted Huu's head. Vo Chi Cong, a 73-year-old southerner who supported production contracts and enterprise autonomy, replaced Huu. Cong was the architect of a series of popular agricultural reforms implemented in the south that introduced contractual relationships with the state.

77. Cited in Nguyen Thi Lieu, "Artistic Freedom in Vietnam," *Vietnam Update* (Winter/Spring 1988): 12.

78. Translated by Nina McPherson and Phan Huy Duong (New York: Hyperion East, 2000).

79. C. K. Nguyen, "Prophets Without Honour," 31.

80. Bao Ninh, *The Sorrow of War,* 2d ed., trans. Phanh Thanh Hao (New York: Riverhead Books, 1996); and Duong Thu Huong, *Novel Without a Name,* trans. Phan Huy Duong and Nina McPherson (New York: Penguin Publishers, 1995). Indeed, Huong could not publish this work in Vietnam and had to send it abroad for publication, an act that got her arrested. Although Bao Ninh's novel was named by the Vietnam Writers' Association as one of the three best novels in 1991, it was trashed by party critics. One, Maj. Gen. Ho Phuong, wrote in *Van Nghe* that "it seems he only sees death and miserable things." In his own defense, Ninh said, "I wrote this novel because most of the other books about the war are inadequate. I'm angry about these novels because they only advertise about the war," or focus on themes such as bravery and camaraderie. See Murray Hiebert, "Even War Heroes Cry," *Far Eastern Economic Review,* 31 October 1991, 54–55.

81. See "Open Letter from Bui Minh Quoc," 3 October 1993, *Vietnam Insight* (May 1994).

3

THE DEBATES OVER
DEMOCRATIZATION AND LEGALIZATION

Today, I can say with certainty that no forces inside or outside the country can destroy the Vietnam Communist Party. Only the party could weaken itself by refusing to adapt.

—General Tran Do

The servant drives in a Volga
The families of the masters wait at the station for a train
The servant has a nice villa
The families of the masters use oil paper to keep out the rain
The servants attend banquets, noon and night
The families of the masters eat greens and pickles every night

—A Vietnamese verse

In the post–Cold War era, exogenous forces are always at work in pushing for greater democratization and political reform. For instance, in President Clinton's speech in which he announced that the United States would establish diplomatic relations with Vietnam, he made clear that a primary motivation was to foster economic growth that would lead to popular demands for greater freedom and political rights. And clearly foreign pressure has had some effect on the treatment of certain dissidents, for example, with the release from prison of Doan Viet Hoat, Duong Thu Huong, and Nguyen Thanh Giang. Although the government refused to admit that their release was brought about by foreign pressure,[1] it is clear that Vietnam hoped to win some economic concessions from the United States through this move. Human rights, whether or not Vietnam agrees with the West's interpretation of it, has to be on the policymakers' agenda. And there is some indication that this is happening. For example, the *Far Eastern Economic Review* reported that in 1992–1993, a high-level interagency group, including representatives from the Ministry of the Interior, the Central Committee and other party organs, the Supreme Court, and the Ministry of Foreign Affairs, met to discuss human rights issues.[2] But despite foreign pressure for political reform and a loosening of the VCP's hold on power, the pressure for democratization and political reform has come from inside the country. Exogenous forces have simply been more of an annoyance than a force for change. Moreover, pressure for political liberalization has come from within the party itself. The origins of the debate over democratization came soon after the Sixth Party Congress in 1986, which elected Nguyen Van Linh as VCP general secretary and heralded the era of economic reform and *doi moi,* or renovation. This chapter discusses the origins of the debate, which was centered in the Politburo, the crackdown in 1989, and the dearth of any official movement toward political reform until the Thai Binh peasant protests erupted in 1998. The chapter then analyzes the demands raised by the National Assembly, the differing views of democracy and pluralism, and their ideological and economic concerns in the 1990s.

Tran Xuan Bach and the
Politburo's Debate over Political Reform

The collapse of communism in Eastern Europe and the former Soviet Union between 1989 and 1991 had a profound influence on the Vietnamese leadership. As with its communist counterparts elsewhere, Vietnam felt some pressure to democratize. Unlike China, though, where democratic pressures came from students and workers, the challenge to the VCP came from its own ranks: democratization was hotly debated in Hanoi from 1986 to 1989. General Secretary Nguyen Van Linh, who had made normalization of relations with China his top foreign policy priority, began to implement Chinese-style economic reforms, based on contracts and market forces at the expense of central planning. The leadership was able to "compartmentalize" the idea of democracy, encouraging democracy in the economy so that political pluralism would not have to be dealt with. As a Politburo member and a top party theoretician, Nguyen Duc Binh, wrote: "Democracy in the economy is the key link along the path of democratizing society. Democratization in other areas will have a greatly reduced significance, and it will be hard to have conditions for adequate and meaningful implementation; indeed we may even encounter obstacles if democratization does not succeed in the economic sphere, the basis for social life."[3] Simply put, if the economy and standard of living grew substantially because of the reform program, popular pressure for political reform would dissipate; only with their economic survival, much less prosperity, in doubt, would the people be emboldened to challenge the state.

Although the party advocated "broadening democracy" as early as 1986, it was not political pluralism that it was embracing. What Linh meant by "democratization" was more debate and discussion over policy within the party itself. For him, democratic centralism was not being practiced, it having been eviscerated in the 1967 purge. All decisions were made by a handful of top leaders who had unchallenged authority but little understanding of details or local circumstances that caused economic stagnation. To emerge from this malaise, there needed to be *doi moi tu duy* ("renovation in thinking") and *coi moi* ("openness"). But in no way was this an embrace of bourgeois multiparty democracy.

The Politburo issued a document in 1988 that divulged its trepidation that individuals would use "democracy" to destabilize the regime. General Secretary Linh argued that multiparty competition was a threat to national security because it would "create conditions favorable for the reactionary forces of revenge within the country and from abroad to rear their heads immediately and legally to operate against the homeland, the people and the regime."[4] The document warned against individuals "taking advantage of democracy and openness to distort the truth, negate revolutionary gains, and to attack the party leadership and state management out of personal motives."[5]

But Linh still had to encourage economic reform because public unhappiness over the continual poverty also posed social instability. The obstacle to reform was the Communist Party bureaucracy that enjoyed its elite status and power through its control of the distribution of scarce resources; thus Linh's market reforms threatened this monopoly of power, and they were fiercely resisted. Linh had to pressure and cajole the bureaucracy into implementing his reforms, and to do this he encouraged the press and other intellectuals in 1987 to criticize middle-level party and state officials who were blocking his reforms. The press was authorized to begin investigative reporting especially to ferret out corrupt cadres. That same year, Linh began to write his own column, "Noi Va Lam" ("Talk and Act"), in *Nhan Dan* and *Sai Gon Giai Phong* to promote his reforms and criticize those cadres who blocked them.

Through Linh's efforts, there was a real loosening of political controls on intellectual discourse, and "the year 1988 brought an unprecedented widening of the boundary of criticism of Vietnam's political system and of its assumptions by party members"[6] who were greatly influenced by their Polish, Hungarian, Czech, and Soviet counterparts. Vietnamese intellectuals and government and party officials followed the debates in Eastern Europe and the Soviet Union very closely, though not always accurately or objectively in their attempt to explain or justify the transformation of the Eastern European polities. They were cognizant that a multiparty system, albeit one in which the Communist Party remained a dominant political force, had emerged in Hungary after regional officials had banded together and founded reform "circles," which evolved into true opposition parties.[7] What made the Hungarian transition possible was a long-term experiment in market reforms that had created sectors and regions with individual economic conditions and needs. It was this aspect that truly alarmed the Vietnamese party. According to one overseas commentator, some southerners in the Central Committee suggested adopting the "Hungarian pattern for developing socialist democracy."[8] Events in Hungary, where opposition parties had the right to not support socialism, therefore, developed very differently than in Poland.[9] The Vietnamese party turned then to the more moderate reforms in the Soviet Union and came up with a very short-lived concept of "socialist pluralism," but even that, as defined by the Soviets, was too radical for Hanoi. In addition to the market reforms being implemented in the economy, the Communist Party of the Soviet Union had begun to tolerate different political viewpoints as long as they "serve[d] the cause of socialist construction" as well as "different opinions and viewpoints . . . including those which do not fit in with and differ from the party's official viewpoints."[10]

Vietnam's intellectuals did not make such bold demands as their Eastern European counterparts, but they were clearly becoming more critical of their regime. One writer and a prominent National Liberation Front official and former Saigon party chief, Tran Bach Dang, complained in the newspaper *Lao Dong* that "freedom of opinion is not respected and open expression is still more restrained."[11] Others called for reenergizing democratic socialism to allow for more freedom of debate within the party. One ideological cadre went even further, calling for a reevaluation of bourgeois democracy. Socialism, he wrote in the party's own theoretical journal, "must include achievements scored by the modern bourgeois state . . . including the systemization of democracy, law and human rights."[12]

Within the party, the political debate in the two years running up to the Seventh Party Congress, in June 1991, was dominated by concerns over political pluralism and the future of socialism. The Central Committee's Sixth Plenum, in March 1989, focused on defining or conceptualizing democracy, that is, the "dictatorship of the proletariat." According to the Plenum's communiqué, "democracy requires leadership, and leadership must be aimed at developing democracy in the right direction and through correct democratic methods. Democracy is applied to the people, but strict punishment must be meted out to those who undermine the gains of the revolution, security, and social order."

By then, senior party officials were warning that calls for "absolute democracy" and "press independence from the party committee and other leading echelons" would "allow the movement to develop a chaotic and anarchic situation and play into the hands of those who opposed the reforms already brought about."[13] Such statements were not as hardline as they may seem: supporters of the economic reform program feared a conservative ideological backlash and counseled restraint. The author, Tran Truong Tan, went on to write that by not cracking down on the forces for political pluralism, party conservatives would gain the upper hand and then roll back the reform program:

> To vigorously advance the movement for democracy and openness in the right direction, we must struggle simultaneously on both fronts— against extreme democracy and openness as well as against conservatism. . . . By failing to correctly and skillfully struggle against extremism, we will allow ourselves to fall into the trap of conservatism and to return to the wrong trail. This is detrimental to the effort to encourage renovation and will create great difficulties for us in the immediate future.[14]

Moderates and conservatives agreed, though not for the same reason, that the debate over political pluralism had gone far enough. After the Sixth Plenum, eight journals that had previously advocated political reform were banned. According to the Thai scholar Thaveeporn Vasavakul, Linh "withdrew his support in 1989 [for intellectuals and critics of the regime] when the political situation in Eastern Europe became unstable and one-party rule was challenged."[15] Linh stopped writing his columns, and Prime Minister Do Muoi restated the party's longstanding position on the role of the media: "The press in our country is the voice of the party," he said, and therefore "should reflect the party's viewpoint and stance."[16]

This debate became urgent with the collapse of communism in Eastern Europe, a traumatic event for Hanoi, which was now convinced that political pluralism was an immediate threat to the regime's survival. In August 1989, the Central Committee issued the "three no's": "no calling into question the leadership of the communist party, no calling into question the correctness of the one-party state, and no movement towards pluralism or a multi-party democracy."[17] In a 25 September editorial in the army daily *Quan Doi Nhan Dan,* the party revealed how seriously it took this threat and how far it would go to defend itself: "The imperialists have failed in their schemes to subvert socialism from within in three cases: Hungary (1956), Czechoslovakia (1968) and Poland (1980)." In each of these crises "revolutionary violence had successfully been used." With the Tiananmen Square incident clearly on its mind, the party sought to ensure the total loyalty of the Vietnamese People's Army and made clear that the military would be called on to defend the regime.

The Central Committee's Ninth Plenum, in March 1990, was one of the longest and stormiest sessions in Vietnam's history and resulted in the rejection of any multiparty system or democratic reform.[18] At that meeting, ninth-ranked Politburo member Tran Xuan Bach was fired, officially for violating party discipline but really for his "advocacy" of political reform. Bach had caused a lot of controversy by giving a speech in which he stated that "one cannot think that turbulence will occur only in Europe while in Asia things remain stable. . . . All socialist countries are now in a process of evolution to move forward, have outstanding differences be solved, and need to break off the long-existing stress and strain of old things."[19] Bach, who was in charge of the Central Committee's External Relations Commission, had traveled widely and was personally aware of the changes taking place across the world. And as the Politburo member in charge of the occupation of Cambodia, he was cognizant of the country's failed foreign policies and the shortcomings of the decisionmaking process, or to his eyes, the absence of meaningful debate in the party over important policies—or the lack of democratic centralism. Bach's emphasis, as it remains for today's party leadership, was how to maintain stability: "We must consistently and firmly maintain stability in the political and economic social domains, especially political stability."[20]

Bui Tin asserts that Bach "accepted the need for discussing differing ideologies and political views. But he stopped short of a multiparty system."[21] In a December 1989 speech published in the *samizdat* newspaper of the Club of Former Resistance Fighters (CFRF), while not calling on the party to voluntarily relinquish its monopoly of power, Bach did encourage it to tolerate greater diversity of political ideas. But he knew that there had to be some political reform. In his widely circulated "Speech to the Union" he warned, "There is still unrest among the people. They are demanding more democracy and social justice."[22] And unlike his colleagues in the Politburo, he scoffed at the idea that you could have economic reform but not political change. For Bach, economic liberalization could only be successful if coupled with political liberalization: "You can't walk with one long leg and one short one, and you can't walk with only one leg," he said in a January 1990 interview.[23] But Bach never suggested "shortening" one leg by taking away party power, much less amputating it. Where party ideologues such as Nguyen Duc Binh believed that by "democratizing" the economy demands for political reform would dissipate, Bach saw just the opposite. He believed that economic growth would create both the demands for greater political participation and the need for such participation. With the development of the economy, the party would have to rely on the advice and expertise of new classes, entrepreneurs, sectors, and nonparty members to manage the increasingly complex economy.

But to a hyperdefensive party, the policies that Bach advocated were controversial and potentially dangerous and therefore were rejected outright. The Central Committee announcement of Bach's expulsion also attributed socialism's collapse in Eastern Europe to "imperialist and reactionary plots" rather than to internal factors. This analysis justified the party's policy of remaining vigilant against foreign plots to undermine the VCP's monopoly of power rather than accommodate different views and interests. It also upheld the VCP's monopoly of power for the sake of stability: "Only with political stability can we stabilize and develop the economic and social conditions [and] step by step reduce the difficulties and improve people's lives."[24]

In the run-up to the Seventh Party Congress, Linh invited people to comment on the draft political report, an opportunity that many used to support Bach. Le Quang Dao, a member of the Central Committee and chairman of the rubber stamp National Assembly, wrote an article in the 8 December 1989 edition of *Dai Doan Ket* entitled "Something Must be Fundamentally Wrong with Socialism; Those in Power Stand Above the People; We Must Apologize Publicly to the People." In it he argued that what was causing Vietnam's malaise, that is, what the Eastern European states did wrong, was overcentralizing. The increasingly critical party intellectual, Nguyen Khac Vien, agreed, arguing that "the party had degenerated because it exercised power directly," for "the Council of Ministers, the National Assembly, the ministries and departments are only executants."[25] The former NLF leader Nguyen Huu Tho weighed in as well: "The root causes of failure are the weight of our conservative bureaucratic system, [and] the lack of democracy on the part of the government."

Despite these and other petitions from such senior officials as Bui Tin and Hoang Minh Chinh, the VCP's Seventh Congress in June 1991 rejected any movement toward political pluralism. Multiparty democracy was anathema because the Communist Party was already "democratic." Indeed, the case of Tran Xuan Bach was not even raised as had been slated. Although Bach was supposed to remain on the Central Committee for the sake of unity, over 50 percent of the body voted to expel him; today he remains a nonperson living in a Hanoi suburb.[26] The congress's Draft Political Programme explicitly rejected Soviet-style political reform, instead calling for the implementation of Chinese-style economic reforms without relinquishing any political power.

After the Seventh Party Congress, there were few if any calls for political reform, and Nguyen Duc Binh appeared to be somewhat vindicated in his analysis. The early 1990s saw some soaring economic growth and popular excitement in the country's reversal of economic misfortunes. Itself confident, the VCP leadership did not address the issue of political reform either, instead the Politburo remained vigilant against foreign (read U.S.) attempts at usurping VCP rule through strategies of "peaceful evolution."[27] As with the Seventh Congress, the Eighth Party Congress, held in June 1996, underlined the need for single-party rule and a commitment to socialist ideals. In a major speech, President Le Duc Anh announced that Communist Party rule would be strengthened—since "various hostile forces have repeatedly attacked the party's guidance, seeking to change the nature of the Communist Party and the State of Vietnam, and derail our revolution."[28] Similarly, former Minister of Defense Doan Khue repeatedly warned that "hostile forces are attempting to wipe out socialism and revolutionary gains of our people."[29] The newly appointed minister of defense, Pham Van Tra, concurred: "Enemy powers still consider Vietnam an important place for their battles. They continue to implement a strategy of 'peaceful evolution, riot, overthrow' in order to eliminate socialism in Vietnam."[30]

Nonetheless, it is important to note that the Sixth, Seventh, and Eighth Party Congresses have seen concrete political reforms. Whether setting age limits, revising the constitution, or separating the functions of the party and state, the party has demonstrated a limited willingness to reform itself. The problem is that the reforms have not gone far enough, and many of the problems that the government failed to deal with have been exacerbated by the economic malaise that has gripped the country since 1996. Indeed, the country's poor response to the crisis can in many ways be explained by the inherent weaknesses of the political system: a system based on consensus, though riddled with factionalism and patron-client ties.[31] Only one event in the 1990s actually forced the regime to confront the problems of its governing style, review its leadership methods, and consider political reform: the 1997–1998 Thai Binh peasant protests.

The Thai Binh Peasant Protests

The peasant protests that afflicted northern Vietnam from late 1997 present an interesting case study for analyzing how the party has responded to the greatest threat to its legitimacy since the early 1980s and, most important, how it actually perceives democracy. The regime's legitimacy has always come from the support of the peasantry. As Prime Minister Pham Van Khai stated: "If rural areas remain stable and farmers are happy with their livelihood, our country will be able to ensure stability however serious the difficulties. Therefore, rural stability is the key to national security."[32] And the regime has always equated national security with its own survival.

Peasants began protesting throughout the north, especially in the densely populated and impoverished province of Thai Binh. In addition to complaining about compulsory labor, they protested arbitrary fees and taxes that ranged from those from land use to "teacher fees" for their children's schooling, an amount that one Vietnamese researcher calculated as 40 percent of an individual peasant's income.[33] In all, the total amount of taxes and levies collected between January 1994 and July 1997 in Thai Binh alone were 176 billion dong (about $16 million) more than had been authorized by the central government.[34] At the same time, loans to local farmers and businesses in the province fell by 40 percent, compared to 1996, and unemployment, which was already at 200,000 people, skyrocketed. In addition, there were concerns about corruption, abuse of power, land seizures, forced contract renegotiations, and "commandism." Since local party secretaries also tended to be the chairmen of the local people's committees, they were in a position of absolute power. Dang Phong explained it this way:

> The role of the state as the only and supreme arbiter in matters of property rights for every type of land throughout the whole country has given local officials the absurd right to give land to this person or that, not least to themselves. This system of administering land rights has created a group of people who have accumulated large land holdings not through land clearing or market transactions, but by abusing their power or their position. This of course is unjust and illegal and causes discontent among the peasants.[35]

Because of this power, the village leaders were able to redistribute communal lands, which averaged between 10 and 25 percent of a village's land area. Legally, this process is supposed to be conducted through auction, but in reality it is conducted out of public view so that the village chief can distribute the land to his family and friends. Although the proceeds from the lease of these "second land use rights" are supposed to be used for social welfare programs, they are often embezzled,[36] so the average peasant lost out in two ways. When the protests in Thai Binh erupted, the party acted quickly, dispatching 1,200 police personnel and several Politburo members to investigate (one of whom's car was torched by angry peasants). In the end, only fifty local police and government officials were arrested, prosecuted, or expelled from the party—fewer than the number of peasants arrested for protesting the corruption.

In the aftermath, the party found no fault with its policies but placed the blame on corrupt local leaders. Village chiefs thus turned "good" policies implemented by the party into means for enriching themselves. As Prime Minister Khai lamented, the problem is in the implementation stage: "According to public opinion, the party, state and government have many correct policies, but these haven't had much result. People agreed with many policies, but don't believe in the implementation results."[37] General Secretary Le Kha Phieu admitted to *Tuoi Tre* that "during the war, our government was always close to the people. Now we should admit that that sacred relation has been dented."[38] He went on to explain that "violations of democracy have appeared" in the countryside. Likewise, former General Secretary Do Muoi argued that "there are many complicated reasons for hot spots, but one common cause is officials involved in corruption, red tape, a lack of democracy, law violations, and intruding on people's legitimate interests."[39] The frankest admission of the party's mistakes came from President Tran Duc Luong who, during a trip to Thai Binh in early 1998, said that the peasant protests had demonstrated that the VCP had "lost its leadership role" and that the protests "exposed shortcomings in the political system under the leadership of the party." Luong continued by warning that the "lack of democracy is driving party, state, political and social organization away from the people resulting in the erosion of the combativity of the entire political system."[40]

The party did not admit that this was a long-standing problem that it consistently failed to deal with. Lack of democratization in the countryside was an inevitable result of decollectivization: with the breakdown of the commune system, commune managers were put out of work. When the state encouraged individual families to work together in cooperatives, the managers stepped back in. Even though direct elections are called for, the former managers often used their concurrent position as the local party secretary to control the elections. This caused problems in a very short time. Rural protests over corruption erupted in 1992, and at the Central Committee's Fifth Plenum in June 1993, the party issued a document acknowledging that "democracy and social justice in rural areas have been ignored" and that "bureaucratism, authoritarianism, and corruption in state apparatuses are still prevalent." The plenum's goal was to guarantee "democracy and social justice" by maintaining political stability. But this is the heart of the problem: cadres interpret the party resolution to equate democracy with stability; therefore, they can justify coercion and heavy-handed tactics to maintain order.

But given the size and scope of the peasant protests, many leaders have come to understand the pressing need for political reform. While some conservatives refused to believe that the protests were the fault of the party and blamed the outbursts on foreign saboteurs,[41] many others in the leadership have used the protests as an opportunity to experiment with new, though limited, policies. President Luong, looking at the positive side of the protests, said: "This is a lesson for us. Our party and state recognize that the discontent of the people in these cases was right."[42] Most leaders talk of the need to improve democracy, but there is no consensus on what democracy is: the definitions and terms used by the individual leaders are often contradictory.

Former General Secretary Do Muoi, leading the conservatives, called for "greater democratization," but what he wants is not democracy in the Western sense. Muoi insists that the party still has to lead at every level of society, but that the party should "encourage the participation of local people in the decisionmaking process." In a November 1998 speech, he publicly chastised Haiphong officials for "not making plans known and allowing discussion, action and management by the people."[43] He does not support the surrender or even the sharing of power with the citizenry. But he has been concerned for many years about the dramatic increase in official corruption, and by calling for greater transparency in the decisionmaking and implementation process, he hopes that the officials will behave more responsibly and ethically for fear of punishment. As he warned Haiphong officials: "We have learned the lesson that the people in some provinces have little trust in the leadership of their party committees and they have petitioned against irresponsibility and corruption among these party members."

President Tran Duc Luong made similar arguments: the country does not need Western-style democracy, it simply needs greater transparency and input from the masses. To this end, Tran Duc Luong called on the party-controlled Vietnam Farmer's Association (VFA) to "promote grassroots democracy and make farmers aware of their democratic and legal rights."[44] More important, Luong wanted the VFA to work with and coordinate policies with local party cells and people's committees. Put simply, Luong is concerned that too much arbitrary power resides in the chairman of the local people's committee and secretary of the local party cell, more often than not the same person. The VFA simply would be a check on their power by encouraging the local government and party cell to adopt the policy "people know, people discuss, people act, people examine, people manage." The problem Luong fails to acknowledge is that the VFA has always been an arm of the state and thus had a rigid, top-down organizational structure. Like Muoi, Luong is not calling for the party to surrender or share power, he just wants the local party officials to be more accountable and therefore less corrupt. The party believes that all democratization must be top-down, hence, controlled by the party.

To this end, in mid-2000 the VFA launched a pilot program with the establishment of the Center for Legal Advice and Information. The center, which is run in conjunction with the Legal Assistance Department of the Ministry of Justice, provides free legal services to train peasants about their legal rights in order to prevent abuse of power and corruption at the local level. It is, however, only a pilot program that has been implemented in only one village, and to date there are no concrete plans to implement the program at the national level.[45]

National Assembly Chairman Nong Duc Manh, who perhaps sees the Thai Binh protests as an opportunity to strengthen the National Assembly, has also pushed forward some local-level political reforms. His policies center on the revitalization of people's councils at the grass-roots level. Manh believed that the protests emerged because the people's council system did not work effectively. Though democratic in name, the people's councils were controlled by a few individuals, often combining government and party responsibilities, hence denying an avenue for the peasants to protest policies or petition the local government. As Manh said: "The councils failed to take the public into confidence, creating favorable conditions for corruption and violations of the law by commune officials" and that the "people's right to democracy was not recognized by the activities of the people's councils." This "caused discontent among the people."[46] In short, "people's councils had not matched the people's aspirations."[47] Manh's proposed solution to the protest is to return to the peasants a way to peacefully, legally, and legitimately petition the government. Revitalizing the people's councils will serve as a release valve that is presently missing. To this end, he asserts that local people's councils "need to have a greater role in real representation" and that "it is essential to continue improving the roles and functions of people's councils and people's committees at all levels and so extend democracy to the village."[48] Yet Manh has not yet come up with any concrete proposals on how the people's committees will be strengthened. The Politburo endorsed a pilot project of democratic village governance in two villages in Hung Yen Province. These local people's councils are intended to share with villagers some decision-making power, at present monopolized by the village's party secretary. To alleviate peasant dissatisfaction, in November 1998 the National Assembly did pass a reformed land law, which sought to further protect the land rights of the peasantry.[49] In late 2000 the National Assembly was drafting a new law on people's committees, although little change will occur in the short term. Revealing the party's own ambivalence toward greater democratization, Manh has reiterated that "the party's leadership must be increased at different levels of government so as to firmly maintain the state's worker environment."[50] At other times, he has asserted that only by strengthening party cells could people's committees themselves be strengthened. Clearly Manh, like the rest of the leadership, envisions greater democratization to come, but not at the party's expense. Indeed, it can only occur under the party's enhanced leadership. As one Western analyst noted: "The party is prepared to countenance more democracy—but it is an elastic term—one that the party interprets as making the party more responsible to the people, but not [political] pluralism."[51] Greg Lockhart agrees, arguing the VCP's conception of democracy is one of "mass engagement and mass consul-

tations," which "make it possible to rejuvenate an autocratic government—and thus elude democracy."[52]

The Vietnamese revolution began in the countryside, and because
Vietnam remains an overwhelmingly agrarian nation, with 80 percent
of its population living in rural areas, it is likely that change will also
begin there. Chinese-style local village elections could be implemented,
but not before several more natural or man-made economic crises force
the peasants to challenge the authority of the state.[53] This is unlikely in
the near future; the party's hold on the countryside remains firm. But
the Vietnamese regime studies Chinese political and economic reforms
with great interest, and if village-level democracy dissipates peasant
protests while not completely diminishing the party's authority in the
countryside, similar reforms may well be adopted.

The Thai Binh protests embody the paradox of political reform in
the country. They erupted because the party holds a monopoly of power
that has been abused for the personal gain of its members, thereby
alienating the party from the people. Some members of the leadership
believe that the way the party can relegitimize itself is to make it more
accountable: they do not propose radical political reform. If anything,
they are supporting what is already constitutional, but which has gone
unimplemented. Legally, local leaders do not have to be party members, though they almost always are, while decisionmaking is never
transparent. The senior party leadership wants to find a way to make
local leaders more accountable for their actions, hoping that they in
turn will be less corrupt and abusive. Ironically, this is similar to the
dissidents' vision of political reform. They too want to make the party
more accountable, encouraging more dialogue and broadening decisionmaking. The difference is that the dissidents believe this has to be
done at the national, not just the local, level.

Envisioning Political Reform

The party's recent attempts to "implement democracy" will remain very
troubling to many for it is clear that the party has no intention of ever
actually sharing power, much less surrendering it. Indeed the party's
calls for greater democratization may even backfire, because such calls
may make the promise seem even hollower. Yet the party's proposed democratization would go a long way in placating the dissidents: the demand for greater democratization comes from not necessarily a belief that

the VCP must be overthrown or that it has to surrender power. Most critics argue that the VCP should use the National Assembly as a means to allow independent voices to be heard in the policymaking process. There are few calls for the establishment of a multiparty system, but near unanimous calls for the end of the totalitarian dictatorship. Gen. Tran Do, one of the most outspoken dissidents, wrote to the Politburo, "I still agree with and support the political leading role of the party. I think such a role is necessary. But leading does not mean imposing. Party leadership does not mean party rule."[54] Le Quang Dao spoke of how essential it was that the "party preserve its role of the vanguard." Another critic, who was jailed for publishing a samizdat paper, *Freedom Forum,* asserted that his group "never aimed to overthrow the government. All we were trying to do was push the process of democratization."[55] In Bui Tin's first statement issued in exile, he spoke of the need to "restore the people's confidence in the party" and suggested that if the party were more willing to listen to ideas offered from outside its ranks and abolish "subjectivism, volunteerism and dogmatism," then "in one word, we will really take root amongst the people."[56]

On one hand, many agree with Duong Quynh Hoa's assertion that "you cannot open only economically. You must open politically, too." A leader of the CFRF (discussed in Chapter 5), for example, stated that the party's refusal to countenance political reform along with economic reform was dangerous. "Our main difference with the leadership is that we favor political change in unison with economic liberalization, whereas they think that they can get away with the latter without addressing the former. Tiananmen should serve as a warning to the party that this is a dangerous line to pursue."[57] But on the other hand, there is a degree of consternation over what democratization may bring. As one of the founders of the NLF, Duong Quynh Hoa personally understands the heavy-handed interference by the party, but even so she shares the party's fear of the destabilizing effects that democracy could have on the country.

> I believe democracy and respect for human rights are necessary things. A country can't be built without them. And if the revolution succeeded it was because it proclaimed a fundamental human right to be free and independent. But if you ask me are we going to have political pluralism here in five years, then I have to say I don't know. Honestly, I'm in favor of pluralism. But honestly, too, I'm afraid of it. You know why? Because the bulk of the Vietnamese population aren't politically aware. I've discussed it with the leaders. I've said

'we have to have democracy. At the moment we don't have democracy. But that doesn't mean just any old kind of democracy. It doesn't mean anarchy.' And when a people have never lived democratically and you suddenly open up, you run the risk of anarchy.[58]

Perhaps because of this fear that full democracy would produce political instability in the nation, few openly call for the establishment of a pluralistic system with contending parties. The demands for democratization come at three levels: the first argues that there has to be greater intraparty debate. The second level says that for the sake of economic development, the party should broaden democracy and include non-party experts and intellectuals. The third level calls for a multiparty election.

At the first level, many of the dissidents are angered by the lack of democracy within the Communist Party, a violation of the party's operating tenet of democratic centralism. For these dissident party careerists, all decisionmaking is monopolized at the senior level of the party. As Tran Do complained, "even inside the party, there have been two layers. One includes party members that are holding power at high positions; the other the majority of members that have to continue to live with the centralized democracy principle, to follow unconditionally all policies, directives, and orders. These members (including senior party members) have no opportunities and cannot discuss their orders."[59] Likewise, in *Writing to Mother and National Assembly,* Nguyen Tran Van stated rhetorically, "Many matters critical to the fate of the country were decided upon by a single individual. Do you know how many people it took to make the decision to invade Kampuchea?" Nguyen Phong Ho Hieu, a southern intellectual who resigned from the party in 1990, similarly complains about the lack of intraparty democracy, let alone democracy:

> No matter how significant its contributions to the country, the Communist Party accounts for only 3 percent of the population, A few have no right to decide the lives of the vast majority. Yet, those few have done that so far—in the name of the working class. Ironically no worker, farmer, street sweeper, soldier, teacher, nor poor person is allowed to participate in the governing process. Even among the rank-and-file of the party, only a handful has the power to be in the process. All the rest need only to be concerned with "learning the party's resolutions."[60]

What Tran Do and others are saying is that the party has made terrible mistakes in both the past and in recent times, mistakes that could be averted if there were more objective debate and discussion within the existing political-legal framework. Since the 1967 purge, though, democratic centralism has been suspended. As Tran Do wrote, "The record of the last several decades showed that the party was not always right. That is the problem of the party holding exclusive power without any institutions or groups to monitor its behavior. That is the source of power abuses and corruption that no correction campaign can stop." It is not just the dissidents who are concerned about this. Former Politburo member Vu Oanh wrote, "The party does not yet deeply understand the people; the people in reality are not closely attached to the party; lower level cadres dare not tell the truth to higher level ones. The atmosphere for democracy, debate and dialogue in order to find the truth is limited. . . . [T]he illness of bureaucratic concentration and arbitrary and autocratic rule still exists."[61]

At the second level, advocates of democratization cite the growing complexity of the economy and the party's own limitations in economic management to justify greater discussion, consultation, and decisionmaking powers for nonparty members. The reason for this is that the party, whose membership only constitutes 3 percent of the population, does not have enough talent or expertise to modernize the economy. The mathematician, Pham Dinh Dieu, has vociferously made this argument, most publicly at an official party function, a Vietnam Fatherland Front (VFF) conference in Saigon in December 1997. There, Dieu demanded democratic reform because the VCP cannot continue to hold a monopoly on power and run a market economy. For Dieu, there is a fundamental contradiction between the needs of the marketplace and the goals of the Communist Party, which "clings to its proletarian principles in the name of political stability and continues to strengthen its monopoly to rule in an absolute manner."[62]

> Instead of pushing harder the process of self-renovation to meet the demands of developing the market economy and the democratization of the society, the party, regrettably, in the name of maintaining political stability, has continued to consolidate its monopolistic leadership with the above principles. And as a result, the fundamental conflict mentioned above has not been resolved satisfactorily to the objective needs of the development. These needs were even further suppressed by the dictatorial authorities to protect the party's exclusive right to the leadership. This has been the case since the Seventh Party Congress, and more clearly and absolutely in the Eighth Congress. The party has continuously proclaimed its complete and absolute leadership of the government and society. The conflict that has been contained, suppressed and unresolved turned into an internal eroding

force with various combinations of a chaotic market and an unlimited
totalitarian dictatorship. That can be considered the main characteristic of our country's social and economic situation in recent years. It
has created tremendous difficulties for the sustained development of
the country.[63]

Dieu predicted that the lack of democratic reforms would hamper economic development by fostering inefficiency, to the point where "failure is obvious" for the economic reform program. He argued that because of the VCP's monopoly of power, the country's leadership lacks
"talent or dynamism to serve the interests of the people." Moreover, the
party has isolated itself from external ideas because "all thoughts contrary to the party line are forbidden" and, therefore, "there is a gap between leaders and intellectuals."[64] Nguyen Khac Vien spoke of the generation gap between the leaders and the youthful Vietnam (over 60
percent the population was born after reunification). For Vien, the party
would not be able to resolve its problems as long as it is "composed of
very old comrades who no longer have physical strength, whose ways
of thinking and doing things are outdated." He continued: "They cannot
be on the same wave-length as the new generation and cannot come to
grips with the new problems."[65]

Gen. Tran Do, the most vociferous campaigner for democratization,
likewise does not explicitly call for a multiparty democracy. What Do
advocates is "the need to reform the party's method of leadership. I
think this reform should include the abandonment of the party's absolute and total control of everything. The party should only keep the
role of political leadership and let the National Assembly, the government and the Fatherland Front have their own responsibilities and independent authorities."[66]

Tron Do believes that the party, while maintaining its leadership,
must become more responsive to the leadership and expertise of other
institutions. What he means by "democratization" is not necessarily the
proliferation of political parties. His goal is to make decisionmaking
within the party more democratic so that a real debate and exchange of
ideas over policies can take place. He complained that

today, we almost always commit to just one measure for each problem, and that measure is supreme just because it is the party's measure. Nobody is allowed to propose another. Nobody is allowed to debate freely about the announced measure. This practice applies to
both general strategies and concrete implementation in separate areas.

I believe our people, particularly our corps of intellectuals inside and outside the country, have many good ideas. If they are allowed to express those ideas, compare them against one another, and debate freely, they can break the current mental block and find an appropriate way out for the country. In other words, the restriction on the intellectuals, the yoke of supremacy over peoples' minds, and the labeling of opinions other than the official one as "rebellion" are among the most important causes of the current stalemate of the strategy for national development.[67]

By allowing more open debate within the party and government, and including intellectuals and experts, the party will become more accountable and responsive to the needs of the people and, hence, strengthened. He warns that if the party does not implement these "democratic" reforms the party will "disintegrate" because it will be too alienated from the masses and lose all legitimacy. In his statement following his January 1999 expulsion from the Communist Party, Tran Do put it this way: "Do we have a way out? I believe we do. One, not to depend on any ideology or dogma. Two, one must have widespread discussion with and among the people, no one can think on behalf of the entire nation. Three, the rulers must be truly of the people, by the people and for the people [meaning, through real elections]."[68]

But again, this is an elitist view of democracy. Tran Do is not advocating a democratic system dominated by a large number of national parties competing for National Assembly seats. He wants a system that encourages experts and committed intellectuals to participate as independents.

There are a few calls for a genuine multiparty system in which the Communist Party is just one of many parties. Few dissidents have actually called on the VCP to surrender its power absolutely. In his essay, "Socialist Vietnam: Heritage, Reform and Economic Development," Lu Phong argues that Vietnam can only develop with a pluralist democracy: "The building of a legalistic government is the basis to establish a multiparty, pluralistic system. . . . The party must relinquish all power to the government, return to a civil society, place itself under the laws and on [an] equal footing with other social, political organizations."[69] But he does not call for its abandonment, merely its inclusion as one of many equal parties. That is the point: the dissident community wants the VCP to share power, not abandon it.

Such calls, however, are not coupled with a well-thought-out plan on how such a transition may take place. The Hungarian transition, though covered briefly (and not at all objectively) in the press, provides one model, but little study of it has actually been conducted. Again, there is a sense that any alternative party to emerge will have been derived from the VCP and start out as being a loyal opposition to the regime, simply using its autonomy to criticize and challenge bad government policies. Many hope that a multiparty system will gradually become institutionalized from an opening of the political system to individuals. Bui Minh Quoc, one of the most outspoken dissidents, has simply argued that for the time being there should be more debates over political reform: "Stop considering the topics of multi-parties and pluralistic systems taboos, but organize public and fair debates on these matters so that people can take appropriate steps together in the effort to democratize the country in peace, stability and development."[70]

Other critics have tried to reassure the party leadership that pluralism is not necessarily going to come at the party's expense. Although the party would have to deal with competitors, that competition would revitalize and enrich the party. In a widely circulated letter, dated February 1998, Nguyen Thanh Giang agreed that greater democratization should be in tandem with the revitalization of the VCP: "Everybody sees the urgent necessity for a real democracy in which people from both the top and the bottom would equally benefit. . . . In order to establish a democracy, there is a need to . . . deeply reform the Communist Party of Vietnam and courageously and cautiously restore multiparty and plural systems in Vietnam."[71]

Yet, simply legalizing other parties would not necessarily solve all Vietnam's problems nor alleviate all of the dissidents' concerns. Phan Dinh Dieu has raised the concern that if the VCP was to eventually allow alternative parties to emerge, they not be controlled in some way by the VCP. He seems aware of models of multiparty systems in which opposition politics, though legal, are controlled by the ruling regime, such as was the case in Suharto's Indonesia. For Dieu, "the essential thing is not only to have many parties or a 'multi-party system,' but to have a real choice. To have a real choice, two parties may be enough, but then there must be real differences between them."[72] But Dieu is emphatic that there should be a multiparty system:

> In this day and age, there should not exist any element that holds exclusive right to leadership, makes any products people must accept, speaks in any way people have to obey as golden rules. In our country's current situation, it is no longer time for anyone to invoke the excuse

of loyalty to impose an outdated ideology on the whole society; neither can one rely on the past glory of the previous generation to assert the monopolistic position of a present generation who claim themselves successors; nor can one force all others to accept forever a path chosen at one time in the past.[73]

Regardless of the level to which the dissidents believe that the country's political system needs to democratize, they feel that there has to be greater dialogue and debate, whether by individuals or an institutionalized multiparty system. More important, each level of democracy can be implemented through existing legal channels and political institutions. The most important of these is the National Assembly.

The National Assembly

Most dissidents and in-house critics have demanded a greater role for nonparty intellectuals in government decisionmaking and a greater tolerance by the party toward disparate political and economic points of view. Few have called for the establishment of a multiparty political system, and even fewer have called for disbanding the VCP. The Hungarian model, in which opposition parties emerged from within the Communist Party that retained its leading role in politics and governance, is an appealing model to many. But most dissidents simply want a depoliticized forum where experts and people with different opinions can openly debate ideas and national policy. For these critics, the natural venue for such debate is the National Assembly. Legally, individuals may become members; thus the VCP could still dominate an open forum without contending with other national-level political parties.

Stillborn: The National Assembly Before Doi Moi

As stated in Chapter 2, one of the dissidents' primary complaints in the 1950s was the impotence of the National Assembly. Although on paper it was the supreme organ of state, in reality it did nothing more than ratify decisions made by the Lao Dong Party. Indeed, the parliament was dormant between the first assembly in 1949 and the second, held eleven years later in 1960, while the other lawmaking organ of the government, the Ministry of Justice, was shut down in 1961 and remained defunct until 1981. During this period, the party simply circumvented the government and ruled by directive and decree, not through legislation. As Carol Rose notes:

> Of the 1,747 legal documents promulgated between 1945 and 1954, only one was an actual law. The only formal law passed during that time was the 1953 Land Reform Law. The rest were "sub-law documents," including 621 presidential orders, 656 government decrees 413 ministry circulars. Between 1955–86, Vietnam issued a total of 7,167 legal documents, of which only 61 were law documents or ordinances—the rest were "sub law" documents, such as executive orders or ministerial instructions.[74]

After the reunification of the country, the National Assembly continued to do little more than rubber-stamp party decisions at its month-long biannual sessions. Gareth Porter notes that the National Assembly was such an ineffective entity that in 1980 the government's Law Commission held a conference on legal tasks for the year without any representatives from the National Assembly—the highest legal organ in the country, and the body constitutionally responsible for lawmaking.[75] Even though the National Assembly was in session during this period, it was clearly an organ under party control. Selection of all candidates, according to a government circular issued in January 1981, had to be undertaken "under close leadership of the party committee echelons."[76]

Nguyen Van Linh and the National Assembly

With the advent of *doi moi* at the Sixth Party Congress, there was a sudden demand for laws to regulate the marketization of the economy. The National Assembly took on new importance, and some reforms, such as secret balloting and allowing press coverage, were implemented to make it a more effective body. General Secretary Linh insisted that the "formalism and bureaucratism" of previous National Assemblies had to be abandoned and he insisted that the body could no longer be a rubber stamp: it had to really debate and question policies.[77] Delegates were told by the Assembly Chairman Nguyen Huu Tho that "henceforth the party's leadership over the Assembly would be through persuasion on the part of party members within the body— i.e., that the party's views would no longer be imposed on the entire membership."[78] At the same time, Tho announced that secret balloting would be allowed for the first time. The National Assembly enjoyed fewer constraints and immediately issued a scathing attack on the

party's management of the economy and the ensuing triple digit inflation. In December 1988, the party, at Linh's prodding, announced that
it would set the general line but allow the National Assembly to legis-
late without any direct interference.[79] The assembly thrived with more
freedom: in 1988 it criticized the government's famine relief efforts,
and required extra sessions because of heated debates over the draft
constitution. In June 1988, 168 of the 464 (an unprecedented 36 percent) delegates defied the party by voting for Vo Van Kiet instead of
the prime ministerial candidate favored by the party, Do Muoi. Mean-
while the Assembly's chairman, Nguyen Huu Tho, announced that the
party would stop "recommending" candidates to "run" for office.[80] Yet
the National Assembly continued to lack sufficient independence.

Like the dissidents in the 1950s, party critics in the 1990s believed
that the National Assembly is an appropriate forum for political, economic, and social debate, and they have demanded both a greater role
for the National Assembly as well as freedom from party interference.
This is essential, as a leading dissident wrote:

> The current National Assembly cannot carry out its duty of monitor-
> ing the government. Neither can it do the duty of "deciding all impor-
> tant national matters." Instead, it is often bypassed by the govern-
> ment. The National Assembly generates laws but what good do those
> laws do when many people consistently do the opposite to the laws.
> The National Assembly watches helplessly for it has no authority to
> intervene. The record of making new laws mean nothing.[81]

Indeed, this should not come as a surprise; nearly all of its members
are either party members or handpicked by the party. This has been a
continual irritant to the dissidents. As Hoang Minh Chinh complained:

> There is no freedom and democracy in this country at all. He [the
> judge] asked me what I had based my conclusion on. I responded that
> among 75 million Vietnamese, there are only 2 million party mem-
> bers. And among the few hundred members of the National Assembly,
> from 93 to 97 percent of them are party members. The National As-
> sembly, therefore, belongs not to the people, but to the party. The
> party draws up even the list of candidates and the people are ordered
> to vote for them or else. They knock on every door and tell people to
> vote according to the party's list. With such a response, the judge
> could not rebut.[82]

La Van Lam agreed, stating, "I want to remind you of your achievement that 95 percent of the members of the National Assembly are

Communist Party members. We cannot say the government is of the people, by the people and for the people with this percentage. The threat to democracy and freedom and happiness is right there."[83]

Even the party stalwart and chairman of the National Assembly, Nguyen Huu Tho, was frustrated enough to vent openly in a speech delivered to the annual VFF conference, in which he chastised the party's continued interference in National Assembly elections. "The Fatherland Front, as indicated by law, has the right to introduce candidates for election. But for years we have blindly obeyed the instructions of the party, nominating the list of officials they send to us. Why has the Front, which is supposed to be a body for the people, simply carried out orders, instead of struggling so that the aspirations of the people can be heard?"[84]

Reforms and Their Limits

With *doi moi*, the National Assembly has had to take on a greater role and has tried to shake the image of being the party's rubber stamp, especially since the Ninth National Assembly of 1997.[85] Institutionally, its role has been strengthened by the promulgation of the country's fourth constitution in 1992.[86] At the Seventh Party Congress, *doi moi* was expanded to encompass legal reform. The Central Committee specifically called on the National Assembly to amend the 1980 constitution and to "improve the skills of lawmakers in promulgating and organizing the implementation of law." Prime Minister Vo Van Kiet asserted that "there must be a complete change from bureaucratic management to running the nation by law."[87]

But for the most part, its role has been strengthened because of the urgency in creating a legal framework to oversee Vietnam's transition from a centrally planned economy to a more market-oriented economy. The National Assembly has asserted itself by passing more laws needed for the reform process and by debating policies made by the party. For example, it has passed some 20,000 pages of laws and ordinances in the past decade, including a comprehensive 834-article civil code in October 1995, and it plannned "to adopt 20 to 30 new laws annually from now until the year 2000."[88] The Ninth National Assembly even refused to endorse the party's nominee for a ministerial position and forced several ministers to resign.

According to one government official, the National Assembly is becoming a "dialogue partner" for the party.[89] In the context of a communist society where the VCP has always monopolized decisionmaking, the more assertive National Assembly is popular. According to a national survey conducted for the assembly, "57 percent of respondents thought that the last assembly performed its legislative functions 'acceptably well.'"[90] But only an unspecified "tiny percentage" felt that the assembly was adequately fulfilling its role of "supervising government."[91] Most still feel that it is a rubber stamp, and even its own delegates would like to see it have more power. Government critics argue the National Assembly should be able to introduce more of its own legislation; currently its Standing Committee drafts only the state budget law.[92] And dissidents, such as Nguyen Ho, argue that the National Assembly has to be still more assertive and "must rigorously oversee and make decisions." Members of the National Assembly are beginning to be more assertive at the local level as well by adopting such Communist Party tactics as inspection tours to find out what voter concerns are and whether previous policies have been implemented effectively.[93]

There have also been changes in the election laws to allow greater participation by nonparty members and independent candidates. The April 1992 election law allowed independent candidates to run for the assembly for the first time. Then in April 1997, the outgoing legislature adopted a new election law that allowed more leeway for "self-nominated" or independent candidates to run their own campaigns. However, little is left to chance. In addition to the rigid quotas of men and women, intellectuals, workers, soldiers, and peasants, the number of nonparty members is also predetermined. During the election for the Ninth National Assembly, for example, thirty of the thirty-two independent candidates were disqualified for technical reasons. Neither of the two remaining independent candidates was elected. Regardless of who nominates them, all candidates must still be officially approved.

The VFF, a party-controlled umbrella organization, manages the elections and oversees three rounds of screening for all candidates. In the first round, organizations, ministries, and other party/state agencies submit their nominees and basically "negotiate and lobby to secure representation."[94] Most candidates are locally nominated, but some 96 and 141 delegates were centrally nominated at the Ninth and Tenth National Assemblies, respectively. In the second round, the candidates have to be approved by their colleagues and neighbors. In the third round, the VFF does a background inspection to "weed out the less morally or politically upright."[95] But after that, an election does occur. Candidates are given limited opportunities to "campaign" and meet with local constituents for about a month preceding the election. And the 1992 electoral law requires that each constituency field at least two candidates per post.

There are plenty of ways for the party to still control the nomination process. A telling example of this was the case of Nguyen Thanh Giang, a prominent geophysicist who works for the government's Geological Survey Department, who was "rejected" by his "co-workers." Although he received 96 percent of the vote at a neighborhood meeting, he only received 30 percent at his office. But despite having 300 colleagues, only 16, most of whom were members of party cells in the department or representatives of the labor or youth unions, were invited to the meeting and allowed to vote.[96]

Even if independent candidates pass through the three nomination stages, they are officially "nominated" by the VFF. "The self-nominated candidate in the long-run is nominated by the Fatherland Front. That's why in the final list of candidates it doesn't say self-nominated or not," stated Nguyen Si Dung, an official of the Office of the National Assembly.[97] The real reason, perhaps, is that the party is afraid there will be a landslide for any independent candidate, thereby embarrassing the party. This prompted one young Hanoi resident to complain that "the candidates are all the same to me. I'll just go down the list, look at their birth dates and chose the youngest guy."[98]

Furthermore, no free campaigning by candidates is allowed for it might give visibility to independent candidates. The 1997 election law gives candidates the right to talk to the voters via the media, but only in meetings organized by the VFF. In a prescient statement, the chairman of the National Assembly and Politburo member, Nguyen Duc Manh, claimed that "we do not use the phrase 'contesting the National Assembly elections.' This is because we do not challenge each other in elections. I should also say that a candidate should not speak ill of other candidates."[99]

Demands for Further Reform

Reforms notwithstanding, the National Assembly continues to be dominated by party members. For example, of the 663 candidates for the Tenth National Assembly 112 (25 percent) were nonparty members, though this was more than twice the number in the election for the Ninth National Assembly (63 of the 601 candidates). Of the 112 nonparty members, 11 were self-nominated. The National Assembly Office's spokesman, Vu Mao, "predicted" that the share of seats held by non-party members would increase from 8 percent at the Ninth National Assembly to 20 percent in the tenth, and the party has indicated that 20 percent is an acceptable number for nonparty members in the future.[100] In the end, they only won sixty-seven seats or 15 percent of the total; and of the eleven self-nominated candidates, only three won seats.[101] Despite the fact that the number of seats held by nonparty members has doubled since the Ninth National Assembly, 15 percent is unacceptable and critics continue to demand a greater share of seats for independent nonparty members. Indeed, one Ho Chi Minh City–based newspaper, *Tuoi Tre,* complained in a blunt editorial that the "opinions [of National Assembly deputies] could be more powerful if new ideas are expressed, and if these are a result of refined wisdom and the initiatives of many people."[102] Even Vu Mao expressed some concern: "We are trying to create a more democratic environment," he said. "We are of the view that even nonparty members can be good."[103]

The party seems unable to cope with its apprehension that allowing more independent candidates will dissipate its control over the assembly. To this end, the party continues to control the selection process, picking loyal party members rather than competent candidates. And this infuriates the dissident community. Critics are openly alarmed about the incompetency and inability of National Assembly delegates, one reason for this inexperience being that for most delegates this is a part-time job. Only members of the National Assembly's standing committee work full-time on legislative issues, clearly not enough to handle the growing number of complex laws that need to be enacted to regulate an economically and socially more diverse system. This, however, concentrates too much power in the hands of the Standing Committee, and so the party, in the person of Nguyen Duc Manh, a senior Politburo member, chairs the committee.

To deal with this problem, the Tenth National Assembly increased the number of delegates in the hope that there would be more full-time delegates to handle the legislative backlog.[104] Nonetheless, the growing number of full-time delegates does not make up for the fact that they are selected by the party by political criteria, not expertise. Nguyen Thanh Giang, in his unpublished "Discussion of the Draft 1980 Constitution," originally raised this issue. In it, he advocated independence of the judiciary and an end to the practice of "dual hats" for National Assembly delegates. Although some of his suggestions have been taken up by other officials and adopted since then, he was identified as a potential troublemaker by the Central Committee's Internal Security Bureau and was again arrested in March 1999 for his advocacy of such reforms.

The party has made a few concessions. The delegates elected to the Tenth National Assembly are younger (an average age of forty-nine), better educated (more than 91 percent had at least a bachelor's degree, compared with only 49 percent in the previous legislature), and have more practical business experience (of the 663 candidates, 100 were entrepreneurs or managers.)[105] But the reforms have merely been window dressing. As the most senior dissident, Gen. Tran Do wrote to the Politburo:

> As for [the right to hold] power, in all official documents the national political power is stated as "of the people, by the people, and for the people," and also "people know, people discuss, people do, and people inspect," but there is no such thing in reality. Everything is decided by the party—actually, by party members in high positions. The election of people's representatives to government institutions, including the highest offices, continue to follow the good old "the party assign [the candidates], people vote" practice with some "variations." And these institutions simply carry out the usual task of "institutionalizing the party's decisions for the government." The party hierarchy, from the top down, has the absolute authority and is under the jurisdiction of no laws. The result is none other than a "party rule" in a totalitarian regime.[106]

In the appendix to his letter, Tran Do carefully outlined the reforms needed to make the National Assembly an effective legislature that could both enact laws and serve as a watchdog to ensure government and party accountability to the people. The first reform was to shift the authority to draw up lists of candidates from the party to two rounds of "general sponsorship and consultation." Any individual would be eligible as long as he or she receives a sufficient number of signatures, just as any other sponsored candidate would have to do. Second, there has to be a "minimum set of requirements" for the candidates, which include ethical standards as well as the expertise, education, and experience to do their job competently. But Do insists that candidates should have "proper political views of his/her task" and he believes the minimum age for a seat on the National Assembly should be forty. Despite the importance of leadership transition, he rejects "installing candidates in their 20s" as a "robotic way to implement rejuvenation."[107]

In short, any political reform or liberalization or decentralization will strengthen the National Assembly. Since 1986, it has become a more independent and vocal organ, challenging the government and demanding greater discretionary and oversight powers. It has assumed a greater role in the reform process because of its lawmaking function; with economic reform alone an entire new series of laws was enacted to regulate the marketplace. The National Assembly has become a remarkably responsive organ of government. Since the outbreak of peasant protests, it has revised the land law and passed a grievance law to regulate conflicts and legalize channels for citizens to air their complaints and petitions, as well as to punish corrupt officials.[108] In the fall 1998 session, deputies fought hard for more agricultural spending, especially for irrigation, roads, and job creation in the 1,715 "poor" villages.[109] The assembly also discussed the "Law of Organizations of People's Councils and People's Committees," as well as a new law on the election of people's council delegates. The assembly has tried to enhance transparency within the government and its state-owned enterprises. The government's budget, for example, was taken away from the scope of the country's secrecy act, and the new law enforces full disclosure of the budget at the local level.[110]

In the June 2000 National Assembly meeting, there was an outpouring of criticism of the government and its handling of the economic crisis. Regional representatives took the central government to task for policies (or lack thereof) that they believe has led to the 65 percent loss in foreign investment since 1996. The prolonged economic crisis has clearly emboldened delegates to be more aggressive in their questioning and oversight of the government and its policies: this assertiveness and several key pieces of legislation have led to improvements in the legislative process. The National Assembly has clearly become far more responsive, and it deserves a lot of credit for pushing for a greater role in the policymaking process. Even though it continues to fall short of the constitutional ideal, we should expect more from this body in the future; it holds the key to political reform in Vietnam.

The Vietnam Fatherland Front

As few dissidents actually call for a multiparty system, their immediate goal seems to be getting the VCP to share power with members of the intellectual elite. Few articulate a Westminster model of formalized political parties competing for parliamentary power. They are looking for a forum for debate in which individuals could also participate. In his 12 December 1997 speech, "On the Need to Continue Reform in the Current Period," Phan Dinh Dieu stopped short of proposing a multiparty system but did call for the establishment of an independent forum where intellectuals could meet and discuss democratization. Another dissident, Bao Cu, responded in an open letter that the party-controlled umbrella organization, the Vietnam Fatherland Front, would be the appropriate venue for such a meeting. As it wrote in its bylaws, the VFF "is a broad political alliance, a voluntary association of organizations, groups, representatives of social classes, minorities, religions, and overseas Vietnamese to represent the aspirations of all sections of the people." Moreover, because Dieu remained on the VFF's presidium, despite his criticism of the party, it would be all the more appropriate host for a conference on democracy.[111]

The motion to have a conference on democratization under the auspices of the VFF is clever. What the dissidents are trying to say is that since democracy can happen even within the existing system of political institutions, there need not be a total revolution or implementation of a multiparty parliamentary system for there to be democracy. The legal framework already exisits. After all, according to the party, the VFF is legally a "major socio-political alliance in the political system of Vietnam that should help protect the legitimate interests of the people."[112] This proposal will obviously fail. To begin with, most know that the VFF hardly lives up to the ideals envisioned in its charter. As Bao Cu complained, the VFF is simply a "front" for the party, and is made up of party members, to "propagate the party's directions and policies."[113] Moreover, most dissidents understand that real democratization, despite party pledges, will not come easily or quickly. It will come slowly and through indirect ways. Simply getting the party to sanction open debates or a forum would be an important first step, but a step that will be long in coming. In mid-1999, the Tenth National Assembly passed a new law to govern the VFF, to codify the "role and status of the VFF and other people's organs" so that dissidents cannot use it in any antiparty matter.

Legalization

Luu Phong's call for the party to place itself "under the laws and on an equal footing" is at the heart of the dissidents' demands. Rather than explicitly calling for political pluralism, most simply demand a strict adherence to the existing law. There are a few aspects to this. First, as discussed above, is giving the National Assembly the independence that it constitutionally is supposed to have. Second, is abolishing article 4 of the 1992 constitution that gives the party extralegal power and allows the party to undermine the existing rule of law. Third, is renovating the legal field in the country, so that the judiciary can serve as an independent arbiter of the law.

At the root of this argument is article 4 of the 1992 constitution that many see as the legalization of the VCP's sole right to rule. Article 4 is controversial, even within the party: during the drafting of the 1992 constitution, it was debated whether the wording of the article should be altered from that of the 1980 constitution, which stated that the VCP was the "only force leading state and society." Article 4 of the current constitution states that the VCP "is a leading force of the state and society," but no one thinks this means that the VCP is willing to relinquish its monopoly of power. The article continues as an object of dissidents' ire. Hoang Minh Chinh, for example, asserted that "the root cause of all miseries of the nation and people of Vietnam is Article 4 of the constitution. It declares the party's exclusive right to rule. The party is therefore placed above the fatherland, nation, and everything else."[114] Most other dissidents agree. For example, in a 3 October 1993 letter to the Central Committee, the writer Bui Minh Quoc demanded that the Central Committee "drop Article 4 of the Constitution and issue a set of laws on the operation of the Vietnam Communist Party" to put the party on a legal par with society.

The last aspect involves strengthening the legal sector. There has been some progress in this area, but many structural obstacles remain. For example, 30 to 40 percent of the judges and legal personnel in the country do not have law degrees or other professional training, but are simply party appointed bureaucrats. And the Vietnamese legal system is ill-equipped to rectify the situation. The first law college was set up only in 1979, and by 1993 there were only fifty members of the Hanoi Bar Association. By the bar's own admission, because of the increased demands that a market economy places on the legal system, Vietnam currently needs between 500 to 1,000 lawyers.[115] Because of the shortage of lawyers, few defendants are adequately represented; their lawyers simply try to negotiate a lighter sentence.[116] Moreover, because the Ministry of Justice was completely defunct between 1961 to 1981 there was an irreparable loss of institutional memory. From 1981 to 1990, the understaffed ministry struggled to create new laws and ordinances, including the 1985 penal code. Despite a growing willingness of the party to create a law-based society, structural impediments have hampered this development.

Related to this is the practice of interlocking directorates whereby a parallel party organ is at every level of the government, a standard practice in communist systems. There have been some attempts by the party to resolve this issue: indeed one of the main goals of General Secretary Nguyen Van Linh (1986–1991) was to break down the system of interlocking directorates that have plagued the VCP. Gareth Porter notes that "although the VCP is supposed to 'lead the state, but not replace the state,' confusion about the division of function between the party and state has been a fundamental problem of the Vietnamese political system from the beginning."[117] Important to Linh was the need to allow expert advice to be heard, in areas of both domestic and foreign issues.

With the collapse of communism in Eastern Europe, in 1989 the key political debates focused on party-state relations.[118] The party daily *Nhan Dan,* in support of Linh, argued that "the Party has interfered too deeply in state management, has reduced the effectiveness of state management, and at the same time, caused its leadership to decline."[119] The 1992 constitution further codified the division between party and state: Although the VCP was to maintain its "guiding" role, "it is no longer allowed to interfere in the day-to-day running of the government or to operate outside the law."[120] In general, there was an attempt to give the government more autonomy, but the VCP continues to set the line and approve all major initiatives. Although more consideration was paid to government experts, final decisions continued to be made by the ministers wearing their Politburo "hats" and other top party officials. A telling example of this is the story of an Asian ambassador who was summoned in December 1999 by General Secretary Le Kha Phieu. Phieu chastised the ambassador for raising complaints about the investment climate to the government and demanded that he speak to Phieu directly because "it's I who make policy."[121]

Party interference that arises from the system interlocking directorates causes a lack of innovation. Because managers and technocrats rank behind their party secretary, they may not be able to make rational economic decisions but be forced to make decisions on political considerations alone. This has alarmed reformers in the party and government as well as the dissidents themselves. But the problem goes even deeper.

Because the VCP has no lawmaking authority, which is the prerogative of the National Assembly alone, it has to rule by decree. Because party decrees are carried out and enforced by party cells at all levels of all organizations, there is no way that they can be challenged and overturned, and this is constitutionally enshrined in article 4. As Tran Do lamented, "The National Assembly generates laws but what good do those laws do when many people consistently do the opposite to the laws. The National Assembly watches helplessly for it has no authority to intervene." Phan Dinh Dieu, likewise, complained that

> the party, or more exactly a small component that controls the party, proclaims its total and absolute leadership over the state and society; devises detailed rules for the party command system to send out guidelines to the National Assembly, the government, the court, the inspectorate institute, and also to grassroots organizations; and thus in fact, transforms the whole government system into implementers of the decrees from a powerful component inside the party. Democracy and laws are also turned into tools to carry out those decrees.[122]

Bui Minh Quoc got to the heart of this issue when he wrote in his memoirs that "if the VCP truly wished to build a legalistic government, its leaders could show their good will by eliminating right away the practice of condemning people with decrees."[123] Bui Tin writes that this has been the regime's standard operating procedure. Rather than dealing with civil crimes, the party simply "labeled" people "reactionaries" and thus was free to deal with them through its own internal disciplinary apparatus.

> After the *Nhan Van-Giai Pham* affair and similar cases, such "political reactionaries" were dealt with in a secret. There were no judgments and no reports in the press or in the radio. Only the top leadership were informed through internal party communications. The organizations specializing in security, particularly those whose duty was to protect the party and the army, acted according to their own whims without any regard for the law.[124]

But the party continues to use the law to maintain its monopoly of power. At the heart of this is a fundamental refusal to separate the powers among the party, state, and judiciary. There is no independent judiciary in Vietnam, and for dissidents such as Nguyen Thanh Giang, this is the most nebulous aspect of VCP rule. Giang has insisted that "separation and full authority must be guaranteed for each government institution in relation with others to carry out its own assigned mission," and that "none of the three branches of government be allowed to dominate the other two."[125] One of the most egregious violations of the principle of separation of powers is resolution 3 of the Seventh Central Committee that directs party officials to interfere in the legal system: "For major lawsuits that entail widespread political consequences, or involve national defense, security, and foreign affairs or involve cadres under the management of the local party leader, the local party leader must contribute his political opinion and direct the trial and sentencing."[126]

The lack of an independent judiciary allows the party to use the laws for its own ends. One of the most striking examples of such abuse, and hence the target of much of the dissident and the international community's scorn, was an April 1997 directive that authorizes arrest without trial.[127] Directive 31/CP gives the minister of the interior "the right to detain individuals for up to two years," without being charged with a crime, a violation of Vietnam's own legal code. Article 2 elaborates a system of "administrative detention": "Administrative detention applies for those individuals considered to have violated the laws, infringing on the national security, as defined in Chapter 1 of the criminal code, but [whose violation] is not serious enough to prosecuted criminally."[128]

And Vietnam has increasingly used 31/CP, having found that detaining individuals brings far less international condemnation than their arrest. Like 31/CP, directive 89/CP also erodes the legal rights of Vietnamese in the name of public stability. The latter was created to deal with potential outbreaks of unrest in the countryside, such as that in Thai Binh province. This directive gives local-level police and military units the right to set up temporary holding centers to quickly apprehend protestors and restore order. But the directive can be used against anyone for any reason, by merely justifying the overwhelming need for public safety.

There is a growing sense among some in government that the legal system, necessary for economic development, will never mature as long as it remains a tool for politics. For example, in a report to the National Assembly, the head of the assembly's own Legal Affairs Subcommittee, Vu Duch Khien, realized that there has been a tremendous abuse of power. According to the report, 28.8 percent of all arrests in 1998 were of innocent people, a number high enough for the National Assembly to warn of egregious "violations of citizen's freedom and democratic rights." Perhaps more important is the committee's remarking that "this situation raises a lot of concern as it does not show the strictness of the law."[129] In a precedent-setting case, in December 1999, a man who was tortured by the police to obtain a false confession to the crime of murder and rape and imprisoned for thirteen months was awarded 56 million dong in compensatory damages.[130]

But the practice of ruling the country by decree rather than by law had another effect: it convinced generations of party officials that their word was literally law. Now that there is a growing body of laws, party members are simply not taking them seriously, if not altogether ignoring them. There is the traditional sense that "The emperor's power stops at the village gate." Thus in addition to a structural impediment to legalization, there is a generational impediment. So conditioned are people to the party's autocratic behavior that no one dares challenge them by asserting their legal rights. A senior member of the ministry of justice also acknowledged such a problem. At a conference on democratization held in Bangkok in 1992, a senior researcher from the ministry, Hoang The Lien, argued that the "historical reality" of Vietnam has made the organization and implementation of democracy a "big problem."[131] Because the Vietnamese people are "passive," according to Lien, "it means that they are doers of 'from top-to-bottom' administrative orders rather than masters with real power to develop their creative abilities." Lien, citing Ministry of Justice surveys on democratization, argued there were two main obstacles to democratization: First, the Vietnamese political system "has not been renovated in a timely fashion for the creation of an active and flexible mechanism in the manifestation and implementation of the people's power." Second, in a system where "a small part of the government officers and members of social political organizations lack professional skills and knowledge of the law," Lien argues, "bureaucracy and authoritarian behavior" are the likely outcomes.[132] Such was the case in Thai Binh.

But placing the party and hence all of its members on an equal legal footing as ordinary citizens will be very difficult to enforce. That the party is above the law and beyond reapproach has caused massive corruption. In a 1994 letter to General Secretary Do Muoi, for example, La Van Lam called for the establishment of a "truly legalistic government," arguing that the legal system is underdeveloped and not well-implemented:

Our current system of laws is not adequate, and the laws that do exist have not been acted upon to guarantee the democratic rights and freedoms of the people in a country "a million times more democratic than any capitalist regime."

Under the leadership of the party, the people "live and work according to the law." Yet in reality, cadres, mostly members of the party, are allowed to take advantage of the current fluid condition to abuse people for personal profit. How can we reduce the national disaster of corruption if we do not have the courage to commit to political reforms, the bases for building a legalistic government?[133]

Carlyle Thayer wrote that article 4 of the 1992 constitution included the sentence, "All party organizations operate within the framework of the constitution and the law," though the attempt to specify that party members were subject to the law was rejected for being redundant.[134] Perhaps, the party chafed at the idea that its members had not always believed themselves to be equal under the law. That party members live above the law leads to another concern raised by the dissidents, that the party has taken on the characteristics and attributes of a "new class."

The New Class:
Corruption, Ideology, and the Future of Socialism

Many dissidents point to a phenomenon first expounded by Milovan Djilas in *The New Class,* who argued that after coming to power the communist party becomes a class in its own right: "The new class obtains its power, privileges, ideology and its customs from one specific form of ownership—collective ownership—which the class administers and distributes in the name of the nation and society."[135] He maintains that "the so-called socialist ownership is a disguise for the real ownership by the political bureaucracy."[136] For Djilas, "Membership in the communist party before the revolution meant sacrifice. Being a professional revolutionary was one of the highest honors. Now that the party has consolidated its power, party membership means that one belongs to a privileged class"[137] because of its administrative monopoly and control over the distribution of scarce resources. Vietnamese leaders and party members have always gotten better opportunities for their children, but by the 1990s they really began to behave like a privileged class. Take, for instance, the case of Pham The Duyet: In the summer of 1998, this Politburo Standing Committee member was investigated for graft and corruption for using state funds to acquire homes for himself and his children after being exposed by disgruntled VCP members.[138] Very clearly, Vietnamese cadres are able to control state resources and pass these privileges on to their children.

What is most alarming to both Djilas and the current Vietnamese dissidents is that the power of the new class grows at the expense of the party: "As the new class becomes stronger and attains a more perceptible physiognomy, the role of the party diminishes."[139] In short, the actions of members of the communist party become more guided by the interests of their class, rather than by the interests of the party or the nation in whose name they rule. Michael Vatikiotis argues that as the party increases their focus on their class interests, political reform will be even harder. The elite's "fear is that by suddenly changing the system, their positions—and not just the primacy of Marxism—will be threatened."[140]

Semantics aside, the concept that the VCP has become a class unto itself that is only out to further its own class interest at the expense of all others has become a focal point for both intra- and extra-party critics. "I put a question to the leaders in Hanoi," Dr. Duong Qunh Hoa told a journalist, "What is your final goal—the final goal of the revolution? Is it the happiness of the people, or power? Then I answered the question. 'I think it is power.' There is too little regard for human rights in Vietnam today."[141] Likewise, Nguyen Thanh Giang denounced the "red capitalist" cadres who use their public positions for personal gain. In his widely circulated 14 February 1998 letter he complained: "After many years of bloody war and sacrifice . . . a great number of well-placed party members have material lives not only better than that of the mandarins of old, but better than those of many capitalists in modern countries." He denounced "those red capitalists . . . promoted, subsidized and protected by a proletarian dictatorship."[142]

> Since society is not based on openness and truthfulness, trust has been extremely damaged. Deception and dishonesty spread from trades to sciences and education; from executive to judicial functions . . . In our country today, workers and peasants are no longer classes, there emerges a new capitalist class based on smuggling and corruption. This class includes powerful officials in the party and government structures at all levels and branches. To accumulate capital, this new class uses power and cunning manipulations to rob people of their possessions . . . They not only trade public properties amongst themselves, but also sell national resources to foreigners . . . Easy money then induces them to a lavish, decadent, unethical, and vulgar lifestyle . . . The difference between the rich and the poor in society is

inevitable, but the difference caused by injustice and producing even more injustice cannot be tolerated . . . Corruption in Vietnam is not simply a by-product of the market economy, but mainly is the heritage of the special power and privileges system.[143]

Nguyen Thanh Giang asserts that this new class, consisting of powerful officials in the structure of the party and government at all ranks and all branches, has been formed around "smuggling and corruption, in close connection with racketeers, thugs and gangsters." Very simply, cadres were stealing state resources that they controlled and were selling them on the marketplace: "The accumulation of wealth by the new capitalist class in Vietnam today is by using authoritarian and deceptive tactics to rob the properties of the government and people."[144]

The most well-known attacks on the "new class" came from the novelist Duong Thu Huong. Although committed to the idealism of the War of National Liberation, she was appalled at the poverty of the nation after the war—especially the growing disparity between the peasants and soldiers, who had suffered terrible deprivations during the many years of war, and the urban cadres. Her second novel, *Paradise of the Blind,* is the story of a young guest worker in the Soviet Union who is confronted by the hypocrisy of her uncle, a dour party cadre responsible for ideology.[145] Though privileged in the communist hierarchy, working abroad and living in a separate compound for high-ranking officials, he must engage in smuggling in order to survive. According to the intellectual historian Hue-Tam Ho Tai, the uncle is "the living symbol of the once self-assured, unyielding party whose moral authority is crumbling amid postwar poverty."[146] Senior cadres' lives revolve around smuggling and corruption in order to get by, yet they shroud their activities in ideological rhetoric, and by living in exclusive compounds they are alienated from the masses.

The book was enormously popular and sold 60,000 copies before the VCP ordered it removed from circulation, and it remains banned to this day, as are her three other novels. The party was further alarmed at a talk she gave in April 1990 to the CFRF in Saigon that drew a crowd of over 1,000. At a June 1989 National Assembly meeting, General Secretary Nguyen Van Linh declared *Paradise of the Blind* to be "anti-communist,"[147] and, though a long-time party member, she was expelled in July 1990 for "indiscipline." She was arrested in April 1991 for having sent a manuscript of *Novel Without a Name* abroad for publication in early 1990. However, the resulting international outcry forced her release in November 1991.

Corruption is out of control and getting worse and, according to Political and Economic Risk Consulting, Vietnam is now the third most corrupt society in Asia, falling in the rating of "clean countries" since 1998.[148] The endemic corruption not only scares away foreign investment but undermines the entire political system. Tran Do believes that the creation of the "new class" has damaged both the party's leadership and its creditability "beyond repair." He laments that "in the past the party and people were one," but now the party is simply "an elite group of rulers," who govern "voiceless subjects."

> It is the concentration of all power in the hands of the party's leading organs that is causing the party to deteriorate and party members holding power to become a new ruling class in society, working for their self-interests and against people's interests. We can assert that many party members with power have really become "new capitalists," hoarding on authority, turning power into private wealth, and causing ever more severe social tension. This condition can lead to social outburst as the incident in Thai Binh.[149]

The party does not deny that there is corruption and smuggling, indeed it makes the point that these are grave social threats. Yet what got Nguyen Thanh Giang into trouble, and eventually arrested on 4 March 1999, was that his explanation differed from the party's. The latter claims that corruption and smuggling are byproducts of the reform program, their having been caused by the corruption of capitalism. According to exiled dissident Doan Viet Hoat, for Giang "corruption is not simply a byproduct of the market economy, but mainly the heritage of privileged power and benefits."[150]

Despite the criticism of rampant official corruption, the dissidents do not necessarily want to dismantle the existing socioeconomic system. Put another way, ideology and the socialist economic model, which give the party its power, are not the subject of scorn that one would expect. Even though the party claims that dissent is an attempt to undermine Vietnam's socialist system, few dissidents advocate the complete capitalization of the Vietnamese economy or the abolition of socialism. Indeed, many complain that the ideals of socialism have been undermined by dogmatic ideological interpretations. Hence, the dissidents attack ideology as the instrument the party uses to maintain its power and to protect its class interests. Regardless of the criticism of ideology, most recognize the role that it played during the war years. Phan Dinh Dieu states that Marxism-Leninism had a "positive effect," Duong Thu Huong called war communism "appropriate," and Bui Tin states that it was a "necessity in that time." Ha Si Phu simply asserts that it was a necessary tool at that time, like a "boat to cross the river, now unneeded on the far shore." Yet all, like Tran Do, while recognizing the role Marxism-Leninism played during the War of National Reunification, believe that its ideological monopoly is holding the country back:

> In the realm of ideology, we maintain a supreme role for Marxism-Leninism not only within the party but also in the entire society. I recognize fully the role of Marxism-Leninism in the revolutionary history of our country. It did play an important role. But today, beside Marxism-Leninism, there are many other schools of thought that deserve to be studied and implemented properly to the condition of our country. Holding on exclusively to Marxism-Leninism only leads to mental retardation.[151]

Ha Si Phu, who has written the most intellectually compelling attacks on ideology in three books and treatises, concludes that the party should abandon socialism under the direct guidance of the VCP and instead use its "people's natural intelligence" to guide and direct social progress and evolution instead of relying on an "archaic method of thought."[152] He continues his Darwinian analysis by arguing that an "outdated ideology" such as Marxism is a step backward in the evolutionary chain: "Marxism-Leninism in Vietnam is just feudalism in disguise. It is dragging down the progress of society and being used to cover up the negative intentions."[153] Using an argument based on Marx's stages of development, he wittily remarked that "the communist movement appeared as a logical phase in history, but it is admittedly just a low rung (intellectually) in the endless struggle for human rights. To find a way out, one must start raising his intellectual eyes to a higher level."[154]

Lu Phuong agrees that for a brief period Marxism was the right tool to utilize for the achievement of independence. But he goes on to complain that "the incompetence in economic development and brutal suppression of politics and culture brought by the socialist model on behalf of Marx and proletarian revolution resulted in Vietnam for many years having independence, but not liberty and happiness."[155] He warns that *doi moi* is bound to fail as socialism because it "drags the nation down into a quagmire, paralyzed and brushed aside while the world is speeding into the future. Socialism is simply an 'illusion that never comes true.' Therefore, any attempts to 'reform' according to the 'socialist' direction, using Lenin's methodology, or based on the proletarian dictatorship to carry out a market economy, are just patching excuses to stay in the Marxist illusion."

Several argue that Marxism should simply be an ideology of choice in a pluralistic context. Bui Minh Quoc states that Marxism should be a choice for both the party and people, not imposed by the party on the people: "Return Marxism-Leninism to its rightful place, the party, instead of continuing to impose it as a choice for the whole population."[156]

From the party's point of view, the most dangerous criticisms of ideology go back to the original debates within the Indochina Communist Party. Common in this line of attack is the argument that Marxism-Leninism failed because the VCP skipped stages of the history, particularly the bourgeois revolution, prematurely inducing the socialist revolution. For Nguyen Thanh Giang, there can not be socialism because "there has never been a worker's class in Vietnam as defined by Marx and Lenin."[157] Hoang Minh Chinh attributes the country's failure to develop to the VCP, which "wants to bypass the capitalist stage of development and move directly into socialism." He rejects the "'Tran Phu platform' of rigid class struggle" that has been adopted by the party in Ho Chi Minh's name, and argues that "we must be determined to restore the 'Nguyen Ai Quoc platform' where success was proved by the Vietnamese Revolution of 1945–1955; that is the bourgeois democratic revolution platform."[158] And yet, according to Chinh, "that bourgeois democratic revolution has just begun." Bui Tin put it this way: "In brief, we wish for nothing more, nothing less, than the implementation of the content of the bourgeois democratic revolution, which the communist parties have owed the people since the time of Stalin."[159]

More daring attacks, like the 1950s essays on the "lime pot," have touched the sacred cow of Vietnamese politics, Ho Chi Minh. Lu Phuong criticized the dogmatic adherence to socialism simply because it was introduced by Ho Chi Minh, who "simply borrowed Leninism as a tool" to fight France and the United States. Ho did not believe that this ideology "would turn intelligent people into foolish ones, turn people with ideals into degenerate ones and bog down the nation in stagnation."[160] Phuong wrote:

> According to the author Tran Dan Tien, who many believe to be the pen name of Ho Chi Minh himself, when Ho chose to follow the socialist path, he did not understand much about this doctrine. He had no idea what class struggle, exploitation, strategy, policy, etc. [meant]. . . . He chose socialism despite his ignorance about it. He did not know that he had tied the fate of the people to an international

organization and an ideology that could not liberate human beings.
. . . The fundamental cause of these sufferings, helplessness, back-
wardness, and autocracy is nothing but slavery to ideology.[161]

Other intellectuals have pointed to socialism's failure in general. At
a 1 August 1993 conference organized by the Ho Chi Minh City Party
Committee's Social Science Committee and the Youth and Students
Club, for example, Nguyen Phong Ho Hieu asserted Marx and Engel's
"theories still have not been proved of any scientific value," and that
"the last century has proved that the predictions of Marx and Lenin are
no more than imaginative figments for utopia."[162] But, more important,
ideology has really stunted economic development. "Have the collapse
of the Soviet Union and the socialist states in Eastern Europe along
with the underdevelopment in China, Vietnam, North Korea, Cuba and
new socialist nations such as Ethiopia, Libya and Mozambique been
enough to provide a failing report card for socialism?"[163]

Other dissidents join the chorus that says socialism is a failed policy that has only hindered Vietnamese economic development and national reunification. Phan Dinh Dieu wrote that "we must admit that
communist theory and 'socialism' with the radicalization of class contradictions and class struggle, with the imposition of a hasty economic
collectivization regime, of centralized management, of monopoly of
leadership of the party have done great harm to the country."[164] Likewise, Ha Si Phu argued that Marxism-Leninism has been "unable to
achieve national reconciliation and the construction of a democratic society and a market economy." [165] Nguyen Ho lamented that he had

joined the revolution for over 56 years, my family has two fallen
combatants. . . . But we must confess: we have chosen the wrong ideology—communism. Because of more than 60 years on this communist revolutionary road, the Vietnamese people have endured incredible sacrifice, yet achieved nothing at the end. The nation is still very
poor, backward; the people are still without a comfortable happy life,
and have no freedom, no democracy. This is a shame.[166]

The other attacks that alarm the party are the accusations that it
uses ideology for the sole purpose of maintaining its monopoly of
power and class interests, rather than as a tool to foster economic development. Lu Phuong argued that

the current leadership, having no ability to create their own, borrowed
foreign ideology first to take over power and later to protect their

position in power. They did not have the vision to self-correct. Their reform policy was the result of looking outward for a solution. And the outside world collapsed, they panicked and found no foundation except the political manipulation learnt during the struggles to take and keep power.[167]

Likewise, Ha Si Phu wrote that "I wonder, once having understood the trend of the era and the aspiration of the people, whether the party, which grew up from a popular movement and now has power in its hands, will shake off the feudal shield for the sake of the people. Will it be able to abandon a regime full of privileges for itself to build a system that truly reflects the will of the people and principles of a pluralistic democracy?"[168]

And he has admonished the party to not "exploit this doctrine as a facade for your personal interests in the last hour of its life": For many, the goals of socialism are not questioned, but ideology is being used to justify the monopoly of power and to serve the interests of one class, namely the party.

Despite the multitude of attacks on the dogmatic application of Marxism-Leninism, only a few intellectuals support a thorough adoption of free-market capitalism in Vietnam. Most still see a role for the state in the economy. Many more are concerned about equity and socioeconomic divisions that could develop because of a wholesale rejection of socialism. Nguyen Thanh Giang's criticizes poor decisions made by the party and government, but he is also critical of capitalism and opening the country to foreign investment; neither of which, according to him, have really helped improve the standard of living of the workers. He was scornful of a statement in the Eighth Central Committee's Seventh Plenum's resolution that said "comparatively cheap labor cost is an important advantage to development." He feels this has led to the poverty of the working class. By making such an assertion though, he is questioning a central tenet of liberal capitalism—comparative advantage.[169] In his 1993 letter to the Central Committee he railed against both capitalism and the party's "red capitalists," who "not only sell public properties among their circle, but also sell natural resources to foreign countries . . . and allow an influx of foreign goods to smother domestic industries."[170] Socialism coupled with the supralegal position of the party and its members have caused massive corruption. This is of obvious concern not just to the dissidents but to the party and society as a whole. But that does not necessarily mean that all want to see socialism's demise: if anything, many dissidents remain starry-eyed idealists.

Duong Qunh Hoa has complained that "we fought for freedom, independence, and social justice. Now all is money. All values have been turned upside down."[171] Duong Thu Huong agrees: "For Vietnamese now the essential interest is money. The money motivation explains everything. They feel that if you have money you can satisfy all desires. The party officials and the leaders are not sufficiently cultivated to refuse money, nor to consider that money may not be the only motivation. There are cadres who are poor, but that is because they occupy positions that they can't turn to profit."[172]

Critics like Nguyen Ho believe that socialism has failed Vietnam, leaving it a poor and backward country, while Vietnam's neighbors have become "imposing tigers." In a December 1988 speech to the CFRF, Ho complained that "Vietnam hasn't advanced to socialism. Vietnam is the poorest and most backward country in the world at present. The influence and prestige of the party and socialism has seriously declined among the people and in the world. That is a great disaster for the party and the people."[173] Yet he does not fault the ideals of socialism, merely its implementation in Vietnam.

Tran Do is more specific, citing the failure and inefficiency of state-owned enterprises. But, more important, he questions why the state has to dominate the economy. Developing a diversified multisector economy, according to Do, must be achieved through the marketplace and "cannot be realized as long as we still insist on the leading role for the state-owned sector."[174]

> Everyone knows the kind of losses the state-owned enterprises generate; the size of government subsidy for them every year; and how horrible a source of corruption and waste they have become. It is understandable this economic sector cannot be eliminated completely because some parts of it are still needed; but holding it in the leading position would mean eliminating or weakening other sectors, including the private sector. One hesitates to discuss the development of the private economic sector for that would be a "deviation from the socialist direction." As a result, the state-owned sector has been a financial burden for the country while resources to develop other sectors are limited.[175]

Bui Tin agrees and states that "we are in favor of the state retaining control of only key economic branches and establishments instead of embracing everything." He suggests that the state take on regulatory functions where "the people will put up capital for business."[176] A handful of dissidents have advocated the complete marketization of the economy. Nguyen Phong Ho Hieu suggests that "there will be a time when Hanoi must officially declare the death of the "socialist market economy" and enter a truly free market. Only then can the nation realize the potential of free enterprise." Phan Dinh Dieu unequivocally argued before senior party members complete enterprise autonomy:

> As the market economy with enterprises, banks, financial structures, etc. was accepted, those institutions should have been given full responsibilities and active roles to run their businesses according to the market structure. Instead, they have been managed and led by the subjective wishes of leaders; and therefore, ineffectiveness, inefficiency, and the creation of corruption and collapse are just the obvious result.[177]

But more than simply not giving state-owned enterprises autonomy or forcing them to equitize, the VCP failed to allow the creation of a large and economically efficient private sector. Although the party committed itself to a multisector economy, it remains poorly capitalized. For example, by mid-1996 the number of joint-stock, limited liability, and private companies was three times greater than the number of state-owned enterprises, but their combined capital was only 10 percent of the latter's. And the state has prevented the private-sector firms' growth by limiting their ability to find foreign partners or investors, and charging them from two to three times the interest rates charged to the state sector.[178] From 1995 to 1998, the private sector grew only at an average annual rate of 6.6 percent, accounting for a mere 7.1 percent of GDP in 1998, and its share of total national output is falling.[179] New policies were issued in 1999 to allow more investment in the private sector, but the regulations merely reinforce the notion that the government is trying to hinder the private sector's growth. For example, foreigners can invest in private enterprises but they can hold no more than 30 percent of equity. And it is no better for domestic Vietnamese investors: institutions can hold 20 percent equity stakes, while individuals can only hold 10 percent.

Instead, the state has pinned its hopes on revamping the state sector, by merging inefficient firms, hoping that they will be able to reap economies of scale. While the government has cut the number of loss-making state-owned enterprises from 12,296 in 1989 to 5,962 in 1995, to around 5,000 in 1999, it is telling that their percentage of industrial output increased from 36.5 percent in 1991 to 41.9 percent in 1995 to 50 percent in 1999. And more important to the state, their contribution to central coffers increased by 135 percent annually between 1991 and 1995; by 1999, contributions accounted for one-third of government revenue. For these reasons, the government is spending much of its efforts and resources promoting a "revitalized" and "renovated" state sector rather than encouraging the growth and development of a more efficient and dynamic private sector. Even when the government announced the equitization of 178 state-owned enterprises in the fall of 1998, it stated that a majority of shares had to be held by the government and 30 percent had to be held by the workers themselves—hardly a privatized system.[180] And this infuriates people like Phan Dinh Dieu who argue:

> We have to realize that whether or not our country is richer and stronger, whether the economy can create outstanding capabilities to compete in the [world] market, depend mainly on our ability to build strong and dynamic enterprises with energetic, committed, educated and creative business people. Such individuals can hardly be coming from the state enterprise management, who, as public officials, must follow the bureaucratic style of the government's administrative machine. The private sector with its own distinctive characteristics, if truly encouraged to develop freely, will be the source to offer the country with such business people. Moreover, encouraging the private sector, forming favorable conditions, legal protection, and providing necessary incentives to this component of the economy, especially in crucial industries, will also have an impact on attracting domestic resources for national development. That will keep these resources from being left idle or spent wastefully.[181]

And wasteful the state-owned enterprises are. In 1999 they were $14.2 billion in debt. To date, only 400 have been fully or partially privatized, although the government announced that the figure would increase to 1,600 by 2005.[182]

Conclusion

Economic development has necessitated the creation of laws and regulations; the economy is simply too complex now to be run by decree. Yet Vietnam is ill equipped to deal with the establishment of a truly legalistic regime, for both structural and political reasons. On the one hand, Vietnam has quickly promulgated a host of laws, but rather than creating a society governed by law, they tend to reinforce the political status quo. The laws are written with the party's interest at heart, not society's, and provide numerous loopholes to place the regime above the law. Although the National Assembly has been strengthened, its power and autonomy remains circumscribed by the party. As the law-making organ of the state, it will become more powerful over time. More important, it will become more willing to act as a watchdog, criticize the poor performance and corruption of government and its officials, and challenge state and party policies. Groupings or factions within the National Assembly may serve as nascent political parties. They do not have to be independent political parties, but the VCP must be prepared to countenance a loyal opposition and become more willing to listen to technocrats and nonparty intellectuals. Ironically, it is in the VCP's long-term interest to allow this, as events in Thai Binh, the parade of high-level corruption trials, and issues such as article 4 of the constitution continue to be a rallying point for public dissent. By having a loyal opposition, which can serve as a watchdog and float alternative policies, the party may actually regain legitimacy and continue its political dominance. Yet the party leadership fears that just the opposite will happen.

What causes grave consternation among senior party members is that once emboldened, the intellectuals and technocrats would push for freedom of speech and greater intellectual freedom in order to continue their dialogue, float new ideas, criticize current policies, appeal to other like-minded individuals, and create independent groupings and political parties. It is the party's long-term control over the flow of information that allows the regime to enjoy its monopoly of power, and it has gone to great lengths to prevent the proliferation of unofficial news organs and limit intellectual freedom.

Notes

1. Reuters, "Vietnam Party Daily Slams Reports on Mass Amnesty," 11 September 1998.

2. Murray Hiebert, "Miles to Go," *Far Eastern Economic Review* (hereafter *FEER*), 29 July 1993, 26.

3. Nguyen Duc Binh, "The Party in the Mission of Socialist Doi Moi," *Nhan Dan*, 5 February 1990, 1.

4. Nguyen Van Linh, "Continuing the Task of Renovation Along the Socialist Path," *Documents of the 7th Party Congress* (Hanoi: The Giao, 1991), 115.

5. Political Bureau, "Conclusions on Some Ideological Work," Hanoi Domestic Service (hereafter HDS), 8 December 1988, in Foreign Broadcast Information Service, *Daily Reports-East Asia* (hereafter *FBIS-EAS*), 9 December 1988, 63.

6. Gareth Porter, "The Transformation of Vietnam's World-view: From Two Camps to Interdependence," *Contemporary Southeast Asia* 12 (June 1990): 8.

7. Patrick O'Neil, "Revolution from Within: Institutional Analysis, Transitions from Authoritarianism, and the Case of Hungary," *World Politics* 48 (July 1996): 579–603.

8. Thai Quang Trung, "Linh and Doi Moi: Prisoners of the Neo-Conservatives?" *Vietnam Commentary* (May–June 1989): 8.

9. Gareth Porter, *Vietnam: The Politics of Bureaucratic Socialism* (Ithaca, N.Y.: Cornell University Press, 1993), 98. Also see Tran Truong Tan, "Why We Do Not Accept Pluralism," Hanoi Domestic Service, 31 May 1989, in *FBIS-EAS*, 6 June 1989, 69.

10. Ha Xuan Truong, "Plurality and Pluralism," *Tap Chi Cong San* (July 1989), in *FBIS-EAS*, 12 September 1989, 69–71.

11. Tran Bach Dang, "Giai Cap Long Nhan va Doi Moi" (The Working Class and Renovation), *Lao Dong*, Special Tet Issue, 1988.

12. Nguyen Dang Quang, "What is Socialism?" *Tap Chi Cong San* (January 1989), in *FBIS-EAS*, 21 April 1989, 55.

13. Tran Truong Tan, "How to Clearly Understand the Vietnam Communist Party Central Committee Political Bureau's Conclusion on Ideological Work," *Nhan Dan*, 23 January 1989, in *FBIS-EAS*, 1 March 1989, 72.

14. Tran Truong Tan, "How to Clearly Understand," 72.

15. Thaveeporn Vasavakul, "Vietnam: The Changing Models of Legitimization," in Multhiah Alagappa, ed., *Political Legitimacy in Southeast Asia: The Quest for Moral Authority* (Palo Alto, Calif.: Stanford University Press, 1995), 285, esp. notes 137–138.

16. Hanoi Domestic Service, 15 October 1989, in *FBIS-EAS*, 16 October 1989, 53–60.

17. See Carlyle Thayer, "Political Reform in Vietnam: Doi Moi and the Emergence of Civil Society," in Robert Miller, ed., *The Development of Civil Society in Communist Systems* (Sydney: Allen and Unwin, 1992), 127.

18. Murray Hiebert, "Against the Wind," *FEER*, 12 April 1990, 12–13.

19. Tran Xuan Bach, "Speech to Union of Vietnam Scientific and Technological Associations," Hanoi Domesic Service, 5 January 1990, in *FBIS-EAS*, 8 January 1990, 67–68. The Central Committee statement said that Bach was purged "for having seriously violated the party organizational principles and discipline, leading to many bad consequences." A report of his purge can be found in Steven Erlanger, "Vietnamese Communists Purge an In-House Critic," *New York Times* (hereafter *NYT*), 1 April 1990, A4.

20. Tran Xuan Bach, "Speech to Union," 67.

21. Bui Tin, *Following Ho Chi Minh: Memoirs of a North Vietnamese Colonel* (Honolulu: University of Hawaii Press, 1995), 161.

22. Ibid., 161.

23. Murray Hiebert, "Survival Tactics," *FEER*, 1 February 1990, 24–25.

24. Cited in Hiebert, "Against the Wind," 12.

25. Nguyen Khac Vien, "Letter to Nguyen Huu Tho, President Vietnam Fatherland Front," 6 January 1991, *Vietnam Commentary* (March–April 1991): 4.

26. Tin, *Following Ho Chi Minh*, 159–160.

27. For example, Politburo resolutions 8A and 8B of 1990 attributed the collapse of communism in Eastern Europe to imperialist and reactionary plots. Other authoritative accounts can be found in Vo Thu Phuong, "A New Step Forward in Vietnam-US Relations," *Tap Chi Cong San* (hereafter TCCS) (August 1995), 47–48; Le Xuan Luu, "Relations Between Building and Defending the Fatherland in the New Revolutionary Stage," Voice of Vietnam (hereafter VOV), 11 June 1996, in *FBIS-EAS*, 13 June 1996, 85–87. The military's perspective can be seen in Phan Hai Ha, "Peaceful Evolution—Victory Without War," *Quan Doi Nhan Dan*, 11 January 1993, in *FBIS-EAS*, 15 January 1993, 56–58, and Senior Lt. Gen. Nguyen Nam Khanh, "Struggle Against Opportunism and Rightism—an Important Part of Party-Building Work at Present," *Tap Chi Quoc Phong Toan Dan* (January 1996), 7–9.

28. "Communist Role to be Strengthened," *Vietnam Investment Review*, 4–10 September 1995, 8.

29. For example, see Doan Khue's article in *Quan Doi Nhan Dan*, 24 November 1993, 1.

30. Originally printed in the army daily, *Quan Doi Nhan Dan;* see Reuters, "Hanoi Warns of Subversion Threat," *International Heral Tribune* (hereafter *IHT*) 16 December 1997, 6.

31. Zachary Abuza, "Debating Globalization: Explaining Hanoi's Bilateral Trade Negotiations," *Problems of Post-Communism* (January 2001).

32. Viet Nam News Service (hereafter VNS), "Manh Wants Stronger People's Committees," *Vietnam News*, 30 September 1998.

33. See Dang Phong, "Aspects of Agricultural Economy and Rural Life in 1993,"in Benedict J. Tria Kerkvliet, and Doug J. Porter, eds., *Vietnam's Rural Transformation* (Boulder, Colo.: Westview Press, 1995), 182–183. A 1996 Oxfam study found in one province eight types of tax imposed by the central government, including land use rights, fishing, salt-making and slaughter, as well as six other local "contributions," including compulsory labor. See Oxfam UK and Ireland, *Report on the Financing and Delivery of Basic Services at the Commune Level in Ky Anh, Ha Tin* (March 1996). Peasants nationwide must contribute, on average, ten days of labor annually to the state.

34. These funds, according to provincial leaders, did not go into their private coffers but rather went to a massive infrastructure investment scheme. The province constructed 4,408 kilometers of roads, including 2,831 paved, and 3,712 kilometers of electric lines, and increased the number of local schools by 90 percent. Yet all this construction led to a debt of 245 billion dong. *Economist* Intelligence Unit, *Vietnam, 2nd Quarter:* 12.

35. Dang Phong, "Aspects of Agricultural Economy," 181.

36. Kerkvleit, "Rural Society and State Relations," in Kerkvleit and Porter, eds., *Vietnam's Rural Transformation*, 75.

37. Dean Yates, "Vietnam Prime Minister Stresses Political Stability," Reuters, 28 October 1998.

38. Reuters, "Vietnam Party Chief Takes Aim at Bureaucrat," 27 April 1998.

39. VNS, "Hai Phong Must Strive for Democracy: Do Muoi," *Vietnam News*, 11 November 1998.

40. Reuters, "Hanoi to Bolster Internal Political Controls," 2 March 1998.

41. Former Minister of Defense Doan Khue, for example, was convinced that the protests occurred because local level cadres were not being vigilant against foreign plots: "To achieve this [political stability in the countryside] we must use all the efforts so that the entire party at all levels is aware of the tricks and plots of enemy forces." Cited in Reuters, "Hanoi to Bolster Internal Political Controls."

42. Adrian Edwards, "Vietnam's President Says Unrest Prompting Rethink," Reuters, 23 February 1998.

43. VNS, "Hai Phong Must Strive for Democracy."

44. VNS, "President Luong Calls on Farmer's Association to Promote Grassroots Democracy," *Vietnam News*, 11 October 1998.

45. VOV, "Legal Assistance Helps Protect Farmer's Rights," 10 September 2000.

46. VNS, "Grassroots Democracy Vital to Effective Governance, Says NA Chairman Manh," *Vietnam News*, 27 July 1998.

47. VNS, "People's Councils Need to Shape Up," *Vietnam News*, 3 October 1998.

48. VNS, "Manh Wants Stronger People's Committees," *Vietnam News*, 30 September 1998.

49. VNS, "Assembly Adopts Long-Awaited Land-Law Changes," *Vietnam News*, 26 November 1998.

50. Deutsche Presse-Agentur (hereafter DPA), "Vietnam Hints at More Local Decision-Making, Under Party Control," 1 October 1998.

51. Chris Brazier, *Vietnam: The Price of Peace*, 56.

52. Greg Lockhart, "Mass Mobilization in Contemporary Vietnam," *Asian Studies Review* 21 (November 1997): 179.

53. Anne F. Thurston, *Muddling Towards Democracy: Political Change in Grassroots China*, Peaceworks No. 23 (Washington, D.C.: U.S. Institute of Peace, 1998).

54. Tran Do, "The State of the Nation," 6.

55. Born in 1932, Pham Duc Kham was arrested in 1990 for his "anti-state" activities. He was arrested along with six other intellectuals for publishing a samizdat newsletter, *Freedom Forum*. He was sentenced in 1993 to sixteen years for "plotting to overthrow the government." His sentence was reduced to twelve years, and in a surprise move, he was released in September 1997 and exiled to the United States, ostensibly released for "humanitarian reasons." The move was seen as an attempt to improve ties with the United States. His release was part of the annual presidential amnesty for national day. See Reuters, "U.S. Says Vietnam Releases Dissident, Welcomes Move," 5 September 1997; Keith B. Richburg, "Vietnam Frees Leading Dissident," *Washington Post*, 5 September 1997, A25.

56. Bui Tin, "A Citizen's Petition," November 1990, *Vietnam Commentary* (November–December 1990): 13–15.

57. Nguyen Phong Ho Hieu, Speech to Ho Chi Minh City Party Committee Social Science Commission," 1 August 1993, in "Dissenting Voice of an Ex-Communist Intellectual," *Vietnam Insight* (January 1994).

58. Quoted in Brazier, *Vietnam: The Price of Peace,* 57.

59. Tran Do, "The State of the Nation," 10.

60. Nguyen Phong Ho Hien, Speech to Ho Chi Minh City Party Committee Social Science Commission.

61. Vu Oanh, "Dai Doan Ket Dan Tong trong Tinh Hinh, Nhiem vu Moi" (Great Unity of the People in Times of New Situations and Responsibilities"), *Nhan Dan,* 1 February 1994, 3.

62. AFP, 14 February 1998.

63. Phan Dinh Dieu, "On the Need to Continue Reform in the Current Period," speech delivered at the expanded Conference of the Presiding Committee, VFF Central Committee, Hanoi, 12–13 December 1997. A translation of the speech can be found at *http://www.fva.org/document/dissident/pddieu.htm*

64. AFP, 14 February 1998.

65. Nguyen Khac Vien, "Letter to Hu Tho," 4.

66. Tran Do, "The State of the Nation," 6–7

67. Ibid., 5.

68. Tran Do, "A Few Words on the 4 January Expulsion," *Vietnam Democracy* (January 1999).

69. Lu Phong, "Socialist Vietnam: Heritage, Reform and Economic Development." Mimeo, n.d.

70. Bui Minh Quoc, "Open Letter to VCP Central Committee," 3 October 1993, *Vietnam Insight* (May 1994).

71. Quoted in Pascale Trouillard, "Vietnam Communist Party Under Fresh Attitude," *AFP* 13 March 1998.

72. "Prof. Phan Dinh Dieu's View of Communism," *Vietnam Democracy* (June 1993), 6.

73. Ibid.

74. Carol V. Rose, "The 'New' Law and Development Movement in the Post–Cold War Era: A Vietnam Case Study," *Law and Society Review* 32 (1998), 97, note 10; also see Hoang The Lien, "On the Legal System of Vietnam," *Vietnam Law and Legal Forum* (September 1994), 34; Mark Sidel, "The Re-emergence of Legal Discourse in Vietnam," *International and Comparative Law Quarterly* 43 (January 1994): 163–174.

75. Porter, *The Politics of Bureaucratic Socialism,* 74.

76. Council of Ministers, Circular No. 20, 16 January 1981, in *FBIS-AP,* 3 April 1981, K6.

77. Nguyen Van Linh, "Address to the National Assembly," Vietnam News Agency (hereafter VNA), 17 June 1987, in *FBIS-EAS,* 17 June 1987, N6-14.

78. Gareth Porter, "The Politics of 'Renovation' in Vietnam," *Problems of Communism* 39 (May–June 1990): 81.

79. Nguyen Huu Tho, "Renovation of Mechanisms in Pressing Needs of the Renovation Process," *Tap Chi Cong San* (March 1989), in *FBIS-EAS,* 5 May 1989, 65. Also see Porter, *The Politics of Bureaucratic Socialism,* 75–76.

80. Nguyen Huu Tho, "Renovation of the Mechanism—Pressing Needs of the Renovation Process," 65.

81. Tran Do, "The State of the Nation and the Role of the Communist Party," 1997–1998, Appendix, 1. A translation can be found at *http://www.fva. org/documents /dissident/trando.htm*

82. Free Vietnam Alliance, "Interview with Hoang Minh Chinh," *Vietnam Democracy* (July 1996).

83. La Van Lam, "Letter to Dao Duy Tung," 6 January 1996, *Vietnam Democracy* (February 1996).

84. Nguyen Huu Tho, "Democracy: A Struggle, Not a Gift," *Vietnam Update*, 2, 1 (Summer 1989): 5.

85. The Ninth National Assembly elected 395 delegates, of whom 362 were party members (92 percent) and 33 nonparty members (8 percent). There were 73 women (18 percent) and 66 minorities (17 percent) elected. And 56 percent of the delegates had university degrees. Of the 395 delegates, 96 (24 percent) were nominated directly by the central government, the remainder were nominated at the local level. In terms of their career backgrounds, 5 percent came from industry, 15 percent from agriculture, 10 percent from the military, and 11 percent from arts and education. *Vietnam Economic Times* (hereafter *VET*), "The National Assembly" (July 1997), 15.

86. For a thorough analysis of the new constitution, see Carlyle A. Thayer, "Recent Political Developments: Constitutional Change and the 1992 Elections," in Carlyle A. Thayer and David Marr, eds., *Vietnam and the Rule of Law* (Canberra: Australia National University, 1993), 50–80, esp. 50–55.

87. Cited in Rose, "The 'New Law' Movement," 99.

88. Ibid., 100–101.

89. Cited in Faith Keenan, "Partners in Dialogue," *FEER*, 24 July 1997, 22.

90. In comparing the Chinese National People's Congress and the Vietnamese National Assembly, Barrett McCormick makes the important distinction that in Vietnam the elections are slightly more competitive than in China. All deputies in Vietnam are directly elected by the electorate. McCormick, "Political Change in China and Vietnam: Coping with the Consequences of Economic Reform," *The China Journal* 40 (July 1998): 135.

91. *VET,* "The National Assembly," 15.

92. Ibid., 15.

93. VNS, "President, NA Chairman Listen to Voter Concerns," *Vietnam News,* 24 October 1998, interactive edition.

94. Thayer, "Recent Political Developments," 56.

95. Faith Keenan, "Partners in Dialogue," *FEER,* 24 July 1997, 22.

96. See Murray Hiebert, "Election Strategy," *FEER,* 9 July 1992, 21.

97. Cited in Keenan, "Partners in Dialogue," 22.

98. Cited in John Chalmers, "Vietnam Gears Up for Low-Key Elections," Reuters, 13 July 1997.

99. Chalmers, "Vietnam Gears Up."

100. Frederik Balfour, "Slouching Towards Democracy: Vietnam Elections Promise Few Surprises," Agence France-Presse (hereafter AFP), 16 July 1997.

101. For more on one of the three, Tran Thanh Trai, see Ian Stewart, "Ex-Vietnam Inmate Becomes Lawmaker," Associated Press (hereafter AP), 11 April 1998.

102. *Tuoi Tre,* 20 July 1997, cited in Adrian Edwards, "Vietnam Hails Elections as Success as Polls Close," Reuters, 20 July 1997.

103. Stewert, "Ex-Vietnam Inmate Becomes Lawmaker."

104. "People and Politics: Interview with Vu Mao," *VET* (July 1997), 20–21.

105. Nguyen Thanh Ha, "The New National Assembly," *The Vietnam Business Journal* (October 1997), 5; VNA, "Conference Reviews 10th National Assembly Election," 19 August 1997; Balfour, "Slouching Towards Democracy."

106. Tran Do, "The State of the Nation," 5.

107. Ibid., 14.

108. VNS, "First Complaints, Petitions Law Passed," *Vietnam News,* 23 November 1998; VNS, "Draft Grievance Law Sparks Heated Debate," *Vietnam News,* 11 November 1998.

109. "Deputies Argue for More Agricultural Spending," *Nhan Dan,* 8 November 1998.

110. Dean Yates, "Vietnam to Act on State Budget Disclosure," Reuters, 14 September 1998.

111. It would be naive to assume that the dissidents actually get along with one another. There is considerable mistrust of Phan Dinh Dieu because he has remained untouched by the party despite his speech and frequent interviews with members of the foreign press. For example, in an open letter Ha Si Phu remarked that "Phan Dinh Dieu himself was invited to sit on the Chairing Committee, but the people who only read of Phan Dinh Dieu were forced to sit behind bars." See "Ha Si Phu's Letter to Phan Dinh Dieu," *Vietnam Insight* (March 1995).

112. VNS, "NA Standing Committee Discusses Proposed Fatherland Front Law," *Vietnam News,* 28 October 1998.

113. Tieu Dao Bao Cu, "Letter to Phan Dinh Dieu," 2 December 1994, in Vietnam Insight (April 1995).

114. "Interview with Hoang Minh Chinh," *Vietnam Democracy* (July 1996).

115. Hiebert, "Miles to Go," 24–26.

116. Murray Hiebert, "Trial and Error," *FEER,* 5 July 1990, 17.

117. Porter, *The Politics of Bureaucratic Socialism,* 84.

118. At the Eighth National Assembly in June 1988, Do Muoi was selected to be prime minister over the reformer and southerner, Vo Van Kiet. His election was described as a "backlash" by conservatives who thought that Muoi would be more willing to put the party's agenda ahead of the state's reform agenda. For more on this, see Louis Stern, *Renovating the Vietnamese Communist Party: Nguyen Van Linh and the Programme for Organizational Reform, 1987-1991* (New York: St. Martin's Press, 1994), 40-42.

119. Quoted in Stern, *Renovating the VCP,* 75.

120. *Far Eastern Economic Review,* Asia 1993 Yearbook, 220.

121. See Nayan Chanda, "The War Within," *FEER,* 4 May 2000, 20.

122. Phan Dinh Dieu, "On the Need to Continue Reform," 2.

123. Bui Minh Quoc, "Think in the Night." Mimeo, n.d.

124. Bin Tin, *Following Ho Chi Minh,* 37.

125. "Letter by Nguyen Thanh Giang to the VCP Central Committee," 20 November 1993, in *Vietnam Insight* (October 1994).

126. See "Letter by Nguyen Thanh Giang to the VCP Central Committee."

127. The directive was first announced in *Cong An Thanh Pho Ho Chi Minh,* No. 689 (10 November 1998).

128. Human Rights Watch argues that "because there is no criminal prosecution, the detainee is not brought to trial and therefore has no opportunity for legal defense." This article is in conflict with both the criminal code and article 72 of the constitution, which states that "no citizens shall be considered guilty and liable to punishment until a verdict has been reached by the court and come into effect." See Human Rights Watch, *Rural Unrest in Vietnam,* 9, 11 (December 1997), 9.

129. DPA, "One-Third of Vietnam Arrests Are of Innocent People Assembly Says," 31 October 1998.

130. AP, "Torture Victim Gets Compensation," 29 December 1999.

131. Hoang The Lien, "Democracy in the Renovation 'Doi Moi' of Vietnam," in Corrine Phuangkasem et al., eds., *Proceedings of the 1992 International Symposium Democratic Experiences in Southeast Asian Countries, 7–8 December 1992* (Bangkok: Thammasat University, 1992), 107.

132. Huang The Lien, "Democracy in the Renovation 'Doi Moi' of Vietnam," 108.

133. La Van Lam, "Letter to General Secretary Do Muoi," 30 April 1994, *Vietnam Democracy* (February 1996).

134. Thayer, "Recent Political Development," 52.

135. Milovan Djilas, *The New Class* (New York: Praeger, 1974), 45.

136. Ibid., 47.

137. Ibid.

138. Faith Keenan, "Dishing the Dung," *FEER,* 13 August 1998, 28. After a three-month-long investigation, the state inspector, Ta Huu Thanh, announced that he had found no wrongdoing by Duyet. See Dean Yates, "Hanoi Probed High-Level Graft Cases," Reuters, 4 November 1998. Members of the inspectorate subsequently intimidated the accusers.

139. Djilas, *The New Class,* 40.

140. Michael Vatikiotis, *Political Change in Southeast Asia* (New York: Routledge, 1996), 101.

141. Ronald E. Yates, "Co-Founder of Viet Cong Unhappy with Communist Party," *Chicago Tribune,* 15 May 1995.

142. Pascale Trouillaud, "Vietnam Communist Party Under Fresh Attack," AFP, 13 March 1998.

143. Cited in "Nguyen Thanh Giang and the Vietnamese Thousand-Year Aspiration," *Vietnam Democracy* (May 1997).

144. "Nguyen Thanh Giang's Letter to the VCP Central Committee."

145. Duong Thu Huong, *Paradise of the Blind,* translated by Phan Huy Duong and Nina McPherson (New York: Penguin Publishers, 1993).

146. Hue-Tam Ho Tai, "Duong Thu Huong," 87.

147. Murray Hiebert, "Mixed Signals," *FEER,* 26 October 1989, 37.

148. Michael Richardson, "Fighting Graft Brings a Net Advantage, Survey Says," *IHT,* 23 March 2000, 16.

149. Tran Do, "The State of the Nation," 5.

150. "Open Letter from Dr. Doan Viet Hoat Regarding the Arrest of Professor Nguyen Thanh Giang in Vietnam," March 12, 1999.

151. Tran Do, "The State of the Nation," 6.

152. Ha Si Phu, "Hand in Hand, Following the Signs of Our Intellect." The article was attacked feverishly by the Central Committee and has been pilloried in the press. According to Tieu Dao Bao Cu, "within two years, more than 30 articles in national and local newspapers and even books were written to attack his writings. . . . Quite a number of theorists of the regime . . . were mobilized in this suppression task."

153. Ha Si Phu, "Excerpts from the Preface of 'Farewell to Ideology,'" in *Vietnam Insight* (May 1996).

154. Ibid.

155. Cited in Murray Hiebert, "Dissenting Voices," *FEER,* 2 December 1993, 26.

156. Bui Minh Quoc, "Open Letter to VCP Central Committee," 3 October 1993, in *Vietnam Insight* (May 1994).

157. Nguyen Thanh Giang, "The Vietnam Worker's Class," in *Vietnam Democracy* (November 1998).

158. Hoang Minh Chinh, "Commentary on the Draft Platform," 21 January 1991, *Vietnam Commentary* (March–April 1991): 6–11, esp. 9.

159. Bui Tin, "The Road Away From Disaster," 16 March 1991, *Vietnam Commentary* (March–April 1991): 15.

160. Cited in Hiebert, "Dissenting Voices."

161. Lu Phong, "Conversation on Socialism." Mimeo, n.d.

162. "Dissenting Voice of an ex-Communist Intellectual," *Vietnam Insight* (January 1994).

163. Ibid.

164. Phan Dinh Dieu, "Petition for an Emergency Program," January 1991, in *Vietnam Commentary* (May–June 1991): 10.

165. Ha Si Phu, "Reflections of a Citizen," *Vietnam Insight* (1988); Cited in Hiebert, "Dissenting Voices."

166. "Dissident Party Member Reveals Own Ordeal," *Vietnam Insight* (June 1994).

167. Lu Phong, "Culture and a Policy to Develop Culture." Mimeo, n.d.

168. Cited in Tieu Dao Bao Cu, "Ha Si Phu: Symbol of Intellect and the Freedom of Thought," *Vietnam Democracy* (February 1996).

169. Nguyen Thanh Giang, "The Vietnamese Workers Class," *Vietnam Democracy* (January 1999): 8.

170. Nguyen Thanh Giang, "Letter to the Central Committee, 20 November 1993," *Vietnam Insight* (September 1994).

171. Harry Kamm, "How Are Vietnamese Doing Now? Viet Cong Doctor Expresses Disgust," *NYT,* 6 May 1993.

172. Cited in Henry Kamm, *Dragon Ascending: Vietnam and the Vietnamese* (New York: Arcade, 1996), 143.

173. Nayan Chanda, "Force for Change," *FEER*, 5 October 1989, 26.

174. Tran Do, "The State of the Nation," 4.

175. Ibid.

176. Bui Tin, "The Road Away from Disaster": 15.

177. Phan Dinh Dieu, "On the Need to Continue the Reform," 2.

178. For more on Hanoi's privatization efforts, see Adam Schwarz, "Reality Check," *FEER*, 3 May 1997, 68.

179. David Dapice, "Point of No Return," *Vietnam Business Journal* (February 2000).

180. VNS, "Government Pushes Quicker Equitization," *Vietnam News*, 11 August 1998. According to the report, 2 state-owned enterprises (SOEs) were equitized in 1993, 1 in 1994, 3 in 1995, 4 in 1996, and 7 in 1997. Decision 44/1998/CP called for the equitization of 178 SOEs. Of the 178, 58 are corporations owned by seven government ministries, 26 are subsidiaries of major corporations, while the remaining 94 are provincial- and municipal-owned firms.

181. Phan Dinh Dieu, "On the Need to Continue the Reform," 2.

182. Huw Watkin, "Foreigners Show Little Interest in Debt-Riddled State Sector," *SCMP*, 23 March 2000.

4

THE BATTLE OVER INTELLECTUAL FREEDOM AND FREEDOM OF THE PRESS

Why do Vietnamese police travel in threes?
One can read. One can write. The third has to control the intellectuals.
—*Vietnamese joke*

The heart of the *Nhan Van–Giai Pham* affair centered on the debate between advocates of free speech, intellectual freedom, the independence of the press, on the one hand, and supporters of socialist realism and party control on the other. The parameters for socialist realism had been rigidly set by Vladimir Lenin,[1] Maxim Gorky,[2] and Mao Zedong, who asserted in his Yenan Talks on Literature and Art that "there is in fact no such thing as art for art's sake, art that stands above classes, art that is detached from or independent of politics. Proletarian literature and art are part of the whole proletarian revolutionary cause."[3] Leaders of the *Nhan Van–Giai Pham* movement were arrested and purged for setting up their own journals as well as creating art and literature that did not support and uphold the correctness of the proletarian revolution. They were seen by the party as "poisonous weeds," a blight on socialist literature and art whose sole purpose was to serve the revolution. It should come as no surprise that one of the issues unanimously agreed upon by the dissidents is intellectual freedom and the means to transmit those ideas. There has been a great flowering of the visual arts since 1986, making Vietnamese art one of the most sought-after commodities in the Asian modern art market, but the freedom of the press and literary expression has been far more circumscribed. Little change in the government's policy should be expected: one of Hanoi's primary means of clamping down on the intellectuals has been to keep them from communicating freely, forcing them to rely on letters and samizdat publications.

Increasingly, they have been able to circumvent the government's control over the press through the Internet, leaving one government official to complain of the "sins of modern communication." But draconian controls over the press remain in place, and a 1999 survey of press freedom across East and Southeast Asia placed Vietnam at the bottom along with Myanmar.

Vietnam is a highly literate society. Despite its being one of the poorest nations on earth, Vietnam has one of the highest literacy rates for both men and women, some 85 percent. To this end, there are some 400 publications, periodicals, journals, and newspapers printed in Vietnam. Although article 69 of the 1992 constitution claims that "citizens are entitled to freedom of speech and freedom of the press," in reality, under the dictates of socialist realism all periodicals and newspapers are owned and controlled by the party or organs of state. Even with the proliferation of journals and publications during the *Nhan Van–Giai Pham* affair, not all journals were independent, and the few that were did not last very long. Since then, there was only one independent newspaper in Vietnam: *Tin Sang (Morning News)*. *Tin Sang* was a left-of-center holdover from the Republic of Vietnam that, as long as it toed the party line, was allowed to remain in business. Because it tried to remain as independent as possible, it became the best-selling paper in Saigon and was sought after throughout the country in the late 1970s. Many party members chafed at its publication, arguing that it only represented the "views of one segment of the masses"—its bourgeois owners and editors.[4] Shortly before the Fifth Party Congress in March 1982, the party decided that with enemies still trying to "sabotage and hinder" Vietnam's development, "complete unity of will and voice were absolutely vital," and *Tin Sang* was shut down.[5] Since then, there have not been any independent newspapers or magazines or alternative sources of news and information except for a few samizdat papers born out of frustration in the late 1980s and through the 1990s. All applications to establish independent journals or newspapers, such as the requests by Gen. Tran Do in 1999, have been rejected outright.

Implementing *Doi Moi:* Nguyen Van Linh and the Press

Although the party has shown absolutely no willingness to allow independent publications since 1986, there have been calls for *doi moi,* or renovation, to take place in journalistic fields as well as the economy. Leaders have used various press organs to further their political agenda in heated factional debates over policy. Indeed, General Secretary Nguyen Van Linh needed the press to help him implement his economic reform program in spite of a stubborn and recalcitrant bureaucracy. And without independent oversight, the abuse of power by and the corruption of party members that had led to their alienation from the masses would only continue. As Linh told a group of journalists on 6 October 1987, "in the days when our party was fighting for power, it depended on the people for support. Now, the possession of power is likely to lead to alienation from the masses, arrogance and high-handedness, greed and embezzlement, bureaucratism and authoritarianism in economic and ideological leadership. All this must be strongly criticized and condemned."[6]

To this end, Linh courted intellectuals and journalists in a way that no senior party official had since the early 1950s. He enlisted their support in investigating and publicizing waste, inefficiency, corruption, and bureaucratism, in what became known as the "Unshackling Days" (*Thoi coi troi*).

The writers and intellectuals supported Linh and his efforts, but they wanted something in return. At the October meeting with Linh, artists and writers complained that the party leadership had been "undemocratic, despotic and overbearing in cultural matters." They called for "untying" culture from party control. In response, Linh admitted that "the party leadership regarding culture, art and literature was, as noted by many, undemocratic, authoritarian, high-handed."[7] He spoke of the "inequity and injudiciousness" that were "impediments to a full development of [the intellectuals'] potential." Most important, he questioned the party's traditional censorship of all works and urged the writers not to give in to please such people. "Formerly a number of critical books were banned and their authors could get into serious trouble. But should we 'bend our pens' to make things palatable to such people? I'm of the opinion that an artist who does this will deprive himself of all revolutionary quality."[8]

Linh then entered into a conversation with the writers: "It seems to me that our achievements in literature and art since liberation day have not been great. Am I right? I would be happy to be wrong, but if I am right, please let me know why. Is it because of the restrictions and censorship of the leadership?" One of the writers, Ho Ngoc, bluntly replied that "culture, art and politics must be separated, not only in the thought of the artists but in organization and in the minds of the leadership, especially those who lead arts organizations." A leading party intellectual who had turned very critical of the party, Nguyen Khac Vien, continued in language reminiscent of the *Nhan Van–Giai Pham* affair:

> In the economy, centralization and bureaucracy has hurt the daily life of the people; in the culture, it has had an even worse effect. The people have been told how many kilos of rice to eat each month; the poets have been told how many poems to write each month. Everything is decided from above—how to write, how to think. It is forbidden for writers to create or to think for themselves. In this situation, human beings lose their nature and become like machines.[9]

In response to this dialogue, in December 1987 the Politburo issued Resolution 5, penned by the liberal-minded culture tsar, Gen. Tran Do, who headed the Central Committee's Cultural Commission. Tran Do, who had tried to mediate a settlement between party hardliners and the intellectuals during the *Nhan Van–Giai Pham* affair, was a staunch advocate of intellectual freedom, for which he would be expelled from the party in January 1999. Resolution 5, which he drafted, outlined new rights and responsibilities for writers and artists, giving them significantly more artistic freedom: "Creative freedom is the vital condition for the creation of genuine values in culture and literature. . . . Literary works that do not violate the law are not reactionary (anti-people, anti-socialist, or anti-peace) and are not degenerate . . . all have the right to be freely circulated, placed under the assessment and judgement of public opinion and criticism."[10]

As a result, in the 1987–1988 period many restrictions on literary works were dropped, and popular works by such anticommunist writers as Nhat Linh and Khai Hung, which had been banned up to that point, were allowed to be published again.[11] Additionally, five of the writers banned during the *Nhan Van–Giai Pham* affair were rehabilitated in 1987 after a party literary and culture critic traveled to Moscow to witness the effect of perestroika on Soviet intellectuals.[12] Although the works of twenty writers and artists remained banned, works of "information aesthetics," the thinly veiled state propaganda that espoused the virtues of heroism, sacrifice, and the collective good, were discarded. Nguyen Ngoc, the editor of the weekly literary magazine *Van Nghe,* was encouraged by Tran Do to publish works by young authors and new fictional accounts of the war.[13] *Van Nghe* became one of the most avant-garde, and hence widely read, publications in the country, showcasing

provocative works such as "The General Retires," a scathing indict-
ment of post-war Vietnamese society.[14] (This story centers on a general
who has just retired after a life of fighting for his country's independence, only to find society more divided by class and a people fighting
for their economic survival.) As a result Nguyen Huy Thiep and other
young authors, such as Duong Thu Huong, Pham Thi Hoai, and Bao
Ninh, as well as Le Luu, came to prominence as the country's best-selling
authors. Such works as *Sorrow of War, Novel Without a Name,* and *A
Time Far Past* portrayed the anti-U.S. war in an entirely new light. The
war was not glorified, and the protagonists of the novels tended to be
anything but the "socialist man" who sacrifices himself for the collective good.[15] They had left for war as patriotic and idealistic young recruits, unprepared for the death and destruction they would live through
in spite of the cynical direction of the party, which was cognizant that
the war was not a holy campaign or just cause. They returned from war
haunted, unable to fit back into society, relate to others, or to love. And
they were disillusioned about the state of society that they returned to,
with the party's promises long unfulfilled. Finally, these antiheroes felt
betrayed by the party and state they had served. As Bao Ninh said,
"Most soldiers thought they were struggling for social equality, democracy, liberty and national construction. But after 16 years few things in
this beautiful picture have been realized. . . . Most soldiers are unhappy
and disappointed."[16] So was society, where these works touched a raw
nerve in speaking for a lost generation.

At the same time, Nguyen Huy Thiep began publishing scathing allegorical attacks on the party and its leadership in *Van Nghe.* Using historical figures such as Nguyen Hue, an eighteenth-century nationalist
hero whom he portrayed as a philanderer in the short story "Chastity,"
he alluded to Ho Chi Minh, whom the party insists remained celibate
despite considerable evidence to the contrary.[17] In "Vang Lua," Thiep
used the historical figure of King Gia Long to attack party officials. Although Giai Long officially is reviled by the VCP for suppressing peasant rebellions, notably the nineteenth-century Tay Son (an uprising considered by the VCP as the precursor of its own twentieth-century
rebellion), and for failing to deal with European threats, Thiep makes
him look like a corrupt party cadre who simply uses his position to enrich himself. As Peter Zinomon explains, "Based on the depiction of
Gia Long, politicians come off as cruel, duplicitous, anti-intellectual,
hypocritical, self-absorbed and egomaniacal. And their pathological
fear prevents them from undertaking the reforms necessary to improve

society."[18] In the same story, Thiep gives a very sad exposition of the state of intellectuals in modern Vietnam. He portrays the author of Vietnam's most famous literary work, *The Tale of Kieu,* Nguyen Du, as a sad figure: underemployed, impoverished, and not taken seriously or respected by the state he serves.

The literature of Thiep, Duong Thu Huong, Bao Ninh, Le Luu, and others is immensely popular. But it was only sympathetic high-ranking officials who allowed this literary renaissance. Zinoman argues that it was the "outspoken reformist Ngoc who, by publishing Thiep's stories in rapid succession beginning in 1987, gave the writer a prestigious and high-profile platform in which to present his work."[19] Without high-level patronage such avant-garde and provocative works could not have been published.

Similar liberalization occurred in the press. Because of pressure from conservatives and the bureaucracy, Linh was having trouble implementing the reform program, so he decided to expand the role of journalists and the press. In a major speech to the editors of newspapers from all over the communist bloc on 28 March 1988, Linh admitted that "renovation is a trend but it will not be an easy process, and will involve struggle."[20] While he confirmed that the press was the primary tool that the party used to disseminate new policies, he stated that "the press is the instrument of renovation, hence it too should be renovated in its personnel (editors, reporters) and its work style."[21] He needed journalists to put public pressure on party cadres and bureaucrats to implement reform and to serve as a watchdog to halt the alarming rise in corruption and abuse of power cases.

At a meeting between the Central Committee's Secretariat and senior editors in June 1988, the newsmen were emboldened by Linh's prodding. They presented a litany of grievances to the Secretariat and tried to redefine journalistic boundaries. *Lao Dong*'s editor in chief, Xuan Cang, asked the Secretariat whether the press could "publish different opinions, even contrary to those of the party, on condition that they are instructive."[22] He was joined by the editor of army daily *Quan Doi Nhan Dan,* Gen. Tran Cong Man, who complained that up until then "debates only concern[ed] the means of applying policies," and not the policies themselves. "Why do we not discuss the correctness or incorrectness of these policies?" he asked.[23] Other editors complained about the party's demand that the media only publish good news: "That produces the illusion that everything is good in our society, when reality shows a number of injustices," complained another editor. "The press announces good harvests, but the population suffers from famine."

As a result of Linh's and Tran Do's efforts, the press had considerably more freedom and, for the first time, journalists were allowed to write about the negative aspects of Vietnamese society and governance. Beginning in 1988, journalists no longer had to get permission for stories from the Central Committee's Ideology and Culture Commission. The major dailies, such as *Sai Gon Giai Phong (Liberated Saigon), Tuoi Tre, Lao Dong, Nhan Dan,* and *Quan Doi Nhan Dan,* began printing investigative stories. In this period, Linh himself penned a weekly column in the major daily in Ho Chi Minh, *Sai Gon Giai Phong,* in which he chastised party and government *apparatchiks* who were holding back the reform program.[24] Exposing corruption was the primary goal, and few were immune. For example, the wife of minister of defense and a Politburo member, Van Tien Dung, was exposed for using her husband's position to engage in smuggling, and as a result Dung was dropped from both positions. There still remained many constraints on the press about whom they could go after.

An interesting case is the example of Ha Trong Hoa, the Communist Party secretary of Thanh Hoa Province who was being investigated for corruption and abuse of power. However, when he was nominated for a permanent seat on the Central Committee, the party clamped down on all investigative reportage in the case. Several newspapers were forced to suspend their publication because of their editors' insistence in following the story.[25] It was evident that the party leadership would tolerate the press targeting low- and mid-level officials who were accused or suspected of corruption and abuse of power, but it would not allow an attack on one of their own. The party protected Hoa this one time, but he continued to engage in corrupt and authoritarian practices so the party unleashed the press and Hoa eventually lost his position.[26]

Although the press still had to contend with high-level interference, in 1988 party watchdogs stopped vetting articles—which only encouraged journalists to demand more freedom. The chairman of the Vietnam Journalist's Association complained about the continual party interference, and the editor of *Quan Doi Nhan Dan* lamented that the press was only allowed to debate "the means of applying policies" instead of the correctness of the policies themselves.[27]

Retrenchment

What little liberalization of the press there was in the late 1980s was very short lived. With the collapse of socialism in Eastern Europe and the Tiananmen Square massacre in Beijing in 1989, General Secretary Linh reversed himself and the VCP cracked down. At the Central Committee's Sixth Plenum in March 1989, Linh denounced the "excesses of liberalism," rejected any movement toward political pluralism, and urged writers to stop writing "only about negative phenomenon." Prerevolutionary works were again banned, and what few freedoms the press had earned in the 1987–1988 period were restrained. The party clamped down on the press, demanding that it again serve solely the party's interests, and advocates of greater press freedom, such as General Tran Do, came under heavy pressure to conform.[28] The Central Committee's Culture Commission shut down eight magazines and newspapers, while the editor in chief of *Sai Gon Giai Phong* was fired and the editor of *Vung Tau Con Dau* arrested for his paper's outspoken and critical reportage. Numerous other editors were also purged: Bui Minh Quoc from *Da Dat Lang Bian,* To Hoa of *Sai Gon Giai Phong,* To Nhun Vy of the literary review *Cua Viet,* and Truong Giang of *Giao duc va Tho dai,* the latter for apologizing to its readers for not publishing a critical response by Phan Dinh Dieu to an article by Le Quang Vinh published first in *Sai Gon Giai Phong* and then in *Nhan Dan.*[29]

In the middle of this crackdown, there was a major congress of journalists on 10 October 1989. Bui Tin writes that advocates of intellectual freedom placed a lot of hope in this congress. Some 300 delegates, representing some 6,000 journalists nationwide, sought—in vain—to confront the party and regain the freedoms they had won since 1986. Tin concedes that there was no confrontation because such senior figures as Tran Do did not attend the congress because they were "under a cloud" for encouraging literary freedom.[30] Indeed, soon after, Tran Do was forced off the Central Committee and the commission he headed, while Nguyen Ngoc was dismissed from *Van Nghe* as well as the executive board of the Vietnam Writers' Association (VWA) in October 1988. Peter Zinoman writes that in the end it was Ngoc's patronage of young writers who had run afoul of the party that "contributed decisively to Ngoc's [being deposed.]"[31]

One of the major confrontations at this conference was over party interference in the leadership of the organization itself. In an overt attempt by the party to control the congress and the election of its leadership, six members of the Politburo and five members in charge of ideological matters for the Central Committee, including Dao Duy Tung, Tran Trong Tan, and Nguyen Duc Tam, attended the conference. Despite the fact that three-quarters of the delegates were party members, the party leadership presented the organization with a slate of candidates for leadership positions that was rejected outright by the congress. In the end, the top three vote getters, including Nguyen Ngoc, were not on the party's short list, and the party's choice for the VWA's general secretary, Anh Duc, did not even get enough votes to win a place on the executive committee.[32]

One final point about the congress that needs to be made is Nguyen Van Linh's conspicuous absence, in contrast to his very high-profile appearance at the 1987 VWA conference when he told the writers not to "bend their pens." The keynote speech was delivered instead by Prime Minister Do Muoi, who warned the writers that "the political responsibility of Vietnamese writers in these times and in the coming years is to affirm by their literary works, the need for socialism and its vital strength in Vietnam."[33]

Frustration among journalists and writers remained high. In late 1988, two southern intellectuals and party members, Bui Minh Quoc[34] and Tieu Dao Bao Cu[35] led a delegation of young artists and intellectuals to Hanoi, stopping along the way to try to recruit other young artists and intellectuals to petition the VCP for the rehabilitation of Nguyen Ngoc. Senior party ideologues declared that Cu and Quoc were violating party discipline and the tenets of democratic centralism: "There are even serious manifestations of factionalism in various activities (such as those groups of persons at the association of writers in Lam Dong province)," wrote one.[36] Though they were not arrested, both were immediately fired and expelled from the party, and *Lang Bian,* the magazine of which they were editor in chief and deputy editor, respectively, was shut down. Another avant-garde literary journal, Hue-based *Song Huong,* was also closed. Expulsion only emboldened Cu and Quoc, and when dissident intellectual Ha Si Phu was first arrested in April 1991, and again in November 1996, they became the leading champions of his cause.[37] Since then, the two have remained active critics of the regime despite being detained in an attempt to intimidate them into silence.

But few others were inspired to take on the party directly. Instead, intellectuals, primarily in the south, began to publish their own journals and samizdat newspapers beginning in the late 1980s. For the most part, these were simply typed pages that were photocopied and passed from friend to friend, colleague to colleague. As Stein Tonneson accurately noted, "The role of the 'photocopy shops' in creating a civil society in Vietnam cannot be exaggerated."[38] There was also a subsequent rise in the number of clandestine publishing houses throughout the

Mekong Delta region. According to a report by the Ministry of the Interior, by 1988 only half of the 400 newspapers in the country were licensed and nearly 40 percent of the books published that year were done so illegally.[39]

The best known samizdat papers were *Freedom Forum* and the news letter of the CRFR, *Truyen Thong Khang Chien* (*Tradition of Resistance*), the subject of the following chapter. The CFRF's newsletter was banned after only three issues,[40] while *Freedom Forum* was first published in January 1990 and shut down by authorities in November 1990 after publishing only four issues. The editors, Pham Duc Kham, Doan Viet Hoat, and six other intellectuals, were arrested for the "anti-state activity" of publishing *Freedom Forum*, in 1990.[41] Although the official *Sai Gon Giai Phong* wrote that *Freedom Forum*'s goal was to "overthrow the people's power" and be a "rallying force to oppose and sabotage our country," the newsletter's editors never advocated violence. In the context of socialism's demise in Eastern Europe, which led to a politically conservative backlash in Vietnam, the government accused *Freedom Forum* of being a "reactionary document to disseminate propaganda about the adverse political developments in Eastern Europe, to exploit Vietnam's economic difficulties, to take advantage of the so-called internal conflicts, and design ways to rally the masses to struggle in the manner of peaceful evolution."[42]

The punishment for the editors of *Freedom Forum* was swift and harsh, with all eight of the editors receiving four- to fifteen-year prison sentences.[43]

Independent publications were not unique to dissident intellectuals. Tran Do was growing increasingly frustrated with the party's control over the literature and the arts, and this would lead to his being sacked. He tried to establish a journal of literature and literary criticism, which in the context of state control over literature and the arts would be ostensibly a journal of political opinion and criticism.[44] The year 1988 saw his journal *Phe Binh va Du Luan* (*Criticism and Opinion*), which came out only once before the party ordered it shut down. Shortly thereafter, the Central Committee reorganized its commissions and merged the Ideology Commission with the Arts and Culture Commission, thereby creating an uncontroversial way to force the increasingly outspoken Tran Do into retirement.

Despite arrests and crackdowns, samizdat publications flourished. Intellectuals and dissidents clearly took heart from the collapse of socialism in Eastern Europe and the former Soviet Union; articles became more critical of the party, its leaders and Marxist ideology in general. The growth of independent publications so angered the party that it warned intellectuals in October 1993 that they would be punished if they were caught distributing or publishing materials "opposing socialism."[45] Overseas Vietnamese groups reported sharp rises in the number of underground publications, including *Nguoi Saigon* (*The Saigonese*), which published thirty issues between spring 1996 and summer 1997; *Noi Ket* (*Link*); a youth paper *Thao Thuc* (*Restlessness*); and *Democracy and the Rule of Law*, published by Free Vietnam Alliance members in Vietnam.

The party was sufficiently alarmed to try to delineate the rights and responsibilities of the press with the promulgation of a press law in December 1989. The law affirmed every citizen's right to free speech and access to information, but the bulk of the law focused on how the state would manage the press.[46] The law specifically forbade the media to "incite the population to oppose the State and the Socialist Republic of Vietnam, or to undermine the national unity bloc." But who is to determine this? Article 2 of the 1989 press law ended state censorship of the media, but the state can still hold the press accountable through licensing and editorial control. Various organs of the party or state own all forms of media in Vietnam, which have to apply for a publication license, thus the organs and their leadership are ultimately held responsible for what their journals publish and can have their licenses revoked. But the real control comes through the editors, who not only stand to lose their jobs but are almost always party members and thus subject to party discipline and personnel appointments by the Central Committee's Organization Department. Despite having ended censorship, the state and party still are able to control the press and to ensure no ideological malfeasance.

All the same, Vietnamese literature had never been better. The VWA defied the party in 1990 by awarding its top prize that year to Bao Ninh's "The Fate of Love," a story about two lovers traumatized by the war. But the crackdown on unregulated writing was real, and conservative ideologues who chafed at the works of Bao Ninh, Nguyen Huy Thiep, Duong Thu Huong, Nguyen Duy, Pham Thi Hoai, and others began to publish scathing criticisms that continued throughout the decade. Nguyen Huy Thiep was condemned for his wanton abuse of history. Bao Ninh was attacked for his bleak portrayal of the war. As one military critic wrote, "The view of the soldier in the novel is so dark and utterly tragic. It seems he only sees death and miserable things."[47]

Critics were also critical of Duong Thu Huong's portrayal of Communist Party members. "The image of communists is distorted," wrote one. "Occasionally, communists are portrayed as heartless and violent people" or "robots, rigid people without morals."[48] The critic continued by issuing a warning to authors of similar style: "We cannot allow a few people to reject the past and, in the name of 'literature,' distort communism and smear Communists and the Communist Party."

A leading party intellectual, To Hoai, the chairman of the Hanoi Literature and Arts Association, wrote a major critique of the literature that appeared in the late 1980s in the party's theoretical journal *Tap Chi Cong San*. He attacked the lifting of the ban on Khai Hung and Nhat Linh, whom he considered antisocialist, and whose works "depicted . . . the 'destruction of bloodthirsty communist soldiers.'"[49] Hoai admitted that in the past some mistakes had been made in the management of arts and literature, but argued that contemporary literature contained "certain deficiencies and unhealthy manifestations" because it "pandered to vulgar tastes for the sake of good business," filled with licentiousness and frivolousness.[50] Hoai singled out seventeen authors by name, including Duong Thu Huong, Nguyen Huy Thiep, Nguyen Duy, Pham Thi Hoai, and Le Luu, who he believed had failed to cherish "what we have already achieved," "revised the decadence of the old south," and included the use of "double entendre" to "belittle someone out of arrogance."

As a result of the attacks, these authors soon found that they were unable to publish their works. Duong Thu Huong's enormously popular work, *Paradise of the Blind,* was banned in 1988. Two years later, she could not find a publisher for her next novel because she had already alarmed too many people. Likewise, after Nguyen Ngoc's fall from grace, Nguyen Huy Thiep could not get his works published after the summer of 1990, despite their not being officially banned.[51] And all this did not happen just to literary dissidents. The war hero, commander of the 1973–1975 campaign that liberated the south, and head of the Military Management Committee in Saigon, Gen. Tran Van Tra, had his memoirs banned by the party.[52] Even such senior party officials as Bui Tin had trouble getting their works published without heavy-handed censorship. Now that press freedoms were being curtailed and ideology was retaking center stage, it was clear that intellectuals would not have an independent voice at home.

A growing number of writers were turning to overseas venues to give them new opportunities to publish their works. With large overseas

Vietnamese communities in France, the United States, and Australia, there were certainly both the means of production and a receptive readership. Overseas publication during the 1990s became the single best way to publish and disseminate works that the party tried to suppress: overseas publications, such as *Que Me* and *Doan Ket,* welcomed such submissions. And the VCP often reacted harshly. For instance, when poet Nguyen Chi Thien smuggled his manuscript of some 400 poems out through the British Embassy in Hanoi for publication abroad, he was arrested (but later released and forced into exile).[53] Volumes of Ha Si Phu's articles appeared,[54] while Duong Thu Huong, after failing to find a publisher for her 1995 *Novel Without a Name,* violated the party's order and sent the manuscript to France, although it was eventually published in the United States as was her latest novel, *Memories of a Pure Spring.* This conduit for unregulated writings very much alarms the party, which still gravely mistrusts the *Viet kieu* (overseas Vietnamese) community that Hanoi sees as innately hostile to the socialist regime. But there is more than the fact that the overseas Vietnamese community is a willing audience for these works. For Hanoi, they are a conduit of subversive materials. For example, the exiled Doan Viet Hoat angered many in the *Viet kieu* community who want to keep Hanoi isolated by supporting normalized trade relations between the United States and Vietnam, maintaining that free trade would entail the unfettered exchange of cultural and intellectual goods.

One hypothesis of why Tran Do was finally expelled from the party in January 1999, after writing many similar open letters in the preceding several years, was that his writings were being used by overseas Vietnamese groups hostile to Hanoi. Tran Do had crossed the line between loyal criticism and sedition. In justifying his expulsion, the party issued a statement that accused him of making the "mistake of disseminating writings and for the fact that they have been widely distributed to the world's news agencies."[55] As one Western journalist commented: "The involvement of outsiders through the Internet gives an increasingly edgy leadership the perfect excuse to move against him at a crucial time."[56]

Although the party had ever less control over publications, it continued trying to stop this practice by going after several authors who were able to publish their works abroad. As already noted, Duong Thu Huong was arrested in April 1990 for sending her manuscript abroad, but was released in November 1991 as a result of French pressure. On 20 July 1992, the Ministry of Culture and Information codified the state's authority over overseas publications in article 3 of Directive 893,[57] and Bui Minh Quoc and Tieu Dao Bao Cu were detained for violating this directive on 28 March 1997. Afterward, along with Ha Si Phu they wrote a joint letter to the National Assembly (on 10 April 1997) protesting that their constitutional right to free speech and expression had been denied, and protested the censorship of any letters or articles sent or published abroad.[58] The three complained that security forces "automatically count the announcement or critique of a domestic writer's works by overseas media as evidence of their bad content," and therefore the directive "can only be used as a tool for certain individuals to harass selected groups while ignoring others."

The Press Under General Secretaries Do Muoi and Le Kha Phieu

With socialism's demise in Eastern Europe and the former Soviet Union, the VCP came down heavily on dissent and applied the brakes on the reform program. At the Seventh Party Congress in June 1991, conservative Prime Minister Do Muoi was elected VCP general secretary. In his first major statement regarding the press, in early 1992, he warned that "information must be guided" and that the press was to remain the "shock force on the ideological and cultural front." He chastised the media for taking advantage of press liberalization: "Not a few press articles and books have appeared that negated the party, distorted realities and history, sowed the seeds of pessimism and advertised a pragmatic way of living, and have had negative effects on society." Other party officials complained about the passivity of the press in its defense of socialist values. The country's leading ideologue, Nguyen Duc Binh, anachronistically spoke of the mass media as "an efficient weapon on the ideological and cultural front" that had to expose "the schemes and maneuvers of the anti-socialist forces who want to negate the party's leadership and divert Vietnam from the socialist path."[59] The press had become less vigilant about defending socialist values, according to the party leadership, because of the negative impact of economic reforms on the media. Suddenly the press was subject to market forces, competition, and the need to increase sales in order to make up for declining state subsidies. At the Central Committee's Fourth Plenum in January 1993, Do Muoi complained that culture, literature, and art had become "commercialized" and sensational.[60] This was used as an excuse to launch a new crackdown on writers and the VWA.[61]

In addition to what was being said in the official media, the party leadership was growing very concerned about the growing number of illegal and unlicensed publications. For example, at the Central Committee's Fourth Plenum, Do Muoi announced that the party would more vehemently "analyze sabotage activities of hostile forces in culture and the arts to counter their conspiracies and tricks positively and efficiently." Although the state would continue to refrain from direct censorship, the party stepped up pressure on the editors to impose self-censorship. In addition, the Interior Ministry established a new department to monitor and control the press, both domestic and international, legal and illegal. At the party's behest, a new law on publications was pushed through the National Assembly in July 1993. The law restated the permission process, spelled out punishments for violators, and banned the following:

- Material detrimental to the Socialist Republic of Vietnam or the unity of its entire people.
- Material inciting violence or wars of aggression; fomenting hatred among nationalities and peoples of various nations; propagating reactionary concepts and culture; disseminating a degenerate or decadent lifestyle; promoting crime, social vice, and superstition; and damaging good Vietnamese morals and customs.
- Material denigrating party, state, military, national security, economic, and foreign policy secrets; secrets involving the personal lives of citizens; and other secrets stipulated by law.
- Material distorting history, rejecting revolutionary achievements, discrediting great Vietnamese men and national heroes, or slandering and damaging the prestige of organizations or the dignity of citizens.[62]

There is little that would not come under this law. With the judicial system so tightly controlled by the party and state, it could be persuasively argued that almost any writing or statement was a violation of this sweeping legislation. Stein Tonneson argues that following the promulgation of this law, there are three factors that determine the scope of free speech: The first is the "degree to which the government *intends* to use the new law in actually repressing cultural and political life."[63] Second is "the *capacity* of the government to actually do so."

Tonneson questions the efficacy of the first two factors, both requiring active policies and enforcement by the state. The final factor, though, is what concerns Tonneson the most: "the amount of fear that the law and certain repressive acts will instill in Vietnamese intellectuals which makes them refrain from writing or publishing texts they would otherwise have produced." It is this passive power of the state, the promotion of self-censorship instilled by fear, that is the implicit ability of the regime to destroy careers.

At the National Congress of the Press and Publishing Houses in August 1997, Do Muoi adopted some of Nguyen Van Linh's attitudes toward the press. He emphasized that the role of the press was to help fight corruption, bureaucratism, smuggling, and other social ills. Yet it was clear that any such reporting would have to be done in accordance with the party's interests and needs, and certainly under its firm leadership. In mid-August, the Politburo announced that it was going to tighten controls over the media. The head of the Central Committee's Ideology and Culture Department, Huu Tho, reiterated that the "press and publications shall operate following the orientation of the party and the laws of the state, in order to reflect and guide public opinion and to encourage the revolutionary spirit."[64] But he warned that the press recently had been showing too much independence and that the party was going to firmly reassert control over wayward organs: "In the time to come, press and publications shall be put under the leadership of the party and operate in the framework of the law."

The Politburo's senior ideologue, Nguyen Duc Binh, soon after wrote an article in *Nhan Dan* condemning the "Westernization" and "commercialization" of Vietnam's press. For Binh, the threat was not necessarily that the newsmen were overtly demanding complete independence from party control. However, as various magazines and newspapers were competing for readership and circulation in an era of declining state subsidies, they were becoming more sensational (i.e., more Western) and less constrained by party discipline. "It's even more dangerous that there are some manifestations of influence of the Western press point of view," he stated.[65] He went on to assert that these Western "tendencies" "destroy the boundaries of social order and national sovereignty in press and information activities. . . . All of these manifestations are strange and unacceptable for our news publications." And he called on the press to revert to its traditional role as a guardian of the people, especially from the negative effects of spiritual pollution: "The press should not just contribute to a correct political orientation, but also prevent and eliminate from social life the harmful germs and poisonous weeds which are trespassing into our country through information channels."[66]

To drive the party's position home, the government sent an unambiguous message. Two months after the conference, Nguyen Hoang Linh, editor of the business daily *Doanh Nghiep* (*Enterprise*), was arrested for publishing an article about high-level corruption in the Department of Customs. The article reported that officials in the Interior Ministry had received kickbacks for the purchase of four patrol boats from Ukraine for which Vietnam paid $4 million. Three of the boats, though, had arrived in unusable condition, and the true market value of the boats was reported to be around $1.5 million. Linh was arrested on the ambiguous charge of revealing state secrets, a violation of article 92 of the constitution. Immediately after his arrest, the Politburo issued a directive on 23 October 1997 that ordered the press to adhere to the party line and warning all others not to "reveal state secrets."

As with all trials of this nature, Linh's fate was determined by high-level political maneuvering. In August 1998, Vietnam announced that Linh's trial would be delayed, and the court stated that he would be charged with "abusing democracy and intruding on the rights of the state, social organizations and the people's interest."[67] Linh was eventually tried on 21 October 1998 and, after recanting, sentenced to time served for "abusing democratic rights," but not the more severe charge of revealing state secrets. He did not have to be charged, because the message to the media was clear: toe the party line and, more important, do not go after sacred cows in the party and government.

A dichotomy became very evident. At the same time that the arrest and trial of Linh were taking place, the press had a very free hand in covering the two largest corruption cases in the state's history. The cases dealt with EPCO-Minh Phung, a textile manufacturer based in Ho Chi Minh City, which had diversified into property holdings to take advantage of rampant speculation in the real estate market, and Tamexco, another party-affiliated trading firm that also was into real estate speculation. Both firms had close ties with the state and the party. A total of seventy-seven defendants from EPCO-Minh Phung and Tamexco were being investigated for fraud, embezzlement, and losses of $280 million, a staggering figure in a country where the average annual income was less than $400. Two executives of EPCO-Minh Phung died in mysterious circumstances, while three executives of Tamexco were executed in January 1998 for graft. During the entire trial the press was relatively unrestricted: obviously the government and party wanted to send a very clear signal to would-be corrupt businessmen. As Human Rights Watch observed:

> Linh's arrest suggests that the widely reported corruption cases of recent months—in January this year Tamexco, a major import-exports company, and in March, EPCO-Minh Phung, a large trading conglomerate, were primarily show-case arrests. Among those arrested in both cases were senior company directors and state officials on charges of misappropriating state assets. The arrest of Linh for reporting alleged high-level misappropriation of funds brings into question the government and party's commitment to exposing corruption when politically inconvenient.[68]

To date the press remains under the party's firm control. For example, during widespread peasant protests in Thai Binh in the 1997–1998 period, mentioned earlier, there was a press blackout for five months, and only after that blackout were the legitimate complaints of the peasants (e.g., about official corruption) summarily reported. The foreign press, of course, was banned from the region altogether. Do Muoi's successor, the hard-line former top political commissar in the army, Le Kha Phieu, immediately held a meeting in that time with top media officials and demanded that they toe the party line and "support revolutionary ideology."[69] He reiterated this position in a November 1998 meeting with senior editors in which he gave this stern admonition: "Being a true journalist, it is necessary to reflect the thoughts and wishes of the public [and be] on the right political track oriented by the party."[70] He warned members of the press not to "give themselves the right to lecture, apportion blame and look at life as black" and to not just "see negative issues." Since then, there has been a spate of new laws affirming that Vietnam is a "law-governed society" but that severely curtail the freedoms of press and speech.

On 19 May 1999, the National Assembly passed a largely rewritten press law that further consolidated control over the media. Under the new law, the Ministry of Culture and Information "will be solely responsible for the issuing of media licenses even if the publication or broadcasting outlet is arranged by another agency."[71] The Ministry of the Interior's Press Department maintains its oversight function as well. The new law also tries to keep the press from any negative reporting by introducing the concept of libel, a tool that is widely used in Malaysia and Singapore to deter the media from challenging the government:

"Any editorial offices or journalists who transmit inadequate information causing damage to others are responsible for compensation according to the provision of the separate civil codes." But libel, as defined or explained here, is ludicrously opaque: there is no clarification of "inadequate information causing damage," and there is no intent to remedy this. For example, if a journalist reports that a shoddily produced product caused injury to a consumer, the producer could sue the journalist or editorial staff for damages relating to a loss of sales.

This measure was followed up in June 1999 by a party decree that tries to reinforce the central governing concept of democratic centralism.[72] Obviously the party leadership is concerned about the lack of discipline in its own ranks and thus prohibits all party members from either speaking out or questioning party decisions (both orally and in writing), or inciting others to do so. The law reiterated that "inciting factionalism and party rifts is also forbidden." Again, this is a very broad concept that could be used against most anyone for most any circumstance, especially in a system that traditionally has been rife with factionalism.

In the run-up to the Ninth Party Congress, set for March 2001, the party has tried to reassert even further control over the news media. There was a major conference of the Vietnam Writers Association in mid-2000, while in April 2000 Prime Minister Phan Van Khai was reported to have ordered a reorganization of the country's cultural sector. In the midst of this a number of books, by both Vietnamese and foreign authors, were banned. In the case of the banned Vietnamese novels, party censors concluded that they were offensive and encouraged "depraved lifestyles," "ideologies of violence," and "social evils and superstition." But the most damning criticism was that they "deny the success of the communist revolution, [slander] and [offend] authority and [ridicule] traditional morality."[73] Clearly, any work that challenges the VCP's interpretation of history and socioeconomic policies is unacceptable. But the Vietnamese government should take heed that dissent can be a "bankable commodity." One only has to look to China to understand that the banning of books has created a vibrant underground cottage industry of illegal publishing houses and distribution networks, as people assume that if the government bans a book, it must be good. Zhou Weihui's *Shanghai Baby* is a case in point: once banned, it became the hottest piece of fiction in the country.[74] Since literary repression in China has become part of the marketing process, in Vietnam a similar phenomenon can occur.

The Dissidents' Rationale and Demands

The dissidents argue that aside from being a violation of article 69 of the constitution, which clearly states that "citizens have the right to freedom of expression; freedom of the press; the right to be informed; the right to assemble, to form associations, [and] to hold demonstrations according the regulation of the laws," censorship and the government's monopoly of the media hurt the country in many ways. For dissidents, independent media will not lead to instability and anarchy, nor will it undermine the party's leadership or challenge its legitimacy. Instead, a free press will make the regime even more legitimate by making the government more accountable and responsive to the concerns of the citizenry.

Tran Do sees the role of the press in much the same light as Nguyen Van Linh did in his first years in office. For Do, it is urgent that the press becomes a watchdog agency because "the current National Assembly cannot carry out its duty of monitoring the government."[75] Freedom of the press would give the people and intellectuals a "real voice" that they could use "to monitor and prevent corruption and other negative conducts, which hundreds of committees and councils cannot accomplish but just complicate the problems even more."

> Allowing these voices is to create a monitoring institution over the government and the party organs, particularly those party organs that are currently under no checking power and have shown signs of power abuses and setting arbitrary laws on the population. Only with this new monitoring means could we actually carry out the motto: By the people, of the people, and for the people; people know, people discuss, people implement, and people monitor.[76]

Tran Do challenges the validity of the party's overriding concern that "a free press will lead to disorder (which is incited by bad people and taken advantage of by the enemies) and political unrest." He argues that "with freedom of expression and freedom of the press," the party will be able to identify those with talents who are able to "solve the country's problems."

> Among the 400 existing periodicals published by [party and government] offices under the "centralized management," if we had just one or two independent papers, that would be enough to make society's intellectual life more lively and beautiful. Intellectuals and experienced citizens have a forum to express their ideas. The party and the

government have a lot more contribution to study and [more warnings of problems] to prevent.[77]

Likewise, Phan Dinh Dieu argues that intellectual freedom is essential to the country's economic development and thus calls for the "liberalization of information exchange." "New ideas and thinking, which are valuable sources for supporting the creation of wealth and prosperity in the new age, if found opposite to the party's lines, have all been prohibited. The modernization of society requires the fundamental democratic rights such as freedom of thought, freedom of expression, freedom of the press, freedom of association, freedom of voting and running for offices."[78]

Dieu frames his argument in economic terms: the marketplace, dominated by economically rational producers and consumers, needs the free flow of information. Vietnam cannot catch up with the rest of the world economically or become integrated into the global economy without a significant change in the information policy of the state. Dieu puts it this way:

> A fundamental factor of the new economy on the global scale is information and intellect, therefore the liberalization of information exchange, strengthening education to uplift citizens' intellectual standard, bringing information and knowledge to everyone, and modernizing informational capabilities for existing manufacturing and service industries, and developing new manufacturing and services industries are opportunities to which we need to pay special attention.[79]

The key to moving up through product life cycles and value-added production is the development of an information-based economy. Although there are only some 45,000 Internet users in Vietnam, a mere .06 percent of the population, the numbers have increased annually and it is estimated that there will be over 1 million users by 2005. There are structural limitations, such as the fact that there are fewer than three telephones per 100 people, but the number of Internet service providers has jumped from one in 1995 to five per 2,000. The Internet will have a profound effect on Vietnam, allowing the country to technologically leapfrog, as long as the government does not feel it must be overregulated.

But this is unlikely because the government has already expressed concern over the anarchic nature of the Internet. Fearing the "sins of modern communication," in January 2000, the government reiterated that all communications over the Internet must comply with the draconian press law, and the Ministry of the Interior now has a department to monitor the Internet and to update its "firewalls," already numbered at over 500. The Ministry of the Interior, moreover, has pushed the government to take control of the Internet from the Ministry of Post and Communications and give it to a committee headed by the Ministry of Interior with members from the Ministry of Science and Technology and the Ministry of Education and Culture. In the end, though, these efforts will fail due to the uncontrollable nature of the Internet and the fact that governments always seem to be a step behind the latest technological advances. Even so, the Vietnamese government seems determined to prevent this from happening.

Having a free press would also serve to facilitate greater debate on policy issues. Even in the context of a tightly controlled press, the senior leadership has always used different news organs as their policy platforms. And individual newspapers, journals, and other media tend to become associated with the thinking of a faction or an individual offical's thinking. As mentioned above, General Secretary Linh had gone further by writing his own column, but others were not so personal. For example, Tran Xuan Bach used *Tien Phong* magazine in his calls for political reform, while the former foreign minister and Politburo member, Nguyen Co Thach, used the magazine *International Relations* to expound his views before the promulgation of Resolution 13 that led to the withdrawal from Cambodia in 1989 and improvement of relations with ASEAN and the West. Despite support and encouragement from senior leaders, with the strict publication laws editors have to be cautious. Many will simply not want to tie their future to the political fortunes of individual leaders when the consequences are incalculable. (If a leader falls from grace, anything leaked to a friendly journal or publication could get the editor a fifteen-year prison sentence for revealing state secrets.)

Dissidents have demanded but two things: an end to state and party censorship, implying the disbanding of the Central Committee's Ideology and Culture Commission, and the freedom to establish independent publications or other media outlets.

Regarding censorship, the dissidents insist that "the press must be allowed to operate independently of the government and is under no control or order from anyone." Although under Nguyen Van Linh, actual press censorship was abandoned, the party continues to control the press through the Central Committee's Ideology and Culture Commission

(ICC). This is done through monthly meetings with the key personnel of the print and electronic media to discuss their performance, and includes meetings with top party leaders themselves, such as at the November 1998 meeting between Le Kha Phieu and senior editors. The editor of *Trui Tre*, Le Van Nuoi, told the *Far Eastern Economic Review* that in these meetings "they [the ICC] directly criticize us. We not only listen to their assessment, but also respond to their criticism."[80] With its editorial boards the party is able to discipline and control the media through instruction and criticism; the resulting fear leads to overcautious self-censorship.

To counter this, Hoang Tien wrote a letter to the party on 6 November 1996 demanding that the ICC be disbanded, because it "is simply an informant's organization to spy on and control the thinking of intellectuals, artists, newspaper staffs, and editors."[81] Disbanding the ICC would have one other profound effect: it would lead to changes in how Vietnamese journalists are trained. The "curriculum at journalism schools here," according to one young journalist, "focuses too much on the party's history and ideology rather than reporting and writing skills."[82] Without the ICC's dictating curricula, Vietnamese journalists would be far better trained to act as independent reporters and watchdogs, rather than as disseminators of party platforms and policies.

The second demand of the dissidents is the abolition of the government and party's monopoly of the media and the concurrent legalization of privately owned and operated news media. This is a major point of the dissidents, many of whom were victims in the *Nhan Van–Giai Pham* affair, and it is really an outrage to those who fought against the French for, even under the colonial regime, private ownership of news media was not illegal—a point noted by Nguyen Van Tran, Tran Do, Nguyen Huu Loan, and others. For Hoang Tien, it is absolutely essential to "recognize people's rights to privately form and publish newspapers," because without this right "discussions on democracy and civil rights are phony." Tran Do, likewise, demanded "new laws to allow private citizens to publish newspapers and to set up publishing houses. They only have to inform the government of their enterprises and obey all the laws of the land. They should not have to ask for permission from anyone [to do so]."[83] To this end, and clearly only to needle the government and the party, Tran Do applied for a license to start a newspaper in early 1999; the application was formally rejected that April.

It is important to note that there would be one additional benefit to the intellectuals in legalizing independent publications. The government has used not only the publishing of underground newspapers or jour-nals, but merely their possession, as a pretext to arrest dissidents. Aside from many like Duong Thu Huong, Ha Si Phu, and Le Hong Ha, who were arrested for possessing the widely circulated October 1995 letter by Vo Van Kiet to the Politburo,[84] authorities have arrested others, such as Nguyen Thanh Giang, just for having a volume of Nguyen Chi Thien's illegally published poems, *Flowers from Hell*. Giang was ar-rested again in March 1999 and charged under article 82 of the crimi-nal code for disseminating "antisocialist propaganda." According to Human Rights Watch, article 82 "criminalizes the mere act of express-ing a political opinion seen as injurious to the state or keeping or circu-lating material that does the same."[85]

Conclusion

Despite its having one of the most literate societies in the world, there is little intellectual freedom or freedom of expression in Vietnam. Al-though there have been vast improvements since 1986 when Nguyen Van Linh implemented *doi moi,* especially in the visual arts, the press and publishing houses are constrained by the party. Stifling controls re-main, as do severe punishments for those who violate the boundaries set by the party. Many authors continue to experience difficulty in try-ing to publish their works.

Freedom of the press and freedom of expression remain the utmost goals of the intellectuals. For them, such reforms would not only better intellectual discourse, but would lead to tangible benefits for society. Unlike the party, which believes that freedom of the press would give a voice to enemies of the state and thus cause instability and anarchy, the dissidents believe that freedom of the press will lead to less corruption and government mismanagement and provide the requisite transparency to run a market-based economy.

External pressure will have some positive effects on human rights and intellectual freedom issues in Vietnam: unlike China, Vietnam just does not have enough leverage to fend off foreign pressure. But we must be clear that exogenous forces will have only a minimal effect. Reform will come about because of the pressure brought by the intel-lectuals, the power of their arguments, and their ability to find allies in the government and party. Prime Minister Phan Van Khai, an advocate of economic liberalization, for example, has shown a greater tolerance for free speech than some of his colleagues. The dissidents will have to convince the party that press reform and intellectual freedom can serve the party's interests by making it more efficient, less corrupt, and more accountable to the people.

Such reforms are unlikely. If the people have a free press and are able to articulate their views, then they will begin to find like-minded individuals and groups with whom they can organize, form alliances, and appeal to a broader audience. Like freedom of the press, freedom of association would undermine the VCP's monopoly of power. To this end, the party has moved quickly to suppress any unofficial newspapers and journals, as well as any autonomous group that is not controlled by the VCP or its umbrella organization, the Vietnam Fatherland Front. This was clearly the case in the late 1980s with Vietnam's first and only independent pressure group, the Club of Former Resistance Fighters.

Notes

1. Vladimir Lenin, "Party Organization and Party Literature," 1905, in Robert C. Tucker, ed. and trans., *The Lenin Anthology* (New York: Norton, 1975), 148–153.

2. Maxim Gorky, "Soviet Literature," Address Delivered to the First All-Union Congress of Soviet Writers, 17 August 1934, in Maxim Gorky, *On Literature: Selected Articles* (Moscow: Foreign Languages Publishing House, n.d.), 228–268.

3. Mao Zedong, "Talks at the Yenan Forum on Literature and Art," 86.

4. "Night Falls on Morning News," *Far Eastern Economic Review* (*FEER*), 17 July 1981, 21.

5. Ibid., 21.

6. Nguyen Van Linh, "Let Writers and Artists Actively Contribute to Renovation," 6 October 1987, in *Vietnam Courier* 1 (1988), 12.

7. Ibid., 11.

8. Ibid., 12.

9. Cited in Nguyen Thu Lieu, "Artistic Freedom in Vietnam," *Vietnam Update* (Winter/Spring 1988): 12.

10. Full text of the Politburo resolution 5, printed in *Nhan Dan,* 5 December 1987, 1.

11. To Hoai, "Salient Features of Contemporary Literature," *Tap Chi Cong San* (hereafter *TCCS*) (April 1989), in Foreign Broadcast Information Service, *Daily Reports-East Asia* (hereafter *FBIS-EAS*), 8 June 1989, 70.

12. *Christian Science Monitor*, 8 June 1988. Also rehabilitated at this time was the musician and composer of the country's national anthem, Van Cao. His rehabilitation was not announced, but his music was published again, while a short article announcing his first recital "after that 30-year silence" was

published in *Vietnam Courier.* For more on his rehabilitation, see Murray Hiebert, "Anthem of Sorrows," *FEER,* 5 September 1991, 52.

13. Bui Tin, *Following Ho Chi Minh,* 145.

14. Nguyen Huy Thiep, *The General Retires and Other Stories,* trans. Greg Lockhart (Singapore: Oxford University Press, 1992).

15. Duong Thu Huong, *Novel Without a Name;* Bao Ninh, *The Sorrow of War;* Le Luu, *A Time Far Past,* trans. Ngo Vinh Hai, Nguyen Ba Chung, Kevin Bowen, and David Hunt (Amherst: University of Massachusetts Press, 1997).

16. Cited in Murray Hiebert, "Even War Heroes Cry," *FEER,* 31 October 1991, 55.

17. There is considerable archival evidence from Moscow that Ho was married to a high-level party cadre. For reporting on these archival findings and publishing a letter in Chinese that was signed "Your maladroit husband— The [Ho's pseudonym at the time]," Kim Khanh, the editor of the newspaper *Tuoi Tre,* was sacked. It is also a common rumor in Vietnam that Politburo member and speaker of the National Assembly, Nong Duc Manh, an ethnic Tai, is Ho's illegitimate son. See Sophie Quinn-Judge, "Ho Chi Minh: New Perspectives from the Comintern Files," *Viet Nam Forum* 14 (1994): 61–81; "Hanoi Editor Sacked Over Ho Chi Minh Report," *FEER,* 14 June 1991, 14.

18. Peter Zinoman, "Nguyen Huy Thiep's 'Vang Lua' and the Nature of Intellectual Dissent in Contemporary Viet Nam," *Viet Nam Forum* 14 (1994): 40.

19. Ibid., 36.

20. Nguyen Van Linh, "The Press and Renovation," speech given to the Regular Conference of Editors in Chief of Newspapers of Communist and Workers' Parties of Socialist Countries, Hanoi, 28 March 1988, in *Vietnam Courier* 6 (June 1988): 21.

21. Ibid., 21.

22. Cited in Gilles Campion, "Wind of Rebellion Blowing Among Newsmen," AFP, in *FBIS-EAS,* 21 June 1988, 63. *Lao Dong* is the official paper of the Vietnamese Confederation of Labor, the umbrella trade organization.

23. Ibid., 63.

24. Vasavakul, "Vietnam: The Changing Models of Legitimization," 285, esp. note 237.

25. Gareth Porter, "The Politics of 'Renovation' in Vietnam," 84.

26. Thai Duy, "An Abscess Has Been Lanced," *Dai Doan Ket,* 2 April 1988, in *JPRS-SEA,* 7 June 1988, 26–28.

27. See AFP, 21 June 1988, in *FBIS-EAS,* 21 June 1988, 63–64.

28. Murray Hiebert, "Mixed Signals," 37.

29. Nguyen Ngoc Giao, "The Media and the Emergence of Civil Society," paper presented at the Vietnam Update 1994 Conference: Doi Moi, the State and Civil Society, Australian National University, Canberra, 10–11 November 1994, ANU, 6.

30. Bui Tin, *Following Ho Chi Minh,* 156. Tran Do did send a letter to the congress in which he reiterated the points he made regarding intellectual freedom in Politburo Resolution 5.

31. Zinoman, "Nguyen Huy Thiep's 'Vang Lua' and the Nature of Intellectual Dissent," 36. Also see C. K. Nguyen, "Left to Write," *FEER,* 17 August 1989, 38; Murray Hiebert, "One Step Backward," *FEER,* 4 May 1989, 15.

32. "The Congress of the Vietnam Writers Association, A Report," in *Vietnam Commentary* (March–April 1990): 13-15.

33. Hanoi Domestic Service, 15 October 1989, in *FBIS-EAS,* 16 October 1989, 53–60.

34. Bui Minh Quoc was born on 3 October 1940, in Ha Tay Province. Along with his wife, Duong Thi Xuan Quy, he joined the VPA and fought for several years in the south. His wife died in battle in 1969. After the war, he became a party-government culture cadre and was appointed chairman of the Writers and Artists Association of Lam Dong Province. He later became editor in chief of *Lang Bian* magazine.

35. Bao Cu was born in Hue in 1945. During the war he joined both the NLF and the VCP. He was a standing member of the Lam Dong Province Artist Association and deputy editor in chief of *Lang Bian* magazine. This editor, poet, and artist now lives in Dalat, where he and his wife are repeatedly harassed by the police.

36. Tran Truong Tan, "How to Clearly Understand the CPV Central Committee Political Bureau's Conclusion on Political Work," 72.

37. Bao Cu, for example, began a letter-writing campaign to free his colleague. He wrote three articles, "Ha Si Phu: Symbol of Intellect and Freedom of Thought" (December 1995), "Ha Si Phu and the Strenuous Journey of the Vietnamese People," and "New Discoveries of the Trial" (September 1996), that were circulated among intellectuals and overseas Vietnamese.

38. Stein Tonneson, *Democracy in Vietnam* (Copenhagen: Nordic Institute of Asian Studies, 1993), Report No. 16, 26.

39. Mai Chi Tho, "Some Urgent Problems on Maintaining Security and Order and Building the People's Police," *TCCS* (December 1988), in *FBIS-EAS,* 10 February 1989, 57.

40. After the publication of the first issue, the club's leadership was ordered to cease publication by the Ho Chi Minh City Party Committee "because there are already too many papers and the situation is very difficult and complex." The membership rejected this and resolved to continue publication.

41. Two other contributing editors, Bui The Dung and Le The Hien, emigrated to the United States before the crackdown.

42. "Smash the Dark Schemes of Reactionary Forces at their Inception," *Sai Gon Gia Phong,* 6 May 1992, 2. Also see Human Rights Watch, *The Case of Doan Viet Hoat and Freedom Forum* 5, 1 (January 1993).

43. Doan Viet Hoat, an academic, former university vice chancellor, and leader of the Buddhist movement, was sentenced to fifteen years in prison. He was released in 1999 with Nguyen Dan Que and exiled to the United States. Nguyen Van Thuan, a poet and journalist, was arrested and sent to reeducation camps from 1975 to 1983. Arrested with Nguyen Dan Que in 1990, and sentenced to ten years in prison and five years under house arrest, he was sentenced to an additional eighteen years for his role in publishing *Freedom*

Forum. After suffering from a stroke in February 1994, he is currently in a prison hospital. Mai Trung Tinh is a poet and former radio commentator and Army of the Republic of Vietnam captain. In 1975 he was sent to a reeducation camp for seven years; he was arrested in November 1990 for his role in publishing *Freedom Forum* and was held for two years before being charged. He was sentenced to four years in prison. Upon release, he emigrated to the United States as part of the Orderly Departure Program. Pham Thai Thuy, a poet and journalist, was arrested in 1975 and held for eleven years. He then became an editor of *Freedom Forum* and was arrested again in 1990. He was released in 1994, and emigrated to the United States in August 1997. Pham Duc Kham was arrested in 1990 for his "antistate" activities and sentenced in 1993 to sixteen years for "plotting to overthrow the government." His sentence was later reduced to twelve years, and in a surprise move, he was released in September 1997 and exiled to the United States. Ostensibly released from detention for "humanitarian reasons," in a move seen as an attempt to improve ties with the United States, Nguyen Mau immigrated to Canada.

44. Tran Dao, "A Work of Art," in *Viet Nam Forum* 14 (1993): 45. See the translator's introduction by Phan Huy Duong and Nina McPherson.

45. Murray Hiebert, "Dissenting Voices," *FEER,* 2 December 1993.

46. Stein Tonneson, *Democracy in Vietnam,* 24.

47. Cited in Hiebert, "Even War Heroes Cry," 55.

48. Le Mai, "Thoughts on the Image of Communists in Literature," *TCCS* (February 1995): 38–40, 56, in *FBIS-EAS,* 15 June 1995, 67.

49. To Hoai, "Salient Features of Contemporary Literature," 70.

50. Ibid., 72.

51. Zinoman, "Nguyen Huy Thiep's 'Vang Lua' and the Nature of Intellectual Dissent," 36.

52. Tran Van Tra, *History of the Bulwark B2 Theater, Vol. 5: Concluding the 30-Years War* (Ho Chi Minh City: Van Nghe Publishing House 1982). Only 10,000 copies were printed before it was quickly banned. Most copies were destroyed, and only volume 5 survived. It was reprinted in JPRS, *Southeast Asian Report* (Document No. 1247), 2 February 1983.

53. Nguyen Chi Thien, *Flowers from Hell* (New Haven, Conn.: Yale University Program on Southeast Asia Studies, 1984). Thien arrived in the United States on 1 November 1995.

54. Ha Si Phu, *Tuyen Tap* (Garden Grove, Calif.: Phong Trao Nhan Quyen Cho Viet Nam 2000, 1996).

55. Cited in Andrew Solomon, "Vietnamese General Hits out at Communist Party," Reuters, 11 January 1999.

56. Greg Torrode, "Internet Gives 'Perfect Excuse' to Oust General," *South China Morning Post* (hereafter *SCMP*), 9 January 1999.

57. Article 3 states, "Before being exported, all cultural items included in the following list must have written consent from the department head at the ministry level (for central offices) or at the provincial level (for local offices) that are charged with authorities to control the content of these cultural items and to issue permits for customs processes: Group A: 1. Documents, papers and published materials for internal circulation, documents belonging to the

State catalog. 2. Documents, papers, articles, drawings, maps that are printed, typed, handcopied, duplicated, photocopied, or by any other means; and of any contents; sent or hand-carried abroad for reprinting, research, teaching, science reports, speeches to international conferences and meetings."

58."We believe item 2, group A, article 3 of Directive 893, dated July 20, 1992 by the Culture and Information Ministry is unconstitutional, violating citizens' right to their freedom of expression, violating their human rights, and especially violating articles 50, 53, 69, 146 of the Constitution and the Universal Declaration of Human Rights which Vietnam solemnly signed and pledged to abide by."

59. VNS, "Nguyen Duc Binh Attends Mass Media Series," 8 December 1992, in *FBIS-EAS,* 8 December 1992.

60. *Nhan Dan,* 16 February 1993, 3.

61. Anh Duc lost his position as chair of the Ho Chi Minh City chapter of the VWA on 11 January 1993; Anh Chuong and Tran Thi Vinh, both members of the VWA executive committee, were expelled and became targets of police investigations; Duong Thu Huong resigned from the organization because of its dictatorial style. See "Crackdown on Writers in Vietnam," *Vietnam Democracy* (April 1993): 6.

62. BBC, Summary of World Broadcasts, FE/1761 B/6, 7 August 1993.

63. Tonneson, *Democracy in Vietnam,* 27.

64. "Vietnam to Strengthen Party Controls Over Press," Reuters, 23 August 1997.

65. "Vietnam Launches Broadside at Western Press Ideals," Reuters, 26 August 1997.

66. Ibid.

67. It was unclear whether he would still be charged for "revealing state secrets" at a later date. See "Hanoi Delays Trial of 'Democracy Abuse' Editor," Reuters, 24 August 1998.

68. Human Rights Watch, *Behind Vietnam's Open Door: A Climate of Internal Repression,* November 1997. Also see Amnesty International, "Newspaper Editor Arrested and Detained," 13 October 1997.

69. "Vietnam's Press Told to Toe the Party Line," Reuters, 21 January 1998. With the launching of Le Kha Phieu's November 1998 anticorruption drive, the media had been directed to lead the attack on corruption, smuggling, and waste. According to Ta Huu Thanh, in five months *Nhan Dan* alone had published "nearly 90 stories reflecting the determination of central authorities and the people to promote thrift and anti-corruption measures throughout society." See VNS, "Media Should Lead Evils Fight," *Vietnam News,* 31 March 1999.

70. "Vietnam Party Leader Warns Press to Toe the Line," Reuters, 28 November 1998.

71. "New Press Law Clarifies Controlling Agency," Vietnam News Service, 20 May 1999.

72. "Vietnam Clamps Down on Free Speech," AP, 7 June 1999.

73. Huw Watkin, "Books Ruled too Hot to Read," *SCMP,* 11 April 2000.

74. John Pomfret, "The New Censorship in China: Anatomy of a Book-Banning," *Boston Globe,* 2 July 2000, A16.

75. Tran Do, "State of the Nation," Appendix, 11.

76. Ibid.

77. Ibid.

78. Phan Dinh Dieu, "On the Need to Continue Reform," 4–5.

79. Ibid., 4.

80. Hiebert, "No Longer Paper Tigers," *FEER*, 1992.

81. Tien was summoned to the Permanent Standing Committee of the National Assembly after writing to the National Assembly's Chairman Nong Duc Manh, in which he demanded freedom of speech and the press. He claims he was interrogated rather than being given a chance to "exchange views" as he had been promised.

82. Huw Watkin, "Reigns on Foreign Media Loosened," *SCMP,* 23 June 2000.

83. Tran Do, "State of the Nation," Appendix, 11.

84. This twenty-two-page document attacked orthodox conservative positions and called for, first, the abandonment of a "class-conflict" view of the world because "the struggle between the socialist and capitalist blocs or the struggle between the classes were" no longer relevant. Second, Kiet called for a greater economic role for private enterprise and the "elimination or any form of business by state-sponsored civil organizations, the party, or armed forces," (i.e., the sacrosanct but inefficient state-owned enterprises). Third, he attacked the slavish copying of the Chinese development model as the conservatives were doing, for the remaining socialist states were "still searching, feeling for a path suitable to each country." Fourth, Kiet advocated greater political reform and democratization. "In order to mobilize the genius of all within the party and promote transparency within the party," Kiet wrote, "there must be uncompromising democracy." Finally, Kiet argued the importance of getting the party out of the routine affairs of the government because "at present, if one examines the history of the development of renovation, one cannot say that our party has played the vanguard role in terms of ideas or has been training or supplying enough cadres to meet demands of the nation. . . . Nor can one say the intellectual and analytical levels of the absolute majority of the party members are compatible with the new demands and tasks of the revolution."

85. Human Rights Watch, "HRW Denounced Arrest of Vietnamese Dissident," 12 March 1999.

5

THE CLUB OF FORMER RESISTANCE FIGHTERS: DISSENSION FROM WITHIN

The basic fact is that in 1975 the leadership became lax, intoxicated with victory.

—*Bui Tin*

Listen land of the three rice growing regions,
Rice is still short for us all.
We have sung too much in praise of our potentials,
Our potentials are asleep.
—*From Nguyen Duy, "Wake Wake Our Sleeping Potential"*

One issue that has persistently beset the VCP since 1976 is criticism over its handling of national reconciliation. "Liberated" in April 1975 and formally "reunified" in 1976, the country still has some deep divisions that the regime refuses to acknowledge despite the passing of twenty-five-years. There are three issues regarding national reunification that the dissidents would like redress: First, there is resentment over Hanoi's handling of the economy, in general, but in particular the "transition to socialism" in the south. Second, Hanoi's political domination of the south and its treatment of former resistance fighters, the Viet Cong. Third, there is lingering resentment over Hanoi's reeducation program for southerners following the liberation of Saigon. As Bui Tin wrote, "National reconciliation, which had been the cornerstone of our policy before our victory, soon turned into recrimination" as over 300,000 southerners were sent off to be reeducated in labor camps.[1] These issues—Hanoi's mismanagement of the economy (the nation's in general, and the south's in particular), the failure to achieve a true spirit of national reconciliation by not recognizing the role of the southern revolutionaries, and treating southerners as the vanquished—became the concern of Vietnam's first independent pressure group, the Club of Former Resistance Fighters. Many of the issues in this chapter, such as legalization, democratization, marketization, and free speech, have already been raised, but I have kept this chapter separate for a reason.

The CFRF is an interesting case study in the limits of political expression and dissent in Vietnam: its membership was made up of exclusively party members, many of whom were very senior in the party apparatus in the south; it presents a test of both the right to organize and to free speech, and how the party will deal with such threats in the future; and it is important because of its goals. CFRF members sought to become an internal loyal opposition to the party, and were by no means advocating a multiparty democracy or an overthrow of the socialist system, but were fighting for the restoration of democratic centralism.

I will begin with a very brief overview of CFRF members' concerns over Hanoi's handling of national reconciliation. This is not meant to be a conclusive analysis of Hanoi's policies, but I include it to present the context in which the club emerged.

The Lingering Issues of National Reconciliation

The ill-conceived decision announced by General Secretary Le Duan at the VCP's Fourth National Congress to rapidly socialize the south to facilitate reunification led to terrible economic dislocations.[2] Despite the National Liberation Front's (NLF's) pledge to maintain the current economic system and gradually reunify the two halves of the country after the defeat of the Saigon regime, Hanoi made the decision to rapidly integrate the country, politically, economically, and socially. There was a sense among members of the Hanoi leadership that because the war was won unexpectedly quickly on their own terms, without a negotiated settlement, that they no longer had to negotiate political and economic integration. This entailed the rapid "socialization of the southern economy." As Politburo member Truong Chinh, who represented the north in the "unification talks," announced: "The strategic mission in our view in this new phase is to accelerate the unification of the country and lead the nation to a rapid, powerful advance toward socialism." South Vietnam would no longer be "a special case." To this end, new policies were implemented governing most every facet of the economy: currency reform that wiped out all personal savings, seizure of private property, nationalization of industry and trade, land reform, and the collectivization of agriculture.[3] In addition, the exodus of nearly a half-million ethnic

Chinese and Vietnamese refugees (resulting in the loss of Chinese aid),[4] as well as the "reeducation" of 300,000 southerners, including much of the intelligentsia, had the net effect of destroying the southern economy. These economic shocks were too much for a fragile economy that since the early 1960s had been geared solely toward the war effort and had been massively subsidized by the United States, distortions all too clear when most U.S. aid was cut after 1973.

With its lofty goals the Second Five-Year Plan estimated that national income would grow at a rate of 13 to 14 percent, but it grew only 0.5 percent, and industrial production, targeted for 16 to 18 percent growth, came in at just 0.6 percent.[5] Hanoi had planned agricultural output to increase by 8 to 10 percent since it now controlled the south, the country's rice basket. But the collectivization of agriculture in the Mekong Delta was disastrous: it was brutally implemented and was met with massive popular opposition. Real agriculture growth was only 1.9 percent during the plan period, and per capita agricultural output actually fell from 274 kilograms in 1976 to 266 kilograms in 1979. Due to the shockingly low economic growth, at the Sixth Plenum of the Central Committee in August 1979 the VCP abandoned its collectivization drive in the south.[6] Tremendous resentment exists to this day of Hanoi's mishandling the economy, a resentment that transcends all socioeconomic classes. Perhaps we should not be surprised that much of the pressure for economic reform, including the policy initiatives of *doi moi*, came from the south. Vo Chi Cong, for example, was the architect of the experimental system of agricultural production contracts that saw the rapid increase in output in the early 1980s, and that was implemented at the national level in 1986.[7] Nguyen Van Linh, who had been dropped in 1982, was quietly brought back into the Politburo in 1985 in recognition of the success of the reforms he had implemented as party chief in Ho Chi Minh City. Four of the top five positions in the Politburo of the Sixth Central Committee Plenum, which implemented *doi moi*, were held by southerners. Southern leaders have a reputation for being far more pragmatic and laissez-faire, perhaps because there is far more lateral interaction in the south between business and government officials.[8] Since *doi moi* was launched in 1986, growth rates in the south have far surpassed those in the north, and southerners take rueful pride in the fact that they have been the engine of growth and that policies emanating from Hanoi hold the south back.

By almost every economic measurement, the south is far more advanced than the north. It has attracted the majority of the country's foreign investment, exports the bulk of the country's manufactured goods and foodstuffs, and has a far higher per capita income. For example, of the top fifteen provincial recipients of foreign investment, the six from the south have received nearly twice the amount of capital than those in the north, $19.86 billion as opposed to $10.45 billion. Indeed, Ho Chi Minh City alone has more foreign investment ($11 billion) than Hanoi, Haiphong, and the other top four provinces in the north combined. Many in the south feel that the more ideological northerners and their majority in the party leadership hold the country back. Hanoi's ideological rigidity and social conservatism infuriates the more freewheeling capitalist south, which believes that politics has greatly interfered with economic development. In May 2000, the Ho Chi Minh City leadership was so frustrated over red tape from Hanoi it felt was driving foreign investors out of the country that it announced unilateral approval of foreign investments if the approval process in Hanoi took more than two weeks.[9] And southern leaders were far more vociferous in their support of the bilateral trade agreement with the United States that would greatly benefit the efficient and export-oriented southern economy far more than the north's, whose inefficient state-owned enterprises would face a barrage of foreign competition.[10]

The second cause for resentment of Hanoi stems from Hanoi's denigration of the role of the southern revolutionaries, the Viet Cong, in the War of National Liberation, and the leadership's betrayal of the Provisional Revolutionary Guard (PRG) and NLF after the war.[11] Hanoi remains transfixed by the devastation U.S. B-52s inflicted on the north, but the south was really the focus of the war. Most casualties, civilian and military, occurred in the south, as did most of the physical destruction. Campaigns such as the Tet Offensive in 1968, which had been planned and ordered by Hanoi, nearly wiped out the Viet Cong forces, so that after 1968 the liberation of the south was primarily conducted by northern regulars. Indeed, the image of North Vietnamese tanks breaking down the gates of the Republic of Vietnam's presidential palace overshadows the role of the *Viet Cong* in the war. While memoirs of Hanoi's senior generals were published, the memoirs of the Viet Cong leaders, such as Tran Van Tra, were either not published or were banned outright.[12]

Duong Quynh Hoa, one of the founders of the NLF and the PRG Minister of Health, considers this one of Hanoi's greatest mistakes: "Without the people of South Vietnam, Hanoi would never have won the war. It was not the forces of North Vietnam that won the war. It was the guerillas and their supporters in the south."[13] However, even in the middle of the Asian economic crisis and a severe economic downturn, the government decided to erect yet another monument to commemorate its liberation of Saigon and build another museum in Hanoi to celebrate the north's victory over the U.S. bombing campaign, and embark on a pomp-filled month-long celebration to commemorate the twenty-fifth anniversary celebrations of its victory in the south.[14]

Since Hanoi never had any intention of abiding by the Paris peace accords, it also had no intention of keeping its promise to the PRG/NLF, which had hoped to establish an independent and neutral southern government that would gradually negotiate reunification with the north. This betrayal stung many leading members of the PRG/NLF. After liberation, the North Vietnamese army's Military Management Committee ran the south, but the shortage of cadres in the south, due to war and outright assassination, was a serious concern for the party. By the end of the war there were only 200,000 Communist Party members in the south, and only 273,000 by the end of 1978, or only 1.3 percent of the south's population. By comparison, there were some 1,533,500 members nationwide, an average of 3.13 percent of the population, and party members constituted 6.3 percent of the population in the north.[15] To make up for this shortage Hanoi began to dispatch cadres to the south en masse. Hanoi was very wary of attempts to recruit in the south because most families had some members with ties to the government and army of the Republic of Vietnam, almost automatically disqualifying most from consideration for membership. Moreover, since the peasants had not yet been collectivized, there was no real proletariat, and students and intellectuals were considered too bourgeois. So, there were no significant groups with the correct class consciousness from which to recruit. In addition, many of the southern party members were treated with suspicion because they were seen as corrupt and tainted by their exposure to capitalism. In short, the north treated the south as conquered territory and southerners as mostly untrustworthy.

The leading PRG/NLF officials were trusted and recruited to serve in the unified government, but according to Truong Nhu Tang, "like me, most of these veteran revolutionaries put up an initial fight, refusing to cooperate once they discovered they were involved in a farce."[16] Hanoi then began to denigrate the independent role of the southerners. As Nguyen Khac Vien wrote before he became critical of the regime, "The PRG was always simply a group emanating from the DRV. If we [the DRV] had pretended otherwise for such a long period, it was only because during the war we were not obligated to unveil our cards."[17] At that point there was no longer any pretense, according to Tang:

> Now with total power in their hands, they [leaders of the DRV] began to show their cards in a most brutal fashion. They made it understood that the Vietnam of the future would be a single monolithic bloc, collectivist and totalitarian in which all the traditions and culture of the south would be ground and molded by the political machine of the conquerors. They, meanwhile, proceeded to install themselves with no further regard for the niceties of appearance.[18]

Indeed, the president of the NLF, Nguyen Huu Tho, who never challenged Hanoi on this point, was the most successful in his rise in the communist bureaucracy, culminating in the chairmanship of the VFF. But even he was never elected to the Central Committee, the party's top decisionmaking body. Others, including advocates of reunification like Duong Quynh Hoa, were angered at Hanoi's "clumsy" handling of reunification. "It was too rapid, it came too soon," she said. And rather than accept the offer to serve as the nation's minister of health, she instead resigned from the party to concentrate on her pediatric practice, disgusted that the party was doing little for the people once it was in power.[19]

Yet if members of the NLF and PRG felt betrayed, they paled in comparison with the sentiments of the southern population in general. In Gen. Tran Van Tra's first speech as chairman of the Military Management Committee, on 7 May 1975, he gave no indication of the retribution that was to come. "Only the U.S. imperialists have been defeated. . . . All Vietnamese are victors. . . . The grandchildren and children of all strata of the new society will from now on be able to grow up with a spirit of national pride, hold their heads high, be happy, be provided for, and be able to work in the most brilliant period of development of this country."

Over 300,000 South Vietnamese were sent to long-term reeducation camps that, in reality, were nothing more than forced labor camps in "new economic zones." Their families were persecuted, and class labels were applied that prevented the offspring of "class enemies" from getting an education, attending a university, or getting a good job with any hope for advancement. For many, this was a terrible mistake, because it was the platform of "National Concord and Reconciliation" that had won the PRG/NLF so much popular support. The original thirty-day reeducation program as conceived by the PRG was usurped by the Politburo, which used it to punish southern collaborators it believed to be war criminals. Bui Tin wrote, "In the eyes of our communist leaders, an 'enemy puppet' whether alive or dead, was always a puppet, a second-class citizen or somebody who had no citizen rights at all."[20] For Tang, the reeducation campaign was an egregious violation of the PRG/NLF's position, and "to my mind vicious and ultimately destructive to the nation."[21]

Bui Tin felt personally betrayed by the policy. As he had commented to President Duong Van Minh upon the surrender of the Republic of Vietnam on 30 April 1975, "You have nothing to fear. Between Vietnamese there are no victors and vanquished. Only Americans have been beaten. If you are patriots, consider this a moment of joy. The war for our country is over."[22] In his memoir, he recounts that soon afterward a medical professor complained to him that

> your mistake is that you have never looked at this question properly. You just put everything in the same basket: Puppets are all worthless and untrustworthy and must be totally discarded, while revolutionaries are all good and better than anyone at all from the previous regime. And you view their offspring in the same rigid way. You are imbued with a firm class viewpoint. So how can you stabilize society, make people feel at ease and help the country develop?[23]

Bui Tin agreed with the criticism and concluded that the party caused irreconcilable harm by dogmatically applying such a policy. He summed up the problem while in exile in France:

> It is regrettable we did not pursue a policy of true national reconciliation after our victory in 1975. . . . Alas, we did not adopt such a course. Instead of declaring a general amnesty and forsaking hatred we applied a very harsh and inhuman policy of revenge. We were full of arrogance, subjectivism, complacency, and total disregard for the need to have good managers (our former enemies) for the country after victory.[24]

It is a sentiment that has diminished with the passage of time and with new generations, but it still lingers. Hanoi has not paid enough attention to the social impact of its policies that caused the exodus of hundreds of thousands of its citizens, including leading intellectuals, bureaucrats, community leaders, businessmen, and economic managers. It should come as no surprise that the first organized opposition to party policies emanated from the south.

The Club of Former Resistance Fighters

The Club of Former Resistance Fighters (Cau Lac Bo Nhung Nguoi Khang Chien Cu) was co-founded by Nguyen Ho[25] and other senior southern revolutionaries, including La Van Lam,[26] Do Trung Hieu,[27] Tran Van Giau,[28] Tran Bach Dang[29] and Tran Nam Trung,[30] in 1986 initially to address veterans' issues.[31] From improving the standard of living of veterans, the CFRF went on to address such issues as corruption, mismanagement of the economy, incompetence of party leaders, and improving the conditions for national reconciliation. The CFRF saw itself as a loyal opposition to the party. This was the first and only attempt to create an organized pressure group within the VCP. Founded in Ho Chi Minh City, its branches spread throughout the south. At its inception, the CFRF claimed 4,000 members and quickly grew to 10,000 by 1988, most of whom were party members.

The club was tolerated for several years but only because of the stature of its members, who included the war hero and chairman of the Military Control Committee that governed Saigon following liberation, Gen. Tran Van Tra, a "senior advisor" to the club. Other high-ranking members included Tran Bach Dang, the former Saigon Party Committee secretary, and Nguyen Ho, the Saigon People's Committee chairman (i.e., mayor). Many of the leaders also had close personal ties to General Secretary Nguyen Van Linh, with whom they had worked during the war when he was secretary of the Central Office for South Vietnam (COSVN,[32] Trung ung Cue Mien Nam) and afterwards when he was the Ho Chi Minh City party chief. They actively supported his promotion to VCP general secretary, anticipating that he would be responsive to the needs and concerns of southerners and implement at the national level the successful economic reforms that had been tested in the south.

The organization maintained a very low profile in its first year of existence. The organization first came to the party's attention in April 1988, when Prime Minister Pham Hung, the last of the first-generation leaders still in office, died and thus forced a leadership contest. The Politburo tapped the dour conservative Do Muoi from Haiphong, the vice chairman of the Council of Ministers and currently the fourth-ranked member of the Politburo. Muoi's selection caused considerable consternation among CFRF members because he was the party official sent to Saigon in 1976 to oversee the disastrous socialization of the southern economy. In a very oblique criticism of the party's candidate, the club urged the National Assembly not to elect people who are "conservative, slow, mandarinal, mechanical, say a lot but do little, say one thing and do another, who has committed serious errors which have led to long term disastrous consequences."[33] In their letter, the CFRF urged the National Assembly to hold truly democratic elections free from party interference and domination. Club members advocated the use of a secret ballot for this and all future decisions rather than the public roll call that deterred members from voting against the party. This letter was signed by 100 officials, including Gen. Tran Van Tra; Gen. Nam Long; Nguyen Van Tran, former ambassador to the Soviet Union; Maj.-Gen. Phan Trong Tue, former minister of transport and communication; Nguyen Khanh, former ambassador to China; and Ha Huy Giap, former vice-minister of education.

Although it was clear that the Politburo's choice would prevail, many in addition to CFRF members were willing to support an alternative to pressure the Politburo to implement further economic reforms. In communist systems shot through with factionalism, competition among informal groups is a common occurrence during periods of leadership transition, but what is uncommon is that the competition becomes so overt. The CFRF publicly supported Vo Van Kiet, the chairman of the State Planning Commission, a fellow southerner, a leading communist official in the south during the war, and a leading proponent of economic reform—and so it openly criticized the party's candidate. The club wrote letters in support of Kiet and actively lobbied members of the National Assembly. That the CFRF was willing to challenge the Politburo earned it tremendous support and tacit sympathy. To that end, of the 464 delegates at the National Assembly, an unprecedented 168 (36 percent) went against the Politburo and voted for Kiet. In the context of a communist system, where the legislature is supposed to be nothing more than a rubber stamp to ratify party decisions, this was a terrible slap in the face for the leadership. However, club members ended up very upset with Nguyen Van Linh, who they thought should have been a forceful advocate for their candidate and fellow southerner Vo Van Kiet; yet Linh, ever the party loyalist, did not join his fellow southerners and supported Do Muoi.

The following year, in 1989, the CFRF became bolder and began a letter-writing campaign to the Central Committee and the National Assembly. General Secretary Nguyen Van Linh was invited to meet with members of the club and actually came to discuss political reforms and improvements in individual freedoms. Until the Communist Party in Eastern Europe came under attack, Linh was willing to meet with such groups to seek input and build consensus for the reform program. Linh did not impose policies; that was not his style. Instead he sought to forge a durable consensus after listening to all groups and sectors. In early 1989, he was willing to meet with this important constituency that was instrumental in his own election as general secretary.

But the CFRF was looking for a wider audience and a more institutionalized role, so it began to publish its own newsletter—even though, almost at the outset, the party banned it. The first one published in September 1988 and entitled *Tradition of Resistance: Voices of the Resistance Fighters,* had a series of articles that lashed out at the party's policy of hasty reunification and the immediate dropping in 1975 of the "united front" relationship with the PRG/NLF. After the publication of the second issue, the party ordered the CFRF to cease publication. Club members unanimously refused, and the third issue was printed clandestinely in a Mekong Delta town in December after the police had seized the original printing plates in Saigon. Also, the CFRF publicly, and angrily, demanded that the minister of information in Hanoi explain why he was violating article 67 of the constitution, which guaranteed freedom of speech. Neither the government nor the party replied and the ban continued.

The December issue of the newsletter contained the boldest attacks to date on the party and political system, "which bred conceit, arrogance, making change more and more difficult as time goes on." In a stinging criticism of the leadership, one commentator demanded their resignations: "We think that to renovate things quickly and efficiently, we must begin at the central echelon and renovate from the top down. Renovations must begin with politics if we want to renovate the economy. If we keep the existing political forces and conservative minds, renovation will be limited or it will not be able to achieve anything."[34]

But the club's outspokenness began to hurt it. At the Central Committee's Third Plenum in March 1989, Linh attacked the CFRF and warned that "any scheme to play down or neutralize the party leadership or create counterforces to the party in the society must be prevented." This, along with the fear caused by the collapse of socialism in Eastern Europe, created a fierce conservative backlash in the party in late 1989 and into 1990, culminating in Tran Xuan Bach's being fired (see Chapter 3). The CFRF was seen as a leading force of intraparty opposition, intolerable in the context of events in Hungary and other Eastern European states, where groupings within the Communist Party had split off and founded independent parties. In an August 1989 Central Committee communiqué, the Vietnamese party warned that a number of cadres and members "have shown some deviations, which if not corrected in time may lead to no small harm." The communiqué urged party members to "firmly oppose any ill-intentioned attack directed at the party's leadership and the state's management."[35]

The CFRF never actually advocated a multiparty democratic system, even though the club was critical of the pace of the reform program, and it did call for greater political openness as well as the independence of the National Assembly from party control. The CFRF also vehemently criticized the election of incompetent cadres and the appointment of "reds" rather than experts. Club members simply wanted to broaden the scope of intraparty debate because any democratic centralism was stifled by a top leadership that was out of touch with the people and unfamiliar with local conditions. Rather than a multiparty system, the CFRF wanted a vigorous debate within the party so that the party itself would be strengthened. It was only through a competitive process that sound socioeconomic policies could be formulated, reversing the unquestioned and unchallenged authority of party leaders that had led to years of policies causing the stagnation of the economy.

The CFRF was not procapitalist by any means: it saw a predominant role for the VCP in any future government. As Nguyen Ho said in a December 1988 speech to the club, "Vietnam hasn't advanced to socialism. Vietnam is the poorest and most backward country in the world at present. The influence and prestige of the party and socialism has seriously declined among the people and in the world. That is a great disaster for the party and the people."[36] The club members' goal was to force the party's hand and to implement meaningful economic reform so that the party would regain the support of the people. "In other peoples' countries," Nguyen Ho complained, "if there is 7–10 percent inflation, the Prime Minister must resign. In our country, they not only don't resign but get promoted." Club members understood that the legitimacy that the party had earned in defeating the Americans would be squandered without delivering economic development to the people. The CFRF was outspoken about internal corruption and launched virulent attacks on the party's failure to eliminate poverty, especially in the countryside, the cradle of the revolution where the VCP's policies had caused "misery and famine." Another article in *Tradition of Resistance* bemoaned the plight of the peasants who are "demonstrating in many provinces, struggling to oppose the new bullies who pressure them, steal their land and beat them, and who are facing serious famine . . . to say nothing of people dying of starvation."

Nguyen Ho was upset that Vietnam's neighbors, at the same time, had surpassed Vietnam by becoming "strong, wealthy and happy." "In the same 13 years [that Vietnam had been reunified], four imposing dragons have appeared in Southeast Asia, which achieved very strong economic performance and enjoyed a high standard of living," and that "through its own economic strength, South Korea was able to successfully organize the Olympics because of their high level of development, technology, standard of living and organizational capacities. A starving country like ours couldn't possibly hold an Olympics."[37]

Such comments, considering from whom they came, deserved a response. In a 19 October 1988 speech to the Vietnamese Trade Union Federation, Do Muoi responded: "We shouldn't compare ourselves to those four dragons because if Vietnam becomes a dragon it will have to lower the flag of Marxism-Leninism." An article in *The Tradition of Resistance* retorted: "The communist party and Marxism-Leninism are still there, but why is it that Vietnam was unable to develop to the point that it has become 201 of 203 countries in the world? From this, people have gained the impression that the flag of Marxism-Leninism in Vietnam has been lowered and that the VCP has been obscured—not by any external pressure but by what it has done to itself."

Many members were highly critical of the monopoly of power at the party's top and the total secrecy in which decisions were made. But any calls for reform were not radical; most simply wanted the party itself, as opposed to society in general, to democratize. Duong Van Dieu wrote that there was a "gang" of "obstructionist elements" that would not allow this. Another member wrote that

> for democracy and openness to be truly realized, I think the example must be set by the Central Committee. . . . If this situation of distrust and even understanding things in a different way continues, it will only create suspicion and a lack of confidence in the leadership and in the direction of the party. I believe the party should give an explanation—better late than never—which would prove that democracy is more than a slogan.

Citing the democratic reforms within the Communist Party of the Soviet Union implemented by President Mikhail Gorbachev, members called for major overhauls of political discourse at party congresses to allow greater debate and the ability to challenge Politburo edicts. Such calls for intraparty political reform touched a raw nerve. The party was alarmed at the club's January 1990 meeting, at which some 600 members met to discuss the situation in Eastern Europe. In particular, the case of Hungary, where a multiparty system had emerged from competing factions in the Hungarian Communist Party, based on regions and economic interests emanating from the country's long experiment with market reforms, was closely analyzed. Club members understood that reform creates competing interests, both regional and economic, which need to have channels to forward their interests. Tang argued that "our main difference with the [party] leadership is that we favor political change in unison with economic liberalization, whereas they think that they can get away with the latter without addressing the former. Tiananmen should serve as a warning to the party that this is a dangerous line to pursue."[38] The party insisted that it alone had the responsibility for articulating the interests of the nation as a whole.

The Party's Response to the Club

The comments and criticism were not easy for the party to countenance, but in the context of the collapse of socialism in Eastern Europe and the conservative backlash that ensued, the party believed that it had no choice but to crack down on the organization. And with the Central Committee's Eighth Plenum about to be convened and the Seventh Party Congress the following year, the leadership moved quickly to silence its most influential group of critics. Nonetheless, because of the organization's popularity and its members' stature, the party had to be very careful in disbanding the CFRF. Instead of heavy-handed tactics, such as banning the group and arresting its leaders, the party set out to first marginalize the CFRF, to make it irrelevant and incapable of winning popular support by removing its charismatic and influential leadership.

The first thing that the party did was a standard Communist Party tactic. To diminish the club's stature, in 1990 the party established its own national-level nonpolitical Vietnam Veterans' Organization (Hoi Cuu Chien Binh Viet Nam) for all veterans, as opposed to a distinctly southern organization for Viet Cong members. The new organization was put under the control and "guidance" of the Vietnam Fatherland Front, the party's umbrella agency for mass organizations. More important, Gen. Tran Van Tra, the CFRF's most famous and influential member, was tapped to serve as the new organization's southern committee chairman. He could not turn down this appointment and thus had no choice but to resign from the CFRF.[39] The party and state threw their weight and resources behind the new veterans' organization, and by the end of 1990 the organization had chapters in forty-four provinces and cities with a total membership of 900,000 people.[40]

The party then orchestrated the removal of CFRF Chairman Nguyen Ho and his vice chairman, Ta Ba Tang. The party claimed that the leadership change was an internal decision made at its 4 March meeting, but one CFRF source told the *Far Eastern Economic Review* that "orders came from the very top," and Ta Ba Tang asserted that "it was party general secretary Linh who gave the order that pressure be brought to bear on the committee."[41] The CFRF would only be allowed to continue if it fell into line and replaced its two leaders with two less well-known members, thought by the party to be more malleable. This vote and the party's bidding were thought to be orchestrated by Nguyen Van Hang, a club member, but also a cadre in the party's mass organization, the VVF. "The Club was too influential to be closed down," Ta Ba Tang explained. "So we have to be toned down instead. The new 10-man provisional committee comprises 'yes men' who are dissatisfied with many things but will always do what they are told in the end."[42]

The change in leadership severely affected the CFRF and its mission. The new leaders were not courageous enough to speak out and criticize the party; they were politically weaker and more pliable. More important, they lacked the charisma of their predecessors. The new chairman, Pham Khai, tried to alleviate the concerns of the members by making a very liberal speech at the 7 January 1990 meeting of the CFRF. But without the stature of a Nguyen Ho or General Tra, he was far more cautious and less able to galvanize members and their sympathizers into action. The two vice-chairmen, Nguyen Duc Hung and Huynh Van Tieng, were also unknown and remained reticent. "This was a serious setback for those of us hoping to see the party reform itself politically," according to Ta Ba Tang.[43] When the controversy started to die down, and it was clear that the new leadership was ineffective, the party quietly banned the organization in March 1990. There was no public protest.

The Aftereffects

Immediately after the CFRF was banned, Nguyen Ho announced his resignation from the VCP on 21 March 1990, after fifty-one years of membership. One month later several leading members, including Ta

Ba Tang, Ho Van Hieu, Do Trung Hieu, and Le Dinh Manh, were arrested. Ho was also detained in September 1990, released, and imprisoned a second time from March 1994 to March 1995. Since then he has been under house arrest. But his resignation and subsequent arrests only emboldened Ho to take on the party more vigorously. On 23 June 1995, he was informed that he was to be arrested again for his continued writings. He turned over two writings, one that called *doi moi* "insincere" and the other that sought to promote real national reconciliation. In *The Solution of Reconciliation and Harmony,* Nguyen Ho attacked the party for failing to reconcile with the people and continuing to divide Vietnamese society.

> So, even though the war had long ended, animosities between sections of the population and the current regime in Vietnam remain wide, deep and have never been defused. And worse, the oppressions, arrests, detainments, imprisonments of the religious (Buddhists, Catholics, etc.), intellectuals, writers, poets, lawyers, physicians, conscientious party members, former resistant fighters, just because they dared to have different opinions from those of the party continued unabatedly.[44]

But what galled Ho the most seemed to be the VCP's foreign policy centered around renormalizing ties with its former enemies, while there were no concurrent moves domestically.

> In the post–Cold War era, reconciliation and cooperation between former enemies have started and quickly multiplied, so the task of bringing reconciliation and harmony back among the Vietnamese people is ever more urgent. . . . Along with the world trend, the VCP has quickly reconciled and unprecedentedly tightly cooperated with former archenemies of the people such as the imperialist Americans, French, Japanese, South Koreans, ASEAN, Chinese. Why could the VCP not reconcile with its own Vietnamese brothers who have been subjected to its oppression and victimization? Have dollars been the condition for reconciliation? Without U.S. dollars, reconciliation cannot exist? If that is the truth, then it is such a sadness and an insult for the unfortunate Vietnamese people. However, I hope that never is the truth.[45]

But Ho understood that the party is resistant to embark on a policy of real reconciliation for three reasons. First, reconciliation would mean an admission of wrongdoing. As Ho noted, the party would have to "reconcile with those that have been victims of false accusations, oppressions, terrorizations, incarcerations, confiscations, and killings by the VCP."[46] Put simply, even if the party decided to reconcile with those who it wronged, it does not have any confidence that if it could start down that road that it could control the process or the outcome.

Second, real reconciliation would entail the two parties' being equals, and the VCP will not countenance democracy or any reforms that could jeopardize its own monopoly of power. The VCP claims to represent all sectors of society, and by negotiating reconciliation it would be giving them de facto autonomy.

Third, national reconciliation would have to include the overseas Vietnamese community, which fled because of the communist takeover of the south. This was an exodus that many in the south believe could have been avoided if the north had not used such heavy-handed tactics. Reconciliation with the overseas Vietnamese should be of paramount importance to Hanoi, according to Ho, for they could play an important role in the country's industrialization and modernization process.

> It is our strategy to maintain independence, to push forth reforms, to open up and merge with the world community. Only on the solid feet of our people can we avoid any foreign subordination. It is, therefore, important and urgent that we can utilize the collective strength of the 2 million overseas Vietnamese, whose total values are on par with a significant nation of the world (their incomes are higher than the GDP of the Socialist Republic of Vietnam: $16 billion from 70 million people). They also include the precious group of professionals (over 300,000) living and working all over the world, especially in Western countries. The experiences from years of rubbing their shoulders in the modern capitalist world have given our brothers and sisters worldclass qualities in various fields to participate in the building of democracy, developing the country, and helping Vietnam fly high. With the abundance of our intellectuals inside and outside Vietnam, why could Vietnam not turn into a 'Dragon' in the near future?[47]

In the same vein, Hoang Tien called on the party to "throw away those class animosities" and "look for common interests" with the *Viet kieu* community, which he calls a "considerable brain trust for the building of the country."[48] Bui Tin agreed, stating that the 2 million overseas Vietnamese "represent a great intellectual potential" because "they have acquired highly valuable experience in the fields of management and business" and are "versed in the social and experimental sciences."[49] He argued that "their potential can be mobilized" if a "policy of respect, overture and concord were pursued."

The relationship between Hanoi and the overseas Vietnamese community is complicated and well beyond the scope of this work. But, if

Mandy Thomas's findings are correct, then the general perception of Vietnamese is that the *Viet kieu* are no less patriotic or nationalistic, nor are they all politically motivated against the regime.[50] For the most part, they emigrated for economic reasons. If this is truly the case, then Hanoi should have less to fear from its compatriots than it does and should be far more willing to court them, especially in the context of the economic downturn and sudden decline in foreign investment due to the Asian financial crisis. The support of the overseas Vietnamese community is essential for the country's development: In 1998, when foreign investment from Asia had collapsed, the *Viet kieu* invested some $200 million in seventy projects.[51] In 1999, they remitted over $1.2 billion through official channels, nearly the same amount as the country received in foreign direct investment that year ($1.48 billion), and it was estimated that at least an equal amount was brought into the country through unofficial channels.

To that end, Hanoi made an important gesture by releasing from prison two overseas Vietnamese, Jimmy Tran and Ly Tong, as part of the general amnesty in September 1998 that also saw the release of dissidents Doan Viet Hoat and Nguyen Dan Que. Jimmy Tran had been arrested in 1993 for planning a grenade attack in Ho Chi Minh City in 1995, while Ly Tong was seized for hijacking an Vietnam Airlines jet, from which he dropped some 50,000 antigovernment leaflets.[52] The release of the two criminals, and both do clearly fall into that category, as distinct from prisoners of conscience, is indicative of Hanoi's need to foster better ties with the overseas community. Again in September 2000, the government released three more *Viet kieu* in its annual general amnesty. In January 2000, the government acknowledged the importance of getting the *Viet kieu* to "actively contribute to the cause of national construction" and eased the process for overseas Vietnamese to receive entry permits. But Bui Tin warns that even though the party is cognizant of the talents and skills of the *Viet kieu*, it truly does not trust them because they are "contaminated with democracy."[53] Hanoi's policies seem to be influenced not by the majority of the *Viet kieu* who seek a mutually beneficial relationship with their homeland, but with the politically active minority that is overtly hostile to the socialist regime.

Summary

The CFRF sought to be a loyal opposition within the VCP. It was frustrated with the pace of economic reforms and with Hanoi's failure to foster true national reconciliation, and with endemic corruption, lack of democratic centralism in the party, and arrogance and secretiveness among its top leaders. The club did not try to overthrow the VCP, but quite the opposite. The CFRF, made up almost completely of party members, was trying to strengthen the VCP by pushing through economic reform and ending official corruption, thus making the party more legitimate in the public's eyes. They understood that the party's hard-won legitimacy on the battlefield meant little to an impoverished populace. The party gained popular legitimacy through its leadership in the anti-imperial wars, but it had squandered that through years of economic mismanagement, economic crisis, and costly foreign policies that left the country isolated. Legitimacy could only be restored through economic development and performance.

The CFRF got away with as much as it did because of the impeccable revolutionary credentials and the positions of its leaders and members. Simply put, the VCP could not crack down on the club without losing more domestic legitimacy, especially in the south where the leaders of the club are considered real heroes. But because of events in Eastern Europe, and Hungary in particular, where groupings in that Communist Party became independent political parties that would go on to challenge the Communist Party for power, the VCP felt it had no choice but to shut the CFRF down. As in the case of Hungary, the club had a regional and economic agenda distinct from the party's. The CFRF had a base of support in addition to a sizable membership, and perhaps the party was also concerned because the club was a distinctly southern organization. Despite the party's publicly claiming that national reunification has taken place, privately many members must know the south still harbors mistrust of and resentment toward Hanoi. It was surprising to see the Viet Cong flag flown during the celebrations for the twenty-fifth anniversary of the war's end in Danang, in March 2000.[54] This was the first open recognition by the party of the role that southern revolutionaries have played since the war's end in 1975. This was powerfully symbolic, but for many it was too little, too late. But most important, Hanoi understands that the greatest threat to its monopoly of power comes not from a Polish-style labor-led movement, but from a Hungarian-style revolution that would emerge from within its own ranks.

The CFRF was the only group inside the political system that tried to apply pressure on the government to reform. But there are several groups outside the political system that also are pressing for change and the development of civil society. The most important of these groups are various religious organizations, especially the underground Unified Buddhist Church and the Catholic Church. Although the central thesis of this book is that pressure for political reform comes from within the Communist Party itself, the role of religious organizations is too important to ignore. Moreover, the demands of church groups are very similar to those of their secular counterparts. Like the CFRF, the various churches demand free speech, freedom of assembly, and the rule of law. Unlike the club, whose leaders were high-ranking party officials and whose of membership was mostly party members, which accorded them a degree of political protection, the churches' clergy has been persecuted mercilessly for their attempts to reform Vietnam's political and spiritual life. This is the subject of Chapter 6.

Notes

1. Bui Tin, *Following Ho Chi Minh,* 89.
2. See Fforde and de Vylder, *From Plan To Market,* 128–131.
3. William Turley, "Hanoi's Domestic Dilemmas," *Problems of Communism* 29 (July–August 1980): 42–61.
4. Khanh estimates that ethnic Chinese controlled the entire wholesale trade and 50 percent of retail trade in South Vietnam by 1975. See Tran Khanh, *The Ethnic Chinese and Economic Development in Vietnam* (Singapore: Institute of Southeast Asian Studies, 1993), 56. King C. Chen believes that the inventory of approximately 50,000 firms was confiscated and some 320,000 ethnic Chinese who remained in Vietnam were sent to New Economic Zones from 1975-1978. See Chen, *China's War with Vietnam: Issues, Decisions and Implications* (Palo Alto, Calif.: Hoover Institute Press, 1987), 64.
5. Fforde and de Vylder, *From Plan To Market,* 167.
6. Ibid., 128–129.
7. Vo Chi Cong, the seventh-ranked Politburo member, was vice chairman of the Council of Ministers until the Sixth Congress, when he was elected chairman of the Council of State (i.e., head of state) and promoted to third in the Politburo. Upon Pham Hung's death in 1988, Cong became the second-ranked Politburo member.
8. Martin Gainsborough, "The Ho Chi Minh City Elite," *Vietnam Business Journal* (May 2000).
9. AFP, "Vietnam's Commercial Capital to Take on Hanoi over Red Tape," 8 May 2000.
10. Although an agreement in principle was reached in July 1999, the full Politburo rejected the Bilateral Trade Agreement with the United States at an October 1999 meeting. Negotiations continued throughout the year, and the agreement was finally signed in July 2000. For more, see Zachary Abuza, "Debating

Globalization: Vietnamese Elite Politics and the Bilateral Trade Negotiations," in *Problems of Post-Communism* (January 2001).

11. For example, Truong Nhu Tang, *A Viet Cong Memoir* (New York: Vintage Press, 1985).

12. Gen. Tran Van Tra's memoirs were immediately banned following their publication in Ho Chi Minh City in March 1982. He was subsequently put under house arrest. His memoirs recounted the debates within the leadership over the post–Paris Peace Accord conduct of the war. Tra, who was the head of Viet Cong forces and led the attack on Saigon during the Tet Offensive in 1968, was very critical of Hanoi's decision and calculations leading to the offensive, which he considered an "illusion based on our subjective desires." Had the Tet Offensive been planned "scientifically," according to Tra, "the future of the war would certainly have been far different." With regard to the reunification campaign, Tra advocated a swift attack before Thieu wiped out the Viet Cong network as Diem had in 1954–1956, following Geneva. In March 1973, Tra was summoned to Hanoi where he clashed with Le Duc Tho, who feared U.S. intervention again, especially following the 1973 cutting off of Chinese and Soviet military assistance. Only after his return to Hanoi in October 1974 did the Politburo agree that "the path of revolution in the south is the path of revolutionary violence." Following Tra's successful capture of Phuoc Luong Province, Politburo member General Van Tien Dung was dispatched to lead the Ho Chi Minh campaign to reunify the country. See Tran Van Tra, *History of the B2 Bulwark Theater.* For examples of published memoirs, see Van Tien Dung, *Dai Thang Mua Xuan* (Hanoi: Nha Xuat Ban Quan Doi Nhan Dan, 1977), trans. John Spraeger, Jr., *Our Great Spring Victory: An Account of the Liberation of South Vietnam* (New York: Monthly Review Press, 1977); or Hoang Minh Thao, *The Victorious Tay Nguyen Campaign* (Hanoi: Foreign Language Publishing House, 1979).

13. Ronald Yates, "Co-Founder of Viet Cong Unhappy with Communist Party," *Chicago Tribune,* 15 May 1995. Also see Truong Nhu Tang, *A Viet Cong Memoir,* 267.

14. The 5,600-square-meter monument, in front of the former presidential palace, was constructed for the twenty-fifth anniversary of the liberation on 30 April 2000. See Ken Stier, "Freedom Memorial," *SCMP,* 18 November 1998.

15. Turley, "Hanoi's Domestic Dilemmas," 53. Also see Le Duan, "Speech to the 4th Party Congress," 17 December 1976, Radio Hanoi in *FBIS-AP,* 23 December 1976.

16. Truong Nhu Tang, *A Viet Cong Memoir,* 267.

17. Nguyen Khac Vien, *Vietnam Press* (Hanoi: Foreign Language Publishing House, 1978), and Truong Nhu Tang, *A Viet Cong Memoir,* 268.

18. Tang, *A Viet Cong Memoir,* 268.

19. See Henry Kamm, "How's Vietnam Doing? Viet Cong Doctor Expresses Disgust," *New York Times,* 6 May 1993, A4; Murray Hiebert, "Ex-Communist Official Turns into Vocal Critic," *FEER,* 2 December 1993, 90.

20. Bui Tin, *Following Ho Chi Minh,* 95.

21. Truong Nhu Tang, *A Viet Cong Memoir,* 274.

22. Cited in Stanley Karnow, *Vietnam: A History* (New York: Penguin, 1983), 683–684.

23. Bui Tin, *Following Ho Chi Minh,* 96.

24. Bui Tin, "The State of the Revolution: An Inside Assessment," *Vietnam Commentary* (July–August 1991), 7.

25. Nguyen Ho was born near Saigon on 1 May 1916. He joined the ICP in 1937 at the age of twenty-one and was arrested by the French in 1940. He was released in 1945. He was a leading Viet Cong official and held many high-level positions in the party and government, culminating as chairman of the Ho Chi Minh City People's Committee.

26. La Van Lam was born in 1919 in Bac Lieu Province. Trained as an economist, he went on to become a military commander in both the Viet Minh and the Viet Cong, including becoming head of military intelligence. He was a leader of the communist underground in the south for three decades. After the war, he served as head of research for the Central Bank of Vietnam's Saigon Office (1975–1981).

27. Born in 1938, Do Trung Hieu became an underground cadre and party official in 1966 in Khanh Hoa Province. Amnesty International reports that he was in charge of mobilizing students and intellectuals and youths during the war. After 1975 he became the standing deputy head of the Religious Affairs Office in Saigon. By 1981 he had become involved with the leadership of the United Buddhist Church (UBC), even though the party issued orders to disband the UBC and to create its own church. Hieu became the head of the Mass Mobilization Department in Saigon in 1984, even though he was increasingly at odds with the party. "The party indeed does not want any influence from the church that could jeopardize the country's independence." Hieu wrote a revisionist history of the UBC and its closure that was published in the CFRF publication. He also wrote a CFRF document that called for a national reconciliation conference, that is, an attack on the party's attempts at reunification and reconciliation.

28. Tran Van Giau was in his eighties when he helped organize the CFRF. He was a leading ICP theoretician and southern party leader in the 1930s, having studied with Ho Chi Minh at the Toilers of the East University in Moscow. In 1956 he railed against the "slavish application of Leninism" in Vietnam, and was purged from the CC. He was made dean of the History Institute in Hanoi, but returned to the south following liberation.

29. Tran Bach Dang was a preeminent NLF organizer in intellectual and religious circles from the 1950s to 1975, and during the 1950s the Saigon party chief.

30. Tran Nam Trung was the minister in charge of veteran affairs until 1984, when he was dismissed for his outspoken demands for better treatment by Hanoi of southern revolutionaries.

31. Nguyen Ho justified the CFRF's founding by stating: "Thirteen years after Liberation Day, 30 April 1975, Vietnam still does not have a veteran's association. This is inadmissible from a country which has gone through 30 years of resistance against imperialist invaders and which has achieved glorious victory."

32. COSVN was the headquarters that controlled all Viet Cong military forces, and it served as the representation of the Lao Dong Party's central committee in the south.

33. Cited in Nayan Chanda, "Force for Change," *FEER,* 5 October 1989, 24.

34. Nguyen Thi Nhu, cited in "First Open Challenge to the Party Leadership: The Southern Former Resistants Raise Their Voices," *Vietnam Commentary* (November-December 1990): 6.

35. Cited in Chanda, "Force for Change," 24.

36. These statements appeared in the third edition of *Tradition of Resistance* and are cited in Chanda, "Force for Change," 26.

37. Chanda, "Force for Change," 26.

38. Cited in Nick Malloni, "Speak No Evil!" *FEER*, 29 March 1990, 18.

39. Bui Tin argues that there were also personal reasons for this decision: Tra had close personal ties with Nguyen Van Linh and President Vo Chi Cong, whose son was married to Tra's daughter.

40. Carlyle Thayer, "The Challenges Facing Vietnamese Communism," *Southeast Asian Affairs 1992* (Singapore: Institute of Southeast Asian Studies, 1993), 355.

41. Cited in Chanda, "Force for Change," 26.

42. Malloni, "Speak No Evil!" 18.

43. Ibid.

44. Nguyen Ho, "The Solution of Reconciliation and Harmony," 11 June 1995, reprinted in *Vietnam Democracy* (July 1995).

45. Ibid.

46. Ibid.

47. Ibid.

48. Hoang Tien, "Letter to the Director of the Press Department, Ministry of Culture of the SRV, 16 June 1990.

49. Bui Tin, "The State of the Revolution," 7.

50. See Mandy Thomas, "Crossing Over: The Relationship Between Overseas Vietnamese and Their Homeland," *Journal of Inter-Cultural Studies* 18 (1997): 153–176.

51. "Overseas Vietnamese Always Think of Their Home Country," *Nhan Dan*, 11 January 1999.

52. Ken McLaughlin and De Tran, "Return to Freedom," *San Jose Mercury News*, 2 September 1998.

53. Bui Tin, "The State of the Revolution," 8.

54. AFP, "Vietnam Tips Hat to Viet Cong," 29 March 2000.

6

RELIGIOUS FREEDOM AND CIVIL SOCIETY

When religion becomes part of the state's political apparatus, the state wields absolute authority.

—*Thich Quang Do*

The central premise of this book is that political dissent in Vietnam tends to come from within the Communist Party elite rather than from other political institutions and agents of change, such as labor unions, student groups, or an urbanized middle class, all of which tend to be weak in Vietnam. This chapter discusses the exception to this: the role of religious organizations in trying to shape party and state policy. Like the Club of Former Resistance Fighters, religious organizations seek to develop civil society, the realm of independent groups autonomous from state control. The debate over religious freedom has little to do with faith and everything to do with the right to organize outside party control.

Religion has always been highly politicized in Vietnam. During the First Indochina War, the Viet Minh ruthlessly targeted Catholics, whom it believed to be French collaborators. Following the Geneva Accords, hundreds of thousands of Catholics fled to the south fearing retribution from the Viet Minh, giving President Ngo Dinh Diem a loyal power base. Yet relying too heavily on fellow Catholics put him at odds with the majority Buddhist population. Diem cracked down on Buddhists and other antiwar activists, whom he considered nothing more than fronts for the Communists, but his inability to effectively cope with the Buddhists led to his and his successors' undoing. Religious persecution continued following the reunification of the country in 1976, when the communist government imposed the same rigid controls in the south that it had imposed in the north since 1954.

With the advent of *doi moi* religion has gradually made a comeback, causing great concern in the Communist Party, which has gone to great lengths to control all religious organizations in the country, including Buddhists, Catholics, Protestants, and the Cao Dai and Hoa Hao sects. This chapter begins by analyzing the growth of religious activities since 1986 and the measures that the regime has taken to control the churches. The heart of this has been the battle between the churches that want independence and the regime that sees religion as an arm of the state. The chapter then focuses on the relationship between the individual religious organizations and the state. It concludes with an analysis of the role of religious organizations in developing civil society.

Religion, Politics, and Power in Vietnam

There is a real paradox with regard to religion in Vietnam. It is possible to argue that there are more religious worshippers in Vietnam today than at any other time in the country's modern history. Of the country's 78 million people, 80 percent are nominally Buddhist, over 8 million are Catholic, while the Cao Dai and Hoa Hao sects claim to have nearly 3.5 million adherents; Protestantism is growing rapidly in the northwest and Central Highlands. Ancestor worship, Buddhist festivals, folk religions, and cults around historical figures, likewise, are commonplace and growing fast. Although veterans of the five decades of war are offered free government funerals, only those who cannot afford a private religious ceremony take the government's offer. It appears that there is an outpouring of faith across the country.

For the individual practitioner or follower, it is true. The government has not imposed any meaningful barriers that would limit an individual's right or even ability to worship. Freedom of religion and belief is guaranteed under articles 69 and 70 of the 1992 constitution. And according to Le Kha Phieu, "Our party truly respects and guarantees the freedom of religion. Our people have the right to join, to switch, to [withdraw], or not to join any religions. No power can block or violate that freedom."[1] As a leader of the state-sponsored Vietnamese Buddhist Church (VBC) said: "I think Buddhism in Vietnam has reached the time of its highest ever development and popularity. People have religious freedom, nobody prevents them from practicing."[2]

However, while the party has shown little concern about individual faith, it is deeply concerned about the growth of organized religion:

their authority structures, nationwide networks, and congregations of adherents. The VCP will not countenance the growth of any autonomous organizations that can potentially challenge the authority of the party. Religion-based organizations are a considerable threat to the regime. In addition to being well organized, having hierarchical structures, and possessing nationwide networks that penetrate to the grass roots and parallel the reach of the state, they have resources and the ability to mobilize resources for relief efforts and social services, ostensibly the sole purview of the state. The threat to the monopoly of distributive power terrifies the regime. Also, religious leaders tend to be well-educated individuals and moral beacons, which is in contrast to the patently corrupt party and government officials. For all these reasons, the party believes that the churches must be rigidly controlled.

Nowhere is this truer than a story about a temple in Vietnam that was built to worship Ho Chi Minh. This temple became very popular with local businessmen, who flocked to it to get Ho's good *qi* (roughly, spiritual power). The authorities were clearly not amused and shut the temple down. Yet this is in a state where Ho is deified: there are portraits of him in every room in every government building, and an entire mythology has been created about Ho even though little is actually known about him. Ho's remains are displayed so that they are holy relics that attract pilgrims from across the land and around the world. But Ho, his name, and his image must be officially sanctioned. To open a temple of Ho on one's own, or to even delve into and explore the mythology is absolutely forbidden.[3] Any other interpretation beyond the doctrinaire portrayal of Ho is heresy. However, in Hanoi they love to do just that, telling the stories of his personal life, his mistresses, his wife, and his love child.

Another aspect of this contradiction has emerged in the past few years. There has been an enormous revival of prerevolution folk religions and cult followings that has caused great consternation in the party. While promising religious freedom, in the same breath it outlaws superstitious activities and has labeled thirty-one religious groups as "illegal cults."[4] Yet the party that has lost so much of its legitimacy in the people's eyes is interested in "Vietnamese culture." Unable to continue peddling anachronistic Marxist dogma, the party General Secretary Le Kha Phieu has launched mass campaigns to highlight the greatness of Vietnamese culture.[5] Clearly the party is alarmed at the Western standards, morals, and consumer preferences of its increasingly youthful population (about 55 to 60 percent was born after 1975 and hence has no recollection of the war years). Spiritual pollution and antisocial evils are portrayed as clearly Western exports to this pure land that were able to take advantage of the reform period. Hence the moral and cultural superiority of Vietnam are put on a pedestal. All the same, grassroot revivals of folk institutions and culture are condemned as threatening to the party—but dissident religious leaders are concerned about these issues as well. Thich Quang Do, one of the leaders of the outlawed Unified Buddhist Church of Vietnam (UBCV), articulates the need for religious freedom to counter the same moral degradation the Le Kha Phieu talks of: "There is the urgent need to stop superstitious practices and social evils as well as the ravaging moral degradation that is hurting us, especially the younger generations."[6] Still the party continues to find ways to clip the power of religion, with Phieu launching another campaign to put "thrift" before religion." This contradiction is not surprising, because it occurs in a socialist state that is trying to implement market reforms while maintaining a Leninist police state.

As Human Rights Watch notes, "Vietnam's 1992 constitution does not guarantee 'freedom of religion' in the fullest sense, but rather 'the freedom to believe or not believe in a religious faith'" (article 70).[7] The same article warns that "no one can violate the freedom of faith or exploit it in a way that is at variance with the law and state policies." Apart from the 1992 constitution, there are five documents that currently regulate official church activities: the 2 July 1998 Politburo "Directive on Religion" and the government's "Decree Concerning Religious Activities," No. 26/1999/ND-CP, 19 April 1999, a directive dated 2 July 1998, Directive No. 500 HD/TGCP of 4 December 1993, and Directive No. 379/TTG.[8] These five documents embody the inherent contradiction in the official attitude toward religion: on the one hand, they guarantee individuals' right to freedom of worship, but on the other they clearly regulate the activities of the church, and ensure that the church remains accountable to the party.

The party and government set out to regulate the various churches through several means. The first is by denying their independence and making them branches of the Vietnam Fatherland Front, the VCP's umbrella for all mass organizations. Although the government's "Decree Concerning Religious Activities" ensures religious freedom, the document goes out of its way to ensure that religion remains an arm of the state. All religions are part of and responsible to the VFF and "must mobilize the faithful and submit rigorously to the policy and legislation of the state."[9] The Politburo's "Directive on Religion" states that all religious persons "have the duties of defending the interests of the socialist Vietnam," but there is clearly a paranoia:

> Any abuses of religious activities to destroy social order and safety, to harm the nation's independence, to sabotage the all-people solidarity policy, to oppose the government of the Socialist Republic of Vietnam, to damage people's ethical values, way of life, and culture, to prevent believers and clergies from carrying out their civil duties will be dealt with according to the laws. Superstitious practices must be criticized and eliminated.

Each church has an officially sanctioned and elected ruling body: for the Catholics it is the Bishops' Council of the Vietnamese Catholic Church (VCC), for Buddhists it is the executive committee of the VBC. In general, these organizations do the state's bidding. For example, Thich Thanh Tu, the vice chairman of the VBC, has publicly justified the government's control over religion, arguing that "if someone goes against state policies, of course the state will impose measures. These people are monks but also citizens of a country, so I think settlement like this is in no way related to repression."[10] But there is often dissent, and the Catholic Bishops' Council has often been critical of the government's slowness in appointing new bishops and priests.

Second, the training, education, ordination, appointment, promotion, and transfer of clergy are the sole responsibility of the state, not the various churches, according to the government decree and directives. Article 18(1) of the government's decree states that only the prime minister has the authority to open seminaries, while 18(2) puts the curriculum under the authority of the Ministry of Education. The ordination of seminary graduates is the responsibility of the chairman of the provincial-level people's committees, while the ordination of bishops, cardinals and *hoa thung* monks must be approved by the prime minister. Directive 379/TTg emphasizes the political screening of all religious personnel and the "importance of selecting persons [to enter monasteries and seminaries] who have fulfilled their civic duties perfectly."[11] The chairman of the provincial people's committee, at the recommendation of the provincial-level Ministry of the Interior and the Bureau of Religious Affairs, must approve the appointment, transfer and promotion of a clergyman. If the transfer involves two provinces, then two provincial people's committees and Ministry of Interior offices get involved.

Third, the government controls the property and assets of the church. Although article 11(1) protects places of worship, article 11(3) confirms that as all religions are officially organs of the state by law, hence all of their property is the property of the state. The government has the legal authority to appropriate any church property—in short, ensuring that no one can reclaim church property appropriated by the state in the north since 1954 and in the south since 1975. The party has expressed concern that the number or incidents of illegal construction and repair of religious sites and disputes over church property ownership have grown tremendously.[12] Major restoration efforts and new construction rests with provincial people's committees. The construction of such religious structures as statues, stelae, and bell towers is likewise regulated by these committees. If a temple is listed as a historic monument, then the central government has authority over the property.

Fourth, under article 14 all church publications, from texts to prayer books, to the writings of the monks and priests, must receive official permission. This is reiterated in Directive No. 379/TTg, which requires the immediate censorship of all religious publications. Article 14 further gives the state broad interpretive powers regarding church publications: "It is prohibited to print, to publish, to commercialize, to circulate, or to possess publications and cultural products whose contents oppose the State of the Socialist Republic of Vietnam, favor the division between religion and nation, and contribute to the destruction of the union in the hearts of the people."

The government directive of 2 July 1998 announced that a religious publishing house would be opened to "mobilize the religious policies of the state."

The Vietnamese government is very concerned about proselytizing by both foreigners, who are more difficult to control, and some of the smaller Protestant sects. Article 25 prohibits foreigners from proselytizing, and the government, while allowing freedom of religion, explicitly bans people from engaging in "superstitious activities." Article 26 reveals the government's concern about foreign control of its churches, specifically regarding the Vatican and the VCC and the *Viet kieu* conferences of the UBCV.

Fifth, although article 8(4) states that religious organizations are able to raise money through the voluntary support of individual members and other "legal sources," for the most part religious organizations, as agents of the state, are funded by the state. Religious institutions, such as monasteries and seminaries, are state schools, and hence fiinanced by the government. Local churches and temples receive money from their local people's committees. The government is clearly concerned that financial independence would encourage churches to take a stronger stance against the government. To that end article 8(4) continues: "In order to organize a fund raising campaign, it is necessary to receive authorization of the chairman of the provincial people's committee."

Sixth, the government curtails all extraclerical activities of any church, such as schooling and the provision of social services, a common activity of clergies elsewhere. Restrictions on what the various churches consider their principal activities and responsibilities, social activism and community service, continue to pit churches against the state. Article 17(1) states that "the clergy and religions can carry out economic, cultural and social activities as all other citizens," but qualifies this in 17(2) by requiring those individuals and institutions to first get government permission to conduct "charitable work." Such permission has never been forthcoming. In reality, a church is forbidden by the government to open schools, orphanages, or offer any other social services that might threaten the monopoly of provision by the state, the authority of the state and its importance and omnipotence to the people being thereby diminished. What gives the communist regime its power is its control of the distribution of goods and services, but it has lost some of this power with the introduction of market reforms. Even though it will allow individuals to fill the void, it is concerned about institutions that try to do so. Individuals, acting in their narrow, self-interested ways, do not threaten the party and state; organizations with a nationwide network, a command and control system, and authority structure that penetrate to the village level can. Hence, the party and government have vehemently struck at both the UBCV and the Catholic Church for trying to provide schooling, orphanages, welfare, relief efforts, and poverty eradication.

What upsets many clergy members is that they do not feel that they are acting politically, or trying to usurp the party's monopoly of power. They are simply trying to improve the lives of the people they serve, and their social goals are, in many ways, the same as the Communist Party's. They do not want to challenge the state or the party. Thich Quang Do is clear to point out that the UBCV has no political goal, and indeed, one of the church's cornerstones is the complete separation of church and state. But the churches do want the party and state to permit other institutions to improve basic human living conditions, especially since the party and state acknowledge that they have limited resources. As Thich Quang Do put it in a fall 1999 letter to the European Union: "If the Unified Buddhist Church of Vietnam were entitled to reestablish the vast network of hospitals, schools, universities, orphanages, social and cultural centers confiscated by the authorities after 1975, it could seriously attack the scourges of poverty, illiteracy, drug addiction, prostitution, child abuse and the many serious problems facing our society today."[13]

In short, at every level, the state injects a layer of bureaucracy, weighing down churches with an incredibly cumbersome bureaucracy. And since the Vietnamese political system is based on consensus, any one ministry or office can throw a wrench into the system. Vietnam does not ban religion, but it makes it operate in a bureaucratic maze and, because most of the funding comes from the state, religious groups have no other choice. There is one additional mechanism of control: punishment and arrest for violators. At present there are some thirty to sixty religious prisoners in Vietnam.

Finally, according to the Politburo's directive, it is the responsibility of "all levels of party leaders" to maintain a close supervision of religions to "carry out this directive, assign the responsibilities of directing, monitoring, inspecting, and driving the task of dealing with religions." What this means is that in a system characterized by interlocking directorates, at every level of the government there is a corresponding party committee structure, so that someone at every level of that party structure is responsible for the day-to-day oversight of religious activities. Even if a government official decides to maintain a lenient policy toward religious activities, he can be overruled by the corresponding party secretary.

The Churches of Vietnam

The Unified Buddhist Church of Vietnam

Buddhism has always been intertwined with politics in Vietnam. Under the French Colonial Decree No. 10, Buddhism was banned from functioning as an official church, simply receiving the status of "association." It was never an organized religion, which is not surprising because Vietnam under the French was a very decentralized state divided into three separate administrative jurisdictions. The first attempt to organize the various Buddhist sects and temples was the General Association of Vietnamese Buddhists. Mistrusted by the Communists, the General Association was disbanded in 1955 by the Viet Minh following the Geneva Accords. In the south, a loose confederation of sects and temples existed until the UBCV's founding in 1964.

Buddhist clergymen were very prominent in the antiwar movement in the south during the 1960s and 1970s. In particular, Buddhist leaders were very critical of President Ngo Dinh Diem's favoritism toward Catholics and increasing repression of the Buddhists. When Diem banned the flying of any flag but the national flag of the Republic of Vietnam, monks in Hue defied the ban by flying Buddhist flags on the Buddha's birthday. Government troops killed nine people during a crackdown on 8 May 1963, after which the Buddhists organized quickly, in a show of political force, to demand that Diem punish those responsible. Diem responded to the Buddhists and their peace movement, both of which he believed to be a front for the NLF, with increased repression. The photograph by AP photographer Malcolm Browne of UBCV monk Thich Quang Duc in fiery self-immolation, on 11 June 1963, to protest Diem's increasing repression against the Buddhist community changed the world's perception of the South Vietnamese regime. After the coup and Diem's assassination, junta leader Duong Van Minh ("Big Minh") released the Buddhist leaders in order to regain popular support and allowed them to hold a conference from December 1963 to January 1964. This conference established the UBCV— "Unified" because it included eleven out of South Vietnam's fourteen separate Buddhist churches and sects. The UBCV became an umbrella organization that was very active in social welfare and activism, but it was not always united, often differing over the best ways to attain social change.[14] But it did found and run a myriad of social institutions, including hospitals, orphanages, and elementary schools.

With each change in the Saigon government came increased persecution and repression. Gen. Nguyen Khanh banned Buddhist flags and outlawed "actions in support of neutralism" in 1964. Nguyen Cao Ky launched an all-out attack on the UBCV and its leadership beginning in May 1966, arresting and executing many. This led to a wave of ten self-immolations by fire, beginning in May 1967. Despite a strong base of support, the organization was weakened by continual repression, including the arrest of one of the most charismatic monks, Thich Tri Quang. After 1967, it never regained the political muscle that it had had from 1961 to 1966.

The organization continued to operate following reunification of the country, but immediately faced problems with the communist regime. Although the new government made overtures to the Buddhist community—for example, a leading UBCV official, Thich Don Hau, being appointed to both the National Assembly and the VFF—at the same time the government began to confiscate church properties and institutions. Thirteen monks and nuns sacrificed themselves in protest against the communist government's restrictions on church activity and confiscation of church property. The Seventh Congress of the UBCV in January 1977 was the last to be held in Vietnam. The March 1977 expropriation by security personnel of a UBCV orphanage led to massive street protests by church supporters in Ho Chi Minh City. Fearful of the church's strength, the government arrested six senior UBCV officials, including Thich Huyen Quang and Thich Quang Do, on 7 April, charging them with "having distorted government policies." Quang and Do were given suspended sentences in April 1978, after spending twenty months in detention without trial. In protest, Thich Don Hau resigned from all government positions and, during the UBCV's Seventh Congress, was elected general secretary of the Supreme Council (i.e., supreme patriarch). But the party could not countenance an independent organization of any type, religious or secular.

In 1979, immediately preceding the UBCV's Eighth Congress, the Communist Party began to crack down on the Buddhists. Most of the UBCV's leadership was put in jail or under house arrest, while several were executed. In early 1980, Hanoi summoned the remaining leadership to Hanoi to meet with the VFF, explicitly to unify all the Buddhist organizations in the north and south of the country, but implicitly to place the church under the VFF's direct control. At the "unification conference" held in Hanoi in November 1981, the VFF presiding chairman, Nguyen Van Linh, announced that the church was a function of the party. Thich Don Hau protested this decision and refused to submit to the party's control, incurring the wrath of Thich Minh Chau, who supported the founding of a state-sponsored church. Chau accused the UBCV monks of "sabotag[ing] the unity effort," and "openly defy[ing] the government and fatherland front." As a result, the UBCV was banned outright by the party and replaced by the state-sponsored and submissive Vietnam Buddhist Church, officially under the direct control of the VFF. The VBC's charter declares that it is the "sole representative of Vietnamese Buddhism in all of its relations both within and outside the country."[15]

With much of the leadership either arrested or in internal exile, and given the overall repressive political regime of the 1980s, the UBCV was all but dormant. Thich Quang Do and several other UBCV leaders were arrested in February 1982 for protesting the expropriation of UBCV properties by the government, including the seizure of An Quang Pagoda in Saigon, the headquarters of the UBCV. The introduction of limited economic reforms, *doi moi*, did not necessarily lead to an easing of religious freedom; but no longer being obsessed with survival, people actually had more time and resources to spend on religion. With the promulgation of the 1992 constitution, restriction of religious activities, such as meetings and worship, were eased.

The turning point in the relationship between the UBCV and the state came in April 1992 at the funeral of their Supreme Patriarch Thich Don Hau. The government attempted to orchestrate his funeral, including posthumously bestowing on him the Ho Chi Minh Medal. This led to a mass hunger strike by thirty monks and the threat by the venerable Tri Tuu, abbot of Linh Mu Pagoda, to threaten to bury himself alive. The VCP backed down, and monks from all over the country came to Hue to attend the funeral.

What really angered the party, though, was the UBCV's continued attempt to operate independently of the party—in particular, the naming by Thich Don Hau of his own successor, a well-known dissident monk, Thich Huyen Quang, already in internal exile in Quang Tri Province. The monks attending the funeral issued a public appeal for the party to give the new patriarch a fair trial and to legalize the UBCV. Quang, himself, had been banned from the funeral, and was only allowed to attend after staging a one-day hunger strike. In a simple ceremony during the funeral, authority was transferred to him. Soon after, on 25 June, he issued an open letter in which he accused Hanoi of persecution and demanded legalization and recognition of the UBCV, the return of its properties and institutions, and the release of its members.[16]

Following the confrontation with the UBCV over the funeral, the Communist Party went on the offensive. On 17 August 1992, the Propaganda Department of the VCP's Central Committee issued a document calling on authorities to "spare no effort in the struggle against Huyen Quang. . . and to step up surveillance of him and . . . [control] all his contacts with people in and outside the country so that punitive measures may be taken in time."[17] More pressure was put on Quang Tri Province authorities to silence the monk. An internal document issued by the provincial security bureau stated that "following directives from the Secretariat of the VCP, the Ministry of Interior is launching a concerted effort to unmask and destroy the authority of reactionaries and their lackeys in the old An Quang Buddhist Church (UBCV). . . . concentrating forces in an all-out offensive from now until October 1992 in the areas of Ho Chi Minh City, Dong Nai, Hue, Quang Nam-Danang, Quang Ngai, and Quang Tri."[18]

The VCP singled out several leading UBCV monks as enemies for their attempts to discredit the government and expose its heavy-handed tactics to control the UBCV.[19] Relations were so tense between the UBCV and the VCP that during Tet in 1993, General Secretary Do Muoi actually gave a speech at Tran Quoc Pagoda in Hanoi. In the speech, he likened the ideals of religion to socialism, thus justifying the VCP's leadership over the various churches.

> The idea of Lord Jesus Christ is mercy, while that of Lord Buddha is great compassion. The ideals of Islamic Lord Allah and of other religions also aim to ensure a bounteous, free and happy life for the people, to oppose oppression exploitations and social injustices. Thus, the ideals of various religions are similar to those of socialism . . . the ideals of socialism and those of various religions do not conflict. . . . We are building a law abiding state. All citizens and organizations are equal before the law. Therefore, in addition to motivating millions of clergy and laymen to build a new society, our state exercises its lawful control over various religions and other organizations in society. Lawful control does not mean using law to constrain religious activities, but rather using the law to ensure regular activities for various religions in accordance with the policy freedom of religion, and using the law to contain and do away with all acts of violating our policy on religion as well as all acts of using religion as a means to undermine national interests.[20]

But despite Do Muoi's attempt to mollify different religious leaders, tensions increased in early 1993. In April and May, three laymen immolated themselves, including fifty-two-year-old Dao Quang Ho, who had traveled 1,260 kilometers from his home in An Giang in the Mekong Delta to Hue where he burned himself to death in front of the tomb of Thich Don Hau. The police dismissed this act as a political protest, denying that he was even a Buddhist and asserting that it was simply the act of a "depressed individual who had quarreled with his wife over an antique vase." The government later claimed that it was the "desperate act of a drug addict with AIDS."[21] The regime then accused the monks of taking advantage of this pathetic man and using his sacrifice to sabotage the government. As a result Thich Tri Tuu, the head of Linh Mu Pagoda, was arrested, causing the first street protests in Hue since the reunification of the country. According to press reports, the crowds blocked the road leading from the pagoda to the police station, surrounded the police car carrying the abbot, released him, and then set the car on fire. Thich Tri Tuu and two other monks, Thich Hai Tinh and Thich Hai Tang, were rearrested on 6 June 1993[22]; and three days later, the government announced that it had arrested over fifty others for disrupting public order—a violation of article 198 of the criminal code. On 15 November 1993 Tuu was sentenced to four years of labor, while the others received between six months and four years for "causing public disorder."[23] During the trial, a senior government official asserted that Tri Tuu "must take responsibility for the death because it occurred at his pagoda," and that the state was still making inquiries into whether the self-immolation was "a murder or a suicide."[24]

It was not just increased religious activism that got the UBCV leaders into trouble with the authorities, but the revival of their former mandate of social activism. In October 1994, the UBCV decided to organize a relief mission to help victims of flooding along the Mekong River, where 400 people had died and thousands had become homeless. The UBCV raised money and bought food, clothes, and blankets. Yet this humanitarian act was seen as an affront by the party and an explicit challenge to the government's handling of its own relief operation, and hence its policies. Never mind the fact that the government had made an international appeal for help in relief efforts, collecting $1.9 million from twenty-one countries, the UBCV was accused of "sow[ing] disunity and insecurity in Vietnamese society."

The relief convoy, which was set for 5 November, never left Ho Chi Minh City: on 29 October, the police made their first arrests at Vien Giac Pagoda in Ho Chi Minh City. The pagoda's abbot, Thich Long Tri, was arrested for being "subversive" and "detrimental to religion and national solidarity." The police warned the six other monks, nuns, and laypersons to abort the relief work. On 6 November three more were arrested, including Thich Khong Tanh, the abbot of Lien Tri Pagoda in Ho Chi Minh City, and Thich Tri Luc, the abbot of Thien Mu Pagoda in Hue.[25] That week the government seized all the relief supplies.

Earlier, on August 4, the people's committee of Quang Ngai Province had sent the patriarch of the UBCV, Thich Huyen Quang, a letter ordering him to stop acting in the name of the outlawed UBCV and demanding the surrender of the Institute of the Dharma, the symbol of the patriarch, which he had been handed during Thich Hon Dau's funeral ceremony.[26] Quang was arrested on 29 December in 1994, after starting a hunger strike to protest the party's treatment of the church, while the secretary general of the UBCV (the second-ranking official), Thich Quang Do, was arrested on 4 January 1995, after authorities raided his Thanh Minh Pagoda in Ho Chi Minh City.[27] Thich Huyen Quang was placed under house arrest at Quang Phuc Pagoda in Quang Ngai province, the government asserting that he had been transferred to another temple "because he often disturbed the other monks at his pagoda and other people" who had requested his transfer.[28] On 16 August 1995, the government announced that it had formally charged the patriarch and would try him in Quang Ngai Province. He was exiled to a remote village in a mountainous region in the north in November.

Thich Quang Do was also never charged and soon after released; but he was rearrested on 15 August 1995 on charges of "sabotaging religious solidarity." He was sentenced along with five other UBCV members, including three monks, after a one-day trial in Ho Chi Minh City, to a five-year term, and released in a September 1998 government amnesty. What infuriated the authorities most, however, was a letter that Thich Quant Do had written to the VCP's general secretary, Do Muoi, in which he condemned the VCP for its "flagrant violations of Vietnamese and international laws."

Coercion increased, especially at temples in the major urban areas. For example, on 22 November 1996, 200 police raided Linh Mu Pagoda and arrested two more UBCV monks, Thich Hai Thinh and Thich Hai Chanh.[29] Linh Mu Pagoda, originally built in 1601, is one of the most prominent temples in the country and one that the government would like to take over. In October 1996 the pagoda was classified as a "historical monument," and thus was shut down as a working temple. The Hue municipal people's committee tried to evict the monks and replace them with VBC monks, while Thich Minh Dao, the superior monk of Long Tho Pagoda in Dalat, was arrested on 30 October 1996. He was arrested at the urging of the VBC's Lam Dong provincial committee for "pursuing superstitious practices that entail serious consequences," by article 199 of the criminal code. The other thirty-four monks and nuns were evicted, and the pagoda was destroyed by security forces.[30]

The VCP has not had troubles just with the UBCV; there have been protests and demonstrations by leaders of the party-controlled VBC as well. The primary reason is that most of the 28,000 VBC monks are sympathetic to or tacitly support the underground UBCV leadership, and they only cooperate with the VBC out of fear of persecution. For example, the VBC-appointed abbot of Son Linh Pagoda near Vung Tau got in trouble with provincial authorities for reading the transcript of Thich Huyen Quang's funeral oration, implicitly supporting the demands for the restoration of the UBCV. In February 1993, the VBC's leading body accused the abbot of "violating the principles of Vietnamese Buddhism," and expelled him.[31] Then on 9 July 1993, 2,000 followers of Thich Hanh Duc clashed with police who came to arrest the abbot.[32] Vu Quang, the head of the government's Religious Affairs Committee, accused the crowd of attacking the police and the pagoda of stockpiling weapons. Duc was sentenced to three years of labor for "crimes against on-duty officials" and "handing out documents hostile to the socialist government of Vietnam." Nine men who had taken part in the demonstrations were also imprisoned.

On 27 November 1994, Buddhist monks protested the politicized curriculum and the arbitrary enrollment criteria at a VBC pagoda school in Hue. As a result of that incident, Thich Thien Su, who was the deputy head of the state-sponsored VBC, turned down the position of headmaster of the school and asked to resign from the VBC. Actually, the entire VBC board in that region resigned. This prompted the VBC's executive board to ask the chairman of the National Assembly and the prime minister to "take stern punitive measures" against the monks. In December 1994, another VBC monk, Thich Thai Hung, was arrested for violating article 198 of the criminal code, while a third, Thich Nhu Dat, was detained but never charged.[33] What really concerned the government was that after the VBC's rejection of the appointed abbot to head the One Pillar Pagoda in Hanoi, the rank and file publicly appealed to the underground UBCV for support.

The government tried to improve relations with the UBCV in 1998. As part of the first annual general amnesty, which saw the release of 5,219 prisoners, the government released Thich Quang Do and several other UBCV monks, including Thich Tri Sieu and Thich Tue Sy.[34] A few weeks later, another senior member of the UBCV was released from labor camp, due to failing health, and put under house arrest.[35] But despite these overtures, the government would not tolerance any attempts by church leaders to organize as an independent entity. For example, in March 1999, the police broke up the first meeting between Thich Huyen Quang (seventy-nine years old) and Thich Quang Do (seventy years old), the top two officials of the Buddhist organization, who had not met with one another in seventeen years. The two were discussing the promotion of younger monks to the UBCV's leadership; they were brought to the police station for questioning and detained for two days, though neither was formally arrested.[36]

Government repression of the UBCV shows no sign of ebbing.[37] With Thich Quang Do's Nobel Prize nomination, growing international profile, and prolific letter-writing campaign, the government is unable to arrest him without serious international repercussions. So it has stepped up its campaign against the UBCV by going after Do's supporters, preventing the growth of the UBCV's authority and popular acceptance. The UBCV attempted to distribute relief aid to the victims of Mekong flooding—which killed over 400 and affected 4 million in Vietnam alone in the summer of 2000—even as they appealed to the international community for assistance.

The Catholic Church

Like the UBCV, the issues that pit the Catholic Church against the state are not found in the freedom to worship, but instead have to do with church autonomy, leadership selection, recruitment, property, and social activism. What really differentiates the Catholic Church from the UBCV, though, is that there is an aspect of foreign control, with neo-colonial overtures, that truly alarms the regime. The VCP believes that the Holy See is active in aiding Catholic goups overthrow communist regimes. According to one party document: "The Vatican directed many overseas religious organizations to provide financial aid and reactionary documents in which the experience of opposing communism in Eastern Europe and the Soviet Union was shared with the Vietnamese Church."[38] In recent years, the government has given unprecedented rights to hold large public masses and organize religious festivals. For example, the Communist Party daily, *Nhan Dan,* reported that a three-day Catholic festival with over 100,000 participants was a success.[39] Yet, at the same time, the party has still not normalized relations with the Vatican, and has even rebuffed attempts by the pope to visit the country, ostensibly over the right to appoint bishops. In this, the Vietnamese have followed the Chinese lead in appointing their own bishops without either approval from or consultation with the Vatican. This became a pressing matter for the Vatican because by the 1990s, there were more than five vacant bishoprics and archbishoprics because of old age, illness, and death.

Catholics are a small but very distinct minority in the country, presently numbering 8 to 10 percent of the population, or somewhere around 7 million, making it the largest Catholic population in mainland Asia, second only to that of the Philippines. Catholicism has always been highly politicized in Vietnam. During the first War of National Liberation against the French, many Catholics sided with the French and were hence targeted by the Viet Minh, especially in the Red River Delta. Following the Geneva Accord in 1954, a large percent of the refugees who fled to the south were Catholic. Unlike in the north where they were persecuted for their religious beliefs, in the south they were the beneficiaries of government largess and protection. President Ngo Dinh Diem came from a prominent Catholic mandarin family; indeed his older brother was the cardinal of Saigon. Under Diem, fellow Catholics were given the best jobs and business contracts, while the Buddhists, under the UBCV, were perceived as mere pawns of the NLF and hence were unfairly persecuted.

With the reunification of the country in 1975 the Catholic Church, like other religions, stagnated under the weight of increased social and political pressures. But even more than the UBCV, it was harassed, being deemed a colonial vestige. In recent years, however, it has attracted more followers. Despite all attempts by the Communist Party to kill it, the Catholic Church has proven remarkably resilient. One party document stated that "the imperialist enemies and their gangs consider using the exploitation of religion as a very important factor in resisting the revolutionary movement."[40] Then again, the Catholic Church has a lot of experience in operating in totalitarian states—and the party seems to have an easier time in working with the hierarchical Catholic Church than the more decentralized Buddhist and Protestant organizations. But negotiations between Vietnam and the Vatican have been tortuously slow.

Vatican envoy Monsignor Claudio Celli traveled to Vietnam in April 1995 to negotiate the appointment of four new bishops, including the successor to the eighty-five-year-old archbishop of Ho Chi Minh City, Nguyen Van Binh. No agreement was reached and bilateral talks were broken off for several years. When Archbishop Binh died in late 1995, the government blocked the appointment of his successor, Bishop Huynh Van Nghi, who was forced to return to his provincial post. In March 1999 a senior Vatican official, Deputy Foreign Minister Monsignor Celestino Migliore, traveled to Hanoi to discuss steps to normalize diplomatic relations between Vietnam and the Holy See. The key sticking point, the right to appoint bishops, is a major one that neither side was willing to give in on. The Vatican argues that it is the pope's decision to make at the suggestion of church cardinals. Vietnam argues that because all religion is state sponsored, and that all religious organizations are responsible to the VFF, only the state has the power to appoint bishops. Hanoi does not automatically approve papal appointments and contends that the Vatican should have no direct influence on the Vietnamese Catholic Church, especially in its day-to-day operations. Accordingly, the highest Catholic organ in Vietnam is the Vietnam Bishops' Council, which reports directly to the VFF.

Although diplomatic relations were not restored, there was a compromise agreement that allowed the pope to appoint six or seven new bishops.[41] Future nominations and appointments, short of an accord, will be made on an ad hoc basis and thus really be influenced by Hanoi's view of the world and perception of threat at the time. But the Vatican was clearly pleased that at least several important vacancies would be filled.

Progress toward full diplomatic relations was made during this trip. For the first time, the Vatican envoy had "substantive talks" with the Ministry of Foreign Affairs, rather than the low-level Commission on Religious Affairs, with whom envoys usually meet. The Vatican pressed for a papal visit in late 1999, when he was to attend the final session of the Asian Synod, a convocation of regional bishops, which began in 1998. To date, the Vatican's requests have been rebuffed by the Vietnamese government, which still considers the church a colonial relic.

In the run-up to the party's Ninth Congress, set for March 2001, relations suffered a setback. In May 2000, another high-level Vatican delegation traveled to Hanoi to negotiate the appointment of bishops for three dioceses that have been vacant for three years. Not only was no agreement reached, but the Vatican announced that overall relations had taken "a step back five years," and that Hanoi's replies to Vatican overtures were "disappointingly scant."[42] The Vatican was very disappointed after the progress that had been made during the 1999 trip and the public diplomacy that the Vatican engaged in that year. In response to the floods that ravaged the central Vietnamese coast in early 2000, the Vatican offered $100,000 in aid, more than three times what it usually sends for disaster relief.

Until relations with the Vatican are restored, the organization and leadership of the Catholic Church in Vietnam is through the Vietnam Bishops' Council that reports to the VFF. It consists of thirty-nine members, most of whom "are in old age and poor health." Although this is the highest church authority in Vietnam, it has not been a completely pliable group. As discussed below, it has sent numerous demands and

complaints to the government, most notably the 11 October 1997 petition to the prime minister in which the council demanded more seminaries and students to fill them, a streamlined process for appointments,
and the right to build more churches, publish a journal, and appoint
bishops. The Bishops' Council meets once a year and writes a report,
which according to a representative of the United States Bishops'
Council, is "half thankful to the state and half critical."

The government treats seminaries as state schools and is thus able
to control their number, size, and enrollment. In the early to mid-1990s,
for example, a new class in the seminaries was only enrolled every
other year.[43] As one priest complained: "Grand seminaries are the government's schools to produce cadres!"[44] The seminary in Saigon had
one class of fifty students, to serve ten dioceses in the south. There are
currently six seminaries for approximately 750 students that may receive additional funding from the Italian Bishops' Council. Moreover,
once the seminarians graduate, the church does not have the authority
to ordain any of them as priests. For example, Father Chan Tin reported
that although 250 priests had died in Saigon Diocese between 1975 to
1998, only 150 priests were allowed to be ordained.[45] One Western
diplomat estimated that there are only 2,000 priests to fill the 5,000
Catholic churches in the country.[46] As a result, many underground
monasteries have emerged. Even though the Vatican reached an agreement with Hanoi in 1999 about opening a new seminary, Hanoi stalled,
and in 2000 it still was not open. Another problem is the appointment
of priests to specific parishes, because often priests are not issued new
residence permits. Further complicating matters is that an individual
diocese encompasses several provinces.[47] Thus several different levels
of government bureaucracy control church activities.

All writings, teachings, and documents of the church are subject to
the publication law of 1993, and the printing and dissemination of any
materials without the government's permission is a violation of that
law. Although leading priests have asserted that the government gave
them permission to publish a journal, in fact they have received no
such permission. There is, however, a Catholic newspaper, *Communion
Newsletter,* that is published by the Bishops' Council.

Like the UBCV, the Catholic Church had extensive landholdings
and properties, especially in the south, but the national, provincial, or
municipal governments during the period of collectivization confiscated most of these. Allegations that Vietnamese authorities have destroyed churches, either to use the property for some other purpose or

to make worship more difficult, continue to this day.[48] The church, furthermore, has not received licenses or approval to repair old facilities or to build new structures.

In 1997 and 1998, for example, Catholics in Dong Nai Province took to the streets when provincial officials refused to return church property confiscated in the previous two decades. Although all states retain the right to seize private property for the collective good, in this case it seems that the local government seized church land to build "a large market." According to one villager, however, only a small market was constructed and the rest of the land was sold off for private plots.

In another case, a northerner who had settled in a predominantly Catholic village in Ba Ria-Vung Tau Province east of Saigon refused to give up his property after an appeals court ruled that the land should be returned to the Catholic Church. His action infuriated other villagers, who began to demonstrate. Violence erupted, and in the end it took fifty policemen to subdue the man along with his "30 axe-wielding family members"; six officers were injured and ten people were arrested. The police actually went to the priests to intervene in the crisis, for there had been the potential for escalation to a much broader confrontation. As one police official said: "It is not our job to go to priests like we did but here among the Catholic community the priests have better credibility and influence than the local government."[49]

Like the UBCV, one of the most troubling issues for the Catholic Church has to do with restrictions on what it considers to be one of its principal activities, social activism and community service. The church is forbidden by the government to open schools or orphanages or to offer any other social services that might threaten the monopoly of provision by the state. Once again, if other agencies provide services that would otherwise be the sole responsibility of the state, the state's importance and omnipotence to the people are diminished.

Many clergy members, like their Buddist counterparts, feel that they are not acting politically. They are simply trying to improve the lives of their parishoners. Their social goals are, in many ways, the same as the party's. According to the editors of *Communion Newsletter*, Nguyen Thanh Cong and Nguyen Nghi, "our own line at the paper is very much in sympathy with the liberation theology of Latin America and its identification with the poor. We wouldn't exactly call ourselves socialists, but we recognize that out human goals are generally better served under socialism than under capitalism. A 'third way' might be the best of all but it has yet to emerge."[50]

Many clergy want the party and state to permit other institutions to work toward improving basic human living conditions, both having admitted their limited resources. As the Cong and Nghi argue, "We need democratization rather than democracy in Vietnam. The Communist Party has liberated Vietnam three times already and it must do it now a fourth time by sacrificing some of its own power, its privileges and monopolies."[51]

Like many other dissidents, they are concerned about the establishment of a multiparty democracy and the instability that it might cause. For them, democracy is not the most applicable or beneficial system for Vietnam, and even if it is the ideal system, it could not be imposed on the country quickly.

> We're not necessarily of the view that a multi-party system would be the right thing here at the moment. Look at the convulsions in Eastern Europe, while they tried to switch over immediately and became very unstable—you can be sure things would be worse in a poor country like Vietnam. We have to change bit by bit. But it will arrive in the end in our own Vietnamese way—which usually means waiting a very, very long time for what you want.[52]

Cao Dai and Hoa Hao Sects

The Cao Dai faith was founded in 1926 by an opium-addicted civil servant, Ngo Van Chieu. The sect, based primarily in Tay Ninh Province, southwest of Ho Chi Minh City, is the amalgamation of some of the great religions of the world: Buddhism, Confucianism, Christianity, and Taoism. Cao Dai members have been perceived by all the governments they have lived under as a threat; beginning in the 1940s, the Cao Dai raised its own army, which angered the French. Later, Ngo Dinh Diem used harsh repression against the sect, as did the Communists after the reunification of the country.

In 1975, Hanoi replaced the sect's leadership with a state-controlled "management council" responsible to the VFF. Much of the Cao Dai's property was appropriated and the seminary was closed. Although the Cao Dai's Holy See in Tay Ninh remains open, the clergy has been intimidated, arrested, and restricted in its freedom to practice. Cao Dai was not formally recognized as an official religion until 1997, and it still remains mistrusted.

In a 1997 report of the Tay Ninh Province party committee, the Cao Dai temple was "where enemies take advantage to stir up political reactionary operations against our revolution."[53] The report continued, "We all agree to fade out spiritualism; to wipe out the Cao Dai system, which was organized like a state within a state." And, to be fair, many exiled groups of anticommunist Vietnamese did operate out of eastern Cambodia, next door to Tay Ninh Province. The Cao Dai sect has an estimated 2.5 million followers, though the government puts the figure at only 1.1 million. The government has established a "management committee" to oversee Cao Dai activities.

The Hoa Hao is another sect that earns the attention of the Vietnamese security forces. An offshoot of Buddhism, like the Cao Dai, it was founded by a southern mystic, Huynh Phu Su. The Viet Minh, who considered the Hoa Hao a rival for the support of the poor peasants in the Mekong Delta, murdered Su in 1947. During the war, the Hoa Hao raised an army and fought both the Viet Minh and South Vietnamese forces. Since then, the relationship between the Hoa Hao and the communist authorities who disarmed its members has been tense. Indeed, because of its militant anticommunist activities, the Hoa Hao has arguably been the most persecuted of all Vietnam's religions. Today, there are approximately 2 million adherents, almost 4 percent of the population, although the government puts the figure at 1.3 million.

Like the Cao Dai, it is not the religious aspect of the movement that is of concern to the authorities, but its organizational capability and authority structure, especially its ties to anticommunist groups based in neighboring Cambodia. The government did allow 160 Hoa Hao delegates to hold a congress in May 1999 in An Giang, but relations remain tense and often deteriorate into armed clashes, such as the December 1999 confrontation between security forces and 300 Hoa Hao followers.

Protestant Evangelism

Although there are only a small number of Protestants in the country, they are alarming to Hanoi for one reason: evangelical and Protestantism missionary activity are taking place in the rugged northwest and central highlands, regions inhabited by hill tribes (who make up about 80 percent of Vietnam's Protestants), especially the Hmong with whom Hanoi has always had a tenuous relationship. The Hmong, a nomadic hill tribe whose population lives in northwestern Vietnam, Laos, Thailand, and southwestern China, have always viewed the Vietnamese as their natural enemy. During the Vietnam War, there was a close alliance between the Hmong and the Americans who clandestinely fought the North Vietnamese in Laos. Hmong were used to conduct guerrilla operations along the Ho Chi Minh trail to interdict the flow of arms, men, and equipment traveling to the south.[54] With the victory of the North Vietnamese and Pathet Lao, the Hmong have been singled out and ruthlessly attacked because of their collaboration with the Americans.[55] With the rise of Western nongovernment organizations (NGOs) in the region, the all-out persecution of the Hmong has been curtailed; however, the Hmong continue to live in the most impoverished regions of Vietnam and Laos and have disproportionately low standards of living. In early 2000, Hmong tribesmen began a violent campaign against the communist regime in Vientiane, causing Hanoi to renew military aid to and cooperation with their Lao counterparts, concerned that minority unrest could spill across the border.

Today, there are an estimated 800,000 Protestants in Vietnam, a four-fold increase since 1975, making Protestantism the fastest growing religion in the country. According to the government's Religious Affairs Committee, there is considerable alarm at the spread of evangelical Protestantism among the Hmong for geographic and political reasons already mentioned.[56] They operate an estimated 300 house churches, which are not legally sanctioned, and receive religious texts and radio transmissions from the refugee communities in the Philippines and Singapore.

Protestant missionaries, as well as many Western NGOs, have operated in Hmong and other hill tribe regions because the government has failed to channel its development resources to these regions. The Lai Chau Province government and the Ministry of Interior's border guards have attacked Protestantism for being "illegal" and "nontraditional" religious practices, and the central government has labeled thirty-one Protestant church groups as illegal cults. They have used the Hmong's traditional role in the opium poppy harvest to justify suppression of "illegal religious activities and drug crimes."[57] Some fifteen Hmong were arrested in Lai Chau in mid-1999 alone for their religious practices, and there have been reports that Hmong have fled Lao Cai and Lai Chau for the Central Highlands.

Theravada Buddhism and Islam

There are some 700,000 to 1 million ethnic Khmers (Cambodians) living in the Mekong Delta region who practice Theravada Buddhism. And there is a small Sunni Islamic population—perhaps only 100,000—spread throughout the country. The Muslim Association of Vietnam, which was banned in 1975, was allowed to reopen in 1992 as part of the VFF. The Muslim Association organizes annual pilgrimages to Mecca, and the government no longer withholds exit visas from followers.

Conclusion

Never in the history of modern Vietnam has religious freedom been so great for the individual practitioner. Yet, the Vietnamese Communist Party considers the spread of independent organized religions as a real threat to its own power. Religious dissent does not come from among the highest echelons of the party, but religious leaders are very influential figures at both the local and national level. On top of their moral authority and the hierarchical structure of their churches, their ability to organize and reach the grass roots causes great concern in the party. This is a development of civil society that the party seeks to curtail, especially since the concerns and demands of the religions echo those of the secular dissidents. If intraparty dissidents are able to link up with a broad-based social movement, the party will have a much more difficult time in maintaining its monopoly of power. Therefore, the party has gone to great lengths to control religion; unlike intraparty dissidents, religious leaders have been persecuted harshly for their refusal to conform to party dictates. Like their lay counterparts, religious leaders demand the right to organize their churches independent of party interference or control; the right to educate, recruit, and appoint their own leadership; and the right to publish freely. Finally, the churches want to provide the social services that the state is unable or unwilling to. They are not out to challenge the state's monopoly or cast doubt on the state's abilities; they are simply trying to help those who fall through the cracks. Yet the state sees itself as the sole provider of social goods, and any other providers as a challenge to the raison d'être of the state's monopoly of power.

Notes

1. Le Kha Phieu, cited in Chan Tin, "Letter to Pham Dinh Tung, Chairman of the Vietnam Bishops' Council," 10 July 1998, in *Vietnam Democracy,* October 1998.
2. Thich Thanh Tu, Vice-Chairman, Vietnam Buddhist Church, cited in Dean Yates, "Key Vietnam Buddhist Defends Controls," Reuters, 18 October 1998.

3. AFP, "Ho Chi Minh Worshippers Religious Sect Banned," 14 December 1995.

4. "Vietnam Has 31 Illegal Religious Cults," Reuters, 23 November 1999.

5. VNS, "Culture is the Nation's Foundation," *Vietnam News,* 13 August 1998; VNS, "Vietnamese Culture Product of Aeons of Creativity, Struggle," 16 August 1998.

6. Thich Quang Do, "Letter to VCP Leaders," 15 January 2000, Translated by Radio Free Asia, 31 March 2000.

7. Human Rights Watch, *Vietnam: The Suppression of the Unified Buddhist Church* 7, 4 (March 1995).

8. This decree replaces Council of Ministers Decree No. 69/HDBT, 21 March 1991.

9. Article 8(5) states that "the religious organizations that carry out activities counter to the ideals of life, to the goals, the religious orientation and the authorized structures by the prime minister, must cease to function. The individuals responsible for these violations will be punished under the law."

10. Dean Yates, "Key Vietnam Buddhist Defends Controls."

11. Directive 500 HD/TGCP of 4 December 1993 reiterates that "civic duties" are the main criterion for the selection of candidates to seminary. Under article 16, any clergyman imprisoned or placed under administrative detention is forbidden to practice or administer his religious duty. Those who were imprisoned after 1975 and have been released must apply for permission to resume their religious activities.

12. "State Claims 'Progress' in Controlling Religious Affairs," Reuters, 13 May 1999.

13. Thich Quang Do, "Letter to the European Union," in *Vietnam Democracy,* September 1999.

14. Human Rights Watch, *The Suppression of the Unified Buddhist Chuch,* 3–4; James H. Forrest, *The Unified Buddhist Church of Vietnam: 15 Years for Reconciliation* (Alkmaar, The Netherlands: International Fellowship of Reconciliation, 1978), 7.

15. Human Rights Watch, *The Suppression of the Unified Buddhist Church,* 5.

16. The party's response can be found in "Text of Government Religious Affairs Commission's Letter to Buddhist Monk Thich Huyen Quang, alias Le Dinh Nhan," Voice of Vietnam, 4 August 1993, in *FBIS-EAS,* 6 August 1993, 40–42.

17. Bertil Lintner, "Vietnam: Coping with Disaffection and Democracy," *International Defense Review* (August 1994): 25–26.

18. Ibid., 26. October 1992 saw the third national congress of the state-controlled VBC. An Quang was the pagoda headquarters of the UBCV.

19. Persecuted monks included Thich Hai Tang, a close associate of the late Thich Don Hau, the head of Kong An Pagoda in Quang Tri, and Thich Khong Tanh, the head of Lien Tri Pagoda, in Ho Chi Minh City. Thich Tri Tuu, head of the famous Linh Mu Pagoda, issued a statement in which he publicly condemned the government's attempts to get him to discredit the late patriarch's final will and testament, and admit that they were forgeries prepared by troublesome monks. Tuu threatened to "offer my body as a torch to light up the truth" to protest the government's coercive policies on 24 December 1992.

20. Cited in Lintner, "Vietnam: Coping with Disaffection and Democracy," 26.

21. VNA, "Clarification of Hue 'Falsehoods' Issued," 31 May 1993, in *FBIS-EAS*, 1 June 1993, 57; VNA, "Man's Family Clarifies Case," 6 June 1993, in *FBIS-EAS*, 7 June 1993, 54-55.

22. Human Rights Watch asserted that four additional monks were arrested.

23. VNA, "Hanoi Reports Sentencing," 15 November 1993, in *FBIS-EAS*, 16 November 1993. Thich Hai Thanh received a four-year sentence for "having played a major role in aggravating the situation," while Thich Hai Thinh and Thich Hai Chanh received three-year sentences. For more on their imprisonment, see Human Rights Watch, *The Suppression of the Unified Buddhist Church*, 8.

24. Vu Quang, head of the government's Religious Affairs Committee, cited in AFP, "Government Denies Senior Buddhist Monk Arrested," 25 May 1993.

25. On 15 August 1995, Thich Khong Tanh, Thich Nhat Ban, and one layperson, Nhat Thuong, were sentenced to five years' imprisonment. They appealed their sentence on 28 October 1995; the following day the court upheld the lower court's ruling. Thich Khong Tan was released from prison on 10 November 1998. The month before his release, he met the UN special rapporteur on religious intolerance, Abdelfattah Amor, who visited the Z30 Reeducation Camp in Xuan Loc, Dong Nai Province. All had served in prison previously. Thich Khong Tanh was released from prison in October 1993, after being detained for a year, while Thich Tri Luc served two months in prison, also in 1992. Tanh had previously spent nine years in prison, from 1976 to 1985, for protesting an order to conscript young monks into the army.

26. "Text of Government Religious Affairs Commissions Letter to Buddhist Monk Thich Huyen Quang," 40–42; VNA, "Hanoi Buddhist Church Criticizes Monk," 5 August 1993, in *FBIS-EAS*, 6 August 1993.

27. Thich Quang Do was held under arrest from 6 April 1977 to 12 December 1978 and then exiled to a commune in Thai Binh on 25 February 1982 for activities "both religious and political," ostensibly for protesting the expropriation of UBCV property. Upon his release he was exiled again, this time to his native province of Thai Binh. In 1992, asserting that his previous arrest and sentence had been illegal because he was never tried in a court of law, he returned to Ho Chi Minh City. He was rearrested in 1995 and sentenced to five years of hard labor. In all, he has spent more than eighteen years in prison camps.

28. "Amnesty International Denounces Buddhist Repression in Vietnam," press release (February 1995).

29. Both were arrested on 5 June 1993 for taking part in a 24 May 1993 demonstration demanding greater religious freedom. They were arrested and sentenced to three years' imprisonment along with the abbots of the temple, Thuch Tri Tuu and Thich Hai Tang, both of whom received a four-year sentence. Thinh and Chanh were released in 1995.

30. Thich Minh Dao had been arrested twice before, once in 1985 and then again in 1980; he has been harassed since 1981 when he refused to join the VBC.

31. Cited in Human Rights Watch, *The Suppression of the Unified Buddhist Church*, 9.

32. Murray Hiebert, "No Middle Path Here," *FEER,* 5 August 1993, 26.

33. "Amnesty International Denounces Buddhist Repression in Vietnam," press release (February 1995).

34. Thich Tri Sieu was released from one of the most notorious prison camps, Z30A, in a general amnesty on National Day in 1998. Originally sentenced to death on charges of attempting to overthrow the government, his sentence was reduced to twenty years. Mark McDonald, "Vietnam Reportedly Frees Buddhist Leaders," *SJMN,* 2 September 1998.

35. Thich Nhat Ban was the abbot of a pagoda in Linh Phong Province. He was sentenced in 1995 to four years after organizing the relief mission for the flood victims in the Mekong Delta, hence his release was only one month early. He had previously served ten years in a labor camp, 1975–1985.

36. Ken Stier, "Police Break Up Buddhist Elders' Talk," *SCMP,* 29 March 1999.

37. In September 1999, Thich Khong Tanh was detained after he met with Thich Quang Do and was charged with "belonging to an illegal organization" that was "conniving with foreign powers" to overthrow the regime. In the same month, Thich Tue Sy, the UBCV's secretary general, was also detained. On 22 September, Thich Quang Do applied for a license to publish a Buddhist journal; his request was denied. The UBCV's Eighth Congress was held in exile in California at the encouragement of the church leaders.

38. Cited in Murray Hiebert, "Secrets of Repression," *FEER,* 16 November 2000, 36.

39. Reuters, "Catholic Festival Gets Party Blessing," 18 August 1998.

40. Hiebert, "Secrets of Repression," 34.

41. Ken Stier, "Vatican Sees Hope of New Bishops," DPA, 20 March 1999. In June 1999, the Vatican formally appointed three new bishops: Pierre Nguyen Soan is now the bishop of Quy Nhon, Joseph Tran Xuan Tieu, archbishop of Long Xuyen, and Joseph Ngo Quang Kiet, bishop of Cao Bang and Lang Son provinces. See Reuters, "Pope Appoints Three New Bishops for Vietnam," 18 June 1999.

42. Jude Webber, "Vatican-Vietnam Links 'Step Back Five Years,'" Reuters, 9 May 2000.

43. Vietnamese Bishops' Council, "Letter to the Prime Minister," 11 October 1997, in *Vietnam Democracy* (January 1998).

44. Tasteo Nguyen Van Ly, "The State of the Vietnamese Catholic Church," Declaration of the Hue Archdiocese, 24 November 1994, in *Vietnam Democracy* (January 1995).

45. Chan Tin, "Letter to Chairman of the Vietnamese Bishops' Council."

46. Dean Yates, "Religious Worship Grows in Vietnam, Controls Stay," Reuters, 19 October 1998.

47. Vietnamese Bishops' Council, "Letter to the Prime Minister."

48. Reuters, "Vietnam Denies Four Churches Pulled Down in South," 19 August 1999.

49. Cited in DPA, "Vietnam Catholics Clash with Police over Land Squabble," 19 January 1999.

50. Cited in Chris Brazier, *Vietnam: The Price of Peace* (Oxford: Oxfam, 1992), 49.

51. Ibid., 49.

52. Ibid.

53. Andy Solomon, "Cao Dai Struggle for Survival in Vietnam," Reuters, 20 April 1999.

54. The two most thorough works on the Hmong's role in the Vietnam War are Jane Hamilton-Merritt, *Tragic Mountains: The Hmong, the Americans, and the Secret Wars for Laos* (Bloomington: University of Indiana Press, 1993); and Roger Warner, *Backfire: The CIA's Secret War in Laos and Its Link to the War in Vietnam* (New York: Simon and Schuster, 1995).

55. Hamilton-Merritt, *Tragic Mountains*, chaps. 23–29.

56. "State Claims 'Progress' in Controlling Religious Affairs," Reuters, 13 May 1999.

57. "Vietnam Province Cracks Down on 'Illegal Religion,'" Reuters, 17 December 1998.

7

THE VCP: COPING WITH INTERNAL DISSENT AND EXTERNAL PRESSURE

The party doesn't hide its mistakes, doesn't hate criticism. The party must accept its mistakes in order to have self-amendments for progress.

—Ho Chi Minh

What makes dealing with the dissidents so difficult for the party is that they raise very legitimate concerns that the party itself acknowledges must be rectified as soon as possible. Corruption, bureaucratism, arbitrary rule, and interlocking directorates are problems that the senior party leadership is cognizant of and deeply troubled by, which makes it difficult for them to crack down on people bringing attention to these issues. Yet, in the party's thinking, it must. The VCP, though not its individual members, is infallible and cannot countenance any dissent. Even if people offer constructive criticism so that the VCP in the end can strengthen itself, it is perceived as an attack on the party's leadership. The party can agree with the issues being raised, but how they are raised is of greater concern to the leadership. Those who have been persecuted, to one degree or another, have been punished not because of the substantive issues and concerns that they raised, but for raising these issues. Despite fifteen years of attempting to restore democratic centralism as the central operating procedure of the party, consensual politics still has not been fully implemented. Unable to openly debate policies, many VCP members have gone outside normal party channels to bring pressing issues to the party's attention.

That the VCP is only willing to listen to limited complaints and criticism from its own members, through very circumscribed and rigid channels is, in itself, evidence that the party is out to maintain its monopoly of power and not serve the national interest. Although a few leaders have tried to defend the right to speak out, most in the VCP leadership want all dissenting voices quelled. It is uncertain what effect the recent criticisms by first-generation leaders, such as Le Giam and Vo Nguyen Giap, will have.[1] On the one hand, they could embolden more mid-level officials to speak out and demand greater reforms. On the other hand, the party may try to preempt such an event to prevent it from happening: and it has justified this in a signed editorial in *Nhan Dan*. "The freedom of each person cannot be a chaotic movement which leads to social disorder," the editorial read, "otherwise society will be unstable and cause harm to the interests of the majority."[2] And Dao Duy Quat, the de facto spokesman of the Central Committee,[3] warned that "ideologically degraded [party] members" should not violate party discipline. He continued by shrugging off pressure from the West: "Each country has its own way to deal with its own problems to maintain stability." Others in the party leadership are looking for "hostile forces from the outside," who have "taken advantage of our weaknesses and negativism to increase their activities aimed at politically and ideologically sabotaging us."[4] The leadership is clearly concerned that internal dissidents will link up with hostile overseas groups.

The government and the VCP have adopted a two-pronged response to deal with the dissidents. First they have gone after the dissidents individually through arrests, expulsion from the party, forced exile, loss of work, interrogation, surveillance, and tirades in the press, all in an attempt to intimidate, isolate, and silence voices. They have used the full powers of the state resources at their disposal: a monopoly of the press, lawmaking and law-interpreting authority, and a powerful security force. Ironically, these heavy-handed tactics have, if anything, resulted in many more dissidents' emerging in the defense of their colleagues, friends, and patrons, whom they feel have been unfairly targeted and vilified. Second, the VCP has responded to many, though not all, of the issues that dissidents have raised through traditional, party-led campaigns to rectify the problems. These campaigns tend to fail because it is the party that is trying to reform itself and root out corruption in its own ranks, and the party has proven incapable of policing itself.

Still, how the regime responds to external criticism is very different. Although the Vietnamese government issues blistering attacks on foreign criticism of its human rights records, basically the regime is vulnerable to foreign pressure and does respond.

Attack

The VCP and government first responded through a systematic campaign of intimidation and terror to silence and isolate critics. By curtailing freedom of association and the press, the regime has gone to great lengths to ensure that a critical mass of dissidents has not been allowed to effectively organize. In this the VCP has been fairly successful. Those who do publicly air their views do not go unnoticed. The regime mobilizes a vast amount of state resources and all political institutions, including the Ministry of the Interior and its police force, the military, and the lawmaking and interpreting bodies of the National Assembly and Ministry of Justice to protect its monopoly of power. The government uses the full weight of the law, while the VCP uses its nationwide grass-roots network to enforce its decisions.

How the party and government have struck at the various dissidents depended on two key factors: first, whether the dissident is a party member and, second, the rank of the dissident. People with impeccable revolutionary credentials, such as Gen. Tran Do and Dr. Duong Quynh Hoa, are fairly immune from persecution. Tran Do was expelled from the VCP in January 1999, though it is unlikely that he will be arrested. High-ranking officials or dissidents with significant revolutionary experience are more immune than others from arrest, but they are often attacked personally or indirectly in the press. Bui Tin was labeled a "liar and distorter of history" by *Quan Doi Nhan Dan,* on 25 May 1992, after the Vietnamese-language publication of his memoirs, *Political Reminiscences.* Lambasting his depiction of Ho Chi Minh, the article avowed that "only an enemy and a traitor could poke holes in that sacred name." Later, in a Voice of Vietnam radio commentary, he was riviled as a "sleeper reactionary" whose writings were a "bigoted negation" that exposed "the intricate psychology of a degraded person posing as a political beggar."[5] Despite his distinguished military career, he was described as a "puppet" in the employ of "overseas reactionaries." Likewise, Duong Thu Huong was labeled by Nguyen Van Linh as the "dissident whore," while Ha Si Phu, Tieu Dao Bao Cu, and Bui Minh Quoc were labeled by *Nhan Dan* as "the attacking troops of the anti-communist front."[6] One leading ideology cadre attacked Bui Minh Quoc and Tieu Dao Bao Cu for being an "absolutist and extreme faction," which played into the hands of the conservatives who criticize all tendencies toward renovation and democratization.[7]

Although Nguyen Ho has not been named in the press, he is attacked obliquely. The first salvo came from *Nhan Dan* in March 1998, when it admitted for the first time that there was real intraparty dissent: "We were surprised, even angry," the commentary said, "at some recent allegations not just from hostile forces but also from a small number of disaffected party members" who use "rich rhetoric" and "want us to give up our way towards socialism."[8] Gen. Tran Xuan Truong warned that "those who want to reject the party line only create illusions for themselves. They have no political future."[9]

In addition to the articles, on two consecutive days *Nhan Dan* then ran letters attacking the calls for greater democracy and political reform.[10] The first equated the dissidents' demands to "democracy like that of the colonial period." The second asserted that "certain people are propagating different opinions which almost completely refute the fundamental experience of the Vietnamese revolution." It went on to note that similar "political reforms" demanded by "opportunists" in the former Soviet Union and Eastern Europe "resulted in the breakup of the socialist regime."[11]

In response to Tran Do's continued letter writing, on 10 August 1998 a front-page commentary in *Quan Doi Nhan Dan* attacked various "hostile forces" and "political opportunists" who have "take[n] the chance to open an attack" to "eliminate socialism in Vietnam and drive us to the capitalist road." The article asserted that "some people have taken advantage of the difficult situation and hastily concluded the reform policies were no longer effective. . . . Their immediate solution is changing direction. It's really illogical."[12] At the same time, however, the party claimed not to pay any attention to him.

For a short essay in which he compared the individual freedoms under the French colonial regime and the communist regime, the poet Nguyen Huu Loan was singled out in an English-language newspaper in April 1998 by Politburo member Nguyen Thi Xuan Mai. Loan's argument was that under the colonial regime there were free elections, less official corruption, a free press, and a legal freedom of expression. Private newspapers were allowed and there was an open examination system for government positions and free education and health care. Loan summed up his argument by stating that "the French colonial regime was horrible indeed, but it is still a far dream for people under regimes that are thumping their chest bragging about independence, and oppressing their own people." In response to Loan and other dissidents, the author of the article in *Vietnam Courier,* Politburo member

Nguyen Thi Xuan Mai, stated that "for me and most other Vietnamese who lived through that era, this slave life was full of misery. We were not treated with human dignity."[13] To this end the author continued, "I thus find it impossible to agree with some 'scholars' who are calling for the removal of the party, blaming it for dragging the Vietnamese into poverty and holding the country back from catching up with the advanced democracies." The author went on to attack the intellectuals Ha Si Phu and Phan Dinh Dieu: "Perhaps these people think that since the party is so good at making sacrifices that all it should do is to lead the nation in wars against foreign aggression. Now that the country is in peace and unified, only science and technology count."

Others have been attacked directly by the party. Nguen Van Tran, for example, was singled out at the Eighth Party Congress by Do Muoi. And when Nguyen Ho was asked why he had left Saigon for the countryside, he replied that it was because the Central Committee had

> directed the whole nation to frame me as a reactionary, a spy having connections with the CIA, pandering . . . to the enemy, abetting the foreign press to propagandize against the party, being paid by the Americans, advocating pluralism and multi-party democracy with the aim to over throw the VCP. All the thoughtless charges against me said that the VCP had trampled me in the mud, buried my whole revolutionary life in ignominy to destroy me totally. Under such circumstances should I return to the city unless Vietnam enjoyed real democratic freedom! Therefore I have decided to live in the countryside until the last day of my life.[14]

The party has used far more coercive measures than pillorying them in the press. As mentioned earlier, of the thirty or so dissidents analyzed in this book, fifteen were party members, nine were expelled from the party, while two resigned. Only eleven of the prominent secular dissidents—Do Trung Hieu, Duong Thu Huong, Ha Si Phu, Hoang Minh Chinh, Le Hong Ha, Nguyen Ho, Nguyen Kien Giang, Nguyen Dan Que, Doan Viet Hoat, Nguyen Thanh Giang, and Pham Duc Kham—were sentenced and imprisoned, although the religious dissidents, especially Thich Huyen Quang and Thich Quang Do, have been persecuted far more systematically. With the September 1998 release of Que and Hoat and Giang's 1999 release, only a few prominent dissidents are currently in prison. But the systematic incarceration of religious and political dissidents continues to be an important means of control. Amnesty International believes there to be fifty-four dissidents in labor camps, while the U.S. Department of State puts the figure at

200. Overseas Vietnamese groups assert that the number of political prisoners is in the thousands.

The VCP has found an effective alternative to arrest, administrative detention. Directive 31/CP authorizes the government to detain individuals for up to two years without trial. The regime has found that not only does this give it a much more effective tool in deterring dissent, it also attracts much less international attention than arrests and trials of dissidents. The international community is increasingly aware of the government's use of this tactic that has become the primary tool for dealing with antigovernment dissent.

But even for those who have avoided labor camp, the party has not made life easy for them. Many, such as Tieu Dau Bao Cu, Bui Minh Quoc, and Nguyen Thanh Giang, have been detained and repeatedly called in for questioning. Giang was only released when he threatened a hunger strike, but was arrested again in March 1998. Security forces continue to harass these people by keeping them under surveillance or ransacking their houses. Tran Do has complained in a second letter to the Politburo that his family members, including his son, a colonel in the army, are now constantly being harassed. As stated above, even those party members who have called on the VCP to investigate corruption among senior party members are intimidated.

It is more than the force of law that the party uses to protect its interests: the government has an enormous infrastructure in place to deal with dissent and maintain its monopoly of power. The Ministry of the Interior is a huge bureaucracy, which in addition to running customs and immigration, operates the police, intelligence, and counterintelligence services and monitors the press, communications channels, and the Internet. The military too is constitutionally bound to defend the socialist regime, and directive 89/CP gives it an internal police role. In short, attacks on dissidents is made possible by an enormous bureaucracy with vast resources at its disposal.

The party has punished dissidents in other ways, primarily by taking away their livelihoods. Duong Thu Huong has been banned from writing or publishing in the country, and is only able to publish her works abroad—an illegal act under Vietnamese law. The academic Ha Si Phu was forced into retirement. Bui Minh Quoc and Tieu Dao Bao Cu lost their jobs at *Lang Bian* magazine and have not been able to work since. Bui Minh Quoc asserts that harassment from security forces has scared away customers from his family's small shop. Lu Phuong, likewise, lost his government job and now makes his living as a photographer in Saigon. Phan Dinh Dieu lost his seat in the National Assembly and in 1993 lost his position as the vice chairman of the National Center for Scientific Research. Tran Do claims that since running afoul of the party, his children have not been promoted and are bypassed for new positions.

Several were forced into exile, such as Pham Duc Kham and Doan Viet Hoat.[15] Bui Tin left voluntarily. Although his early release was supposed to have been in return for a pledge to leave the country and not return, Nguyen Dan Que has refused to leave and has vowed, instead, to remain in prison.[16] He is currently "convalescing" in Ho Chi Minh City, while Hoat has actively campaigned among Vietnamese exile groups in Europe and the United States to link development assistance and bilateral aid to improvements in Vietnam's human rights situation.[17]

At other times, the VCP has been conciliatory and made overtures to certain dissidents, perhaps suggesting that the party is not of one mind when it comes to how to deal with the dissidents. For example, nonparty mathematician Phan Dinh Dieu participated in a roundtable discussion of Marxism-Leninism in the party's main theoretical organ *Tap Chi Cong San* (*Communist Review*). In the article, which ran shortly before the Seventh Party Congress, he openly questioned whether Marxism-Leninism was an appropriate socioeconomic model for Vietnam.[18] That September, General Secretary Do Muoi invited Phan Dinh Dieu to talk about political reform.[19] He was invited by both the Institute of Social Science and the Marxism-Leninism Institute to discuss the crisis facing world communism. Indeed, his most stinging criticism of the regime was a speech delivered to the Extended Conference of the VFF Central Committee in December 1997. The most notable meetings came in the midst of the economic crisis in the late 1990s. Le Kha Phieu, during his "campaign" to become VCP general secretary in the fall of 1997, had a fairly well-publicized meeting with Hoang Minh Chinh—clearly a bid to win support from more liberal party members who were alarmed at the idea of a military man leading the party.[20] Le Kha Phieu soon afterward called on Tran Do during Tet in 1998, asking him to resolve his differences through proper party channels, not through open letters. Likewise, in May 1998 it was rumored that General Do was invited to meet with three members of the Politburo. The meeting came just a few months after he submitted his letter to the Politburo and Central Committee, which was widely circulated in the party and among dissidents and intellectuals. Clearly the party hoped that by giving him an audience he would agree to stop writing and criticizing the government. He was warned, in his words, that "the politburo considered that my opinions were not in line with the party's policies, and were therefore unacceptable."[21] He was ordered to stop writing, but refused. And on 20 June 1998, he submitted another open letter to the press. Though it was not published, it was widely circulated. He asked, "Do we need a developed country with enough food and clothes, freedom and happiness (i.e., democracy), or do we need a country with socialist orientation that it very poor?"[22] Six months later he was expelled from the party.

Ironically many of the harsh tactics have backfired on the VCP; many colleagues, friends, sympathizers, and patrons have sent letters to the party Central Committee condemning the attacks on people they feel have legitimate concerns. Many of these dissidents have unassailable revolutionary credentials; they spent their lives in the service of their country and fought to improve the standard of living of their compatriots. The former head of the Ministry of Defense Institute of Military History, Col. Pham Que Duong, for example, resigned from the VCP in protest over Tran Do's January 1999 expulsion. In his letter of resignation to the Central Committee, Colonel Duong wrote that a party that would expel a loyal revolutionary such as Tran Do was no longer a "worthy place for honest members."[23] A former Central Committee member and party boss of Haiphong, Hoang Huu Nhan, likewise wrote a blistering attack on the party's actions toward Do. In a letter to the Central Committee, Nhan complained that the campaign to vilify Do in the press throughout 1998 was "calumnious, brutal and dictatorial," and that Do was not attacking Marxism, the party's leadership, or the socialist system in Vietnam. But just the opposite, he was trying to make suggestions to strengthen the party: "I understand both the words and the heart of Tran Do in trying to rebuild the Party so that it can truly fortify and maintain its leadership role, to revive the party's credibility and its image in people's hearts as they were during the revolution and resistance time. In those days, the party and the people are one."[24]

To that end, Nhan argued that Do's proposal "should be treated with respect and it deserves careful study by the leading organ." That the party simply attacked the author without considering the substantive issues was, in Nhan's mind, "simpleminded."

Two other senior military cadres, Gen. Nguyen Van Dao and Lt. Gen Pham Hong Son, have also lashed out at the continuing crisis of corruption and the party's suppression of whistle blowers and internal critics, such as Tran Do. Echoing Tran Do's criticisms, the two attacked corruption in the senior echelons of the VCP, military, and state and advocated monitoring the businesses of the leaders' families, as well as banning all businesses owned by the party and security and military apparatuses.[25] For Pham Hong Son, continued corruption was only going to lead to a collapse of VCP rule as it did in the Soviet Union, where "people did not support party leadership as a result of a lack of democracy and too many privileges for the leaders."[26] Pham Hong Son has also attacked the overlapping roles of the party and state, which are redundant and wasteful and cause interference in the workings of government: "Our party's machinery is larger than the publicly elected administration, both of which receive taxpayer's money." Yet that machinery is not used to protect the people's interests. According to Son, "We should understand that government at all levels is the servant of the people. It means we gave to shoulder the common task of the people, not to dominate people like under the French and Japanese rulers."[27]

With the recent spate of attacks, the VCP announced that any further comments and criticism, both from within and outside the party, will not be tolerated. In February 1999, the party issued a directive for its members that guarantees "ideological freedom" on the one hand, but ensures that any public dissent will be severely punished, on the other: "[Party committees should] strictly criticize and punish those party members who . . . after being assisted by the party organization keep disseminating their own opinion or distributing documents contrary to the platform, statutes and resolution of the party.[28]

The party can be critical of itself, in proper forums, directed by the leadership, but it often is unable to effectively punish transgressors. But party rank and file and nonmembers are prohibited from raising any criticism that could lead to rifts in the VCP. Maintaining party unity and social stability remain the party's paramount concerns.

Defense

Aside from proactive attacks and arrests to silence dissidents and in-house critics, the party has also adopted a number of defensive strategies to counter the concerns of the critics. The most obvious is implementing new policies and laws to ameliorate the negative condition. In some cases this has happened. For example, the Vietnam Farmer's Association recently implemented a legal assistance program in conjunction with the Ministry of Justice to teach farmers their legal rights and to prevent abuse of power by local officials. There has also been an experiment in village democracy. But clearly there is a lot of trepidation in the VCP. Although potentially significant, these are both very small pilot programs with limited resources. Likewise, the party authorized the National Assembly to reform itself to become a more effective body. Since 1986, the National Assembly has become a more independent body that does indeed question government policy. National Assembly members are younger, better educated, and with more diverse professional experience. Still these are cosmetic changes: the VCP cannot let go and give the National Assembly the authority it needs to effectively formulate policy and serve as a government watchdog; its power is far short of its constitutional mandate and what will satisfy the dissidents. In short, the VCP refuses to embark on meaningful political reform. It has always taken a very cautious approach, far more reactive than proactive. And despite fifteen years of structural economic reforms, there have been almost no parallel political reforms.

A second strategy is the use of public campaigns led by the VCP to ameliorate negative conditions. The most common is the campaign against "spiritual pollution" that targets the negative effects of the reform program and opening the country up to the outside world. According to the party, with trade and investment come foreign ideas, unethical practices, pornography, drug addiction, and conduct that goes against revolutionary morality. In the first half of 1996, for example, the Politburo issued decree 87/CP, which authorized a nationwide campaign against spiritual pollution, in which videocassettes, illegal publications, and pornography were confiscated and destroyed, while brothels, gambling halls, massage, and karaoke parlors were closed. These public campaigns are short-lived and only address the symptoms of the problem that continues to grow, further disillusioning the populace.

A parallel to the campaign was a public crusade to inculcate the population with a sense of Vietnam's cultural grandeur and uniqueness; equating culture with socialist realism and ideology. At the Fifth Plenum of the Eighth Central Committee, in May 1988, for example, Le Kha Phieu called for the creation of an advanced culture with a strong sense of traditional Vietnamese identity. He elucidated several important tasks in this endeavor:

- Building the model Vietnamese citizen who is patriotic, righteous and law-abiding

- Creating an environment that promotes a healthy cultural life in each social unit
- Creating cultural and art works of high ideological and aesthetic value
- Preserving cultural heritage
- Managing the mass media[29]

The Central Committee resolution went on to state that "the preference for anything foreign, the disdain for national cultural values and the pursuit of an egoistic lifestyle have harmed the nation's fine traditions and customs." Here VCP adopts the language articulated in the debate over Asian values. Yet Asian leaders, including the Vietnamese, who espouse "culture" and "traditional values" want it both ways. They want to promote traditional values as opposed to the Western values that chafe them. But traditional values can be a Pandora's box for the regime. There is a terrible irony that the dissident Vietnamese monk Thich Quang Do shares the same concern as the hardline general secretary of the Vietnamese Communist Party Le Kha Phieu regarding moral degradation in society: "There is the urgent need to stop superstitious practices and social evils as well as the ravaging moral foundation that is hurting us, especially the younger generations."[30] For Do, traditional values cannot be separated from religion, but this is unacceptable to the Communist Party, which has launched its own campaigns to promote traditional values. In these campaigns, spiritual pollution and social evils are portrayed as Western exports to the pure land, hence the moral and cultural superiority of Vietnam must be put on a pedestal. So, General Secretary Le Kha Phieu launched a mass campaign to highlight the greatness of Vietnamese culture, but this spawned a revival of cult religions that the government seems unable to control. And it has allowed young intellectuals like Nguyen Huy Thiep to delve into history, using allegory to attack the government.[31]

Perhaps the most prescient acknowledgment of the dissidents' concerns is in the constant anticorruption campaigns. The VCP is clearly concerned with corruption in the party, and this has been the focus of the past few meetings of the Central Committee. Huu Tho, the head of the Central Committee's Ideology and Culture Commission, recently admitted that "the Party Central Committee showed great interest in the depravity in living styles of a part of our cadres and party members," since such practices "will be harmful to economic development and will make us lose the trust from the people."[32] To that end, Phieu launched a two-year "regeneration drive" of criticism and self-criticism in May 1999 to restore the party's soiled image that included disciplining errant members. Soon after the campaign began, in July 1999, the party had already expelled 200 members and disciplined 1,550.[33] By November 1999, the courts had heard 526 cases of graft involving 1,100 government officials and businessmen in the first nine months of 1999 alone, while 1,500 local and provincial officials were purged in the year after launching the anticorruption drive in May 1999.

As already discussed in detail in Chapter 4, the VCP has encouraged the press to report on several high-profile corruption trials, such the commercial fraud case involving an import-export firm owned by the Ministry of the Interior, which implicated seventy-four people in smuggling worth $64.8 million.[34] Similar cases include the fraud trials involving officials of EPCO-Minh Phung, who embezzled $280 million for land speculation,[35] and the 1997 Nam Dinh textile mill trial, in which fourteen people were imprisoned after corruption caused $17 million in losses. Yet despite these cases, however, corruption continues unabated, and one report concluded that the Ministry of Finance could not account for $6 billion—or nearly one-third of all state assets.[36] There is also the issue of who guards the guards. Some of the worse corruption scandals have occurred in the Ministry of Interior itself, several senior ministry officials being implicated in running drugs from Laos. Smuggling is so endemic that the head of the Customs Department, Phan Van Dinh, was sacked by the prime minister on 13 October 1999, as a corruption trial implicating seventy-four defendants got under way.

The party also recognized that to assuage the bad feelings of the peasantry, it will have to continue purging corrupt local officials, such as with the dismissal of fifty cadres after the peasant riots in Thai Binh in the 1997–1998 period and 100 party members (nearly the entire district-level administration) following demonstrations in Thanh Hoa Province in the mid-1990s. Even so the party anticipated more peasant protests throughout the country, thus it issued directive 89/CP, in November 1998, which authorizes local police and military units to establish temporary detention units in which people can be held without trial. This decree was promulgated simply to deal with mass detentions to prevent any peasant protests from escalating beyond control.

Vietnam has long deluded itself that corruption is a problem only at the lower echelons of the party and state apparatus. This was evident in the case in Thai Binh Province, where corrupt low-level cadres who failed to implement the party's line correctly were blamed, without there ever being an analysis of the effectiveness of party policies. Prime Minister Phan Van Khai announced that "corruption is seen among state officials and enterprise owners but it is not like in other countries where corruption climbs up to government levels."[37] Yet the party is beginning to acknowledge the problem is broader than previously acknowledged. Prime Minister Khai announced new regulations in the fall of 1998 for officials to annually disclose their assets, but not surprisingly, there is a loophole.[38] Although officials are told to disclose their assets of over 50 million dong ($4,500), they do not have to reveal their sources of income unless there is a radical difference from one year to the next. The regulation also bans the relatives of senior officials from holding certain positions, as well as banning senior officials from establishing or coestablishing private enterprises, joint stock or limited liability corporations, private schools, private hospitals, or research establishments.

At the Sixth Plenum in February 1999, which focused almost exclusively on the issue of corruption, General Secretary Le Kha Phieu warned that "each individual cadre from Politburo member, Central Committee member, minister provincial and city party secretary, provincial and city chairman down to the ordinary cadre and party member will be subject to criticism."[39] And as an integral component of its anticorruption strategy, the VCP decided at the Sixth Plenum in February 1999 to launch an intensive short-term campaign to "renovate" itself "politically, ideologically and organizationally." As part of "party-building" activities, according to Dao Duy Quat, the Central Committee voted to enhance the authority of internal inspection and discipline committees, as well as the authority of law enforcement agencies, elected bodies, and the media over party members.[40] Quat called for an intensive period of criticism and self-criticism for party members over the following two years. Le Kha Phieu explained that the two-year campaign would help to create a "strong and transparent party and government apparatus."[41] Other leaders have jumped on the bandwagon. But when Politburo member Pham The Duyet, who was himself the subject of a high-level investigation into allegations surrounding graft and nepotism before being exonerated, argues that the VCP has not been stringent enough against corrupt party members, he makes a mockery of the process. Until the senior leadership itself is willing to hold itself accountable, corruption will continue at all levels of the system.

"Party-building" activities are an acknowledgment of a problem, but they are clearly not enough to remedy Vietnam's current malaise. Rooting out some corrupt cadres, punishing those who abuse their power, and making the criteria for party membership stricter are important, but they are symptoms of the problem, not the root cause. It is still to be seen whether the party is really able to reform itself. It has never before been so forthcoming about internal problems. The problem with party building is that the VCP believes that if it is stronger, more hierarchical, and more centralized, then the country's problems will be solved. It is precisely not allowing alternative voices to be heard that got the country into its current political situation. Moreover, there will continue to be abuses of power so long as such a small elite monopolizes absolute power. For example, of the total population of 79 million there are only 2.5 million party members, approximately 3 percent of the population, yet it claims to speak and act in the interest of all. What is most alarming is the growing generational gap in the party. Although the party inducted 141,000 new recruits in 1999, the largest yearly increase in a decade, the number of new members under the age of 30 was at an all-time low. Moreover, most joined for reasons of career advancement, not because of a commitment to ideology or public service. As such, the likelihood of stemming corruption within party ranks seems bleak.

In sum, the dissent, especially from within the party's own ranks, is a conundrum. The VCP knows that the criticism is on the mark and that there are problems that the party has so far been unable to resolve, but the party is unsure of how to cope with the dissenters. On the one hand, it is forced to go on the defensive and address the issues raised: it has launched anticorruption campaigns and tried to improve party-building work, which will lead to a stronger, more unified party. But this is exactly the kind of response that continues to raise the dissidents' ire for it is top-down, controlled by the leadership, and never goes above the mid-level of party ranks. The party is corrupt, in the dissidents' eyes, because it holds a monopoly of power and refuses to allow organizations, individuals, or the press to serve as a watchdog or to force accountability on the senior leadership.

On the other hand, while tacitly acknowledging such concerns, the party has attacked the dissidents, pillorying them in the media, forcing them out of their jobs, denying them their livelihoods and outlets for their work, expelling them from the party, intimidating them, and, finally, detaining and arresting them. By assailing individuals who, for the most part, have loyally served the party and revolution and who have nothing to gain personally by such acts of provocation, the party reveals how self-serving it is. That the VCP will countenance no dissent or challenge to the rule reinforces the fictition of infallibility and reveals the hollowness of its pledges of democracy.

But dissent can also be politically useful for the various factions at both ends of the Vietnamese political elite. For ideological conservatives, a small but vocal dissident group allows them to demand greater discipline and justifies campaigns against spiritual pollution and party-building campaigns. They give the conservatives the proof they need that there are groups of saboteurs who are out to undermine the leading role and monopoly of power held by the VCP. As long as there is dissent, the party is under attack and must remain vigilant. For example, in early 1999, conservatives circulated a 7-page letter that warned: "The nation is in danger. Our party is facing the threat of a leadership split." To that end, only ideological purity and party discipline can combat these insidious attacks and threats to unity. Reformers, likewise are able to use the dissidents to further their political agenda. They can use the dissidents' calls for reform and warnings of the party losing legitimacy to justify continued and deeper economic and political reforms, as Prime Minister Pham Van Khai has done. One reformist Central Committee member, Nguyen Van Dao, has clamored for the ending of attacks on whistleblowers who raise allegations of corruption against party members.[41] As long as it is politically expedient, then it is likely that some dissent will be permissible. But it will also be very dangerous, subject to the quickly vacillating balances of power in the factional world of Vietnamese elite politics.

Exogenous Forces

One cannot simply look at endogenous explanations for how the regime responds to the dissidents. In the post–Cold War era and the age of interdependence, exogenous forces are always at work in pushing for greater democratization and political reform. The VCP's reactions to the dissidents will always be influenced by foreign pressures. Even though it chafes at foreign pressure, which it characterizes as blatant interference in Vietnam's internal affairs, it is unlikely that the Vietnamese government will be able to withstand international pressure and deny international monitors access to the country. The government is very concerned about foreign pressure; it is plain that more contact with the West will increase such pressure on Vietnam's human rights conditions and record.

There are Vietnam's international commitments, as a signatory and party to various human and social rights documents, including the Universal Declaration of Human Rights. Although the Vietnamese government annually commemorates its signing of the UN Declaration of Human Rights, the leadership has warned that not only do "we need to selectively absorb human values in accordance with Vietnam's political, economic, cultural and social conditions," but that "we also have to take measures to prevent those who take advantage of 'human rights and democracy' to interfere in Vietnam's internal affairs and sovereignty."[43] Vietnam has repeatedly asserted that "each country has its own way to deal with its own problems in order to maintain stability."[44] So, it has resisted foreign monitoring of its active commitment to human rights.[45] But this has not always been possible. For example, Vietnam signed the International Covenant on Civil and Political Rights in 1982, and article 18 of the covenant guarantees freedom of religion, belief, and thought. But pressure from the international community tends to come from bilateral sources—particularly the United States, as well as Australia and France, and from NGOs rather than any multilateral institutions. This changed with the October 1998 visit of UN Special Rapporteur on Religious Intolerance Abdelfattah Amor. His ten-day trip had taken three years to arrange, and probably happened only after Hanoi read Amor's 1994 report on China, which offered little criticism of the regime.

Despite promising Amor free and unfettered access to all religious sites and church leaders, his trip was highlighted by several direct confrontations with security forces, such as at the Thanh Minh zen monastery in Ho Chi Minh City, and being barred from entering Thich Quang Do's temple. In the former instance, the police tried to force the monks to turn the UN envoy away until the abbot threatened to burn himself to death on the spot. Though allowed in the temple, Amor was still not allowed to meet with the recently detained abbot.[46] Amor was also prevented from entering the Z30A labor camp, in southern Dong Nai Province, in which numerous clergymen are held. All in all, he was prevented from meeting with various clergy from the Buddhist, Catholic, Hoa Hao, Confucian, and other faiths.

In his written report to the UN Commission on Human Rights, Amor made it clear that every religious community in Vietnam was prevented from practicing its faith freely. "Religion appears as an instrument of policy rather than a component of society, free to develop as it wishes, something which is ultimately contrary to freedom of religion or belief as governed by international law."[47] While it was important for Vietnam to be publicly chastised for its repression, Amor's report had a very negative consequence: the Vietnamese government was so outraged that it announced that it would no longer admit international inspectors into the country.

The most significant pressure that can be brought to bear on the Vietnamese government comes from bilateral sources. For instance, in President Clinton's speech in which he announced that the United States would establish diplomatic relations with Vietnam, he made it clear that a primary motivation was to foster economic growth that would lead to popular demands for greater freedom and political rights. During his November 2000 visit to Vietnam, Clinton not only spoke about human rights to the Vietnamese leadership, but mentioned it publicly in a television address. More alarming to Hanoi was the reference Clinton made to Eastern Europe: "Increased contact between Americans and Vietnamese will advance the cause of freedom in Vietnam just as it did in Eastern Europe and the former Soviet Union."[48] Likewise, during a visit to Hanoi, U.S. Secretary of State Madeleine Albright told her Vietnamese hosts that "human rights is a permanent issue for us. It is not going to go away."[49] The U.S. State Department's 1997 annual report on human rights stated that the Vietnamese government's "human rights record continues to be poor" and that the government "continued to repress basic political and some religious freedoms and to commit numerous abuses."[50] Subsequent reports have been just as critical.

In addition to the law that obligates the State Department to conduct an annual survey of human rights violations, there is a 1998 U.S. law that requires the president to impose sanctions on any state that fails to meet Washington's standards for religious freedom. This law was immediately condemned by Vietnam. The *Quan Doi Nhan Dan* editorial was one of outrage: "With this new law on religion, one has the impression that American lawmakers intend to make laws for the entire world." This law instructed the State Department to compile its Annual Reports on International Religious Freedom. The first report, while acknowledging the improved climate for religion in civilian life, concluded that "government regulations control religious hierarchies and organized religious activities, in part because the VCP fears that organized religion may weaken its authority and influence by serving as a political, social, and spiritual alternative to the authority of the central government."[51]

Such acts have led Vietnam to conclude that the United States is trying to undermine Communist Party rule through "peaceful evolution." The army daily, *Quan Doi Nhan Dan*, stated that the United States was seeking "the victory in peace that eluded it in war." As another commentator explained: "It is clear that the United States and other Western countries have, in the name of pluralism and human rights, used their familiar trick of 'peaceful evolution' to overthrow the socialist regime and undermine the socialist construction of many countries."[52] But there seems to be little else that Vietnam can do other than protest and use such pressures to justify internal repression.

Direct U.S. involvement has led to the release of many dissidents. In June 1997, the case of Doan Viet Hoat, editor of *Freedom Forum*, who was serving a fifteen-year sentence, was raised by Secretary of State Albright. In September 1998, the government released several prominent dissidents and religious figures, as well as some Vietnamese-Americans, as part of the general amnesty. Doan Viet Hoat, Nguyen Dan Que, Nguyen Thah Giang, Thich Huyen Quang, and Thich Quang Do have all been released midway through their sentences. Although the government refused to admit that their inclusion was brought about by foreign pressure,[53] it is clear that Vietnam hoped to win some economic concessions from the United States through this move. And even though Hanoi was angered by a June 2000 letter from thirty-two members of the U.S. Congress calling for the immediate release of Ha Si Phu, it has little power to stop such attacks.

Bilateral pressure comes not just from the Americans. With the hosting of the November 1997 Francophone Summit, Hanoi found itself under intense French pressure to release forty dissidents whose names the French foreign minister presented to his Vietnamese counterpart, Nguyen Manh Cam. To present a better face to the international community, journalists were less constrained, which allowed one French TV crew to film the remote prison camp where a prominent dissident was being held. In November 1994, France awarded Duong Thu Huong its highest literary honor, the Chevalier of the Order of Arts and Letters, despite strong protests from the Vietnam Writers' Association. Indeed, Huong was freed from prison only at French Foreign Minister Roland Dumas's urging. The secretary general of the VWA, Vu Tu Nam, stated that this was a "political act" that could "only create suspicion toward the goal of French cultural policy in Vietnam." Likewise,

Germany took up Huong's case in early 2000, after Vietnamese authorities denied her a passport so she could travel to Germany where she would be awarded a prestigious literary award.

Vietnam pays more attention to international NGOs, such as Amnesty International and Human Rights Watch. It chafes at their annual reports, calling them biased and a violation of Vietnam's sovereignty, but the government knows that it is held accountable by the international community.[54] In the past few years, much of the attention of both the international community and human rights organizations has focused on Vietnamese writers. For example, the World Association of Newspapers awarded its highest honor, the Golden Pen of Freedom award, to Doan Viet Hoat. Again Vietnam complained: "We think that WAN's giving the Golden Pen of Freedom Award to Doan Viet Hoat, a delinquent who is serving his sentence, is a mistake," a foreign ministry spokesman said.[55] The foreign pressure must have had some affect: Hoat was given an amnesty, along with human rights activist Nguyen Dan Que in September 1998, only five years into his fifteen-year sentence, even though he was forced into exile in the United States. Human Rights Watch has also been active in singling out Vietnamese writers for recognition. Between 1991 and 1998, twenty-seven of more than 200 Hellman/Hammett grants, which are awarded to writers who face political persecution, anything from imprisonment to censorship to jeopardizing their livelihood, went to Vietnamese writers (see Table 7.1). Recipients have included Duong Thu Huong, Nhu Phong, Nguyen Ho, Doan Viet Hoat and Bui Minh Quoc, as well as religious figures such as Catholic priest Chan Tin and Unified Buddhist Church leaders Thich Tri Sieu and Thich Tue Si.

In addition to pressure from NGOs and multilateral and bilateral sources, there are other exogenous forces that shape the debate in Vietnam. Foreign radio transmissions, such as those from the BBC, Voice of America, Radio Free Asia, and Radio Irina in Russia, not to mention the proliferation of satellite TV dishes, all have helped to pierce the veil of state-controlled media and information. More important, they have helped to raise the standards for Vietnam's own journalists.

The foreign media also bring light to issues of press freedom in Vietnam through their own reporting. For example, the temporary closing of the *Far Eastern Economic Review*/Dow Jones office, because its correspondent Adam Schwarz was unable to renew his visa after unflattering reportage on Vietnam's economy and state-owned enterprise reform, sent a clear message to the international community. The April

Table 7.1   Hellman Hammett Awardees

1991	Duyen Anh
1992	Duong Thu Huong
	Nguyen Kim Tuan (aka Duy Lam)
1994	Doan Viet Hoat
	Nguyen Chi Thien
	Tien Thanh Dinh (aka To Thuy Yen)
1995	Nguyen Van Ho (aka Nguyen Ho)
	Nguyen Ban Thuan (aka Chau Son)
	Nguyen Xuan Ty (aka Ha Si Phu)
	Nguyen Thieu Hung (aka Mai Trung Ting)
1996	Do Trung Hieu
	Hoang Minh Chinh
	Thich Quang Dao
	Tieu Dao Bao Cu
1997[a]	Bui Minh Quoc
	Chan Tin
	Nguyen Dinh Huy
	Nguyen Ngoc Lan
	Nguyen Van Tran
	Phan Thanh Hoai
1998[b]	Hoang Tien
	Le Duc Vuong
	Lu Phuong
	Nguyen Huu Loan (aka Huu Loan)
	Nguyen Ngoc Tan
	Pham Thai Thuy
	Thich Tri Sieu

Notes: This is a partial list because some recipients requested anonymity.

a. Nguyen Dinh Huy is a journalist serving a fifteen-year term for planning to hold an international conference to promote democracy. Nguyen Ngoc Lan is a philosophy professor who has been under surveillance for writing articles and calling for freedom of expression and political pluralism. Chan Tin is a Catholic priest who was imprisoned for five years for demanding the release of political prisoners. Phan Thanh Hoai is a physician turned author who has been banned from writing.

b. Nguyen Ngoc Tan is a journalist and novelist who was an opposition MP during the Republic of Vietnam era, and arrested for fifteen years in 1975. He was sentenced again on 12 February 1995 for eleven years for attempting to overthrow the government. Pham Thai Thuy is a poet and journalist, and also a southerner. He joined Doan Viet Hoat to edit the samizdat journal *Freedom Forum* and was imprisoned from 1990 to 1994. He now lives in exile in the United States. Thich Tue Si and Thich Tri Sieu are both Buddhist monks and leaders of the banned UBCV. Both were arrested in April 1984 for "activity aimed at overthrowing the people's government."

2000 arrest and expulsion of the correspondent for the French weekly *L'Express,* Sylvaine Pasquier, again highlighted the inability of foreign journalists to report freely in the country and to operate without official handlers. Even when it is not as extreme as these two cases, several journalists have told me about being detained and interrogated by the Ministry of the Interior personnel for having written specific stories or interviewing certain individuals.

In conclusion, human rights, whether Vietnam agrees with the West's interpretation of it or not, has to be on the policymakers' agenda. And there is some indication that this is happening: there is now a high-level interagency group, including representatives from the Interior Ministry, the Central Committee and other party organs, the Supreme Court, and the Ministry of Foreign Affairs, that meets to discuss human rights issues.[56] The regime will have to respond to foreign pressure. Simply put, Vietnam is too small and vulnerable, too dependent on foreign development assistance and direct investment to shut out the international community. It does not have the political and economic leverage that China has. Nonetheless, despite foreign pressure for political reform and a loosening of the VCP's hold on power, the pressure for democratization and political reform has come from within. Exogenous forces will continue to be more of an annoyance to the regime than a force for change. Pressure for political liberalization has to come from within the party itself.

Notes

1. Huw Watkin, "Hero Takes Leadership to Task," *South China Morning Post (SCMP)*, 20 June 2000.

2. Reuters, "Vietnam Justifies Clampdown on Dissidents," 18 March 1999.

3. Dao Duy Quat is the deputy director of the Central Committee's Ideology and Culture Commission. He is the son of the late party ideologue and Politburo member, Dao Duy Tung.

4. Andy Solomon, "Vietnam Communist Party Faced Sabotage in 1998," Reuters, 9 March 1999.

5. See *Voice of Vietnam,* 13 June 1995, Foreign Broadcast Information Service, *East Asia-Daily Reports (FBIS-EAS)*, 15 June 1995, 59-60.

6. *Nhan Dan*, 5 May 1997.

7. Tran Truong Tan, "How to Clearly Understand the Vietnam Communist Party Central Committee Political Bureau's Conclusion on Ideological Work," 72.

8. Cited in Adrian Edwards, "Party Chief Rejects Calls for Reform," Reuters, 11 March 1998.

9. *Quan Doi Nhan Dan,* 16 March 1998.

10. *Nhan Dan*, 10–11 March 1998.

11. Cited in AFP, "Vietnam Has No Need to Democratize, Say Party Newspaper Readers," 11 March 1998.

12. Cited in Reuters, "Vietnam Army Daily Takes Aim at 'Hostile Forces,'" 10 August 1998.

13. Nguyen Thi Xuan Mai, "Is Democracy Better Under a Colonial Regime?" *Vietnam Courier,* No. 240, 5–11 April 1998, 10.

14. Nguyen Ho, *Ideology and Life,* excerpted in "Dissident Party Member Reveals Own Ordeal," *Vietnam Insight* (June 1994).

15. Hoat stated, "I wanted to stay but they would not let me. I love my country. I want to contribute to freedom and democracy in my country." "Freed Activist 'Forced to Leave Country,'" *SCMP,* 2 September 1998.

16. "Vietnamese Dissident Refuses to Leave," BBC World Service-Asia Pacific, Interactive *http://www.bbc.co.uk,* 29 August 1998.

17. A. Lin Neuman, "A Life Apart," *FEER,* 11 February 1999, 27–28; AFP, "Link Aid to Human Rights: Vietnamese Dissident Tells France," 1 February 1999.

18. Murray Hiebert, "Higher Criticism," *FEER,* 2 May 1991, 17-18.

19. Hiebert, "Dissenting Voices," 26.

20. For more on the leadership selection, see Zachary Abuza, "The Unfinished Congress: Leadership Transition in Vietnam Since the 8th Party Congress," 1105–1121.

21. Andy Solomon, "Dissident Vietnam General Fires New Broadside," Reuters, 29 June 1998.

22. Ibid.

23. Radio Free Asia, "Military Historian Turns in Party Card to Protest General Tran Do's Expulsion," 19 January 1999. Colonel Duong was the editor in chief of the influential *Tap Chi Lich Su Quan Su (Journal of Military History).* He retired in 1987.

24. Hoang Huu Nhan, "An Inconceivable Treatment," *Vietnam Democracy* (February 1999).

25. Ken Stier, "Party Grapples with Surge of Internal Dissent," *SCMP,* 20 February 1999.

26. Cited in Stier, "Party Grapples with Surge of Internal Dissent."

27. AP, "Second Vietnamese General Openly Criticizes Party," 13 February 1999.

28. Cited in Reuters, "Crackdown on Members Who Go Against Party Line," 26 February 1999.

29. VNS, "Culture is the Nation's Foundation," *Vietnam News,* 13 August 1998; VNS, "Vietnamese Culture Product of Aeons of Creativity, Struggle," 16 August 1998.

30. Thich Quang Do, "Letter to VCP Leadership, 15 January 2000," translated and published by Radio Free Asia, 31 March 2000.

31. See the following three short stories for examples of allegorical attacks on the regime: "Kiem Sac (A Sharp Sword)," "Vang Lua (Fired Gold)," and "Pham Tiet (Chastity)," translated by Peter Zinoman, *The Vietnam Forum* 14 (1994): 7–17, 18–25 and 26–35, respectively.

32. Andrew Soloman, "Vietnam Says Corruption Causes Loss of Trust," Reuters, 16 July 1998.

33. Huw Watkin, "Concerned Communists Keep Purging," *SCMP,* 22 July 1999.

34. Reuters, "Two Major Criminal Trials Set for Vietnam's Courts," 10 February 1999.

35. The trial concluded in August 1999, resulting in the death sentence for six former officials and lengthy prison sentences for the other seventy-one people on trial.

36. Huw Watkin, "Death Sentences Fail to Inspire Financial-Sector Confidence," *SCMP,* 6 August 1999.

37. Andrew Solomon, "Vietnam Talks Tough but Corruption Seems Ingrained," Reuters, 29 March 1998.

38. Decree 64/1998/CP was signed on 17 August 1998. See VNS, "New Decree Issued to Fight Corruption," *Vietnam News,* 21 August 1998.

39. DPA, "Vietnam Communist Party Boss Launches New Anti-Corruption Push," 5 January 1999.

40. *Nhan Dan,* "Sixth Plenum Passes Resolution on Party Building Work," 4 February 1999.

41. VNS, "Drastic Measures Pledged to Beat Corruption and Waste," *Vietnam News,* 5 January 1999.

42. Ken Stier, "Party Grapples with Surge of Internal Dissent."

43. "Vietnam Says Must Be Selective Over Rights," Reuters, 10 December 1998.

44. "Vietnam Justifies Clampdown on Dissidents," Reuters, 18 March 1999.

45. According to Foreign Ministry spokesman Le Sy Vuong Ha, "We will not accept any foreign individual or organizations that wish to travel in Vietnam to carry out rights investigations into religious or human rights issues." The statement came after the UN Special Rapporteur on Religious Intolerence, Abdelfattah Amor, released his report on Vietnam that accused the regime of restricting religious freedom. Amor accused Hanoi of hindering his investigation in October 1998. Reuters, "Hanoi Says Human Rights Investigators Unwelcome," *SCMP,* 18 March 1999.

46. Ken Stier, "Little Faith Shown in Religious Freedom," DPA, 30 October 1998.

47. Abdelfattah Amor, "Civil and Political Rights, Including the Question of Religious Intolerance," Report Submitted by the Special Rapporteur to the UN Commission on Human Rights, 29 December 1998.

48. Adam Schwartz, "Now What," *FEER,* 17 August 1995, 23.

49. Albright told her hosts, "It is our view that Vietnam is holding itself back from greater international participation and respect through its failure to permit organized political opposition and a free press." Cited in Thomas W. Lippman, "Vietnam Rejects U.S. Reproach on Human Rights," *IHT,* 28–29 June 1997, 1.

50. U.S. Department of State, Bureau of Democracy, Human Rights, and Labor, "Vietnam Report on Human Rights Practices for 1997," 30 January 1998, electronic dissemination, *http://www.vinsight.org/.*

51. U.S. Department of State, Bureau of Democracy, Human Rights, and Labor, "Annual Report on International Religious Freedom for 1999: Vietnam," 9 September 1999.

52. Ha Xuan Truong, "Plurality and Pluralism," *TCCS* (July 1989), in *FBIS-EAS,* 12 September 1989, 69-70.

53. Reuters, "Vietnam Party Daily Slams Reports on Mass Amnesty," 11 September 1998.

54. See, for example, Human Rights Watch, *Vietnam: The Silencing of Dissent* (2000).

55. AFP, "Vietnam Labels Recipient of Golden Pen Award 'Delinquent'," 3 June 1988.

56. Murray Hiebert, "Miles to Go," 26.

8

CONCLUSION

My words could be hard for the authorities to hear, but bitter medicine can stop diseases. I just want to contribute to the advancement of this country and catch-up with other neighboring countries and the world.

—*Hoang Tien*

In writing about the Club of Former Resistance Fighters, Nayan Chanda stated that "what the Vietnamese leaders fear is not a Chinese-style, student-led movement for democracy or a Polish-style, anti-party Solidarity trade union, but a challenge from party veterans angered and humiliated by the disastrous state of the country's economy."[1] A decade later, the party's concerns remain the same: opposition from within its own ranks and the emergence of overt factional infighting, a nascent democracy.

The development of civil society has been weak, and there are few independent agents of change in Vietnam. The VCP has tried to curtail civil society's growth and maintain full control over "mass organizations" such as professional associations, labor unions, and religious organizations. There is obviously growing concern, and the party expends a vast amount of resources to control civil society and prevent autonomous organizations from emerging. This is critical because without broader links to the general populace, the dissidents pose a much smaller threat to the regime. As soon as they can mobilize a critical mass of people in society, then the VCP will face the first real test of its monopoly of power. A group like the CFRF, with its regional following of closely bound veterans who share similar concerns and a charismatic leadership that can mobilize its following, is troubling to party leadership. This is also true of religions with their nationwide network of churches and adherents, a hierarchical authority structure, and charismatic and morally upright leader who are able to disseminate information and mobilize their congregations. It was disappointing to see that with the worst floods in the Mekong Delta in four decades in the fall of 2000, the VCP, while courting international relief aid for the nearly 4 million affected people, not only shunned relief support mobilized by local Buddhist temples, but waged an all-out campaign against the monks trying to contribute to relief efforts. While Australia, the UN World Food Program, and the International Committee of the Red Cross have all been active in relief aid for the 190,000 people in need of emergency assistance, there is little that the international community can do for the approximately 4 million people who have lost homes, livestock, or crops.[2] Yet, at the domestic level, the state feels that if it were to lose its monopoly on the distribution of goods and services, its political authority would dissipate.

Civil society is growing in parallel with the country's economic development, and professional organizations and associations are being formed, autonomous from the party.[3] But civil society's development is limited for three reasons. First, the VCP fears the development of civil society and its constituent parts and tries to curtail their autonomy, making them responsible to organs of the party and state. Second, there is no legal framework in which they can operate, and, while the existing laws may technically support independent organizations, the interests of the party remain paramount. Third, although the private sector is legal, the government has hampered its development, as well as obstructing the major advocates for civil society and legalization, favoring instead the state-owned sector of the economy.

Until civil society is more thoroughly developed, dissidents will remain the primary articulators of political and legal reform. This alone is cause for alarm for the VCP. The dissident movement in Vietnam is nascent and still small, yet its power is in its membership. As lifelong members of the party, veterans have unassailable revolutionary credentials, as well as the finest intellectual minds in the country; they speak with moral authority and reason. These are people, who for the most part, have given their entire lives to their nation; they are true patriots and want only the best for their country.

Although they are by no means a uniform group, they share several moderate goals. Most want to work within the current legal-constitutional structure by empowering the National Assembly to govern in a legalistic society, in which a free press provides information and serves as a public watchdog. Few advocate a truly pluralist system. They want to strengthen the current system, not undermine it. But their frustration over the party's monopoly of power, control of the National Assembly, corruption, and refusal to liberalize and reform the economy, as well as the lack of intellectual freedom and freedom of the press, have led them to challenge the party's methods and goals. The dissidents wish to serve as a loyal opposition in order to contribute to the development of the nation. But to an insecure regime that has rested on its laurels and employed coercion to maintain its monopoly of power, these dissidents are a threat to not only the regime, but to the nation.

What is it they want? First, they support the development of a law-based society. But it is more than creating a legal framework or ending rule by decree. They want a total adherence to the rule of law, in particular the abolition of article 4 of the constitution that places the party above the law. Existing laws that provide loopholes to protect the party's interests must be abolished. For instance, right now press laws or laws that guarantee freedom of association or religion are hollow because they have caveats in which the party's interests trump individual rights and freedoms.

Second, the dissidents articulate the broadening of democracy. They either stop short of calling for a Western-style bourgeois democracy or suggest a gradual transition to it. Most are looking for a broader forum in which open debate can take place. Very simply, the VCP's monopoly on decisionmaking has led to ill-conceived and executed policies that have led to economic mismanagement and stagnation as well as diplomatic isolation. The dissidents call for the constitutional authority of the National Assembly to be restored, and for the party to relinquish its control over the parliament and the selection of its members. Rather than calling for the immediate establishment of political parties, the dissidents see a role for individual members, nonparty experts, and intellectuals to have a meaningful debate over policies, free of party interference. There is a precedent for this, the case of Nguyen Xuan Oanh. Oanh, a Harvard-trained economist who briefly served as prime minister in the Republic of Vietnam regime in 1964, went on to serve the communist regime, eventually becoming the deputy governor of the Bank of Vietnam. Respected by many senior party members, including former Prime Minister Vo Van Kiet, Oanh has been very candid in his critique of the quasi-market system and has advocated a laissez-faire free-market system. In a forthcoming book, Oanh questions whether

proletarian revolution and class struggle are "still undisputed truths in
the new millenium."[4] Oanh is politically protected, and is thus an
anomaly. But he is a model of the type of "broadened democracy"
many of the dissidents are looking for.

"Broadening democracy" will have three net effects. First, it will
reinforce the notion of a law-based society. Second, open debates
should foster better policies. Third, the National Assembly can serve as
a watchdog, a constitutional check on the abuse of power by the party,
helping to end the endemic corruption. The "broadening of democracy"
is simply about governance style. As La Van Lam said, "The Party's
way of ruling the nation has shown its sincere ineffectiveness since
1955. It's time for change, to bring prosperity to the people, strength to
the nation and justice to our society." Likewise, another veteran revolutionary, Do Trung Hieu, complained about the party's style of leadership:

> For 40 years I had fought under the flag of the VCP out of love for
> this country and people and out of hope that the party would build a
> powerful country with social justice. Reality has proved otherwise.
> The party leads the country closer to a dead end. The VCP must seri-
> ously review its methods. . . . We raise this issue with leaders of the
> VCP simply to clear the way to advance the country and have no
> other purposes.

The third, and perhaps the most widely disseminated demand of the
various dissidents, has been for freedom of the press and intellectual
freedom in general. The party's continuous monopoly of information
has hindered the country's development. This monopoly has prevented
accountability: without the watchdog function of an independent press,
official corruption has continued unabated and failed policies remain in
place. Without a free press, there can be no free and meaningful debate
over policy. The lack of a free press is going to adversely affect the
country's economic development; the free flow of information has become the sine qua non of knowledge-based economies.

Many of these concerns can be summed up in one way: the dissidents are aghast that the VCP equates its own survival with national security, patriotism with communism. As Do Trung Hieu put it, "Without
Vietnamese patriotism there would be no Vietnamese Communist Party.
The party is only great when it stands in the hearts of the people and
carries out the people's wishes." If the party was really patriotic, it
would not "equate the survival of the party with that of the nation" and
would "stop building the communist reality for just the party Central

Committee." The party has become a new class and by refusing to reform, the party has convinced the dissidents that now it is only existing to perpetuate its monopoly of power.

Related to this is the party's xenophobia that keeps the country in a state of self-imposed isolation. The regime believes that the international community is very hostile, and is trying to undermine the VCP's monopoly of power through strategies of "peaceful evolution." At a mid-1998 party plenum, for example, the military released a list of enemy states, with the United States at the top, that were trying to undermine Vietnam and the VCP's monopoly of power. Concerns over the United States' ulterior motives played a large part in delaying Hanoi for one year in signing the Bilateral Trade Agreement.[5] Le Hong Ha articulated the absurdity of this type of thinking:

> From the momentum of normalization of relations with the US and the joining of ASEAN, the party should have focused the strength of the country into integrating with the world economy, community, and culture to develop the nation. A number of leaders, to the opposite, have wasted a bit of time and energy on political security against the enemies' peaceful evolution and psychological warfare. They hold thousands of meetings across the country. They think that doing so will solidify the support of the classes; instead they simply show panic, fear, and cringing.

The party uses this fear of foreign intervention to justify harsh crackdowns on the dissident community and tolerates no dissent or opposition. It has arrested, detained, harassed, exiled, and denied livelihoods to those who question its rule and policies. In the dissidents' eyes, "arresting and terrorizing comrades who contributed greatly to the long resistance, and who have been warning the party against its mistakes," is a very shortsighted policy. Yet the regime continues to use the vast state resources at its disposal—legal and physical—to do just that.

And the future? The dissident community will remain small and besieged by a hostile regime until civil society becomes more developed. Until then, the VCP will not face any credible threat to its power. In addition to its ability to mobilize all state resources to defend its monopoly of power, the VCP still has considerable legitimacy, especially in the countryside. No dissident will deny the role that the party played during the thirty years of war and the drive for independence and reunification. The party led with a large degree of moral authority and public support, and at that time it could call on the population to make enormous sacrifices. But none will forgive the party for failing to develop the nation, improve people's livelihoods, democratize, forgo its monopoly of power, and end the rampant corruption, or for equating its own interests to those of the people. The party has become entrenched, alienated from the people, abusive of its power, and increasingly embattled. Poor decisionmaking and policy choices have delegitimized the regime. Although the economic reform program that began in late 1986 saw great initial results, the economy has been in a recession since 1997, and shows little sign of rebounding unless difficult and unpopular policies are implemented. Yet ideology aside, the regime can be very pragmatic when it has to be. The regime has squandered legitimacy, not lost it. Where does this leave the regime at the start of the new century?

The literature on political transformations gives us some indication on what the future holds. If there is growing social unrest there are three courses of action: crackdown, surrender, or a negotiated accommodation. The regime could attempt a crackdown, to crush any existing opposition and deter future opposition, and it certainly has the power to do so. Yet this option may not be pursued for the following reasons. First, advocates of such a course of action may be in the minority; there might not be the political will to undertake such a severe initiative. Second, it would be enormously detrimental to Vietnam's international standing and image. Such an egregious violation of human rights would be sharply criticized, and Vietnam simply does not have the economic leverage to withstand isolation. The result would be more akin to the present situation of the military junta in Myanmar, a state of continued economic and political isolation, rather than what the Chinese leadership found itself in following the 4 June 1989 Tiananmen massacre. Third, such a crackdown would require the full compliance of the military. Although the armed forces are constitutionally bound to defend the regime, and there is an officer corps that is very loyal to the VCP (most officers are party members), the rank and file may be unwilling to use force against an unarmed population.

The second course of action, surrender, is most unlikely. Few regimes voluntarily relinquish all political power. Moreover, such a scenario would be disastrous because there is nothing now to fill the void, no group or movement with a nationwide network or sufficient resources. The VCP remains the strongest political institution in the country, while the second strongest is the military, which does not bode well for the future of democracy and a peaceful political transition from an authoritarian regime.

The third option is the likeliest: a negotiated transition over a long period. This will happen as the unitary façade of the Vietnamese political system breaks down and more open factionalism emerges, coupled with the development of civil society. There will not be a sudden collapse as there was in Eastern Europe. The party is not going to "wither away." As Ha Si Phu wrote, "I'm sure that the 'farewell' will come. It will be, however, an unusual goodbye. There won't be a handshake and each [parting in] to an opposite direction. In Vietnam, it will be a gradual process. A number of changes already took place in the economic area. This is the result of reality and not the Marxist-Leninist direction. I think the remaining Marxism-Leninism in Vietnam is a parasite on the back of that reality."

With economic development there will be greater demands for individual, economic, and political freedoms, and the development of autonomous organizations to articulate demands for the newly emerging and competing sectors. It will be a gradual process, but it is the most likely scenario for Vietnam. As in Hungary, pressure to reform the economy and liberalize speech and politics will come from competing political factions from within the ruling body itself, with their divisions over regional differences and economic-ideological proclivities, not from unions, disgruntled workers, and students protesting in the streets.

But in the short run this is terrible for the country. So fearful is the regime of being divided, that it is, at present, unwilling to undertake bold policies for fear of unbalancing the ideological status quo. No one has forced the resolution of pressing issues for fear of opening up a broader ideological and philosophical debate in which factional infighting will becomes overt. Since the Asian economic crisis began in the summer of 1997, there have been almost no policy responses from Hanoi, which seems determined to ride out the storm. Simply no consensus could be reached, and the leadership has responded in piecemeal fashion. Indeed, the Central Committee's Fifth Plenum in July 1998 emphasized the mobilization of $7 billion in domestic capital to supplant the fall in foreign investment. Conservatives in Vietnam's leadership blamed the Asian economic crisis on capitalism and believed that Vietnam's lack of integration was a blessing in disguise. Reformers, on the defensive, blamed the crisis on "crony capitalism," imperfect markets, and too much government intervention. For three years there was no major decision by the Politburo, which has been completely deadlocked since the Eighth Party Congress in 1996. Within the conservative-dominated Politburo there is tremendous resistance to implementing these necessary reforms. This, too, was seen in the case of the Bilateral

Trade Agreement with the United States. The Politburo voted against the deal in October 1999, after an agreement in principle had been reached that July, because of a political deadlock between the advocates of globalization and liberal economic reform and the ideological conservatives. Reformers believed that in the context of declining exports, a drastic fall in foreign investment, and a surging trade deficit, Hanoi needed this deal for its economic recovery. Conservatives saw it as a threat to state-owned enterprises, which, though inefficient, are at the heart of the socialist system. The trade deal would also have broken the state's monopoly on foreign trade and increased Vietnam's interdependence, making it more vulnerable and susceptible, for example, to the economic contagion that swept East Asia after the summer of 1997. Ideological conservatives in the leadership carried the day in October and refused to embark on a course they sensed could threaten political stability. Only after ten months of rancorous debates and bargaining did the Politburo reach a consensus and give its support to the agreement. The entire time, there was considerable consternation on the part of the party leadership that their much cherished unity was being challenged.

Much of the problem is the fault of the Vietnamese political system. Vietnamese politics are highly factional, yet still operate on the basis of consensual decisionmaking. The leaders today are weaker than their predecessors and seem far more concerned about maintaining power than implementing meaningful reform. The constant striving for balance within the leadership, in terms of age, region, and sector, further plays to consensual politics.

The fact is, responding to the Bilateral Trade Agreement or the Asian economic crisis, or reforming state-owned enterprises, or coping with rebellious peasants, are very divisive issues. Yet the VCP is terrified at the idea of being divided, and hence fails to effectively deal with them. Policies are stopgap measures, reactive rather than proactive, cosmetic rather than structural. The lingering issues that plague society, such as abuse of power, corruption, and economic mismanagement, will remain unresolved until there is a fundamental change in the way policy is made in Vietnam. There needs to be open debate, including input from nonparty elites, to introduce new ideas and to hold the party accountable. Yet the VCP leadership sees even this limited political reform as the first step in the loss of its monopoly of political power. Since Hanoi does not have to worry about independent agents of change that brought down communist regimes in Eastern Europe, such as large student movements, a large and independent church presence, and independent unions, it does worry about intraparty dissent and division. Because of calls for a "Hungarian pattern for developing socialist democracy," the leadership at present is unwilling to take on major ideological policy issues that could jeopardize the unity of the party and encourage the transition of informal factionalism to a more institutionalized political system. To that end, the party will not countenance any dissent within its own ranks, from those who simply want to serve as a loyal opposition to the country that they have served throughout its tumultuous modern history.

Notes

1. Nayan Chanda, "Force for Change," *FEER*, 5 October 1989, 24.
2. AP, "Red Cross Steps up Vietnam Relief as Flood Deaths Top 300," 10 October 2000.
3. Carlyle Thayer, "Mono-Organizationalism Socialism and the State," 39–64.
4. Michael Sheridan, "City Last Hurrah for Vietnam's Old Red Guard," *Sunday Times*, 23 April 2000.
5. Zachary Abuza, "Debating the Future."

BIBLIOGRAPHY

Abbreviations Used in this Bibliography

AFP	Agence France-Presse
AP	Associated Press
DPA	Deutsche Press-Agentur
FEER	*Far Eastern Economic Review*
FBIS-AP	Foreign Broadcast Information Service, *Daily Reports-Asia Pacific*
FBIS-EAS	Foreign Broadcast Information Service, *Daily Reports-East Asia*
HDS	Hanoi Domestic Service
IHT	*International Herald Tribune*
JPRS	Joint Publication Research Service
ND	*Nhan Dan*
NYT	*New York Times*
QDND	*Quan Doi Nhan Dan*
SCMP	*South China Morning Post*
SJMN	*San Jose Mercury News*
TCCS	*Tap Chi Cong San*
VBJ	*Vietnam Business Journal*
VET	*Viet Nam Economic Times*
VIR	*Viet Nam Investment Review*
VNA	Viet Nam News Agency
VNS	Viet Nam News Service
VOV	Voice of Vietnam radio network

245

Abuza, Zachary. "The Unfinished Congress: Leadership Transition in Vietnam Since the 8th Party Congress." *Asian Survey* 38 (December 1998): 1105–1121.

———. "Human Rights and Culture in Southeast Asia." Paper presented to the International Studies Association, 30–31 August 2000.

———. "Debating the Future: Vietnamese Politics and the United States Trade Deal." *Problems of Post-Communism* (January 2001).

Allaire, Marie-Benedict. "Chirac Brings Human Rights Issue to Vietnam." Reuters. 12 November 1997.

Amnesty International. *Annual Report, 1997, http://www.amnesty.org//ailib/*

———.*Country Report—Socialist Republic of Vietnam: The Case of Le Hong Ha and Ha Si Phu* (1996).

———."Newspaper Editor Arrested and Detained," 13 October 1997.

Amor, Abdelfattah. "Civil and Political Rights, Including the Question of Religious Intolerance," Report Submitted by the Special Rapporteur to the UN Commission on Human Rights, 29 December 1998.

Balfour, Frederik. "Slouching Towards Democracy: Vietnam Elections Promise Few Surprises." AFP, 16 July 1997.

Bao Ninh. *The Sorrow of War*, 2d ed., translated by Phan Thanh Hao (New York: Riverhead Books, 1996).

Boudarel, Georges. "Intellectual Dissidence in the 1950s: The Nhan-Van Giai-Pham Affair." *Vietnam Forum* 13 (1990): 154–174.

———. *Cent Fleurs aecloses dans la nuit du Vietnam: Communism et dissidence, 1954–1956* (Paris: J. Bertoin, 1991).

Brazier, Chris. *Vietnam: The Price of Peace* (London: Oxfam UK and Ireland, 1992).

Bui Minh Quoc. "Open Letter to VCP Central Committee," 3 October 1993, *Vietnam Insight* (May 1994).

Bui Minh Quoc, Ha Si Phu, and Tieu Dao Bao Cu. "Letter to the National Assembly," 20 April 1997. *Vietnam Democracy* (June 1997).

Bui Tin. "A Citizen's Petition," November 1990. *Vietnam Commentary* (November–December 1990): 13–15.

———. "The Road Away From Disaster," 16 March 1991. *Vietnam Commentary* (March–April 1991): 15.

———. "The State of the Revolution: An Inside Assessment." *Vietnam Commentary* (July–August 1991): 7.

———. *Following Ho Chi Minh: Memoirs of a North Vietnamese Colonel* (Honolulu: University of Hawaii Press, 1995).

Bui Xuan Quang. "The End of Glasnost? The Tightening of Ideological Control." *Vietnam Commentary* (September–October 1989): 7–9.

Campion, Gilles. "Wind of Rebellion Blowing Among Newsmen," AFP, in *FBIS-EAS,* 21 June 1988, 63.

Chalmers, John. "Vietnam Gears Up for Low-Key Elections." Reuters, 13 July 1997.

Chan Tin. "Letter to Pham Dinh Tung, Chairman of the Vietnam Bishops' Council." 10 July 1998. *Vietnam Democracy,* October 1998.

Chanda, Nayan. "The War Within." *FEER,* 4 May 2000, 20.

———. "Force for Change." *FEER,* 5 October 1989, 24, 26.

Chen, King C. *China's War with Vietnam: Issues, Decisions and Implications* (Palo Alto, Calif.: Hoover Institute Press, 1987).

Chirot, Daniel. "What Happened in Eastern Europe in 1989?" Daniel Chirot, ed., *The Crisis of Leninism and the Decline of the Left: The Revolution of 1989* (Seattle: University of Washington Press, 1991): 3–32.

Council of Ministers. Circular No. 20, 16 January 1981, in *FBIS-AP,* 3 April 1981, K6.

Currey, Cecil. *Victory at Any Cost* (Washington, D.C.: Brassey's, 1997).

Dahl, Robert, *Polyarchy* (New Haven, Conn.: Yale University Press, 1971).

Dang Thai Mao. "Vietnamese Literature." *Europe,* 387–388 (July–August 1961): 91.

Dang Phong. "Aspects of Agricultural Economy and Rural Life in 1993." Benedict J. Tria Kerkvliet and Doug J. Porter, eds. *Vietnam's Rural Transformation* (Boulder, Colo.: Westview Press, 1995), 165–184.

Dapice, David. "Point of No Return." *Vietnam Business Journal* (February 2000).

Djilas, Milovan. *The New Class* (New York: Praeger, 1974).

Drummond, Larry. "Rethinking Civil Society: Toward Democratic Consolidation." *Journal of Democracy* 2 (July 1994): 4–17.

Duiker, William. *The Communist Road to Power in Vietnam* (Boulder, Colo.: Westview Press, 1981).

Duong Thu Huong. *Paradise of the Blind,* translated by Phan Huy Duong and Nina McPherson (New York: Penguin Publishers, 1993).

———. *Novel Without a Name,* translated by Phan Huy Duong and Nina McPherson (New York: Penguin Publishers, 1995).

———. *Memories of a Pure Spring,* translated by Phan Huy Duong and Nina McPherson (New York: Hyperion Books, 2000).

Durand, Maurice M., and Nguyen Tran Huan. *An Introduction to Vietnamese Literature* (New York: Columbia University Press, 1985).

Edwards, Adrian. "Vietnam Hails Elections as Success as Polls Close." Reuters, 20 July 1997.

———. "Vietnam's President Says Unrest Prompting Rethink." Reuters, 23 February 1998.

———. "Party Chief Rejects Calls for Reform." Reuters, 11 March 1998.

Elliott, David W. P. "Dilemmas of Reform in Vietnam." William S. Turley and Mark Selden, eds., *Renovating Vietnam: Doi Moi in Comparative Perspective* (Boulder, Colo.: Westview Press, 1993), 53–96.

Erlanger, Stephen. "Vietnamese Communists Purge an In-House Critic." *NYT,* 1 April 1990, A4.

Ermolaev, Herman. *Censorship in Soviet Literature, 1917–1991* (New York: Rowman Littlefield, 1997).

Fforde, Adam, and de Vylder, Stefan. *From Plan To Market: The Economic Transition in Vietnam* (Boulder, Colo.: Westview Press, 1996).

Forrest, James H. *The Unified Buddhist Church of Vietnam: 15 Years for Reconciliation* (Alkmaar, The Netherlands: International Fellowship of Reconciliation, 1978).

Freeman, Charles. "Human Rights, Asian Values and the Clash of Civilizations." *Issues and Studies* 34 (October 1998): 48–78.

Gainsborough, Martin. "The Ho Chi Minh City Elite." *Vietnam Business Journal* (May 2000).

Goldman, Merle. *China's Intellectuals: Advice and Dissent* (Cambridge, Mass.: Harvard University Press, 1981).

Goll, Sally. "Art in the Time of *Doi Moi*." *FEER,* 7 May 1992, 36–37.

Gorky, Maxim. "Soviet Literature." Address delivered to the First All-Union Congress of Soviet Writers, 17 August 1934. Maxim Gorky, *On Literature: Selected Articles* (Moscow: Foreign Languages Publishing House, n.d.), 228–268.

Gurtov, Melvin. *The First Indochina War: Chinese Communist Strategy and the United States* (New York: Columbia University Press, 1967).

Ha Si Phu. "Hand in Hand Following the Signs of Our Intellect." (1988).

———. "Reflections of a Citizen." *Vietnam Insight* (April 1994).

———. "Letter to Phan Dinh Dieu," 2 September 1994. *Vietnam Insight* (March 1995).

———. *Tuyen Tap* (Garden Grove, N.J.: Phong Trao Nhan Quyen Cho Viet Nam Nam 2000, 1996).

Ha Xuan Truong. "Plurality and Pluralism." *TCCS* (July 1989), in *FBIS-EAS,* 12 September 1989, 69–71.

Hamilton-Merritt, Jane. *Tragic Mountains: The Hmong, the Americans, and the Secret Wars for Laos* (Bloomington: University of Indiana Press, 1993).

Hantover, Jefferey. "Distant Shores, Common Ground." *An Ocean Apart: Contemporary Vietnamese Art from the United States and Vietnam* (Boulder, Colo.: Lynne Rienner Publishers, 1995), 13–17.

Harris, Nigel. "New Bourgeoisie?" *Journal of Development Studies* 24 (January 1988): 237–249.

Hiebert, Murray. "One Step Backward." *FEER,* 4 May 1989, 15.

———. "The Joy of Marx." *FEER,* 31 August 1989, 23.

———. "Against the Tide." *FEER,* 14 September 1989, 28–30.

———. "Mixed Signals." *FEER,* 26 October 1989, 37–38.

———. "Eat First, Talk Later." *FEER,* 11 January 1990, 18–19.

———. "Survival Tactics." *FEER,* 1 February 1990, 24–25.

———. "Against the Wind." *FEER,* 12 April 1990, 12–13.

———. "Trial and Error." *FEER,* 5 July 1990, 16–17.

———. "Higher Criticism." *FEER,* 2 May 1991, 17–18.

———. "More of the Same." *FEER,* 11 July 1991, 10–11.

———. "Anthem of Sorrows." *FEER,* 5 September 1991, 52.

———. "Even War Heroes Cry." *FEER,* 31 October 1991, 54–55.

———. "Election Strategy." *FEER,* 9 July 1992, 21.

———. "Miles to Go." *FEER,* 29 June 1993, 24–26.

———. "No Middle Path Here." *FEER,* 5 August 1993, 26.

———. "Dissenting Voices." *FEER,* 2 December 1993, 26.

———. "Ex-Communist Official Turns into Vocal Critic." *FEER,* 2 December 1993, 90.

———. More of the Same. *FEER,* 10 February 1994, 15.

Ho Chi Minh. *Selected Writings (1920–1969)* (Hanoi: Foreign Language Publishing House, 1973).

———. "To the Artists on the Occasion of the 1951 Painting Exhibition." Ho Chi Minh, *Selected Writings (1920–1949)* (Hanoi: Foreign Language Publishing House, 1973): 133–134.

———. "On Revolutionary Morality." (1958) *Selected Writings,* 195–206.

———. *On Revolution, Selected Writings, 1920–66.* Bernard B. Fall, ed. (New York: Praeger, 1967).

———. *Selected Articles and Speeches, 1920–1967.* Jack Woddis, ed. (New York International Publishers, 1969).

Ho Tai, Hue-Tam. "Duong Thu Huong and the Literature of Disenchantment." *Vietnam Forum* 14 (1994): 82–91.

Hoang Cong. "Some Perceptions on Human Rights Issues." *TCCS* (August 1993): 46–49, in JPRS, *Report-East Asia,* 9 November 1993, 9–11.

Hoang Giang. "La Révolte des Intellectuels au Viet Nam en 1956." *The Vietnam Forum* 13 (1990): 144–153.

Hoang Huu Nhan. "An Inconceivable Treatment." *Vietnam Democracy* (February 1999).

Hoang Minh Chinh. "Commentary on the Draft Platform," 21 January 1991. *Vietnam Commentary* (March–April 1991): 6–11.

Hoang The Lien. "Democracy in the Renovation 'Doi Moi' of Vietnam." Corrine Phuangkasem, et al., eds., *Proceedings of the 1992 International Symposium Democratic Experiences in Southeast Asian Countries, 7–8 December 1992* (Bangkok: Thammasat University, 1992).

———. "On the Legal System of Vietnam." *Vietnam Law and Legal Forum* (September 1994), 34.

Hoang Tien. "Letter to the Director of the Press Department, Ministry of Culture of the SRV," 16 June 1990.

———. "The Case of Ha Si Phu and the State of Justice in Vietnam Today." *Vietnam Democracy* (December 1996).

Hoang Van Chi. *The New Class in North Vietnam* (Saigon: Cong Dan Publishing Co., 1958).

———. *From Colonialism to Communism* (London: Pall Mall Press, 1964).

Hoang Van Hoan. *A Drop in the Ocean: Hoang Van Hoan's Revolutionary Reminiscences* (Peking: People's Liberation Army Press, 1987).

Honey, P. J., ed. *North Vietnam Today: Profile of a Communist Satellite* (New York: Praeger, 1962).

———. *Communism in North Vietnam: Its Role in the Sino-Soviet Dispute* (Cambridge, Mass.: MIT Press, 1963).

Hue-Tam Ho Tai. "Duong Thu Huong and the Literature of Disenchantment," *Vietnam Forum* 14 (1994): 82–91.

Human Rights Watch. *The Case of Doan Viet Hoat and Freedom Forum: Detention and Dissent in Vietnam,* 5, 1 (January 1993).

———. *Vietnam: The Suppression of the Unified Buddhist Church* 7, 4 (March 1995).

———. *Behind Vietnam's Open Door: A Climate of Internal Repression,* November 1997.

———. *Rural Unrest in Vietnam* 9, 11 (December 1997).

———. "HRW Denounced Arrest of Vietnamese Dissident," 12 March 1999.

———. *Vietnam: The Silencing of Dissent* 12, 1 (May 2000).

Huntington, Samuel P. *The Third Wave* (Norman: University of Oklahoma Press, 1991).

Jamieson, Neil. *Understanding Vietnam* (Berkeley: University of California Press, 1993).

Jeong, Yeonsik. "The Rise of State Corporatism in Vietnam." *Contemporary Southeast Asia* 19, 2 (September 1997): 152–171.

Kamm, Harry. "How Are Vietnamese Doing Now? Viet Cong Doctor Expresses Disgust." *New York Times,* 6 May 1993, A4.

Karnow, Stanley. *Vietnam: A History* (New York: Penguin, 1983).

Kausikan, Bilahari. "Asia's Different Standard." *Foreign Policy* 92 (Fall 1993): 24–41.

Keenan, Faith, "Partners in Dialogue," *FEER,* 24 July 1997, 22.

———. "Steam Rises." *FEER,* 2 April 1998, 28–29.

———. "Dishing the Dung," *FEER,* 13 August 1998, 28.

———. "Opening the Door," *FEER,* 11 February 1999, 24, 26.

Kerkvliet, Benedict J. Tria, and Doug J. Porter, eds. *Vietnam's Rural Transformation* (Boulder, Colo.: Westview Press, 1995).

Khanh, Huynh Kim. *Vietnamese Communism, 1925–1945* (Ithaca, N.Y.: Cornell University Press, 1982).

Khanh Toan. "Interview with Senior Lieutenant General Pham Van Tra, Minister of National Defense." *QDND* 11 January 1995, 3, in *FBIS-EAS,* 29 January 1999.

Kokko, Ari, "Vietnam: Ready for Doi Moi II," *ASEAN Economic Bulletin* 15 (1998): 319–327.

Kolko, Gabriel. *Vietnam: Anatomy of a Peace* (New York: Routledge, 1997).

Kurihara, Hirohide. "Changes in the Literary Policy of the Vietnamese Workers' Party, 1956–1958." Takashi Shiraishi and Moto Furuta, eds., *Indochina in the 1940s and 1950s* (Ithaca, N.Y.: Cornell University, Southeast Asia Program, 1992), 165–196.

La Van Lam. "Letter to Dao Duy Tung," 6 January 1996. *Vietnam Democracy* (February 1996).

Laothamatas, Anek, ed. *Democratization in Southeast and East Asia* (Singapore: Institute of Southeast Asian Studies, 1997).

Larimer, Tim. "Disquiet Among the Quiet," *Time,* Asia Edition, 18 January 1999.

———. "Sensing an Opening: Vietnam's Outspoken Ones." *Time,* Asia Edition, 9 March 1998, 18–19.

Latimer, Thomas. *Hanoi's Leaders and their South Vietnam Policies, 1954–68.* Ph.D. Diss., Georgetown University, 1972.

Le Duan. "Speech at the 4th Party Congress," Radio Hanoi, 17 December 1976, in *FBIS-AP,* 23 December 1976.

Le Luu. *A Time Far Past,* translated by Ngo Vinh Hai, Nguyen Ba Chung, Kevin Bowen, and David Hunt (Amherst: University of Massachusetts Press, 1997).

Le Mai. "Thoughts on the Image of Communists in Literature." *TCCS* (February 1995): 38–40, in *FBIS-EAS,* 15 June 1995, 67–68.

Le Minh Quoc. "On the Necessity to Build a Socialist Law-Governed State in Vietnam." *Vietnam Social Sciences* 5 (1997): 27–33.

Le Xuan Luu. "The Ideological Destructive Nature of the Reactionary Forces' 'Peaceful Evolution' Strategy." *TCCS* (April 1993): 19–22, in *FBIS-EAS,* 21 May 1993, 52–55.

———. "Relations Between Building and Defending the Fatherland in the New Revolutionary Stage." Voice of Vietnam, 11 June 1996, *FBIS-EAS,* 13 June 1996, 85.

Lenin, Vladimir. "Party Organization and Party Literature," 1905. Robert C. Tucker, ed. and trans., *The Lenin Anthology* (New York: Norton, 1975), 148–153.

Lintner, Bertil. "Vietnam: Coping with Disaffection and Democracy." *International Defense Review* (August 1994): 25–26.

Lippman, Thomas W. "Vietnam Rejects U.S. Reproach on Human Rights." *IHT,* 28–29 June 1997, 1.

Lipset, Seymour. "Some Social Requisites of Democracy: Economic Development and Political Legitimacy," *American Political Science Review* 53 (March 1959): 69–105.

Lockhart, Greg. "Mass Mobilization in Contemporary Vietnam." *Asian Studies Review* 21 (November 1997): 174–179.

Lu Phuong. "Civil Society: From Annulment to Restoration." Vietnam Update Conference, "Doi Moi, the State and Civil Society," 10–11 November 1994, Australian National University, Canberra.

———. "Letter to Do Muoi." 30 April 1994. *Vietnam Democracy* (February 1996).

Ly, Tasteo Nguyen Van, "The State of the Vietnamese Catholic Church," Declaration of the Hue Archdiocese, 24 November 1994. *Vietnam Democracy* (January 1995).

Mai Chi Tho. "Some Urgent Problems on Maintaining Security and Order and Building the People's Police." *TCCS* (December 1988), in *FBIS-EAS,* 10 February 1989, 57.

Malloni, Nick. "Speak No Evil." *FEER,* 29 March 1990, 18, 20.

Mao Zedong. "Talks at the Yenan Forum on Literature and Art," May 1942. Mao Zedong, *Selected Works,* vol. 3 (Peking: Hanoi Foreign Language Publishing House, 1965), 69–98.

Marr, David G., "The Vietnamese Communist Party and Civil Society," Vietnam Update Conference, "Doi Moi, the State and Civil Society," 10–11 November 1994, Australian National University, Canberra.

Marr, David G., and Rosen, Stanley. "Chinese and Vietnamese Youth in the 1990s." *China Journal* 40 (July 1998): 145–172.

McDonald, Mark. "Vietnam Reportedly Frees Buddhist Leaders." *SJMN,* 2 September 1998.

———. "U.S. Queries Hanoi About Inmates Fate." *SJMN,* 14 July 1999.

McLaughlin, Ken, and De Tran. "Return to Freedom," *SJMN,* 2 September 1998.

McCormick, Barrett L. "Political Change in China and Vietnam: Coping with the Economic Consequences of Economic Reform." *The China Journal* 40 (July 1998): 121–143.

Miller, Rena. "Taking Liberties." *FEER,* 10 September 1998, 9–10.

Ministry of Defense. *Vietnam: Consolidating National Defense Safeguarding the Homeland* (Hanoi: Ministry of Defense, 1998).

Mohammed, Mahathir. "Let's Have Mutual Cultural Enrichment." *New Straights Times,* 16 March 1995: 10–11.

Neier, Aryeh. "Asia's Unacceptable Standard." *Foreign Policy* 92 (Fall 1993): 42–51

Neuman, A. Lin. "A Life Apart." *FEER,* 11 February 1999: 27–28.

Nguyen Chi Thien. *Flowers from Hell* (New Haven, Conn.: Yale University Program on Southeast Asia Studies, 1984).

Nguyen Chuong. "May diem Sai Lam Chu Yen Trong bao Nhan Van va tap Giai Pham Mua Thu." *Nhan Dan,* 25 September 1956.

———. "Co Can Cu Hay Khong Co Can Cu." *Nhan Dan,* 15 October 1956.

Nguyen Dang Quang. "What is Socialism?" *TCCS* (January 1989), in *FBIS-EAS,* 21 April 1989, 55.

Nguyen Duc Binh. "The Party in the Mission of Socialist Doi Moi." *Nhan Dan,* 5 February 1990, 1.

Nguyen Duy. *Distant Road,* translated by Kevin Bowen and Nguyen Ba Chung (Willimantic, Conn.: Curbstone Press, 1999).

Nguyen Ho. "Ideology and Life" (1994).

———. "The Solution of Reconciliation and Harmony." 11 June 1995, reprinted in *Vietnam Democracy* (July 1995).

Nguyen Huu Tho. "Renovation of Mechanisms in Pressing Needs of the Renovation Process." *TCCS* (March 1989), in *FBIS-EAS,* 5 May 1989, 65.

———. "Democracy: A Struggle, Not a Gift." *Vietnam Update* 2, 1 (Summer 1989): 5.

Nguyen Huy Thiep. *The General Retires and Other Stories,* translated by Greg Lockhart (Singapore: Oxford University Press, 1992).

———. "Kiem Sac (A Sharp Sword)," translated by Peter Zinoman. *The Vietnam Forum* 14 (1994): 7–17.

———. "Vang Lua (Fired Gold)," translated by Peter Zinoman. *The Vietnam Forum* 14 (1994): 18–25.

———. "Pham Tiet (Chastity)," translated by Peter Zinoman. *The Vietnam Forum* 14 (1994): 26–35.

Nguyen, C.K. "Left to Write," *FEER,* 17 August 1989, 38.

———. "Prophets Without Honor," *FEER,* 4 April 1991, 31–32.

Nguyen Khac Vien. *Vietnam: A Long History* (Hanoi: The Gioi Publishers, 1993).

———. "Letter to Nguyen Huu Tho, President Vietnam Fatherland Front," 6 January 1991. *Vietnam Commentary* (March–April 1991), 4.

Nguyen Nam Khanh. "Struggle Against Opportunism and Rightism—an Important Part of Party-Building Work at Present." *Tap Chi Quoc Phong Toan Dan* (January 1996), 7–9.

Nguyen Ngoc Bich, ed. *One Thousand Years of Vietamese Poetry* (New York: Columbia University Press, 1975).

———. *Six Studies on Vietnam* (Washington, D.C.: unpublished manuscript, 1971).

Nguyen Ngoc Giao. "The Media and the Emergence of 'Civil Society.'" Paper presented at the Vietnam Update 1994 Conference: Doi Moi, the State and

Civil Society, Australian National University, Canberra, 10–11 November 1994.

Nguyen Phong Ho Hieu. "Speech to Ho Chi Minh City Party Committee Social Science Commission," 1 August 1993. "Dissenting Voice of an Ex-Communist Intellectual." *Vietnam Insight* (January 1994).

Nguyen Thanh Giang. "Letter to the Central Committee of the Vietnam Communist Party," 20 November 1993, *Vietnam Insight* (September 1994).

———. "Open Letter to Bui Minh Quoc and Friends," 2 April 1997. *Vietnam Democracy* (April 1997).

———. "The Vietnam Worker's Class." *Vietnam Democracy* (November 1998).

———. "Open Letter," 14 October 1999. *Vietnam Democracy* (November 1999).

Nguyen Thanh Ha. "The New National Assembly." *Vietnam Business Journal* (October 1997), 5.

Nguyen Thi Xuan Mai. "Is Democracy Better Under a Colonial Regime?" *Vietnam Courier* 240, 5–11 April 1998, 10.

Nguyen Thu Lieu. "Artistic Freedom in Vietnam." *Vietnam Update* (Winter/Spring 1988): 12.

Nguyen Van Linh. "Address to the National Assembly," VNA, 17 June 1987. *FBIS-EAS,* 17 June 1987, N6-14.

———. *Doi Moi De Tien Len* (*Renovating to Move Forward*) (Hanoi: Nhat Xuat Ban Su That, 1987).

———. "Let Writers and Artists Actively Contribute to Renovation," 6 October 1987. *Vietnam Courier* 1 (1988).

———. "The Press and Renovation." Speech given to the Regular Conference of Editors-in-Chief of Newspapers of Communist and Workers' Parties of Socialist Countries, Hanoi, 28 March 1988. *Vietnam Courier* 6, June 1988.

———. "Speech to the Closing Session of the 7th National Congress," 24 August 1999. *FBIS-EAS,* 29 August 1989, 66–70.

———. "Speech on the Occasion of National Day," 1 September 1989. *FBIS-EAS,* 8 September 1989, 63–70.

———. "Continuing the Task of Renovation Along the Socialist Path," *Documents of the 7th Party Congress* (Hanoi: The Giao, 1991).

Nhan Nguyen. "Why is the Management of the State By Law Still Weak." *QDND,* 13 June 1997, 3.

Nhu Phong. "Intellectuals, Writers and Artists." P. J. Honey, ed., *North Vietnam Today: Profile of a Communist Satellite* (New York: Praeger, 1962): 70–92.

O'Neil, Patrick. "Revolution from Within: Institutional Analysis, Transitions from Authoritarianism, and the Case of Hungary." *World Politics* 48 (July 1996): 579–603.

Oxfam UK and Ireland. *Report on the Financing and Delivery of Basic Services at the Commune Level in Ky Anh, Ha Tin* (London: Oxfam UK and Ireland, 1996).

Phan Dinh Dieu. "Petition for an Emergency Program," January 1991. *Vietnam Commentary* (May–June 1991): 10.

———. "On the Need to Continue the Reform in the Current Period." Speech delivered at the expanded conference of the presiding committee, VFF Central Committee, Hanoi, 12–13 December 1997.

Phan Hai Ha. "Peaceful Evolution—Victory Without War." *Quan Doi Nhan Dan*, 11 January 1993, in *FBIS-EAS*, 15 January 1993, 56–58.

Phan Khoi. "Criticism of the Leadership in Arts and Letters," *Giai Pham Mua Thu* (September 1956). Hoang Van Chi, ed., *The New Class in North Vietnam* (Saigon: Cong Dan Publishing Co., 1958), 74–84.

Pike, Douglas. *Vietnam and the Soviet Union: Anatomy of an Alliance* (Boulder, Colo.: Westview Press, 1987).

———. "Political Institutionalization in Vietnam." Robert Scalapino, Seizaburo Sato, and Jusuf Wanandi, eds., *Asian Political Institutionalization* (Berkeley, Calif.: Institute of East Asian Studies, 1986), 42–58.

Political Bureau, "Conclusions on Some Ideological Work." Hanoi Domestic Service, 8 December 1988, in *FBIS-EAS*, 9 December 1988, 63.

Pomfret, John. "The New Censorship in China: Anatomy of a Book-Banning." *Boston Globe*, 2 July 2000, A16.

Porter, Doug J. "Economic Liberalization, Marginalization and the Local State." Benedict J. Tria Kerkvliet and Doug J. Porter, eds., *Vietnam's Rural Transformation* (Boulder, Colo.: Westview Press, 1995): 215–246.

Porter, Gareth. *Vietnam: The Politics of Bureaucratic Socialism* (Ithaca, N.Y.: Cornell University Press, 1993).

———. "The Transformation of Vietnam's World-view: From Two Camps to Interdependence." *Contemporary Southeast Asia* 12 (June 1990): 1–19.

———. "The Politics of 'Renovation' in Vietnam." *Problems of Communism* 39 (May–June 1990): 72–88.

Przeworski, Adam. *Democracy and the Market* (New York: Cambridge University Press, 1991).

Quinn-Judge, Sophie. "Ho Chi Minh: New Perspectives from the Comintern Files." *Viet Nam Forum* 14 (1994): 61–81.

Richardson, Michael. "Fighting Graft Brings a Net Advantage, Survey Says." *IHT*, 23 March 2000, 16.

Richburg, Keith B. "Vietnam Frees Leading Dissident," *Washington Post*, 5 September 1997, A25.

Robin, Regine. *Socialist Realism: An Impossible Aesthetic*, translated by Catherine Porter (Palo Alto, Calif.: Stanford University Press, 1992).

Rose, Carol V. "The 'New' Law and Development Movement in the Post-Cold War Era: A Vietnam Case Study." *Law and Society Review* 32 (1998): 163–174.

Schwarz, Adam. "Just Do It." *FEER*, 2 February 1995, 48.

———. "For Better or Worse." *FEER*, 9 February 1995, 61–62.

———. "Now What." *FEER*, 17 August 1995, 22–23.

———. "Arrested Development." *FEER*, 7 September 1995, 34, 36.

———. "Nation Builders: Assembly Lays Foundation for Rule of Law." *FEER*, 16 November 1995, 22.

———. "Reality Check." *FEER*, 3 May 1997, 68.

Sidel, Mark. "The Re-emergence of Legal Discourse in Vietnam." *International and Comparative Law Quarterly* 43 (January 1994): 163–174.

Soloman, Andrew. "Vietnam Talks Tough but Corruption Seems Ingrained." Reuters, 29 March 1998.
———. "Dissident Vietnam General Fires New Broadside." Reuters, 29 June 1998.
———. "Vietnam Says Corruption Causes Loss of Trust." Reuters, 16 July 1998.
———. "VCP Expels Outspoken General." Reuters, 7 January 1999.
———. "Vietnamese General Hits out at Communist Party." Reuters, 11 January 1999.
———. "Mixed Signals from Hanoi General's Ouster." Reuters, 13 January 1999.
———. "Vietnam Communist Party Faced Sabotage in 1998." Reuters, 9 March 1999.
———. "Vietnam Dissident's Arrest Seen as Warning?" Reuters, 11 March 1999.
———. "Cao Dai Struggle for Survival in Vietnam." Reuters, 20 April 1999.
Stern, Louis. *Renovating the Vietnamese Communist Party: Nguyen Van Linh and the Programme for Organizational Reform, 1987–1991* (New York: St. Martin's Press, 1994).
Stewart, Ian. "Ex-Vietnam Inmate Becomes Lawmaker." AP, 11 April 1998.
Stier, Ken. "Little Faith Shown in Religious Freedom." DPA, 30 October 1998.
———. "Freedom Memorial." *SCMP*, 18 November 1998.
———. "Party Grapples with Surge of Internal Dissent." *SCMP*, 20 February 1999.
———. "Vatican Sees Hope of New Bishops." DPA, 20 March 1999.
———. "Arrest of Key Dissident Reminder of Dark Reality." DPA, 24 March 1999.
———. "Police Break Up Buddhist Elders' Talk." *SCMP,* 29 March 1999.
———. "Interview with Dr. Nguyen Dan Que: Jail 'Abuse' of Political Prisoners." DPA, 14 April 1999.
Taylor, Keith. "Locating and Translating Boundaries in Nguyen Huy Thiep's Short Stories." *Vietnam Review* 1 (Autumn–Winter 1996): 439–465.
Templer, Robert. *Shadows and Wind: A View of Modern Vietnam* (New York: Penguin, 1998).
Thai Duy. "An Abscess Has Been Lanced." *Dai Doan Ket.* 2 April 1988, in JPRS, *Southeast Asian Report,* 7 June 1988, 26–28.
Thai Quang Trung. "Linh and *Doi Moi:* Prisoners of the Neo-Conservatives?" *Vietnam Commentary* (May–June 1989): 8.
Thayer, Carlyle. "Political Reform in Vietnam: Doi Moi and the Emergence of Civil Society." Robert Miller, ed., *The Development of Civil Society in Communist Systems* (Sydney: Allen and Unwin, 1992).
———. "Recent Political Developments: Constitutional Change and the 1992 Elections." Carlyle A. Thayer and David Marr, eds., *Vietnam and the Rule of Law* (Canberra: Australia National University, 1993), 50–80.
———. "The Challenges Facing Vietnamese Communism." *Southeast Asian Affairs 1992* (Singapore: Institute of Southeast Asian Studies, 1993), 355.
———. "Mono-Organizationalism Socialism and the State." Benedict J. Tria Kerkvleit and Doug J. Porter, eds., *Vietnam's Rural Transformation* (Boulder, Colo.: Westview Press, 1995): 39–64.

256

.

Bibliography

ZZZ

.ZZZ

Trouillaud, Pascale. "Vietnam Communist Party Under Fresh Attack." AFP, 13 March 1998.

———. "Vietnam Tries to Polish its International Image." AFP, 22 October 1998.

Truong Chinh. "Marxism and Vietnamese Culture" (report delivered at the 2nd National Culture Conference, July 1948). Truong Chinh, *Selected Writings* (Hanoi: Foreign Languages Publishing House, 1977).

Truong Nhu Tang. *A Viet Cong Memoir* (New York: Vintage Press, 1985).

Turley, William. "Hanoi's Domestic Dilemmas." *Problems of Communism* 29 (July–August 1980): 42–61.

——— and Mark Selden, eds. *Reinventing Vietnamese Socialism: Doi Moi in Comparative Perspective* (Boulder, Colo.: Westview Press, 1993).

U.S. Department of State, Bureau of Democracy, Human Rights, and Labor. "Vietnam Report on Human Rights Practices," annual reports, 1986–1999.

Van Ta Tai. *The Vietnamese Tradition of Human Rights* (Berkeley, Calif.: Institute of East Asian Studies, 1988).

Vasavakul, Thaveeporn. "Vietnam: The Changing Models of Legitimization." Multhiah Alagappa, ed., *Political Legitimacy in Southeast Asia: The Quest for Moral Authority* (Palo Alto, Calif.: Stanford University Press, 1995), 257–292.

Vatikiotis, Michael. *Political Change in Southeast Asia* (New York: Routledge, 1996).

Vickerman, Andrew. *The Fate of the Peasantry: The Premature "Transition to Socialism" in the Democratic Republic of Vietnam* (New Haven, Conn.: Yale Center for International and Area Studies, Monograph No. 28, 1986).

Vietnamese Bishops' Council. "Letter to the Prime Minister," 11 October 1997. *Vietnam Democracy* (January 1998).

Vietnam Insight. "Dissenting Voice of an ex-Communist Intellectual" (January 1994).

———. "Dissident Party Member Reveals Own Ordeal" (June 1994).

Vo Thu Phuong. "A New Step Forward in Vietnam-US Relations." *TCCS* (August 1995), 47–48

Vu Oanh. "Dai Doan Ket Dan Tong trong Tinh Hinh, Nhiem vu Moi" ("Great Unity of the People in Times of New Situations and Responsibilities"), *Nhan Dan,* 1 February 1994, 3.

Warner, Roger. *Backfire: The CIA's Secret War in Laos and Its Link to the War in Vietnam* (New York: Simon and Schuster, 1995).

Watkin, Huw. "Concerned Communists Keep Purging." *SCMP,* 22 July 1999.

———. "Death Sentences Fail to Inspire Financial-Sector Confidence." *SCMP,* 6 August 1999.

———. "Foreigners Show Little Interest in Debt-Riddled State Sector." *SCMP,* 23 March 2000.

———. "Books Ruled too Hot to Read." *SCMP,* 11 April 2000.

———. "Hero Takes Leadership to Task." *SCMP,* 20 June 2000.

———. "Reigns on Foreign Media Loosened." *SCMP,* 23 June 2000.

Webber, Jude. "Vatican-Vietnam Links 'Step Back Five Years.'" Reuters, 9 May 2000.

White, Christine Pelzer. "The Vietnamese Revolutionary Alliance: Intellectuals, Workers and Peasants." John D. Wilson, ed., *Peasant Rebellion and Communist Revolution in Asia* (Palo Alto, Calif.: Stanford University Press, 1974), 77–98.

Womack, Brantly. "Political Reform and Political Change in Communist Countries: Implications for Vietnam." William S. Turley and Mark Selden, eds., *Reinventing Vietnamese Socialism* (Boulder, Colo.: Westview Press, 1993): 277–308.

Woodside, Alexander. "Exalting the Latecomer State: Intellectuals and the State During the Chinese and Vietnamese Reforms." *China Journal* 40 (July 1998): 9–36.

———. "Freedom and Elite Political Theory in Vietnam Before the French." David Kelly and Anthony Reid, eds., *Asian Freedoms: The Idea of Freedom in East and Southeast Asia* (New York: Cambridge University Press 1998), 205–224.

Yates, Dean. "Viet Assembly Opens, Hears Blunt Economy Report." Reuters, 21 April 1998.

———. "Vietnam to Free Key Critics in Mass Amnesty." Reuters, 28 August 1998.

———. "Vietnam to Act on State Budget Disclosure." Reuters, 14 September 1998.

———. "Key Vietnam Buddhist Defends Controls." Reuters, 18 October 1998.

———. "Religious Warship Grows in Vietnam, Controls Stay." Reuters, 19 October 1998.

———. "Vietnam Prime Minister Stresses Political Stability." Reuters, 28 October 1998.

———. "Hanoi Probed High-Level Graft Cases." Reuters, 4 November 1998.

———. "Hanoi Rights Record Red Flag for Business." Reuters, 14 April 1999.

———. "U.S., Vietnam in 'Serious Rights' Talks." Reuters, 13 July 1999.

Yates, Ronald, "Co-Founder of Viet Cong Unhappy with Communist Party." *Chicago Tribune,* 15 May 1995.

Young, Stephen B. "Vietnamese Communism in the 1990s: The End is in Sight." *Vietnam Commentary* (November–December 1989): 5–6.

Zagoria, Donald. *Vietnam Triangle: Moscow, Peking, Hanoi* (New York: Pegasus Books, 1967).

Zakaria, Fareed. "Culture is Destiny: A Conversation with Lee Kwan Yew." *Foreign Affairs* 73 (March/April 1994): 109–126.

Zinoman, Peter. "Nguyen Huy Thiep's 'Vang Lua' and the Nature of Intellectual Dissent in Contemporary Viet Nam." *Viet Nam Forum* 14 (1994): 36–44.

INDEX

Agents of change, 9–15, 183, 235;
  Asian, 10–12; growth of, 10;
  independent, 11; Vietnamese, 13–15
Agriculture: Chinese-style, 17;
  collectivization of, 16, 17, 53, 162,
  163; communal, 3; family-level, 17;
  growth in, 163; output, 17, 163
Aid: Chinese, 42–44; development, 3;
  Soviet, 17
Albright, Madeleine, 30, 227, 233n45
Amnesty International, 14–15, 24, 66,
  181n27, 215, 229
Amor, Abdelfattah, 37n18, 208n25,
  226, 227, 233n45
Anarchy, 90
Anh Duc, 139, 159n61
An Quang Pagoda (Saigon), 193
Aquino, Corazon, 11
Arrests: for antistate activities, 124n55;
  of dissidents, 56, 175; of
  intellectuals, 52, 54, 138; of religious
  leaders, 192, 195, 196; without trial,
  108; of writers, 143
Art, 18; for art's sake, 44, 131
Asian values, 22, 36n2, 57
Association of Arts and Letters, 46
Aung San Suu Kyi, 11
Australia, 226
Authoritarianism, 5, 16, 109, 133;
  absence of legislation and, 49;
  decisionmaking and, 12; prevalence
  of, 85

Authority: moral, 27; respect for, 22;
  rule of law and, 33; structure, 33

Bac Lieu province, 181n26
Bao Ninh, 46, 67, 73n80, 135, 136, 141
Ba Ria-Vung Tau province, 202
BBC, 229
Boudarel, Georges, 44, 48, 70n29
Brezhnev, Leonid, 61
Buddhism, 7, 14; antiwar activities,
  191; charitable work, 191;
  confiscation of properties, 192;
  persecution of, 183, 191, 192, 194,
  195, 196, 197, 198, 207n19, 208n23,
  208n25, 208n27, 208n29, 208n30,
  209n34, 209n37, 228; Theravada,
  205–206; Vietnamese Buddhist
  Church, 187
Bu Duch Khien, 108
Bui Cong Trung, 56
Bui Minh Quoc, 68, 94, 105, 107, 115,
  138, 139, 144, 157n34, 213, 216,
  229
Bui The Dung, 157n41
Bui Tin, 52, 80–81, 82, 89, 107, 113,
  115, 118, 138, 142, 156n30, 161,
  167, 176, 177, 182n39, 213
Bureaucracy, 109, 133, 134;
  conservative, 82; National Assembly
  and, 96; prevalence of, 85
Bureau of Religious Affairs, 187
Burma: military regime in, 11

Cambodia, 4, 17, 80, 204
Campaigns: amelioration of negative conditions by, 220; anticorruption, 32, 35, 221; antilandlord, 53; cultural, 185; of intimidation, 213; literary, 53; problem-rectification, 212; promotion of socialist realism, 57; rectification, 43, 71n43; as response to dissent, 7; for socialist realism, 47
Cao Dai sect, 203–204
Capital: domestic, 30; foreign, 10; short-term, 10
Catholicism, 7, 14, 198–203; appointment of bishops, 198, 199; autonomy issues, 198; Bishops' Council, 187; foreign control aspect, 198; liberation theology and, 202; persecution of, 183, 199, 200; in Philippines, 11; publications of, 201–202; social activities, 202; underground monasteries, 201; Vietnamese Catholic Church, 187
Celli, Monsignor Claudio, 199
Censorship, 46, 142, 150, 152; of church publications, 188; questioning, 133
Center for Legal Advice and Information, 86
Central Committee, 19; Arts and Culture Commission, 140; Culture and Education Committee, 63; Culture Commission, 25, 134, 138; External Relations Commission, 80; Ideology and Culture Commission, 146, 152, 153, 221; Ideology Commission, 140; Internal Security Bureau, 25, 62, 63, 102; Organization Commission, 61, 141; policymaking by, 4; Propaganda Department, 193; Subcommittee for Arts and Letters, 55; "three no's" of, 80; Vietnam People's Army on, 19
Central Office for South Vietnam, 168
Chanda, Nayan, 235
Change: agents of, 9–15, 183, 235; constitutional, 10; political, 9, 10, 11, 12, 81, 89

Chan Tin, Father, 201, 229
"Chastity" (Nguyen Hue), 135
Che Lan Vien, 58, 73n73
Che Van Lien, 65
China: aid to Vietnam, 16, 42–44, 60; antirightist campaign in, 53; conflict with, 4; Cultural Revolution in, 71n62; economic institutions in, 42; menace to territorial integrity from, 22–23; normalization of relations with, 76; political institutions in, 42; relations with, 2, 59; Tiananmen Square massacre in, 11, 80, 89, 138, 173; underdevelopment in, 116; underground publishing in, 149; war with, 17
Chirot, Daniel, 12, 32, 36n6
Chu Ngoc, 52
Class: alliances, 9; consciousness, 165; contradictions, 116; enemies, 67; feudal, 43; labels, 16, 53; landlord, 53; landowning, 43; middle, 10–12, 13, 14; new, 110–120; privileged, 110; reactionary, 43; social, 43; struggle, 115, 116; working, 21, 90, 117
Clientelism, 83
Clinton, Bill, 75, 227
Club of Former Resistance Fighters, 7, 81, 89, 112, 118, 161–179, 235; criticism of national candidates, 168–169; democratic views of, 171; founding, 25, 168; issues addressed, 168; letter-writing campaign of, 169; National Assembly and, 169; north-south conflict and, 35; party response to, 173–174; pressure on, 173–174; publishing efforts, 170
Coexistence, peaceful, 60, 62, 63
Coi moi, 17, 18, 29, 58, 77
Collectivization, 16, 17; agricultural, 53, 162, 163; economic, 116; peasant, 165
Communion Newsletter (newspaper), 201, 202
Communism: Eastern European collapse of, 1, 2, 18, 29, 32, 76, 80, 106, 137–138; factions in, 60; international, 60; peaceful

coexistence and, 60, 62, 63; revisionism in, 60

Conflict: north/south, 7, 35, 72*n61*, 161, 162, 165; regulation of, 103

Congress on Arts and Literature, 54

Constitution (1992), 19, 98; adherence to, 33; article 4, 68, 105; leading role for party in, 34; religion in, 184, 186, 193

Corruption, 2, 5, 7, 32, 83; as byproduct of reform, 113; campaigns against, 32; causes, 109; endemic, 113; EPCO–Minh Phung case, 147, 148, 222; exposure of, 17; high-level, 111–120, 147, 222–223; incentive for, 31; increase in, 86; investment and, 31, 113; official, 86; pervasiveness of, 32; political legitimacy and, 22; press exposure of, 137; prevalence of, 85; protests over, 31; punishment for, 103; rural protests over, 85; Tamexco case, 147, 148

Council of Ministers, 168, 179*n7*

Council on Mutual Economic Assistance, 17

Criticism and Opinion (journal), 140

Cua Viet (journal), 138

Cuba: underdevelopment in, 116

Culture: commercialization of, 144; laws, 2; party control of, 133; political, 4

Currency: overvaluation of, 30; reform, 3, 16, 66, 162; stabilization, 17

Czechoslovakia, 27, 80; Soviet intervention in, 13

Da Dat Lang Bian (newspaper), 138

Dahl, Robert, 33

Dang Kim Giang, 63

Dang Phong, 83–84

Dao Duy Anh, 50–51, 55

Dao Duy Quat, 212, 223

Dao Duy Tung, 138

Dao Quang Ho, 194

Decisionmaking, 2; authoritarianism and, 12; consensual, 32–33, 68; decentralization of, 17; democratic, 92; economic, 18; factionalism and,

19; monopolization of, 42; National Assembly and, 33; nonparty, 91; political, 18; transparency in, 12, 66, 86, 88; village, 87

Decollectivization, 85

Democracy: absolute, 79; "Asian values" and, 22, 36*n2*, 57; bourgeois, 67; compartmentalization of, 76; conceptualizing, 79; demands for, 81, 90; to destabilize regime, 77; elitist views of, 93; grassroots, 86; implementation of, 34, 88; lack of consensus on defining, 85; multi-party, 33, 34, 80, 82, 92, 203; perceptions of, 83; pluralist, 93; risk of anarchy and, 90; socialist, 78; stability and, 85; top down, 21, 86; transition to, 13; urbanization and, 11; Western style, 21, 22, 33, 34, 67, 86

Democracy and the Rule of Law (Free Vietnam Alliance), 141

Democratic centralism, 32, 42, 44, 59, 77, 90, 139, 171, 178; demise of, 68; lack of, 80; pre-decision debate in, 21, 59; reinforcing, 149; suspension of, 91

Democratization, 66; Asian, 10–11; broadening, 237, 238; calls for, 33; containment of, 20; debates over, 75–121; destabilization and, 89; exogenous forces for, 75, 76; indicators of, 12; internal pressure for, 76; intraparty, 68; lack of, 84, 85; obstacles to, 109; peaceful evolution and, 22, 38*n35;* pressure for, 76

Detention of dissidents, 24, 128*n128,* 216

Development: aid, 3; civil society, 35, 236; economic, 11, 12, 90, 92, 108, 116, 164, 171; private sector, 31; renovation and, 23; societal, 10; stability and, 23; stunted by ideology, 116

Dien Bien Phu, 16, 46, 70*n36*

Dissent: from within, 161–179; agents of change and, 9–15; by clergy, 1; corruption and, 7; exogenous influences, 29; free speech and, 7;

growth of, 1; issues of, 32–36; legacy of, 65–68; limited, 41; religious, 7; rise of, 5

Dissidents: age of, 24; attacks on, 25; broadening of democracy and, 237; demands by, 104, 150–154, 235–238; divisions among, 34; emergence of, 29–32; expulsion from party, 25, 112, 134, 139, 143, 215; gaining followings by, 28; geographic representation, 24; government dealings with: 213-219; identity of, 23–29; links to population, 9; as loyal opposition, 27; military and, 51; occupations, 24–25; party membership of, 27; rationale of, 150–154; release of, 75; religious, 24; seen as dangerous by regime, 27, 28; treatment of, 75; in War of National Liberation, 25; working together, 29, 127n111

Djilas, Milovan, 110, 111

Doanh Nghiep (newspaper), 147

Doan Khue, 82, 124n41

Doan Viet Hoat, 24, 26, 75, 113, 140, 143, 157n43, 176, 177, 215, 217, 228, 229, 232n15

Do Duc Kien, 71n64

Doi moi, 3, 4, 6, 18, 20, 29, 35, 76, 77, 98, 132–137, 163, 184, 193

Do Muoi, 63, 66, 79, 84, 85, 97, 109, 127n118, 139, 144–149, 168, 169, 172, 194, 196, 215

Dong Nai province, 202, 208n25, 226

Don Hau, Thich, 192, 193, 194, 207n19

Do Trung Hieu, 168, 175, 181n27, 215

Dubcek, Alexander, 27

Dumas, Roland, 228

Duong Quynh Hoa, 25, 89, 111, 118, 164, 213

Duong Thi Xuan Quy, 157n34

Duong Thu Huong, 26, 46, 67, 75, 112, 113, 118, 135, 136, 141, 142, 143, 154, 213, 215, 228, 229

Duong Thu Huuong, 216

Duong Van Dieu, 172

Duong Van Minh, 167, 191

Durand, Maurice, 73n73

Eastern Europe: civil society in, 12–13; collapse of communism in, 1, 2, 18, 29, 32, 76, 80, 106, 123n27, 137–138; corruption in, 32; exogenous forces and, 12; reactionary plots in, 81, 123n27; repression in, 13

East Germany, 12

Economic: collectivization, 116; crises, 10–12, 30, 88, 103; decisionmaking, 18; development, 11, 12, 90, 108, 116, 171; dislocations, 162; growth, 75; integration, 162; interdependence, 3; liberalization, 23, 31, 66, 89, 154; malaise, 83; mismanagement, 2, 5, 7, 91, 161; reform, 3, 12, 17, 30, 76, 103, 163, 169, 193; stagnation, 77

Economy: centrally planned, 3, 76, 98, 134; complexity of, 91; foreign-trade based, 3; information-based, 151; market, 3, 14, 76, 91, 98, 105, 113, 118–119; multisector, 118, 119; northern dominance in, 35; Stalinist, 16; state-dominated, 118

Elections, 93; Asian, 10; campaigning for, 99–100; candidate screening, 99; Chinese-style, 88; competition in, 126n90; control of, 85; laws, 99, 100; local, 88; multiparty, 90; participation by independent candidates, 99; party control of nominations, 100

Enterprise (newspaper), 147

Estrada, Joseph, 10

Ethiopia, 116

Exports, 3, 17, 163; declining, 30; encouragement of, 17

Factionalism, 83, 169; decisionmaking and, 19; in policymaking, 2; in socialist regimes, 13

"The Fate of Love" (Bao Ninh), 141

Film industry, 2

Flowers from Hell(Nguyen Chi Thien), 154

France, 226; colonial rule by, 15, 16; defeat at Dien Bien Phu, 16; wars against, 2

Francophone Summit (1997), 30, 228

ML

Freedom, artistic, 18, 134

Freedom, intellectual, 7, 34, 42, 66, 131–155

Freedom, religious, 34, 37*n18*, 183–206

Freedom, restrictions on, 37*n18*

Freedom Forum (newspaper), 89, 124*n55*, 140, 157*n43*, 228

Freedom of association, 151, 213

Freedom of expression, 2, 15, 33

Freedom of opinion, 78

Freedom of the press, 7, 12, 14, 33, 66, 131–155

Freedom of thought, 151

Free Vietnam Alliance, 141

General Association of Vietnamese Buddhists, 191

Geneva Accords (1954), 16, 46, 53, 62, 183, 191, 199

Germany, 229

Gia Long (King), 135

Giao Duc Va Tho Dai (newspaper), 138

Golden Pen of Freedom Award, 229

Gorbachev, Mikhail, 13, 172

Gorky, Maxim, 44, 131

Gross domestic product, 1–2, 3, 31, 119

Gulf of Tonkin, 22, 61

Habibie, B.J., 10

Ha Huy Giap, 169

Hanh Duc, 197

Hanoi Literature and Arts Association, 142

Ha Si Phu, 25, 26, 51, 56, 116, 117, 129*n152*, 139, 143, 144, 154, 157*n37*, 213, 215, 216, 228

Ha Trong Hoa, 137

Havel, Vaclav, 9

Hellman/Hammett grants, 229, 230*tab*

Hoa Hao sect, 203–204

Hoai Thanh, 48, 52

Hoang Huu Nhan, 218

Hoang Minh Chinh, 62, 63, 82, 97, 105, 115, 215

Hoang Minh Giam, 62

Hoang The Lien, 109

Hoang Tien, 153, 176, 235

Hoang Van Chi, 70*n25*

Ho Chi Minh, 15, 16, 19, 22, 41, 42, 43, 44, 56, 68*n1*, 181*n28*, 181*n31*, 211; acknowledgment of excesses, 71*n43*; allusions to, 50, 135; class struggle and, 115; cult of, 21; on educating intellectuals, 54; introduction of socialism, 115; marriage, 156*n17*; "On Revolutionary Morality" article, 57; presidential prerogatives and, 60; worship of, 185

Ho Chi Minh City People's Committee, 181

Ho Chi Minh Communist Youth Union, 20

Hong Dieu, 70*n23*

Ho Ngoc, 133

House arrest: of intellectuals, 47; of writers, 47

Ho Van Hieu, 175

Hue-Tam Ho Tai, 26, 112

Hu Feng, 47, 48

Human Rights Watch, 128*n128*, 148, 154, 186, 229

Hungary, 27, 80; economic reform in, 12; market reform in, 78; multiparty system in, 78, 173; political transition in, 93–94; Soviet intervention in, 13, 53

Hung Yen province, 87

Huntington, Samuel, 13

Huy Can, 58, 65

Huynh Phu Su, 204

Huynh Van Nghia, 199

Huynh Van Tieng, 174

Imprisonment: advocacy of reform and, 18; political prisoners, 14; religious prisoners, 14

Individualism, 22, 57

Indochina Communist Party, 15, 43, 68*n1*, 115

Indonesia: elections in, 10; political change in, 11; student protest in, 10, 14

Industrialization, 3

Inflation, 3, 17, 97

Information: access to, 141; alternative,

48, 49; exchange, 151; free flow of, 151; guidance of, 144; independent sources of, 48; policy, 151
Infrastructure, 20
Institute of the Dharma, 195–196
Institutions: political, 18–22
Intellectuals: in anticolonial struggle, 44; arrest of, 56, 57, 138; banned, 134; challenges to state by, 28, 29; as "class enemies," 43; constraints on, 44; control by party, 45; crackdown on, 6, 46–59, 131, 138–144; criticism by, 78; issues of truth and, 48; national security laws and, 57; obligations of, 27; organizations for, 54; party control of, 44, 57; reeducation courses for, 55, 157n43; self-criticism and, 48, 55, 222; self-publishing by, 48, 141; sent to labor, 56; in Viet Minh, 43; withdrawal of support for, 79
International Covenant on Civil and Political Rights, 226
Internet, 132, 151, 152; as subversive force, 30
Investment: corruption and, 113; decline in, 30, 176, 177; foreign, 3, 17, 30, 31, 103, 113, 119, 163, 164, 176, 177; infrastructure, 123n34; loss of, 103; speculative, 10
Islam, 205–206

Khanh Hoa province, 181n27
Khmer Rouge, 4
Khrushchev, Nikita, 48, 60, 61, 62, 63
Kim Dae Jung, 10
Kim Khanh, 156n17
Kong An Pagoda (Quang Tri), 207n19
Kosygin, Andrei, 61

Labor: camps, 215, 226; compulsory, 123n33; costs, 117; movements, 12, 13; study through, 56; unions, 183
Land: laws, 87, 103; leases, 3, 84; redistribution, 43, 84; reform, 16, 43, 49, 53, 87, 96, 162; rent reductions, 43; rights, 84, 87; seizures, 83
Land Reform Law (1953), 96

Langbian (magazine), 139, 157n34, 216
Lao Dong, 73n73
Lao Dong Party, 16, 43, 46, 53, 54, 55, 95, 181n31
La Van Lam, 26, 66, 97, 109, 181n26, 238
Law Commission, 96
Law of Organizations of People's Councils and People's Committees, 103
Laws: adherence to, 104; culture, 2; electoral, 99, 100; existing, 104; formal, 96; grievance, 103; land, 87, 103; national security, 57; press, 2, 141, 148, 152
Leadership: age of, 50; calling into question, 80; collective, 19; criticisms of, 71n62; generation gap with country, 92; influence of collapse of communism on, 76; lack of talent in, 92; outdated worldview, 4; rigidity of, 50, 51; transition, 169; Viet Minh, 43; wars of national liberation and, 21
Le Dat, 47, 49, 50, 52, 55, 56
Le Dinh Manh, 175
Le Duan, 53, 60, 62, 66, 71n65, 162
Le Duc An, 82
Le Duc Tho, 28, 60, 61, 62, 180n12
Legalization, 34, 104–110; debates over, 75–121; of society, 6
Le Giam, 212
Legitimacy: performance, 21–22; political, 21, 67, 83
Le Hong Ha, 56, 63, 154, 215
Le Kha Phieu, 32, 84, 106, 144–149, 148, 153, 159n69, 184, 185, 186, 217, 220, 221, 223
Le Luu, 135, 136, 142
Le Minh Nghia, 71n64
Lenin, Vladimir, 44, 116, 131
Le Quang Dao, 81, 89
Le Quang Vinh, 138
Le Sy Vuong Ha, 37n18, 233n45
Le The Hien, 157n41
Le Trong Nghia, 63
Lhai Hung, 134
Libel, 148, 149

Liberalization: demand for, 11; economic, 23, 31, 66, 89, 154; of information exchange, 151; political, 1, 5, 23, 76, 81; press, 17, 136, 144; of socialist regimes, 13

Liberated Saigon (newspaper), 137

Libya, 116

Lien Tri Pagoda (Ho Chi Minh City), 195, 207*n19*

"Lime pot," 49, 50, 115

Lin Biao, 71*n62*

Linh Mu Pagoda, 193, 195, 196, 207*n19*

Link (newspaper), 141

Literacy, 2, 132

Literary Association for National Salvation, 45

Literature, 18; achievements in, 133; banned, 134, 138, 149; bourgeois tendencies in, 66; Marxist development of, 66; proletarian, 44, 131; relaxation of censorship, 134, 135; restrictions on, 134; self-criticism and, 48, 55; socialist realism and, 57, 73*n73;* unavailability to populace, 52

Lu Dingyi, 48, 52

Lu Phuong, 25, 115, 116, 216–217

Luu Phong, 93, 104

Luu Thi Yen, 56

Luu Trong-Leuu, 73*n73*

Luu Trong Lu, 58

Ly Tong, 176, 177

Mai Chi Tho, 28

Mai Trung Tinh, 157*n43*

Malaysia: dissent in, 11; political change in, 10; student protest in, 14

Mao Zedong, 44, 47, 131

Marx, Karl, 116

Mass Mobilization Department, 181*n27*

Memories of a Pure Spring (Duong Thu Huong), 143

Migliore, Monsignor Celestino, 199

Military: budget, 17; defense of regime by, 80; missions in the south, 60; power of, 2

Military Control Committee, 168

Military Management Committee, 142, 165, 166

Minh Can, 63

Ministry of Culture and Information, 143–144, 148

Ministry of Defense: Institute of Military History, 218

Ministry of Education and Culture, 152, 187

Ministry of Finance, 222

Ministry of Foreign Affairs, 200

Ministry of Justice, 68, 95, 105, 220; Legal Assistance Department, 86

Ministry of Post and Communications, 152

Ministry of Science and Technology, 152

Ministry of the Interior, 30, 147, 152, 187, 216; Press Department, 148

Morning News (newspaper), 132

Movements: chaotic potential, 79; labor, 12, 13; literary, 65; revolutionary, 65

Mozambique, 116

Muslim Association of Vietnam, 205–206

Nagy, Imre, 27

Nam Long, 169

National Assembly, 6, 95–104; bureaucratism and, 96; call for greater role for, 33; calls for freedom from party control, 49; civil code and, 98; competition for seats, 93; decisionmaking and, 33; demands by, 76; demands for reform of, 100–103; democratization of, 21; as dialogue partner, 98–99; domination by party, 100; "dual hats" of delegates, 101–102; economic regulation and, 96–98; formalism and, 96; government bypassing of, 97; independence of, 97; land laws and, 87; Land Reform Law (1953), 96; lawmaking authority, 107; Law of Organizations of People's Councils and People's Committees, 103; law on people's committees, 87; Legal

Affairs Subcommittee, 108; membership control of, 20; party delegates in, 126*n85;* party intervention in, 97, 98; period of liberalization in, 97; Permanent Standing Committee, 160*n81;* policymaking and, 89; press laws, 148; prior to *doi moi,* 95–96; provincial domination of, 38*n28;* reform in, 220; responsiveness of, 103; as rubber stamp for party decisions, 2, 19, 68, 81, 82, 95–96, 99; strengthening of role of, 98; as watchdog, 238

National Concord and Reconciliation, 166

Nationalization, 162

National Liberation Front, 7, 25, 78, 157*n35,* 162, 164, 165, 166, 181*n29*

National reconciliation, 7, 161, 162–167, 168, 175, 176, 199

New Economic Zones, 41, 56, 166, 179*n4*

Nghe An province, 71*n43*

Ngo Dinh Diem, 5, 16, 24, 53, 183, 191, 199

Ngo Dinh Nhu, 53

Ngo Van Chieu, 203

Nguoi Saigon (newspaper), 141

Ngu Phong, 229

Nguyen Ai Quoc, 115

Nguyen Cao Ky, 191

Nguyen Chi Thanh, 60, 62

Nguyen Chi Thien, 143, 154

Nguyen Co Thach, 152

Nguyen Dan Que, 24, 26, 66, 157*n43,* 176, 177, 215, 217, 228, 229

Nguyen Dinh Huy, 230

Nguyen Duc Binh, 76, 81, 144, 146

Nguyen Duc Hung, 174

Nguyen Duc Man, 101

Nguyen Duc Manh, 100

Nguyen Duc Tam, 138

Nguyen Duy, 141, 142, 161

Nguyen Ho, 99, 116, 118, 168, 171, 172, 174, 181, 214, 215, 229

Nguyen Hue, 135

Nguyen Huu Dang, 49, 56

Nguyen Huu Loan, 51, 153, 214

Nguyen Huu Tho, 82, 96, 97, 98, 166, 221

Nguyen Huy Thiep, 135, 136, 141, 142

Nguyen Khac Vien, 65, 67, 82, 92, 134, 165

Nguyen Khanh, 169, 191

Nguyen Kien Giang, 63, 215

Nguyen Manh Cam, 228

Nguyen Manh Tuong, 49, 55

Nguyen Mau, 157*n43*

Nguyen Minh Nghia, 71*n64*

Nguyen Nghia, 202

Nguyen Ngo, 142

Nguyen Ngoc, 134, 136, 138, 139

Nguyen Ngoc Tan, 230

Nguyen No, 25

Nguyen Phong Ho Hieu, 26, 90, 116, 119

Nguyen Si Dung, 100

Nguyen Thanh Cong, 202

Nguyen Thanh Giang, 25, 75, 94, 100, 101, 107, 111, 112, 113, 115, 117, 154, 215, 216, 228

Nguyen Thi Xuan My, 214, 215

Nguyen Tran Van, 90

Nguyen Trung Thanh, 62

Nguyen Van Binh, 199

Nguyen Van Dao, 218

Nguyen Van Hang, 174

Nguyen Van Linh, 17, 18, 25, 67, 76, 77, 78, 79, 96–98, 106, 112, 132–137, 139, 146, 147, 152, 163, 168, 169–170, 174, 182*n39,* 192, 213

Nguyen Van Thuan, 157*n43*

Nguyen Van Tran, 26, 153, 169, 215

Nguyen Xuan Oanh, 237

Nhan Dan (newspaper), 25, 60, 137, 146, 159*n69,* 198, 212

Nhan Van–Giai Pham affair, 6, 7, 32, 41–59, 134

Nhat Linh, 134

Nhat Thuong, 208*n25*

Noi Ket (newspaper), 141

Nong Duc Manh, 86, 87, 156*n17,* 160*n81*

Non-governmental institutions, 229

North Korea: underdevelopment in, 116

Novel Without a Name (Duong Thu Huong), 112, 143

100 Flowers Speech, 48, 52
"On Revolutionary Morality" (Ho Chi Minh), 57
Opposition: popular, 3
Orderly Departure Program, 157*n43*
Organizations: anticolonial, 43; autonomy of, 35; civil, 160*n84;* independent, 35; mass, 20; municipal, 20; political, 93, 109; professional, 12, 14; provincial level, 20; religious, 35, 183–206, 185, 188–189, 200; social, 93, 109; umbrella, 14, 54, 68*n1,* 99, 104, 186, 191; voluntary, 104
Ownership: collective, 110; media, 141; socialist, 110

Paracel Islands, 22
Paradise of the Blind (Duong Thu Huong), 142
Paris Peace Accord, 165, 180*n12*
Party Military Affairs Commission, 19
Paternalism, 12
People's councils, 86, 87
Persecution, 7
Pham Duc Kham, 124*n55,* 140, 157*n43,* 215, 217
Pham Hong Son, 218, 219
Pham Hung, 168, 179*n7*
Pham Que Duong, 28, 218
Pham Thai Thuy, 157*n43*
Pham The Duyet, 110, 128*n138*
Pham Thi Hoai, 135, 141, 142
Pham Van Dong, 62, 66
Pham Van Khai, 83, 174
Pham Viet, 63
Phan Dinh Dieu, 25, 51, 91, 92, 94, 103–104, 107, 113, 116, 119, 120, 127*n111,* 138, 151, 215, 217
Phan Hoi, 49
Phan Khoi, 47, 48, 50, 52, 54, 70*n23*
Phan Trong Tue, 169
Phan Van Dinh, 222
Phan Van Khai, 149, 154, 223
Phe Binh va Du Luan (journal), 140
Philippines: Catholic Church in, 11; elections in, 10
Phung Quan, 48, 70*n29*
Phuoc Luong province, 180*n12*
Poland, 80; opposition parties in, 78

Policy: debate, 152; foreign, 80; information, 151
Policymaking: factionalism in, 2
Politburo, 4, 6, 16, 17, 19, 55, 167, 168, 172, 179*n10;* debate over political reform and, 76–88; Directive on Religion, 186, 187; legality of power to condemn by, 68; Resolution 5 of, 134, 156*n30;* resolutions, 123*n27;* Standing Committee, 19, 110
Political: change, 9, 10, 11, 12, 81; compromise, 4; culture, 4; debate, 79; decisionmaking, 18; diversity, 81; institutions, 5, 18–22; legitimacy, 21, 67, 83; liberalization, 1, 5, 23, 76, 81; organizations, 93, 109; parties, 11; pluralism, 23, 76, 77, 79, 80, 82, 89, 104, 138; prisoners, 71*n43,* 216; reform, 1, 2, 5, 9, 17, 23, 75, 76–95, 169; rights, 11, 75
Political Reminiscences (Bui Tin), 213
Politics: factional, 59; northern dominance in, 35; stagnation of, 49; Vietnamese, 9–36
Poverty, 29–30, 31, 32, 77., 112, 117; government blame for, 32; public dissatisfaction and, 77
Press: antistate activities of, 140; blackouts, 148; censorship, 152; clandestine publishing, 139, 140, 141; commercialization of, 146; constraints on, 137; crackdown on, 137–144; foreign, 127*n111,* 148; freedom of, 7, 12, 14, 33, 66; independence of, 79, 131; investigative reporting by, 77, 133, 137; laws, 2, 141, 148, 152; libel charges, 148, 149; liberalization, 136, 144; overseas publication, 142, 143; retrenchment of liberalization of, 137–144; samizdat papers, 89, 124*n55,* 131, 132, 139, 140; self-criticism and, 48; socialist realism and, 132; socialist values and, 144; state monopoly of, 21; underground publications, 141, 154; "Unshackling Days" of, 133; as voice of party, 79; as watchdog agency, 150

Press and Publishing Houses, 146
Price(s): centrally planned, 17;
    controls, 3; reform, 3
Privatization, 3, 31, 130n180
Production: contracts, 3; land reform
    and, 16
Protestantism, 204–205
Protests: peasant, 6, 31, 35, 84, 87,
    148, 222; religious, 24, 192, 202;
    student, 14; Thai Binh, 6, 31, 148,
    222
Provisional Revolutionary Government,
    7, 25, 166
Provisional Revolutionary Guard, 164
Przeworski, Adam, 13
Purges: antirevisionist, 67; intraparty,
    6, 42, 59–65; of Khrushchev, 61;
    legality questioned, 63; military,
    59–65; over policy, 62; reeducation
    and, 42; re-emergence of, 63–65;
    rehabilitation from, 67; roots of,
    59–62
Putnam, Robert, 12

Quan Doi Nhan Dan (newspaper), 136,
    137, 213, 228
Quang Ngai province, 195
Quang Phuc Pagoda (Quang Ngai), 196
Quang Tri province, 193

Radio Free Asia, 229
Radio Irina, 229
Ramos, Fidel, 11
Reform: agricultural, 3; currency, 3, 16,
    66, 162; demands from within for,
    23; democratic, 92; economic, 3,
    12, 17, 76, 92, 103, 163, 169, 193;
    ideological differences over, 19;
    land, 16, 43, 49, 53, 71n43, 87, 96,
    162; legal, 49, 98; limits to, 98–100;
    literary, 66; market, 17, 77, 78;
    obstacles to, 77; political, 1, 2, 5, 9,
    17, 23, 75, 76–95, 169; price, 3;
    resistance to, 31; structural, 3
Regionalism, 20
Religion, 183–206; ancestor worship,
    184; Buddhism, 7, 14, 190–198; Cao
    Dai sect, 203–204; Catholicism, 7,
    14, 183, 198–203; charitable work,

189; church property, 188, 201–202;
    clergy issues, 187; folk, 184, 185,
    186; freedom of, 34, 37n18; funding,
    189; growth of, 184–190; Hoa Hao
    sect, 203–204; organized, 184;
    persecution of, 183; politicization of,
    7, 183, 199; Protestantism, 204–205;
    publications, 188; state control of,
    14, 184–190, 200; Theravada
    Buddhism, 205–206
Religious Affairs Commission, 181n27,
    197, 200, 208n24
Renovation period, 23, 41, 76, 109
The Resistance Will Win (Truong
    Chinh), 43
Restlessness (newspaper), 141
Reunification, 16, 20, 41, 53, 59, 67,
    161, 165, 166; National Assembly
    and, 96
Revisionism, 60, 62
Revolutionary Youth League, 15
Rights: democratic, 86, 109–110; to
    freedom of expression, 15; human,
    15, 22, 23, 30, 37n18, 75, 76, 212,
    226, 227; individual, 22; during
    investigations, 37n18, 49; land, 84,
    87, 123n33; legal, 86, 108, 109; to
    organize, 14; political, 11, 75;
    property, 11; second land use, 84

The Saigonese (newspaper), 141
Sai Gon Giai Phong (newspaper), 137,
    138
Saigon Party Committee, 168
Saigon People's Committee, 168
Sector, cultural, 149
Sector, financial, 30
Sector, legal: need to strengthen, 105
Sector, private, 3, 31, 119, 120
Sector, state, 3, 30, 31
Sector alliances, 9
Self-criticism, 48, 55, 222
Smuggling, 112, 113, 137, 222
Social: activism, 191, 195, 202; class,
    43; conservatism, 164; duty, 22;
    instability, 77; institutions, 191;
    justice, 26, 81, 85; order, 11, 146;
    organizations, 93, 109; pressures, 13;
    services, 185; welfare, 84, 191

Socialist pluralism, 78
Socialist realism, 18, 44, 45, 47, 48, 52, 57; press and, 132; rebellion against, 66
Society: civil, 7, 12–13, 35, 93, 183–206, 235, 236; complex, 11; development of, 10; group/individual rights and, 22; legalization of, 6; modernization of, 151; order in, 22; radicalization of, 53
The Solution of Reconciliation and Harmony (Nguyen Ho), 175
Song Hao, 62
Song Huong (newspaper), 139
Son Linh Pagoda (Vung Tau), 197
South Korea, 10; economic performance in, 172; labor unions in, 11; student activity in, 11; student protest in, 14
Soviet Union: aid from, 17; collapse of communism in, 1, 29, 76; Council on Mutual Economic Assistance, 17; disengagement from Vietnam, 60; intervention by, 13, 53; moderation of policy in, 60; peaceful coexistence with United States, 60; policies toward intellectuals, 48
Spratly Islands, 22
State: autonomy of, 106; challenges to, 28, 29; control of church property, 188; control of press, 132; control of religion, 184–190, 200; economic role, 117; enemies of, 70*n23;* inefficiency of, 118; interventionist role of, 18; ownership, 30; party intervention in, 106; regulatory functions of, 118; subsidization of, 31, 119, 120; as supreme arbiter, 84; transparency in, 103
State Planning Commission, 169
Surveillance of dissidents, 24, 216

Ta Ba Tang, 174, 175
Ta Huu Thanh, 128*n138,* 159*n69*
Taiwan: elections in, 10; political parties in, 11
The Tale of Kieu (Nguyen Du), 136
Tap Chi Cong San (journal), 142
Tay Ninh province, 203

Tay Son rebellion, 135
Te Hanh, 65
Tet Offensive, 164, 180*n12*
Thai Binh protest, 6, 31, 109, 148, 222
Thailand: currency defense in, 10; political change in, 10
Thanh Hoa province, 137, 222
Thanh Minh Pagoda (Ho Chi Minh City), 196; monastery, 226
Thao thuc (newspaper), 141
Thich Hai Chanh, 196, 208*n23*
Thich Hai Tang, 195, 207*n19,* 208*n29*
Thich Hai Thanh, 208*n23*
Thich Hai Thinh, 196, 208*n23*
Thich Hai Tinh, 19
Thich Hon Dau, 196
Thich Huyen Quang, 192, 193, 196, 197, 215, 228
Thich Khong Tanh, 195, 207*n19,* 208*n25,* 209*n37*
Thich Long Tri, 195
Thich Minh Chau, 192
Thich Minh Dao, 208*n30*
Thich Nhat Ban, 208*n25,* 209*n35*
Thich Nhu Dat, 197
Thich Quang Do, 24, 183, 186, 189, 192, 193, 196, 197, 208*n27,* 209*n37,* 215, 221, 226, 228
Thich Quang Duc, 191
Thich Thai Hung, 197
Thich Thanh Tu, 187
Thich Tri Luc, 195
Thich Tri Quang, 191
Thich Tri Sieu, 197, 209*n34,* 229
Thich Tri Tuu, 193, 195, 207*n19,* 208*n29*
Thich Tue Si, 229
Thich Tue Sy, 197, 209*n37*
Thien Mu Pagoda (Hue), 195
Thien Su, Thich, 197
Thieu Dao Bao Cu, 28, 104, 129*n152,* 139, 144, 157*n37,* 213, 216
Tiananmen Square massacre, 11, 80, 89, 138, 173
Tien Phong (magazine), 152
Tin Sang (newspaper), 132
To Hoa, 138
To Hoai, 142

To Huu, 46, 47, 52, 54, 55, 58, 65, 66, 70n27, 73n73
To Nhun By, 138
Trade: deficit, 30; foreign, 3; retail, 179n4; wholesale, 179n4
Tradition of Resistance (newspaper), 140, 170, 171
Tran, Jimmy, 176, 177
Tran Bach Dang, 78, 168, 181n29
Tran Chau, 63
Tran Cong Man, 136
Tran Dan, 46, 47, 52, 55, 56, 70n25
Tran Dan Tien, 115
Tran Do, 25, 28, 52, 75, 89, 90, 91, 92, 93, 102, 113, 118, 132, 134, 137, 138, 140, 143, 150, 153, 156n30, 213, 216, 217–219
Tran Duc Luong, 23, 84, 85, 86
Tran Duc Thao, 55
Tran Hieu, 63
Tran Nam Trung, 168, 181n30
Tran Phuong, 73n76
Tran Quoc Hoan, 62
Tran Quoc Pagoda (Hanoi), 194
Tran Thieu Bao, 56
Tran Truong Tan, 79, 138
Tran Van Giau, 168, 181n28
Tran Van Tra, 82, 142, 164, 166, 168, 169, 173, 180n12
Tran Ve Lan, 49
Tran Xuan Bach, 23, 76–88, 122n19, 152, 170
Trotsky, Leon, 9
Trui Tre (newspaper), 153
Truong Chinh, 16, 43, 44, 62, 70n36, 71n43, 71n48, 162
Truong Giang, 138
Truong Nhu Tang, 165, 167
Truyen Thong Khang Chien (newspaper), 140
Tuoi Tre (newspaper), 137, 156n17

UN Declaration of Human Rights, 15
Unemployment, 3, 31, 83
Unified Buddhist Church, 181n27, 186, 189, 190–198, 192, 193; protest by, 24
Union of Arts and Letters, 54, 56
United States: diplomatic relations with Vietnam, 75; involvement in

Vietnam, 61, 164, 228; peaceful coexistence with Soviet Union, 60; wars against, 2, 164
United States Department of State, 215, 227; human rights report, 24, 227
Universal Declaration of Human Rights, 226
"Unshackling Days," 133
Urbanization, 11, 12

Van Cao, 54, 71n49, 155n12
"Vang Lua" (Nguyen Hue), 135
Van (journal), 54, 55
Van Nghe (newspaper), 48, 57, 134, 135, 138
Van Tien Dung, 137, 180n12
Vatican, 198, 199, 200
Vien Giac Pagoda (Ho Chi Minh City), 195
Viet Bac, 45, 46
Viet Cong, 25, 164, 173, 180n12, 181, 181n26
Viet Kieu, 176, 177
Viet Minh, 15, 16, 41, 43, 68n1, 181n26, 183, 191, 199, 204
Vietnam: agents of change in, 13–15; aid from China, 60; bureaucratic system in, 82; clientelism in, 83; commitment to socialism, 2; dangers to regime existence, 22–23; debt crisis in, 30; diplomatic relations with United States, 75; disengagement from Soviet Union, 60; economic issues in, 3, 10–12; factionalism in, 83; French colonial rule in, 15, 16; gross domestic product, 1–2, 3, 31, 119; interference in internal affairs of, 23; labor movements in, 12, 13; legal system in, 104–110; liberation of the south, 16; literacy rates, 2; malaise in, 30; military budget, 17; overcentralization in, 81–82; people's courts in, 16; political institutions in, 18–22; political prisoners in, 24; politics in, 9–36; population growth, 30; poverty in, 29–30, 31, 32, 112, 117; privatization in, 31; relations with China, 2, 4, 16, 17, 18, 42–44, 59; religion in, 14, 183–206; reunifica-

tion, 16, 20, 41, 53; standard of living, 1; student protest in, 14
Vietnamese Bishops Council, 200, 201
Vietnamese Buddhist Church, 184, 192, 197
Vietnamese Communist Party: accountability of, 93; Central Committee, 19, 25; conception of democracy, 87–88; concern over religious growth, 184, 185; consolidation of power by, 15–18; continuous rule of, 1; defensive strategies, 219–225; democratic claims, 21; external pressure on, 211–231; factionalism in, 169; hold on countryside, 88; identification of threats to, 22–23; internal dissent and, 211–231; international pressure on, 53, 226; legitimacy of, 67; literary policies, 52; membership, 19, 43, 90; monopoly of power by, 2, 5, 9, 14, 81, 91, 92, 105, 107, 172, 239; negotiations with United States, 61; as obstacle to reform, 77; opposition to, 68; party-building activities and, 224; policymaking by, 4; position above the Laws, 6; rejection of political pluralism, 79, 80, 82; response to Club of Former Resistance Fighters, 173–174; response to dissent, 7, 51–56; revitalization need, 94; rise to power, 5; rule by decree, 107, 109; Secretariat, 19, 136, 194; sole right to rule of, 105; survival of, 4; threats to legitimacy of, 83; xenophobia of, 239
Vietnamese Literary Association: 1956 Conference, 47
Vietnamese Trade Union Federation, 172
Vietnam Farmer's Association, 86, 219–220
Vietnam Fatherland Front, 20, 91, 98, 103–104, 166, 200, 203; electoral role, 99, 100; as front for party, 104; professional associations and, 14; religious control and, 186
Vietnam General Confederation of Labor, 13, 20
Vietnam Journalist's Association, 137
Vietnam Peasants Association, 20
Vietnam People's Army, 157*n34;* on Central Committee, 19; defense of regime by, 80; loyalty of, 80; Political Affairs Department, 62; Political Department, 61; as political institution, 19; resentment of party in, 51, 52; sympathy for dissenters, 51; White Paper, 23
Viet Nam Quoc Dan Dang, 68*n1*
Vietnam Veterans' Organization, 173
Vietnam Women's Union, 20
Vietnam Writers' Association, 73*n80,* 138, 141, 145, 149, 159*n61,* 228
Visual arts, 2, 131
Vo Chi Cong, 73*n76,* 179*n7,* 182*n39*
Voice of America, 229
Vo Nguyen Giap, 28, 60, 61, 70*n36,* 71*n61,* 212
Vo Van Kiet, 20, 32, 38*n28,* 71*n72,* 97, 98, 127*n118,* 154, 169, 237
Vu Mao, 101
Vung Tau Con Dau (newspaper), 138
Vu Oanh, 91
Vu Quang, 197, 208*n24*
Vu Tu Nam, 228

War of National Liberation, 6, 25, 67, 112, 164, 199
Wars: anticolonial, 2, 25; against France, 2, 25; guerilla, 15, 16, 71*n62;* protracted, 62; with United States, 2
"When You Have Purpose" (Che Lan Vien), 58
World Association of Newspapers, 229
World Bank, 3, 31
Writers and Artists Association, 157*n34*
Writing to Mother and the National Assembly (Nguyen Van Tran), 63

Xuan Cang, 136
Xuan Dieu, 47, 57, 58, 65, 70*n27,* 73*n73*

Youth and Students Club, 116

ABOUT THE BOOK

Moving from the 1950s to the present, Zachary Abuza explores Vietnamese politics and culture through the lens of the internal debates over political reform.

Abuza focuses on issues of representation, intellectual freedom, the rise of civil society, and the emergence of a "loyal opposition," assessing the prospects for change. He finds that, while some mildly dissident groups may add impetus to the effort, internal party protest remains the most legitimate—and most likely—form of political dissent in the country. His analysis offers a compelling portrayal of the extraordinary contradictions that are at the core of contemporary Vietnam.

Zachary Abuza is assistant professor of political science and international relations at Simmons College.